MASTER YOUR DATA

with Power Query in Excel and Power BI

Leveraging Power Query to Get & Transform Your Task Flow

Formerly 'M is for Data Monkey'

by
Ken Puls &
Miguel Escobar

Holy Macro! Books
PO Box 541731
Merritt Island, FL 32953

Master Your Data with Excel and Power BI

Authors: Ken Puls and Miguel Escobar

Layout: Jill Bee

Copyediting: Deanna Puls

Cover Design: Shannon Travise

Indexing: Nellie Jay

Ape Illustrations: Walter Agnew Moore

Cover Illustration: Pavel Goldaev

Published by: Holy Macro! Books, PO Box 541731, Merritt Island FL 32953, USA

Distributed by: Independent Publishers Group, Chicago, IL

First Printing: September, 2021 Typo corrections: 11/30/2021. Reprinted Feb 2023 with corrections

ISBN: 978-1-61547-058-7 Print, 978-1-61547-241-3 PDF, 978-1-61547-358-8 ePub, 978-1-61547-141-6 Mobi

Library of Congress Control Number: 2021942985

Table of Contents

Foreword

How Power Query Changed OUR Lives
Ken's Story: "Coffee & Power Query"

It's the name on the meeting in my Outlook calendar from back in November 2013. It was during one of the Microsoft MVP summits, the product had recently had its name changed from Data Explorer, and I was meeting with Miguel Llopis and Faisal Mohamood from the Power Query team over coffee to talk about the good and the bad of the tool from an Excel users' perspective.

In that conversation, I told them both that Power Query was great, but it was a lousy replacement for SQL Server Management Studio. I distinctly remember that part of the conversation. I'd been working with SSMS and Power Query a lot at the time and was struggling with the fact that Power Query did some of the same tasks, but not all. I was frustrated, as I was struggling with the tool, trying to make it behave the same, but it just wasn't doing it.

What happened after I laid out my concerns flipped my complaints on their head. I'm paraphrasing from my memory, but the response was something like this:

"Ken, this tool isn't a replacement for SSMS. We built this for Excel people... our intent is that they never need to use or learn SQL at all."

For anyone that knows me well, they know that I'm very seldom left speechless, but that was just about enough to do it. That statement upset the balance of my world.

Understand that I'm not a normal Excel pro. I know enough SQL to be dangerous, I'm extremely accomplished with VBA and had also worked with VB.NET, C#, XML and a few other languages. And while I love technology and challenges, the true reason I know as many languages as I do today is that I taught myself out of necessity. Typically, my needs were complicated, and that involved a painful journey of jumping into the deep end with a "sink or swim" approach.

That meeting changed my view of Power Query forever. I took a step back and looked at it in a new light. And I started to use it as it was intended to be used... on its own, driving everything through the user interface, avoiding writing SQL wherever possible. And you know something... it started working better, it allowed me to go more places, it allowed me to solve things I'd never been able to do before.

I love this tool. Not just because of what I can do with it, but because of how easy it makes it to get things done for a business pro without the need for coding. Yes, there is a coding layer within the tool that you can learn, but it is entirely optional. That is what makes this tool so special: it has one of the best user-interface designs I've seen in a long time, which essentially writes code for you as you click buttons. I love this tool because the people we teach can pick it up rapidly and build complex solutions that add real business value in an incredibly short amount of time. This product is truly centered around the business professional.

On a personal note, Power Query has allowed me to quit my full-time corporate job and build my own business. We deliver live training (in-person or online), as well as our own commercial Excel add-in – Monkey Tools – which can help make your life even easier when working with Power Query and Power Pivot in Excel. Ultimately, there is nothing that gets me more excited than seeing someone find that magic moment that significantly impacts their workflow and saves them time.

Miguel's Story: A new beginning

Before starting my business as a freelancer in 2013, I had a reputation in my past jobs of being the "power user", so I kept that nickname even after leaving those jobs and that's how I named my YouTube channel and now my new website 'The Power User'.

I was never in IT, but I was usually the guy trying to push things forward in terms of how technologically advanced we were and how much value we could get from the tools that we had at hand, which was usually just Excel (and not even the latest version). Pivot Tables and Excel formulas ended up becoming like second nature to me.

Fast forward to 2013 and I got introduced to Power Query. I can't really remember how I got to it, but things like simply filtering data, removing columns, promoting headers, and unpivoting columns had a huge impact on my day to day. I had no knowledge of VBA (and I still don't), so Power Query literally opened completely new data wrangling opportunities for me which were previously impossible. I no longer needed to become a VBA or SQL Expert – I just needed Power Query and my data preparation issues would be gone.

The Power Query user interface was **the hook** for me. It felt intuitive and is the type of interface that puts you right in the driving seat in front of what matters most to you - your data. However, since it was a new tool and a new language, there was little content or information on the web about how to get the most out of Power Query, so I started my journey to be "the very best, like no one ever was" on this new technology and started creating content for it.

Through this new content creation (blogging, videos, emails, etc.), I ended up meeting people like Rob Collie and Bill Jelen who later introduced me to Ken who was also big on Power Query. Ken and I never met in person, but we decided to work together because we felt we complemented our views on Power Query and we both wanted to "preach" about how amazing Power Query is. We started a project called PowerQuery.Training which ended up fostering the content that got published in the first edition of our book. During that period of writing the first edition and even before that, we realized the true potential of Power Query and how it could change the lives of most Excel users for the better. For us, **Power Query was and still is a major breakthrough as far as self-service tools go.**

Ever since we published the first edition of our book, readers, friends, and colleagues have reminded us that some of the pictures and the content in that first edition was getting outdated, but that the content was still a solid foundation, and it opened their eyes to see the potential that Power Query has. That has been our north star since the very beginning – we're on a mission to change people's lives the same way that this tool changed our lives and made data preparation simple and straightforward.

From 2015 to 2021, Ken and I received more and more confirmation from the readers of our book that Power Query is changing people's lives; either directly or indirectly. Hearing that type of feedback always put a smile on our faces. It's reassuring and it's also the main motivation why we decided to write a second edition of the book the way that we did. We wanted it to be done just right and for that, we needed to wait for the right time.

In May of 2021, I was asked if I would be interested in joining Microsoft as a Program Manager on the Power Query team. To me, this means taking a new role but following the same mission – to bring Power Query to more people and have a positive impact in the way they work.

As this book is going to print we are still working out the formal contractual details and start date of the position, but I can't put into words how motivated I am for this new role. And if you needed an example of how Power Query can change people's lives, I'm one example of how much it can.

Author Acknowledgements

As with any book, there are a bunch of people who are quite influential with making things happen. Without the influence of the people below, this book would never have come to fruition:

Bill Jelen – We cannot imagine working with someone who is more accommodating than Bill. Writing a book involves a huge amount of time and effort. Just balancing that against our own business needs is tough, but when the book is based on technology that changes as quickly as Power Query is changing… And then, with very short notice, we dropped a book on his lap that was twice the length of what we had originally promised. Bill accepted every delay and change with grace and understanding, encouraging us on a regular schedule to get the book finished.

Miguel Llopis – From the very first meeting over coffee, Miguel has been our go-to guy at Microsoft, even joking that his full-time job is answering Ken's emails. He's been incredibly supportive since day one, has responded to feature design requests, bugs and so much more.

Curt Hagenlocher, Ehren Von Lehe, Matt Masson, and all the others on the Power Query/Power BI team – We cannot begin to express how willing this team has been to talk to us and answer our questions and emails. Their help and clarifications have been incredibly helpful in turning out the finished product.

Wyn Hopkins, Cristian Angyal and Matt Allington – For the feedback and opinions on some material that we were particularly concerned that we had pitched correctly.

The countless people that have commented on our blogs and videos, attended our training sessions, and shared their own creative and alternate solutions with the world. Each of you has helped challenge us to explore new methods, develop better techniques, and have a lot of fun with this program.

Ken would like to thank:

Our previous book started with an email on Mar 6, 2014, introducing me to Miguel Escobar. He had a dream; to write a book on Power Query. Despite the fact that we'd never met in person – and still wouldn't for several years – Miguel's ideas and energy have had a profound impact on me. They led to the creation of our initial book (M is for Data Monkey), an online Power Query Workshop, our Power Query Academy, and now a second edition of the book. Without his inspiration and devotion to these projects, none would have come to fruition. His passion has continued to push my personal growth with Power Query, particularly when working with the M language itself. I am still trying to figure out how he can work 24 hours per day though!

This book would never have been finished without the support of my family. Even more than being a rock in my corner, my wife Deanna did the initial proof-read of every page of this book, (several times), fixing my spelling and clearing up the odd wording that I sometimes write down when my brain is a paragraph ahead of what my fingers are typing. I also need to give a shout out to my daughter Annika who taught me all about the Oxford comma (including the fact that Taylor Swift doesn't use them). I only wish she'd shared that wisdom with me more than 72 hours before the manuscript was submitted!

We now have a team of people at Excelguru who held down the fort as I locked myself away to complete this manuscript: Rebekah Sax – who handles *everything* we throw at her with grace, Abdullah Alharbi – who gets tossed a rough idea for Monkey Tools that he has to bring to fruition in code, and Jim Olsen – my friend, mentor and former manager who now looks after our accounting for us. Without each and every one of you doing what you do, there is no way that we would be as successful as we are, or that I would have been able to finish this project.

Anyone who works on the Excel team can tell you that I deliver fairly passionate feedback about the product. I'm fairly certain no one has been on the receiving end of that more than Guy Hunkin, who lives at the nexus of both Power Query and Excel, tasked with the integration of the two technologies. Guy's endless patience absolutely amazes me, and I can't thank him enough for always taking my feedback professionally, but never personally. Beyond our emails and calls, I'm lucky enough to have had Guy attend a couple of my training courses where he took copious amounts of notes which have led to several things being fixed or changed.

Finally, I'd like to thank our business partner Matt Allington. Matt joined Miguel and I at the beginning of the COVID pandemic in mid-2019, in order to expand the Power Query Academy and our business operations. Since then, we have re-branded to become https://skillwave.training – and now offer both self-paced and coached training in Power Query, Power Pivot, and Power BI (among other topics). Matt has been a friend for many years, but of particular importance to this book was some advice on scheduling and prioritizing that actually allowed us to get it over the finish line.

Miguel would like to thank:

I'd like to thank YOU for reading this. Yes...YOU! You're a crucial part of our main objective and our intention with this book is to provide you with the resources so you can become a Data [M]aster, Data [M]agician, and, above all, a great Data [M]onkey in the most positive way possible. I'd like to thank you in advance for making this world a better place – at least in the context of business decision making and the world of data.

I'd also like to thank all of the Excel and BI practitioners worldwide that have shown their support towards our book and our Power Query related endeavors. It is truly an honor to be part of this worldwide community and I invite you to join us by simply using this tool.

Let's not forget about a crucial part of my life: Friends and Family. I'm not putting names in here as I'm afraid I might leave someone out of it – so I'm playing it safe here! :)

Special thanks to Ken for being extremely supportive and being able to overcome the language barrier at times with me! "Spanglish" gets me sometimes, yet Ken distinguishes what I'm trying to say and makes a better version of it.

Also, special thanks to Curt Hagenlocher, Ehren Von Lehe, Matt Masson, and Miguel Llopis from the Power Query team who I've been spamming with questions, bugs, rants, suggestions, ideas and overall complaints about Power Query since 2013 and, to this day July 4th 2021, they still haven't ignored me or just told me to stop – if you need some classes about patience and customer service, you should speak with them someday :). They are the real MVPs.

Our Loyal Supporters

There are a great many of you who pre-ordered this book when it first went on sale at Amazon, and/or you signed up for the Power Query Academy at https://skillwave.training (or https://powerquery.training). Each of you has been promised a copy of this book and has been waiting a LONG time to actually see it arrive at your door. THANK YOU for both your support *and* your patience. We truly hope that you feel that it was worth the long wait.

And finally...

A huge thank you to our Power Query Academy members at Skillwave.Training who jumped on the opportunity to proof-read the book on a very tight schedule. We especially want to throw a shout out to Seth Barron, Randall McHenry, Stanton Berlinsky, John Hackwood, Mitchell Allan, Nick Osdale-Popa, Mike Kardash, and Lillian, each of whom submitted over a dozen spelling and grammar fixes through the book.

We'd also like to thank YOU. For both buying the book, putting your trust in our teaching methods, and for becoming part of the Power Query movement.

This book was written for you, in an effort to help you master your data. We truly hope it does, and that you'll find it to be the most impactful productivity book you've ever purchased.

We'd like to thank YOU. For both buying the book, putting your trust in our teaching methods, and for becoming part of the Power Query movement.

Chapter 0 - The Data Revolution

The Common Scenario of the Data Analyst

Whether we are performing basic data entry, building simple reports or designing full-blown business intelligence solutions using VBA, SQL and/or other languages, we all deal with data to a certain extent. Our skill sets vary greatly, but the overall jobs we are usually trying to perform include:

- Extracting the data from a data source,
- Transforming the data to our needs,
- Appending data sets,
- Merging multiple data sets together, and
- Enriching our data for better analysis.

We are Information Workers. And no matter what you call yourself in your formal job description, our role is to take our data, clean it up, and turn that data into information. Our job may not be glorious, but it is essential, and without our work done correctly, the end results of any analysis are suspect.

Naturally, our tool of choice for years has been Microsoft Excel. And while tools like Excel have amazing functionality to help us build business intelligence out of data, converting raw data into consumable data has been a challenge for years. In fact, it's this issue that we can often spend most of our time on; prepping the data for analysis, getting it into a nice tabular format so that it can be consumed by analytical and reporting tools.

Behind the curtains, we are all information workers trying to reach our desired goal with data

To those who have done our jobs, they'll know that we are more than just Information Workers; we are Data Magicians. Our data seldom enters our world in a ready-to-consume format, instead it can take hours of cleaning, filtering and re-shaping to get things ready to go.

Once our data is prepared and ready, we can perform a vast array of powerful analytical processes with ease. Conditional formatting, filters, pivot tables, charts, slicers and more, each of these tools will open up to us and let us weave the true magic to impress our audience.

Our issue comes much earlier in the process. We're served dirty data, held in collections of text and Excel files (maybe a database if we're VERY lucky) and we somehow have to clean it up and get it ready to use. Ultimately our end goal is simple: get the data into a tabular format as quickly as possible, while ensuring it is scoped to our needs, and accurate. And with every solution needing a different combination of data coming from different sources... it takes magic.

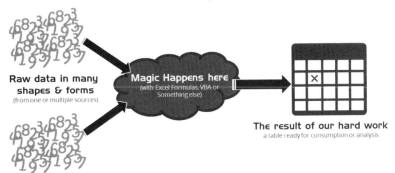

Black Magic: What really happens to data before consumption

The Benefits and Dangers of Black Magic

And the true wizards of Excel use many different techniques to weave their magic; sometimes on their own, and sometimes in combination with other tools. These types of magic include:

- **Excel formulas** – These are some of the first techniques that the magician will often reach to, leveraging their knowledge of formulas such as VLOOKUP(), INDEX(), MATCH(), OFFSET(), LEFT(), LEN(), TRIM(), CLEAN() and many more. While formulas tend to be used by *most* Excel users, the complexity of these formulas varies by the user's experience and comfort.
- **Visual Basic for Applications (VBA)** – A powerful language that can help you create powerful and dynamic transformations for your data, these techniques tend to be used by *advanced* users, due to the discipline required to truly master them.
- **SQL Statements** – Another powerful language for manipulating data, SQL can be extremely useful for selecting, sorting, grouping and transforming data. The reality, however is that this language is also typically only used by *advanced* users, with many Excel Pros not even knowing where to get started with it. This language is often confused with being the sole domain of database professionals, although every Excel Pro should invest some time in learning it.

Each of these tools has something in common; they were essentially the only tools that we had in order to clean and transform our data into something useful.

Despite their usefulness, many of these tools also had two serious weaknesses: the time needed to build the solution and the time needed to master the techniques.

While it's true that the truly savvy magicians could build solutions to automate and import raw data in a clean format, this took years of learning advanced languages, and then a significant amount of time scoping, developing, testing and maintaining the solutions. Depending on the complexity of the solutions built, fixing the solutions for a minor change in the import format, or extending them to embrace another source could be horrendous.

Which leads to a third danger of having a true wizard in the company; they build an incredible solution which works until long after they've left the company. It's only then that the company realizes that they didn't understand the solution, and don't have anyone to fix it.

On the flip side, many people tasked with this data cleanup didn't have the time or opportunity to learn these advanced magic techniques. And while we could say that maybe they're better off never having a massive system collapse without anyone to fix it, instead they waste hours, days, weeks, months and years of labor time and money performing repetitive data cleanup and imports on a regular basis.

Take a moment and think about how many hours are consumed on a monthly basis in your company simply performing repetitive data import and cleanup tasks in Excel. Multiply those hours by the average wage rate in your company. And by the number of companies in your industry world-wide and... do we need to go bigger? The cost of lost productivity in this area is staggering.

We need a better way. We need a product that is easy to learn, that others can pick up and understand with limited instruction. We need a product which lets us automate the import and cleanup of data, letting us focus on turning that data into information, adding true value to our company.

That product is finally here. It's called **Power Query**.

The Future Transforms

Power Query is the answer to our data issues and solves the earlier issues of each of the toolsets. It is very easy to learn, having one of the most intuitive user interfaces we've ever worked with. It's easy to maintain, as it shows each step of the process, which can be reviewed or updated later. And everything done in Power Query can be refreshed with a couple of clicks.

From the perspective of two people who have spent years building solutions using black magic techniques, Power Query is a game-changer for many reasons. One of those is the speed with which it can be learned.

When specifically trying to import, clean and transform data to get it ready for analysis, Power Query can be learned faster than even Excel formulas, and handles complex sources much more easily than VBA:

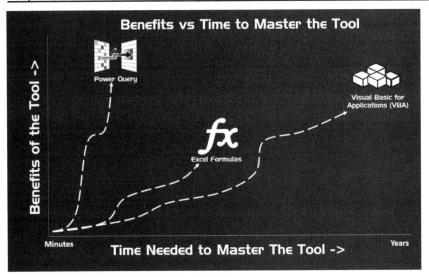

Power Query was designed to be an easy-to-use Data Transformation and Manipulation tool

The ease of use is actually the reason we believe that this tool is the answer to the issue of the vanishing data magician that faces so many businesses. Even if that magician builds something complex in Power Query, you can have someone up to speed to be able to maintain or fix the query with minimal training, (as in hours, not weeks).

As hard as it is for true Excel Pros to understand, many users actually don't *want* to master Excel formulas. They simply want to open up a tool, connect it to their data source, click a few buttons to clean it up and import it, then build the chart or report they need. It's for exactly this reason that Power Query's reach will be even broader than those users who master formulas. With the menu-driven interface, a user never has to learn a single formula or line of code in many cases.

TRANSFORMATION TOOLS REACH

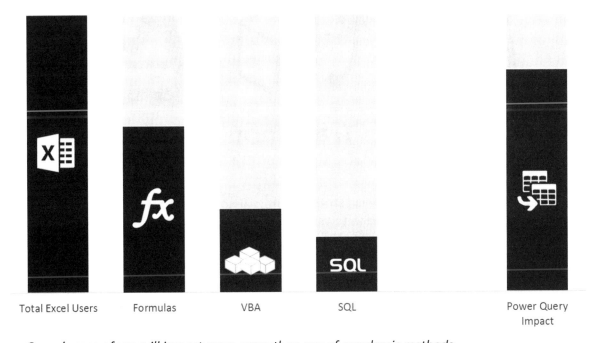

Power Query's ease of use will impact more users than any of our classic methods

There is no doubt in our minds that Power Query will change the way Excel Pros work with data forever.

We also want to make it quite clear here that we are not discounting the value of formulas, VBA or SQL. In fact, they are tools that we could not live without. Formulas can be knocked out quickly outside the tranformation context to do many things that Power Query will never do. VBA has a far greater reach in sheer capability and power, allowing us to reach to other applications, create programs to pull and push data, and so many other things. And a SQL query written by a SQL wizard will always be faster and better than that created by Power Query.

In the context of simply connecting to, cleaning and importing data, however, Power Query offers more for less, allowing us to automate the job more quickly and with less investment in time. And with the constant improvements made by the Power Query team, those gaps between the SQL pro and the Power Query generated queries are shrinking.

As impactful as this is for Excel users, it's important to recognize that Power Query is not just about Excel. In the past, if you'd built a system in Excel to transform and load data, it would need to stay in Excel or be totally re-written in a new language. But Power Query offers your data transformation process a "grow-up" story. The reason is that the same Power Query technology is in use in Excel, Power BI Desktop, Power Automate and Power BI Dataflows. So today, when you've built a solution using Power Query in Excel, you can simply import it into Power BI Desktop, or copy it into Power BI Dataflows.

Beyond creating portable and scalable solutions, this means that as data pros, we can learn a new portable skill and re-use it many times across various different software products. And even better? We have no reason to expect that Power Query won't expand beyond these footprints.

And with its solid integration into other software, we get the best of both worlds. We can provide our own SQL queries to Power Query if needed, refresh it with VBA in Excel or schedule the refresh via Power BI when desired, load our Power Queries directly into data models or entities, and so much more.

Why Power Query IS Magic

The number one issue facing the data pro when building robust and stable solutions has been accessing, cleansing and transforming the data. What we've needed, and yet many of us have never heard of, is an ETL tool:

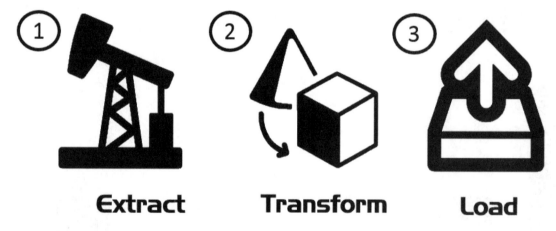

ETL: Extract, Transform, Load

Power Query is an ETL tool; its function is to Extract data from almost any source, Transform it as desired and then Load it. But what does that truly mean to us as functional data pros?

Extract

Extraction can be targeted against one or more data sources including the following: Text files, CSV Files, Excel Files, Databases and Web pages. In addition, the Power Query team has built many connectors to data sources that have otherwise been tough to get at: Microsoft Exchange, Salesforce and other "Software As A Service" (SAAS) sources that you'd never have expected. And naturally, there are ODBC and OLEDB connectors for those databases that haven't yet been covered by the team. No matter where your data lives today, there is a very solid chance that you can extract it and use it with Power Query.

Transform

When we talk about transformation, we include each of the following areas:

1.   **Data Cleansing –** This includes filtering out departments from a database, to removing blank or garbage rows from a text file import. Other uses include changing cases from uppercase to lower case, splitting data into multiple columns and forcing dates to import in the correct format for your country. Data cleansing is anything you need to do to your data to clean it up to be used.

2.   **Data Integration –** If you use VLOOKUP(), INDEX()/MATCH() or the newer XLOOKUP() formulas in Excel, then you're probably integrating multiple datasets. Power Query can join data in either vertical or horizontal fashion, allowing you to append two tables, (creating one long table), or merge tables together horizontally (without having to write a single VLOOKUP() function). You can also perform other operations such as grouping and more.

3.   **Data Enrichment -** These tasks include adding new columns or doing calculations over a set of data. From performing mathematical calculations like creating Gross Sales by multiplying Sales Quantity * Sales Price, to adding new formats of dates based on your transaction date column, Power Query makes this easy. In fact, with Power Query you can even create entire tables dynamically driven based on the value in an Excel cell, SQL dataset or even a web page. Need a dynamic Calendar table that runs five years back from today's date? Look no further than Power Query.

What is truly amazing about Power Query is how many transformations can be performed through menu commands, rather than having to write formulas or code to do it. This tool was built for end-users and requires no coding experience whatsoever in order to perform transformations that would be incredibly complex in SQL or VBA. That's a great thing!

If you are the type of person who likes to get under the covers and tinker with formulas or code, however, you can. While there is no requirement to ever learn it, Power Query records everything in a language called "M" (we joke that languages A through L were taken). And for those wizards who decide to take advantage of this language, we can build even more efficient queries and do even more amazing things.

No-code, low-code or pro-code: the option is totally up to you. But no matter which way you choose to go, you'll be floored with just how much can be done in the no-code world.

Load

As each program that supports Power Query has different uses, the locations you can load your data to will vary:

1.   Excel: Load to Excel Tables, the Power Pivot Data model, or only to Connections

2.   Power BI: Load to the Data Model, or only to Connections

3.   Power Automate (Flow): Load to Excel workbooks (and we expect more destinations in future)

4.   Dataflows: Load to Azure Data Lake Storage, Dataverse, or to Connection Only

The "Connections" might seem a bit mysterious, but it simply means that we can create a query that can be used by other queries. This allows for some very interesting use cases that we'll explore more fully in the book.

While it's interesting to look at where the data loads, that really isn't the important part of the Load process in this ETL tool. It's **how** it loads, or rather how to load it **again**.

Power Query is essentially a macro recorder, keeping track of every step you use when you work through the Extract and Transform steps. This means that you define your query once and determine where you'd like to load it. After you've done that you can simply refresh your query.

Define once   Consume anytime

Define the transformation process once and consume anytime

Consider this for a moment. You import your text (.TXT) file, the one it used to take you 20 minutes to import and clean each month before you could use it. Power Query makes it easy, allowing you to accomplish the same task in 10 minutes, saving you 10 minutes the first time you use it. Then next month comes along and you get a new file...

Until now, you'd roll up your sleeves and re-live the 20 minutes of Excel exuberance where you show Excel that you're a master at reliving the past, performing those exhilarating steps over and over again each month... wait... you **don't** find that exhilarating?

In that case, just save your new .TXT file over the old one and click Data → Refresh All in Excel (or Home → Refresh in Power BI). You're finished. **Seriously**. And if you've published the file to Power BI or set it up in Power BI Dataflows, you can just schedule the refresh to avoid even that hassle!

This is the real power in Power Query. Easy to use, easy to **re-use**. It changes your hard work into an investment and frees up your time next cycle to do something worthwhile.

Power Query Experiences & Product Integrations

Power Query is a technology that is revolutionizing the world. It officially started in Excel back in 2013 as a COM add-on and it is now in over 8 different products ranging from Excel and Power BI Desktop, to SQL Server Integration Services, Azure Data Factory, and is probably being integrated in your favorite data-related Microsoft product as you are reading this book.

The impact that Power Query is having is phenomenal and is dramatically changing the lives of many data professionals across many different software products. The downside is that being integrated into so many products comes at a cost. The difficult situation that the Power Query team faces on a daily basis is balancing parity of functions, features and experiences throughout all these product integrations. They have to strike the sweet spot between consistency as well as features that are specific to the product that is hosting the Power Query feature set.

The Components of Power Query

You can think of Power Query as somewhat of an onion – it has layers – which are effectively the core components that make Power Query, well... Power Query.

Whenever we look at physical things, we see them at face value. As you progress through this book, you'll learn that there is a lot that happens behind what we first see from Power Query. There is M code – which is visible to us – as well as the actual M Engine that you might never see as an end-user. Let's take a quick look at the onion that is Power Query:

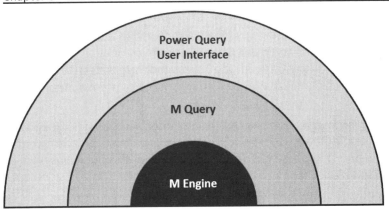

The layers behind Power Query

There are a total of three possible layers in Power Query, but some product integrations might only have the first two layers. These layers are:

M Engine - The underlying query execution engine that runs queries expressed in the Power Query formula language ("M").

M Query - A set of commands written in the Power Query M formula language.

Power Query User Interface – Also known as the Power Query Editor, serves as a graphical user interface that helps the user with actions such as but not limited to:

- Creating or modifying M queries by simply interacting with the user interface
- Visualizing queries and their results
- Managing queries by creating query groups, adding metadata, etc…

At the bare minimum, a product integration might have at least the M engine and the M query components. But as you can see from the table below, not every integration will contain all three layers of the Power Query onion:

Product	M Engine	M query	Power Query User Interface
Excel	Yes	Yes	Yes
Power BI Desktop	Yes	Yes	Yes
Power BI Dataflows	Yes	Yes	Yes
SQL Server Integration Services	Yes	Yes	No

Not all Power Query integrations contain all of its components

Experiences by Product Integration

If during the first half of 2021 you tried to compare the experiences found in Power Query for Excel against the Power Query experience found in Power BI Dataflows, you might have noticed some differences. Power BI Dataflows leverages the Power Query Online user interface, where Excel and Power BI have an experience based on the Power Query Desktop user interface. While the user interfaces do have differences, the underlying process of using them is similar.

If you try doing this again in the first quarter of the year 2024, you might notice that the gap is not as big as it was before. That's primarily because the Power Query team is trying to work towards a single and unified core experience for the Power Query User Interface which will then be used across all user experiences and products.

Of course, there might still be some unique features per product integration in the future. Things such as grabbing data in a table directly from an active workbook might still be something unique to the Power Query experience found in Excel, but the core of the experience will be quite similar across all product integrations. Some of these differences translate into differences in the M engine, M code and the Power Query User Interface layers, while others might only impact something like the user interface. (An example might be different icons between different experiences.)

One thing which is certain is that, currently and for the past few years, Microsoft has been making a huge investment to push things to the Power Query Online experience first. Once they've iterated and tested enough, they then move those features into preview in the Power Query Desktop experiences, followed by eventual general release. This means that if you ever want to try out the "latest and the greatest" from Power Query, your best option is to use the Power Query Online experience through any of its product integrations such as Power BI Dataflows.

It is no secret that this tool is evolving quickly, both in features as well as user interface changes. Due to this fact, we have concluded that writing a book about Power Query with screenshots of the user interface that will remain current for the rest of our lives is simply impossible; in fact, the release of this book was delayed for two years while we waited for one user interface change to become live in Excel.

While we provide a great deal of click-steps through this book, we need you to recognize that the actual steps that you need to take when this book is in your hands may differ – both by product integration as well as by product if the user interface gets an update. But what won't change is the goal, theory or recipes behind the examples. That is the core we are attempting to teach here; how to master your data, not necessarily the specific user interface you've been presented with. In this way, we hope to achieve our mission of writing a book that can be relevant for several years to come.

The Power Query Update Cycle

Before we tell you where to get Power Query, let's talk about the updates. Yes, that may seem like putting the cart before the horse, but there is a pretty solid reason for this.

The Power Query team releases monthly updates. We're not talking bug fixes (although those are certainly included); we're talking new features and performance enhancements. While some are small, others are much larger. In early 2015 they released an update that cut query load time by 30%. In July 2015 they released one that solved some very serious issues with refreshing to Power Pivot. We've seen Join Types, Conditional Columns and so much more released over the ensuing years. In the last three years specifically we saw the introduction of Columns from Example and Fuzzy Matching, among other new features.

So how do you get your hands on them? The answer is, it depends on the end point where you are consuming Power Query.

Power Query Online

Power Query Online refers to any instance of Power Query used in an online experience in programs such as Power Automate, Power BI Dataflows and others. These are all web-based services and there is nothing you need to update in any of them. Fixes and features are released on an ongoing basis, so you just need to review them every now and then to see what's been added.

Microsoft 365

Our preferred way to consume Excel (or any other Office product) is via an Microsoft 365 subscription. If you are on subscription, the software will just update automatically with new bug fixes and features on a regular basis based on the "Channel" that your version of office is using.

> ✎ Learn more about Channels at the following link:
> https://docs.microsoft.com/en-us/deployoffice/
> overview-of-update-channels-for-office-365-proplus

Excel 2016/2019/2021

Power Query is a product under constant development. If we look back at Excel 2016 (originally released in Sep 2015), it finally brought Power Query into Excel natively, but it also shipped with a named range bug as well as a legacy experience for combining files. In addition, the Join Types, Conditional Columns and Column From Examples feature hadn't even been released at that point.

The good news is that even though the Excel 2016 and 2019 products were never on subscription, they did receive some Power Query updates after their initial releases. And we highly recommend that you update your software to get the new experience that we illustrate in the book.

The secret to getting these deployed on your system is to ensure that your system also gets updates for "other Microsoft products" when it downloads its Windows Updates. To check this setting in Windows 10:

- Press the Windows key and type Windows
- Select the Windows Update Settings
- Go to Advanced Options
- Check the box next to "Give me updates for other Microsoft products when I update Windows"

Excel 2010 & 2013

Unlike Excel 2016 and higher, where it is built-in as part of the product, Power Query must be manually downloaded and installed from https://go.microsoft.com/fwlink/?LinkId=317450. The final update for Excel 2010 & 2013 was released in March 2019.

Power BI Desktop

Power BI Desktop has two delivery mechanisms. If you installed it via the Microsoft Store, then it will continue to update for you automatically. If, on the other hand, you downloaded and installed it via the advanced options at https://powerbi.microsoft.com/en-us/downloads/, you'll have to manually download and install updates.

> ✎ The cool thing about Power BI is that this is the first place we see new Power Query releases. They're usually hidden in Power BI's options window under the Preview Features tab. But if you want to see what's coming to Excel, check there. New features are typically released to Power BI Desktop first, and then come to Excel 2-3 months after they hit General Availability (they are no longer in preview) in Power BI Desktop.

How to Use This Book

This book is intended to be your #1 resource in order to understand Power Query and the M language from a practical point of view, no matter if you are new to the tool or a seasoned ETL pro. Our goal is to address common problems that affect the everyday user and show you how we can use Power Query to solve them. We'll also cover some more advanced scenarios as well, incorporating Power Query and M best practices throughout, to help you understand not only how to build Power Query solutions, but how to make them last.

The vast majority of the scenarios, illustrations and cases used through the book will be shown using the Microsoft 365 version of Excel. Unless otherwise stated, the illustrated scenario will work in either Excel or Power BI.

Where to Find the Power Query Commands

The key to locating the Power Query commands is simply to know where to look:

Excel 365

In versions of Excel released as part of a Microsoft 365 product, (which we refer to as Excel 365), the Power Query commands are found on the Get & Transform group of the Data tab. While there are some one-click shortcuts to common sources, you can find all the Power Query data sources available to you under the Get Data button.

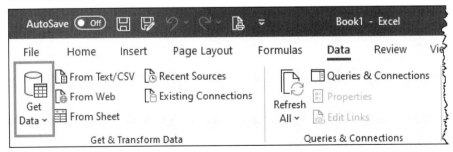

Locating Power Query in Excel

Power BI Desktop

In this software, you don't even have to leave the Home tab. Notice the huge Get Data button that is right there waiting for you to click it.

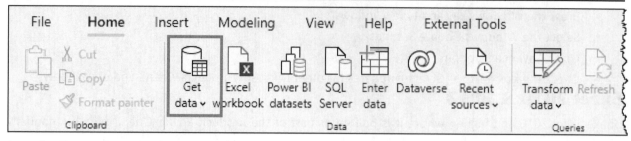

Locating Power Query in Power BI Desktop

Previous Excel Versions

While this book focuses on the Microsoft 365 version of Excel, the majority of the features are compatible with earlier versions. The thing to recognize however is that the commands may be in different areas:

- **Excel 2019:** For the most part, Excel 2019 will look very similar to Excel 365. The one big exception at the time of printing was that the "From Sheet" button you will be directed to and see pictured in this book was called "From Table/Range".

- **Excel 2016:** Like in Office 2019/365, the Power Query entry point is found on the Data tab, however you'll find them under the New Query button (in the middle of the Data tab) instead of under the Get Data button you'll find pictured throughout this book.

- **Excel 2010/2013:** You'll find Power Query on its own tab once you have downloaded the installer. Where the steps in the book will point you to go to the Get Data button on the Data tab, you'd need to go to the Power Query tab and locate the command there.

"Get Data" Click-Steps

Power Query can connect to a wide variety of data sources, which you can explore by clicking the Get Data button found on the Data tab in Excel, or the Home tab in Power BI Desktop. While Excel's data sources are subcategorized in menu subfolders, you'll find that in order to see the subcategorized list in Power BI Desktop, you'll need to click the More... button.

For the sake of consistency, we will use the following method to describe how to connect to a CSV file:

- Create a new query → From File → From Text/CSV

The actual Excel click path would be:

- **Go to the Data tab → Get Data → From File** → From Text/CSV

This would be equivalent to the following in Power BI Desktop:

- **Go to the Home tab → Get Data → More...** → File → Text/CSV

If you are still using Excel 2016 or earlier, these click-steps would read as follows:

- Excel 2016: **Go to the Data tab → New Query** → From File → From Text/CSV
- Excel 2010/2013: **Go to the Power Query tab** → From File → From Text/CSV

Special Elements

> 🍌 Notes will appear in an indented paragraph with a banana icon. These delicious paragraphs point out special features, quirks, or software tricks that will help increase your productivity with Power Query.

🙈 Warnings appear in a shaded paragraph with a "see-no-evil monkey" icon. Ignore these at your peril, as they call out potential pitfalls and problems that could cause queries to break in the future.

Example Files

Before reading further, we highly recommend you download all the Workbooks used in this book so you can follow along with us. You can get them all at the following webpage:

        https://www.skillwave.training/book-master-your-data-examples/

It's time to explore this amazing tool in-depth. Let's get started.

Chapter 1 - Power Query Fundamentals

The purpose of Power Query is to collect and reshape data into the desired format, before loading it into tables for consumption by the business analyst. The basic overview of the process, which Power Query will attempt to follow without your intervention, can be visualized as follows:

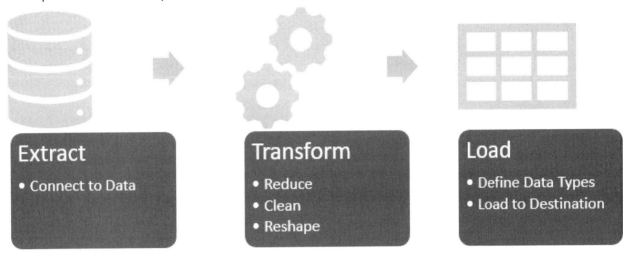

An overview of the Power Query process

Of course, we can manipulate any part of this process at any time. And indeed, in this book we will do a lot of that. But to begin with it is helpful to walk through and understand the overall method that Power Query is attempting to follow.

Before You Begin

Before you launch into your Power Query journey, there are some defaults that we suggest you change in the Power Query interface. Why? Microsoft turned certain features off to avoid overwhelming you, but unfortunately some of these items are critical in order to use the tool properly. And since you have this book, you'll be guided through the correct use here anyway!

Adjusting Excel's Default Power Query Properties

To adjust your default settings in Excel:

- Go the Data tab → Get Data → Query Options
- Under Global → Data Load, ensure that Fast Data Load is checked. (This setting will lock Excel's user interface during a refresh but will ensure that you have up to date data before continuing.)
- Under Global → Power Query Editor, ensure that every box here is checked. We especially want to make sure the Formula Bar is showing but checking every box will make sure you have all the options that you'll see throughout this book.
- Click OK

There are other options within this area, but for now the default settings will work just fine.

Adjusting Power BI's Default Power Query Properties

To adjust your default settings in Power BI Desktop:

- Go the File tab → Options & settings → Options
- Under Global → Power Query Editor, ensure that every box here is checked. We especially want to make sure the Formula Bar is showing but checking every box will make sure you have all the options that you'll see throughout this book.
- Click OK

> ✎ While in the Power BI Desktop options, you may also want to check the Global → Preview Features tab to see if any new features look enticing. As features are released to Power BI Desktop first, this is a great place to see what is coming to Power Query in Excel.

Extract

In this chapter, we will look at importing a simple CSV file into Power Query in Excel or Power BI to show just how Power Query approaches the tasks above, how they look in the user interface, and how they are identical between the two programs.

The ETL process all begins with the Extract step. Inside this step are four distinct subtasks as follows:

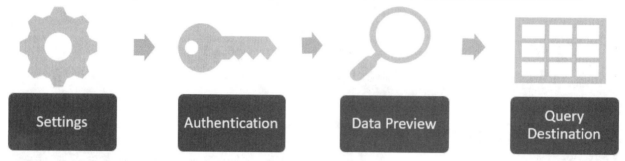

The four sub-steps of the Extract process

Configure Connector Settings (Choose Your Data)

The first step is to choose and configure the data connector we want to work with. In this case, we'll start by creating a new query that uses the CSV connector in Excel:

- Go to Get Data → From File → From Text/CSV

This would be equivalent to the following in Power BI Desktop:

- Go to Get Data → More... → File → Text/CSV

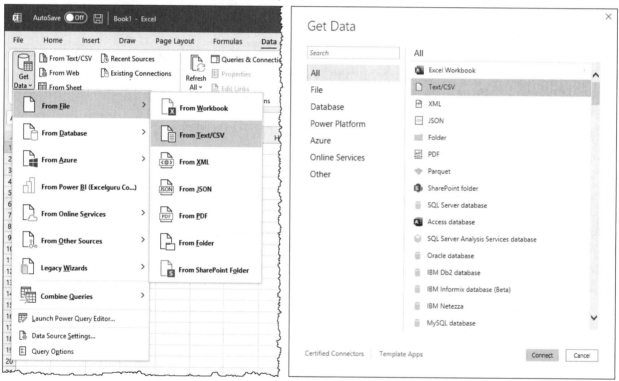

Connecting to a Text/CSV file in Excel (left) or Power BI Desktop (right)

It is worth recognizing that you could attach to a Text/CSV file in less clicks in either program. As Text/CSV files are a common data source, they surface in the user interface much more quickly than drilling down into the sub-menus. In Excel you'll find this connector right beside the Get Data button on the Data tab. And in Power BI the connector is on the very first level of the menu, with no need to drill down into the More... sources. This, however, won't always be the case as we move into other data sources later in the book, so we've standardized on the full path to the data source.

🔨 Power BI Desktop can actually connect to a larger set of data sources than Excel. The intention of the team here is to release beta connectors into Power BI and – once they have passed beta stage – eventually bring them to Excel.

Once we've selected the connector we wish to use, we'll be able to browse to and locate the file. In this case, we'll connect to the following sample file:

```
Ch01 Examples\Basic Import.csv
```

Authentication

Many data sources will require authentication before you'll be allowed to connect to them. Should that be the case, you'll be prompted to provide authentication at this stage. Fortunately, this is a CSV file stored in your local file system and the mere fact that you have access to it implies authentication.

The Preview Window

Once you've selected your file, you'll be taken to a window that looks similar to the following:

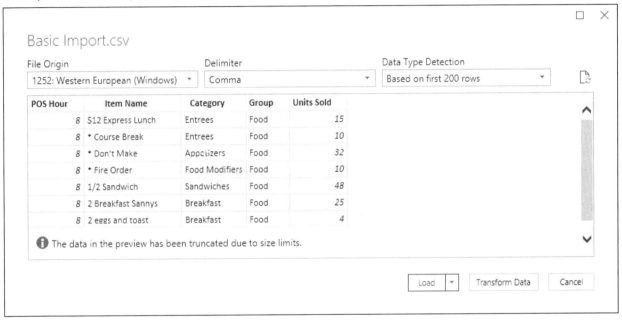

The Preview window for Power Query

The purpose of this window is to present you a view of the data as Power Query will interpret it, allowing you to make any necessary changes before Power Query starts the transformation process. Overall, we find that you rarely need to change anything here, as Power Query is fairly good about making the correct default choices in most cases. Having said that, you'll notice that there are options at the top which will allow you to toggle the settings for:

- **File Origin**. This would allow you to change the file encoding standard. It is unlikely that you will ever need to change this setting.
- **Delimiter**. It is also quite rare that this needs to be changed, as Power Query usually gets this right. If required, however, you could manually set this to one of a variety of options including a list of common characters, custom characters or even fixed column widths.
- **Data Type Detection**. This selection allows you to tell Power Query to detect data types based on the first 200 rows, entire data set or not at all.

Another important thing to be aware of is the message about the data preview being truncated. This is super important to be aware of as there is a limit to how much data can be shown in this window.

Choosing the Query Destination

At the end of the day, it's unlikely you will change anything in this preview. The main purpose of the preview window is really to give you a look at the state and shape of the data and allow you to decide if this data meets one of three criteria:

1. Is it the wrong data set? If so, click the Cancel button.

2.   Is it perfect? Then click Load.

3.   Does it need reshaping or enriching? Then click Transform Data.

> 🏹 It is our belief that 80%-90% of data needs some kind of transformation before it can be used. The degree of transformation may be simple (just renaming a column), or much more complex. Regardless of what is required, however, the default option here should not be "Load", but rather "Transform Data".

Now that we've had a preview and decided that this is the data we need, we'll click the Transform Data button to launch Power Query, which will launch you into a new window as shown here:

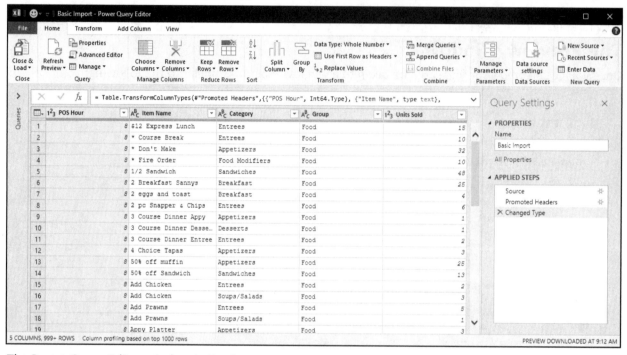

The Power Query Editor window in Excel

Transform

The next step of the ETL process is to Transform your data. Unlike Excel's classic methods for importing data however, Power Query allows you to see and modify the default transformations that the system has assumed for you in the ETL process. These are managed in the Power Query Editor window, which launched upon clicking the Transform Data button.

The Query Editor Window

There are seven main areas of the Power Query Editor that we will be referring to within this book, each of which are numbered in the image shown here:

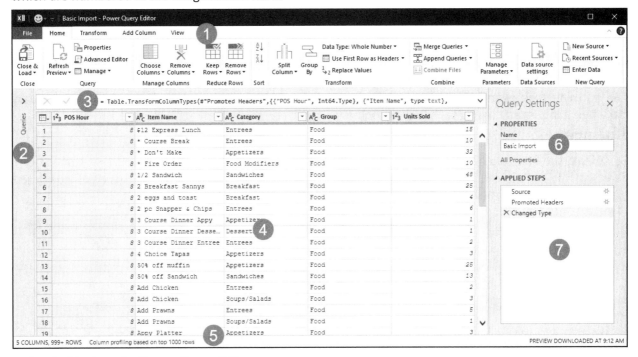

A detailed look at the Power Query Editor

The terms for each of these areas are:

1. **The Ribbon**: Located at the top of the screen, the Power Query ribbon has four tabs: Home, Transform, Add Column and View.

2. **The Query Navigator Pane**: In versions of Excel prior to 365 this pane was collapsed by default. You can always click the > just above the word Queries in order to maximize it, showing a list of all Power Queries in the project. (Note that in Excel 365 and Power BI, this window is expanded by default, and can be collapsed by clicking the < button instead.)

3. **The Formula Bar**: If this area is not showing, it means that you didn't follow our advice earlier in the chapter on setting your defaults correctly. As this is an essential tool, it's a good idea to hop over to the View tab on the Power Query Ribbon and check the "Formula Bar" checkbox now.

4. **The Current View Window**: This area is your working area to execute and preview data transformations. But while it can display a data preview, it may also allow viewing a schema view or diagram view.

5. **The Status Bar**: Located at the bottom of the screen, this provides a quick summary of the column count, row count and indicator of how many rows are being used to drive column profiling statistics, as well as an indicator on the far right as to when the preview was last updated.

6. **The Properties Window**: This area provides the name of the query and is inherited from the query's data source.

7. **The Applied Steps Window**: This area will become very important to you in your Power Query journey, as it shows the transformations that have been applied to your data preview, and that will be applied to the entire data set upon import.

Default Transformations

Upon first extracting data from a file, it is helpful to understand what Power Query has already done for you. To do this, we'll focus on the steps that are listed in the Applied Steps window on the right side. You'll notice that there are currently three steps listed:

1. Source
2. Promoted Headers
3. Changed Type

The key thing to be aware of is that each of these steps is selectable, so you can see exactly what Power Query did when it imported the file. Let's look at each one:

Source

By default, the first step of every query will be called "Source", no matter what data source it comes from. Selecting it in the Applied Steps window will change the preview to show you Power Query's original interpretation of the raw data it extracted:

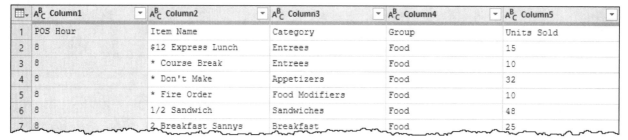

The visual representation of the Source step

At this stage of the ETL process, Power Query has identified each comma in the original data set should be used as a column separator, and it has done so. But no further transformations have been made.

At this point Power Query's internal algorithms determine something about this data: Row 1 looks different than the next few rows... it looks like a header.

Promoted Headers

When you click on the Promoted Headers step, you'll see the effect of Power Query's assumption. It uses the values from row 1 as column headers, replacing the generic Column1, Column2, etc... headers that were there previously:

	POS Hour	Item Name	Category	Group	Units Sold
1	8	$12 Express Lunch	Entrees	Food	15
2	8	* Course Break	Entrees	Food	10
3	8	* Don't Make	Appetizers	Food	32
4	8	* Fire Order	Food Modifiers	Food	10
5	8	1/2 Sandwich	Sandwiches	Food	48
6	8	2 Breakfast Sannys	Breakfast	Food	25
7	8	2 eggs and toast	Breakfast	Food	4

The results of the "Promoted Headers" step

Changed Type

The final step in the current query is called "Changed Type", and it looks as shown here:

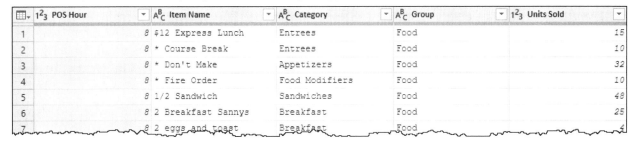

1²₃ POS Hour	AᴮC Item Name	AᴮC Category	AᴮC Group	1²₃ Units Sold
1	8 $12 Express Lunch	Entrees	Food	15
2	8 * Course Break	Entrees	Food	10
3	8 * Don't Make	Appetizers	Food	32
4	8 * Fire Order	Food Modifiers	Food	10
5	8 1/2 Sandwich	Sandwiches	Food	48
6	8 2 Breakfast Sannys	Breakfast	Food	25
7	8 2 eggs and toast	Breakfast	Food	4

Column headers showing the results of the "Changed Type" step

The logic behind this step is that Power Query has scanned the first 200 values in each column and made a judgement as to what types of data the columns hold. It then adds this step to "lock in" those data types prior to loading the data to a destination. The most common data types you'll see are:

- DateTime (indicated with a calendar/clock icon),
- Whole number (indicated with a 123 icon),
- Decimal number (indicated with a 1.2 icon), and
- Text (indicated with an ABC icon).

  🔦 There are actually many more data types available in Power Query, but we will discuss these in more detail in future chapters.

Making and Modifying Transformations

So far, Power Query has been super helpful, and appears to have done everything correctly. But what if we wanted to make some more changes to our data?

Let's start by removing a column that we don't need: the "POS Hour" column. (We're never going to analyze data in this data set at that level.) To do this you have two choices:

1. Select the POS Hour column, right-click it and choose Remove, or
2. Select the POS Hour column and press the DEL key on your keyboard

Notice that whichever choice you made, the column goes away, and we get a new step called "Removed Columns" showing up in our Applied Steps window:

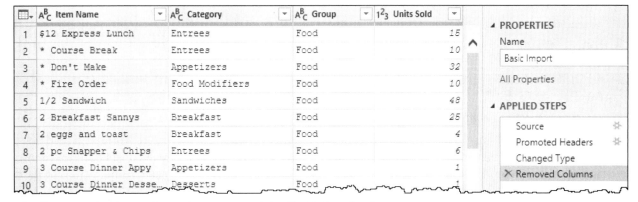

AᴮC Item Name	AᴮC Category	AᴮC Group	1²₃ Units Sold
1 $12 Express Lunch	Entrees	Food	15
2 * Course Break	Entrees	Food	10
3 * Don't Make	Appetizers	Food	32
4 * Fire Order	Food Modifiers	Food	10
5 1/2 Sandwich	Sandwiches	Food	48
6 2 Breakfast Sannys	Breakfast	Food	25
7 2 eggs and toast	Breakfast	Food	4
8 2 pc Snapper & Chips	Entrees	Food	6
9 3 Course Dinner Appy	Appetizers	Food	1
10 3 Course Dinner Desse...	Desserts	Food	1

PROPERTIES
Name
Basic Import
All Properties

APPLIED STEPS
Source
Promoted Headers
Changed Type
✕ Removed Columns

The "Removed Columns" step has removed the "POS Hour" column

But wait... what if we needed that column after all? No problem, we could just delete the step! We're not going to do this now, but if you wanted to, you would go to the Applied Steps window and click the X to the left of the Removed Columns step. The step would disappear immediately, and all the data from that column would be visible again. You can basically view this as an "Undo" feature with Power Query, only better. Unlike the Undo feature, which loses its memory when you close the application, this Undo stack persists until you modify it!

🖐 While being able to Undo a step is very important, there is an even bigger implication of this feature… it gives you license to click anything at any time, just to see what it does. Power Query is always working on a copy of your data, so it is impossible to compromise your data source. This gives you the ultimate ability to look at any button and answer the question "I wonder what that does?" Just click it, and if you don't like the outcome, simply delete the step. We encourage you to do this with any command you don't recognize. Not only will you discover new functionality, you'll start to learn how to match the descriptions in the Applied Steps with the feature that generated them!

Now, getting back to modifying our data… how about we simplify our column names, starting with Item Name:

- Right-click the Item Name column → Rename → Item

A new step called "Renamed Columns" will appear in the Applied Steps window, and you'll have uncovered a trend: each time an action is performed in Power Query, a new step is added to the Applied Steps window.

The implications of this are rather important. Unlike the classic Excel world, where data can be transformed with absolutely no trail at all, Power Query gives a full audit trail of transformations. By default, each step you take through the user interface will be added to this window. While you may not know where the command is that drove this transformation, you can at least see what type of transformation took place and – if you select the previous step – you can even see what the state of the data looked like before the transformation was applied. (Then simply select the later step to see the effect of the transformation.)

Now, what will happen if we decide to rename another column? Will we get a new step again? Let's find out. Just as there are multiple ways to do things in Excel, there are multiple ways to do things in Power Query. To rename our column this time, take the following actions:

- Double click the Units Sold column header
- Change the text to "Units"

Notice how the change takes place, but this time we do NOT get a new step. We still only have one step called "Renamed Columns":

	ABC Item	ABC Category	ABC Group	123 Units		PROPERTIES
1	$12 Express Lunch	Entrees	Food	15		Name
2	* Course Break	Entrees	Food	10		Basic Import
3	* Don't Make	Appetizers	Food	32		
4	* Fire Order	Food Modifiers	Food	10		All Properties
5	1/2 Sandwich	Sandwiches	Food	48		
6	2 Breakfast Sannys	Breakfast	Food	25		APPLIED STEPS
7	2 eggs and toast	Breakfast	Food	4		Source
8	2 pc Snapper & Chips	Entrees	Food	6		Promoted Headers
9	3 Course Dinner Appy	Appetizers	Food	1		Changed Type
10	3 Course Dinner Desse…	Desserts	Food	1		Removed Columns
11	3 Course Dinner Entree	Entrees	Food	2		✕ Renamed Columns

The two rename actions have been combined into a single "Renamed Columns" step

Be aware that whether you right-click and rename the column or double click it, the result here would have been the same. When performing two "like" actions in sequence, Power Query will consolidate them into one step. The reason for this is simple: it keeps the steps list shorter and easier to read. As many files require significant data cleanup, this can be a real blessing.

🖐 Naturally, there can be a flip side to this feature as well. Let's say that you renamed six columns, then realized that you accidentally renamed the wrong column. While you could delete the step, that would remove the *entire* step, including the five rename actions that were correct. Alternately, you could rename the column back to its original name, or – as you'll learn later in this book – edit the M code formula.

Load

At this point, we have a query which has performed the following actions:

- Connected to the CSV data source
- Promoted the first row to headers and set data types
- Removed an irrelevant column
- Renamed two columns to make them more friendly

For this data set, that's enough. The data is in a clean tabular format, and it is ready to be used to drive business intelligence. It is time to finalize the query and do exactly that.

Set Data Types

Before finalizing your queries, it is a very good idea to re-define the data types for each column in the data set. The reasons for this will be discussed in a later chapter, but we want you to set good habits right from the beginning of your Power Query journey. In fact, so does Microsoft, and that is the reason that Power Query adds data types by default as the last step of each query.

While you can click the icon in the top left of each column to choose the appropriate data type, this can take a fair amount of time, especially if you have a ton of columns to deal with. Another trick is to let Power Query set the data types for all columns, then override the ones you want to change. To do this:

- Select any column
- Press CTRL + A (to select all the columns)
- Go to the Transform tab and click Detect Data Type

This will result in a new Changed Type step called "Changed Type1" being added to the query as shown here:

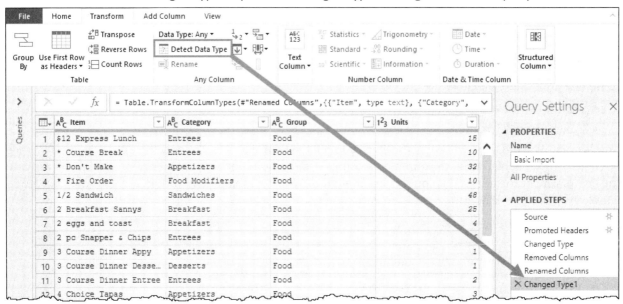

Visualizing the results of (re) setting the column data types

Why "Changed Type1"? The answer is that the query already has a Changed Type earlier in the steps list (the step that Power Query automatically added after the initial promoting of headers). This step helps underscore a few more important things to understand about how Power Query works:

1. Each step name in the query must be unique,

2. The Power Query engine will increment a number at the end of any step name that already exists, and

3. While performing two "like" actions in succession results in the steps being combined (as we saw with the Renamed Columns step), similar actions will not be combined into a single step if there is a different step between them.

Are we stuck with that step name? Not at all. While we generally encourage leaving the steps as is, and learning which user interface commands generate those steps, you are absolutely able to rename them if you'd like to:

- Right-click the Changed Type1 step → rename
- Change the name to "Lock in Data Types"

🖐 The only step that cannot be renamed in this way is the Source step. To rename the source step, you need to edit the query's M code.

Name Your Query

By default, a query assumes the name of the data source as the query name. Since "Basic Import" is far from ideal, we'll change that to something more logical.

- Go to the Query Settings Pane → Properties → Name
- Change the name to "Transactions"

The final query now looks as follows:

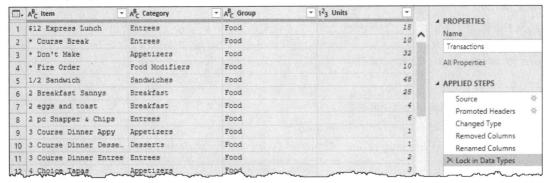

The results of renaming the query and the final query step

Loading the Query - Excel

To finalize your query and load the data in Excel, you need to:

- Go to the Power Query Home tab
- Click Close & Load

At this point, Power Query will apply the steps you built in your query to not only the data preview you have been working with, but rather the entire data source. Naturally, depending on the size of the data source and the complexity of the query, this could take some time. When complete, you should see your data loaded to a table on a new worksheet:

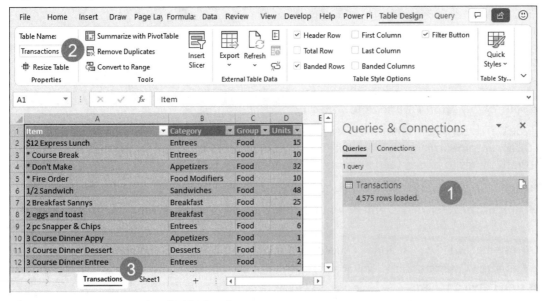

The Transactions query loaded in Excel

In the image shown here, we have highlighted three individual elements in the Excel user interface:

1. The Query pane. This will always match the name of the Query as defined inside the Power Query editor.
2. The Table name. This will usually match the name of the Query, but illegal characters will be replaced with the _ character, and conflicts with other worksheet names will be resolved by appending a numeric value at the end of the query name.
3. The Worksheet name. This will usually match the name of the Query, but illegal characters will be replaced with the _ character, long names may get truncated, and conflicts with other existing tables will be resolved by appending a numeric value within parenthesis at the end of the query name.

🐾 Each of the three elements may be renamed, and do not need to stay in sync with each other in order to continue working.

Loading the Query – Power BI

The only real difference between loading a query in Power BI vs Excel is the name of the button:

*   Go to the Power Query Home tab
*   Click Close & Apply

Just like with Excel, Power Query will apply the query steps to the entire data source. The main difference is that – in Power BI – the data will end up loaded into the Power BI data model. Once complete, you'll see your table show up in the following locations:

*   The Fields list (on the right side of the Reports pane)
*   The Data tab (pictured below)
*   The Model tab

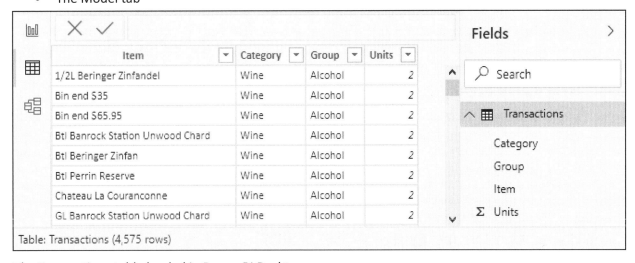

The Transactions table loaded in Power BI Desktop

While Excel shows a summary of the total count of rows loaded in the Queries & Connections pane, Power BI does not. Fortunately, you can still see this information when you switch to the Data tab by selecting a table from the Fields list on the right. When you do this, the total count of rows loaded will be shown in the bottom left-hand corner of the page.

🐾 Unlike Excel, Power BI will sort the data by the first column by default. To replicate this in Excel, you would need to add an explicit step to sort the data before loading.

Refreshing Queries

As you learn more about Power Query's capabilities, you'll realize that it can be used to clean up data much more efficiently than classic methods we used to employ in Excel. But the real benefits come when you get to take advantage of Power Query's ability to refresh a query when the source data file is updated. At that point,

Power Query will perform each of its steps against the updated data source, landing the updated output to the load destination. And the best part? Making this happen is super easy.

- In Excel: Go to Data → Refresh All
- In Power BI: Go to Home → Refresh

After that, all that is left is waiting for Power Query to read the data from the file, process it, and land it to the Excel table or Data Model.

While Power BI will always show a dialog when data is loading, seeing that a refresh is taking place may not be quite as obvious in Excel. It will show in the status bar (at the very bottom of the Excel interface) but this is very subtle and easy to miss. The most obvious way to watch a refresh process is to make sure the Queries & Connections pane is showing, as the refresh process is displayed on the queries listed here. The figure below shows the queries being refreshed in Excel and Power BI respectively:

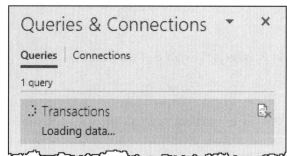 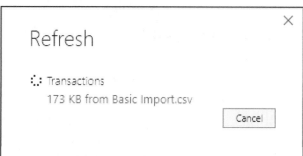

Query load progress displays in Excel (left) and Power BI Desktop (right)

Once the data has been loaded, Excel will show the total number of rows loaded in this tile, and you can check the Power BI row counts by switching to the Data tab and selecting the table (as described in the previous section).

This feature works very well for data files that get updated on a regular basis. Whether the source file is an Excel file that multiple people are updating, or a CSV that you extract every month-end, and just save over the prior month's version, you're a quick click away from a full refresh.

Editing Queries

While the one-click refresh is amazing, we often build solutions that need to be repointed to a different file before refresh. For example, let's assume that we've built a query against a file called Jan.CSV which holds January's data. Then you receive a new data file called Feb.CSV. Obviously just clicking refresh isn't going to achieve the desired result, as it will only refresh the January transactions, and not give you the February transactions from the Feb.CSV file. In this case, we need to change the file path before we trigger the refresh, and that means editing our query. And to edit our query, we need to get back into the Power Query editor. The steps to do this depend on the program you are using.

Launching the Query Editor – Power BI

Launching the Power Query Editor is super easy in Power BI. All you need to do is go to the Home tab and click on Transform Data. This will open the Power Query editor, allowing you to modify any existing queries (or even create new ones).

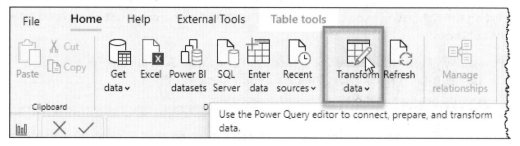

Click the Transform Data button to edit queries in Power BI

Launching the Query Editor – Excel

In Excel, there are actually three options for launching the Power Query editor, and two of them rely on the Queries & Connections pane being active. Unfortunately, this pane needs to be opened manually when a new Excel instance is started, and this can trip people up. Since the vast majority of Excel solutions we build today involve Power Query, you'll find that one of the first steps after opening Excel is to display this pane. You can do that via the following click-path:

- Go to the Data tab → Queries & Connections

As far as options for launching the Power Query editor in Excel, these are your choices:

- Go to the Data tab → Get Data → Launch Power Query Editor
- Go to the Queries & Connections pane → Right-click any query → Edit
- Go to the Queries & Connections pane → Double click any query

🐒 Since we leave the Queries & Connections pane open most of the time, we typically use the latter two methods. We also joke that the difference is really whether you would like to wear out your mouse buttons evenly or put more stress on the left mouse button.

Reviewing Steps

Once you have returned to the Power Query editor, you now have the ability to review any step in the query simply by selecting it in the Applied Steps window. As you select each step, the data preview will refresh to show you the effect of the given step.

🐒 Data previews do take advantage of caching. If you ever notice that the data is out of date, or if you want to ensure that it isn't, you should force a refresh of the previews. To do this, click the Refresh Preview button on the Power Query Home tab.

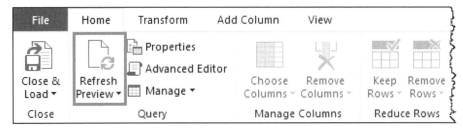

The Refresh Preview button can be found on Power Query's Home tab

Reconfiguring Steps

As you have returned to the editor, you now have the full ability to add new steps, delete steps, and even modify steps within the query. In the case of this example, what we'd like to do is reconfigure the query to point to a new data file.

🐒 If you open the completed Excel or Power BI example files for this chapter, you'll notice that they will fail to refresh. The reason for this is that the Source step is pointed to the path of where the data file lives on our system. Following the steps in this section will allow you to repoint the solution to use the correct data file.

Let's look at the current query steps:

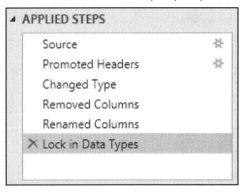

The current steps of the Transactions query

In this image we can see something very important... two of these steps have a little gear icon to the right side of the step name. This gear icon allows you to reconfigure a given step using a user interface.

🖋 As a general rule of thumb, if you are prompted with a dialog when you perform an action in Power Query, you will get a gear icon which will allow you to reconfigure the step. (If you don't get prompted with a dialog, it's likely you won't see the gear icon.) There are exceptions for every rule, of course, as you can see in the case of the Promoted Headers step.

In looking at the query, we know that the original data source must be referenced at the very beginning of the query, and fortunately, the Source step has one of those gear icons!

- Select the Source step
- Click the gear icon

You'll be taken to a new dialog which will allow you to reconfigure key components of this step:

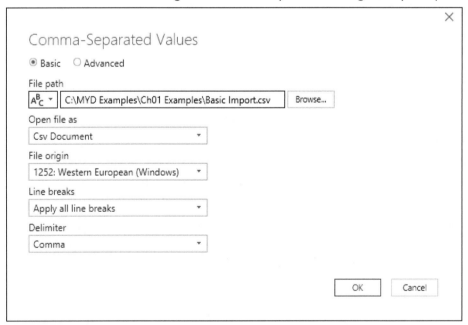

Reconfiguring the Source step

The very first field in this list is the File Path, which just happens be the field we want to update. So let's do exactly that:

- Click Browse
- Locate the following sample file:

      Ch01 Examples\New Data.csv

🖋 Power Query did a pretty good job of configuring the correct choices for us when we first imported the data, so there is nothing else we need to change here. But what if it had picked the wrong delimiter (say Comma instead of Tab). Notice the Delimiter field at the end? You could change that choice here if you needed to!

- Click OK to close the dialog

If the data is significantly different, you'll see it right away in the preview window. But in this file things look identical. So how can we tell if the change was effective? To further complicate this question, the data set has more than the 999 rows that fit in the data preview window. So... what do we do?

We load the data!

> 🔧 While you can certainly select each step in the Applied Steps window to verify that things still work, there is no requirement to do so here. Since this data has an identical structure to the previous file, each of the steps will be applied without issue. There is no need to select them to make that happen.

- On the Home tab, click Close & Load (Excel) or Close & Apply (Power BI)

The data will load, and you can then verify the effect via the Excel Queries & Connections pane (or the row count on the Data tab in Power BI):

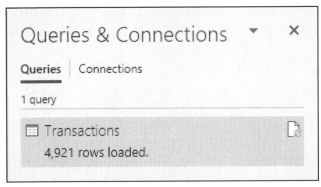

Our data has changed from 4,575 rows to 4,921 rows loaded

The Impact of Power Query

Once you embrace Power Query, you'll find that it will have a huge impact on your workflow. Some of the key things to remember about this amazing technology are:

- It can connect to a wide variety of data sources
- It records each action you take, building up a Power Query "Script"
- It never changes the source data, allowing you to try different commands, and delete the generated steps if you don't like/need them
- It can be refreshed in future when the data changes

The impacts here are huge. Consider a solution where you have built a Power Query script to perform some significant data cleanup, landing the results into a table on an Excel worksheet. You've then created a bunch of charts and reports based on that data table. In the past, when you received an updated data file, you would need to re-do all of the data cleanup steps manually, then copy and paste the clean data into the data table.

With Power Query, all that re-work is gone; you just click the Refresh All button and you are done. It is just that simple. Not only is it faster but the process is guaranteed to be applied consistently each and every time, removing the human factor that can cause errors.

Even if you don't need to take advantage of the refresh capabilities, you'll find that Power Query gives you a wide variety of tools to make your data cleanup easier and faster. As you'll learn throughout this book, historically complex data cleanup tasks can now be performed with ease, allowing you to get to the task you're actually being paid to do: analyzing the data.

The final thing you want to recognize here is that you aren't learning one ETL tool for Excel or a (different) ETL tool for Power BI. The Power Query toolset exists in Excel, Power BI Desktop, Power BI Dataflows, Power Automate and other Microsoft products and services... so far. Microsoft has been quite clear to us that they see this as a growth area and have goals on seeing Power Query in many more places. While learning how to use a new tool is always a journey, isn't it better if that tool can be used in many places?

Chapter 2 - Query Management

Before we dive into the incredibly vast world of Power Query data transformations, it is a good idea to make sure that you set yourself up for success in future. One of the things we know about solutions is that most start small and end up growing and getting more complicated over time. The methods outlined in this chapter will help ensure that you can set up or manage your queries as the size and complexity of your solution grows.

Using a Multi-Query Architecture

As you've learned in the Introduction and Fundamentals chapters, Power Query is a program that provides you with ETL functionality for your solutions. As shown in Chapter 1, Power Query actually works through this entire process in each query that it creates. The only challenge? This doesn't necessarily set you up well for maintenance or when your solution scales in size. For this reason, you may wish to add some additional query layers to the solutions you build.

Separate Queries for E, T & L

Rather than performing all of your query steps in a single query, we can also break the tasks down into multiple queries. For example, consider the following structure:

- **Raw Data**: This query is used to Extract the data from the data source. Very little transformation is done here. In fact, we typically only remove unusable columns or rows in this step. The end goal is a clean table of ALL records in the data set, whether you plan to use them or not. This gives you a single place to view (and change) the original data source, and see what records are available to you.

- **Staging**: The purpose of a staging query is to handle the majority of the Transform portion of the ETL process. In these queries we reduce the data, and make whatever cleanup or transformations are needed in order to create clean tables for later use. While the staging layer should consist of one query at a minimum, it is entirely acceptable to break it down into multiple queries, should you be able to or need to do so.

- **Data Model**: You can view these queries as the final step before the Load stage in the ETL process. These queries always assume the name of the table you wish to create in an Excel worksheet or the Data Model, and their main function is to perform any final steps before loading. Typically, these will include appending and/or merging staging queries together (if required), as well as setting the final data types for each column in the table.

At first glance, this might seem like overkill. Do you really need three separate queries to collect, manipulate and load data for a single Excel table? As it turns out, Ken and Miguel have differing opinions on this…

The Benefits of a Single Query

Miguel prefers to build all steps in a single query or in the least number of queries possible. This is following the same minification concept that is used in other programming languages where you try to optimize your code and its outcome by stripping out any unnecessary pieces inside your solution, keeping things as tidy as possible. Here are some of the benefits from this method:

- It is very easy to find the query you need when there are only a few in your queries list. As the Query Navigator doesn't have a search feature, a huge list can make it difficult to locate the specific query you are after.

- The more queries you have, the harder it is to trace the lineage of them, as Power Query doesn't have a great toolset to do this.

- There are times where splitting queries can trigger a "Formula Firewall" error. This can be super frustrating and there are some instances where you must declare all your data sources in a single query to get past this.

- Other programs that make use of Power Query – such as SSIS and Azure Data Factory – only support a single query. If your goal is to port your solution to one of those platforms, it is a better idea to stick to a single query.

- You always have the benefit of seeing how everything ties together in a single view and make fundamental changes to your query so that the transformation process can be in its most optimal form.

This is incredibly beneficial when you are using the Query Diagnostics tools and checking for more advanced things such as Query Folding and checking the Query plans.

The Benefits of Separating Your Queries

Ken prefers using separate queries and argues that there are several benefits to structuring your queries as described above. While this is not an exhaustive list, here are just a few of the benefits:

- It is very easy to select your Raw Data query, see what data is available to you from the data source, and to update that query if the data source changes.
- You can re-use prior queries (from Raw Data to Staging) multiple times, saving you from having to duplicate work.
- Maintenance of your solution becomes easier when the file path to your data source changes, as you only have one file path to update in your solution, no matter how many times you've used it.
- Updating to a new data source type is also much easier, as you can create a new Raw Data connection in parallel with the old source, make sure the columns are named the same, and then just swap it in place of the original connection.
- While there are instances that required keeping your data sources in one query to avoid the Formula Firewall, there are also instances where you must separate your queries to bypass it.

Again, Ken feels there are many more benefits to this setup. And when you move into using Power Query to serve up the data for a dimensional model in Power Pivot or Power BI, you'll love how easy this setup makes it to build good Fact and Dimension tables. It's for this very reason that the Dimensional Modeling course at https://skillwave.training begins by covering this very topic!

> ⚓ One of the great benefits of Power Query and Power Pivot is the ability to rapidly prototype Business Intelligence solutions without having to get IT involved. Even if you start from an Excel table as a data source, why not set up the solution so that you can easily repoint a query to a SQL database table when the time comes?

Does Separating Queries Impact Performance?

One concern you may have about separating your queries relates to performance. Will this kind of a setup slow down the refresh in any way?

In both Power BI and Excel 2019 and higher (including Microsoft 365), the answer is no. These versions of Power Query take advantage of a technology called "Node caching", which caches the results of the first refresh in a sequence, then re-uses it for other queries in the same refresh session.

Assume for a moment that we have a query setup which retrieves data from a CSV as shown here:

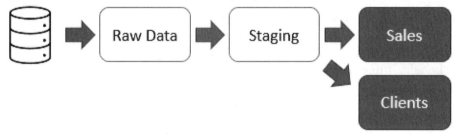

A simple query chain where the results of the Staging query are re-used

Assume also that very little happens in the Raw Data query, but that there is a complex multi-step set of transformations required to get the Staging query into a clean format. From there, the Sales and Clients queries are both quite short, simply pulling their data from the Staging query, then removing the columns and rows that are not relevant for their outputs.

When refreshed, the Staging query will be generated once and cached. The Sales query will reference that cache, perform any additional transformations required, and load that data to the end destination. Next, the Clients query will then go back and reference the cached version of the Staging query, apply any of its own transformations, then load the Clients table to its destination. The key thing to recognize here is that the Staging query results only get generated once, as it is used by multiple queries.

Now, compare that with the setup shown here for the same data source:

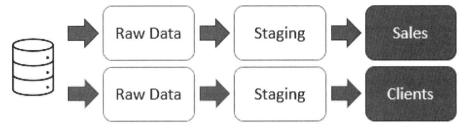

Separate query chains despite calling from the same data source

In this case, when Sales is loaded, it must call the data from the CSV, perform the complex transformations in the Staging query, then finish the steps in the Sales query before being loaded.

Next comes Clients which, as it is completely independent of the Sales query chain, executes the same workflow. Not only must Power Query call the same data from the CSV file, but it also must process all of the steps of the Staging query before it can process and load the results of the Clients query.

As you can see, referencing queries and re-using them can actually help performance, rather than hinder it.

> 🐵 Caution! In the above scenarios, it is important to recognize that the Raw Data and Staging queries should be set up as staging queries. If these queries are loaded to a table or the data model, then you will have created "linked entities", which will take longer to process.

Referencing Queries

So how would you set up queries to follow this pattern? Let's walk through that process by re-creating the query from the previous chapter.

Creating the Base Query

Begin by opening a new Excel workbook or Power BI file. Then:

- Create a new query → From Text/CSV
- Browse to and select \Ch01 Examples\Basic Import.csv
- Click Transform Data to enter the Power Query Editor
- Rename the query to "Raw Data" via the Query Settings pane

At this point, your query should look similar to that shown here:

Power Query's first impression of the Basic Import.csv file

Have you ever built a solution, only to have your boss ask you to expand it a few months later? Are you left wondering if your data set even contains the data they want you to report on? That is one of the goals of this query: a one stop preview of the data available to you.

As it happens, the default set of steps that were recorded when we connected to this data set get us to that point. We have a clean table that shows all of the columns in the data set, and all the rows that fit in the data preview.

> 👠 Remember that each data source needs to be reviewed on a case-by-case basis when setting up your Raw Data query. There will be times that you can just accept the initial query from Power Query, but there will also be times that you'll need to remove the Changed Type step, filter out data, or even expand columns. These will become more apparent as you work through the book.

Referencing Queries

With the initial Raw Data query set up, it is now time to reference it and create our first Staging query. To do this you will need to have the Query Navigator pane expanded. This is easy in Power BI, as this is the default state, but in Excel this pane always starts off collapsed. To do this:

- Make sure the Queries pane is expanded (click the > above the word Queries if needed)

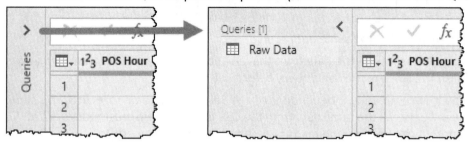

Expanding the Query Navigator in Excel

With the Query Navigator expanded, we can now see all the queries in the solution, and do the work we need to do:

- Right-click the Raw Data query → Reference

This will create a new query called "Raw Data (2)". We want to rename this as "Staging", and there are three different options to do so:

1. Right-click the query in the Query Navigator → Rename
2. Double click the query name in the Query Navigator
3. Change the Name in the Properties area of the Query Settings pane

Each option will result in the query being renamed, so use whichever route you prefer.

While we're here, let's also create that final query that will load our data to the end destination:

- Right-click the Staging query in the Query Navigator → Reference
- Rename the new Staging (2) query as "Sales"

Now, let's take a look at some important elements of what we've accomplished so far:

1. The Query Navigator shows that we now have three queries, of which the currently selected query is "Sales"
2. Unlike our original Raw Data query, which had three steps, the Sales query only has a single step called "Source"
3. The formula bar shows the contents of the Source step, which says the Source step is equal to the output of the Staging query

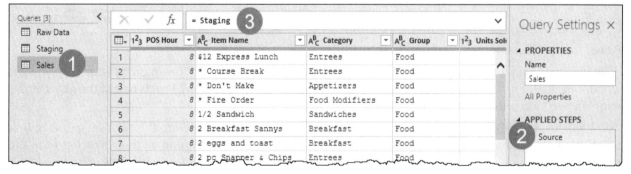

The current state of our solution

The implications of the formula bar are very important to understand here. Whatever happens in the Staging query will flow through to the Sales query. Let's prove that out...

- Select the Staging query
- Select the POS Hour column and press the DEL key (or right-click it and choose Remove)

- Double click the Item Name column to rename it as Item
- Double click the Units Sold column to rename it as Units

The results of the Staging query should now look as shown here:

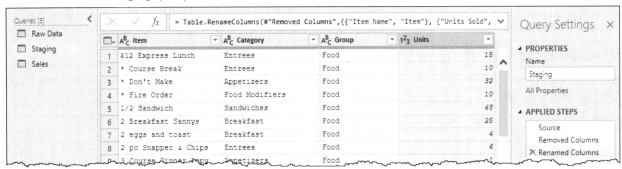

The Staging query after cleaning up the data

Now, return to the Sales query by selecting it in the Query Navigator:

Has anything changed in the Sales query?

If you look closely, you can see that the structure of the Sales query has not changed:

It still has only a single step (Source)

The formula in the formula bar still calls the results of the Staging query (just like it did before we modified the Staging query.

But there is a change, isn't there? The data now reflects exactly what you see in the Staging query. The POS Hour column, which was originally displayed in the Sales query, is no longer there. In addition, what were previously the Item Name and Sales Units columns also bear their names as defined in the Staging query.

Despite not making changes to the Sales query, we are seeing different data here. But this is to be expected as we made a change to the query that Sales is referencing. Any change that happens in the Staging query *must* flow through to the Sales query since the source of the Sales query is the Staging query.

Let's add a new step to the Sales query, to lock in the data types before finalizing this query chain:

- Select the Item column → press CTRL + A (to select all columns)
- Go to the Transform tab → Detect Data Type

So... what have we accomplished? We have rebuilt the ETL process into three separate queries which work in the following manner:

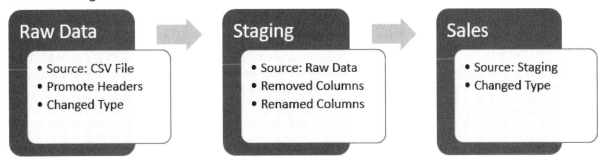

One single ETL process spread across three queries

Again, while this may seem like a lot of work for a very simple query, creating a query chain with distinct steps for each of these phases will set you up to easily scale your solution in future.

⚓ One of the questions you will eventually end up asking yourself is "which transformations should I put in which query?" The answer to this is subjective and is something that you'll develop a preference for over time.

Visualizing the Query Dependency Tree

You should also be aware that Power Query has a dependency viewer built-in to the software, so that you can see how your queries are chained together. To see this:

- Go to the View tab -> Query Dependencies

For this solution, the result will look as shown here:

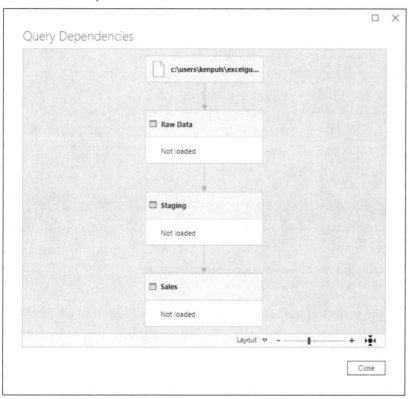

The Query Dependencies viewer

To make best use of this tool, you'll want to click the box in the bottom right corner with the four arrows pointing into it. This is the Zoom feature that will expand the query chain to fix the window. You can then zoom in or out with the zoom slider beside the Zoom control.

🐵 While the Query Dependencies tool looks very useful at first glance, the version that was included with Power Query at the time of publication lacks useful features. And while these aren't critically important in simple models, this view becomes almost useless for larger models with many dependencies. Microsoft has begun working on this in Power Query Online, providing a much more interactive and detailed dependency viewer called Diagram View.

Viewing Dependencies with Monkey Tools

Should you run into an issue where you have a complex query structure and need tools to trace and understand it, you may want to check out Monkey Tools: an Excel add-in that Ken developed in part to solve some of the challenges with this viewer. While it offers many features for both creating and auditing queries, one key feature is the Query Sleuth which provides a robust query tracer as shown here:

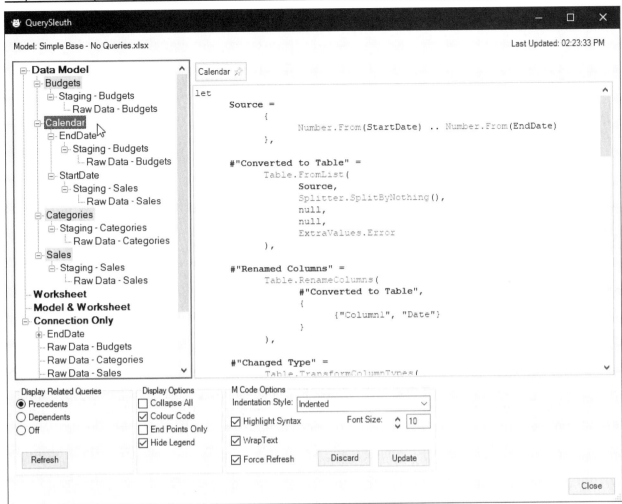

Monkey Tools QuerySleuth displaying the dependency tree and M code behind the Calendar query

You can learn more about this add-in, and download a free trial at Ken's website:

```
https://xlguru.ca/monkeytools
```

Choosing Query Load Destinations

With the queries all created properly, it is now time to load them. But in truth, we only need one of these queries to load to the Excel workbook or Power BI model: the Sales query. The Raw Data and Staging queries are simply helper queries to get to the end result, but we don't really want or need to store their data in our solution.

The good news is that Power Query has a method to deal with this. In Power BI, we accomplish this by disabling the load of the query, and in Excel, we tell the query to load as Connection Only. The effect of these terms is the same in that Power Query will never execute the steps of the query unless called by another query in the query chain. Throughout this book you'll find that we refer to any "Connection Only" query as a Staging query, as that is the point of a Staging query: Stage the data for use by another query.

Choosing a Load Destination in Power BI

By default, all Power BI queries will load to the data model. If you'd like to change this, all you need to do is:

- Right-click the query in the Query Navigator → Uncheck the Enable Load option

As you can see here, queries that are not flagged to load are each shown in italics:

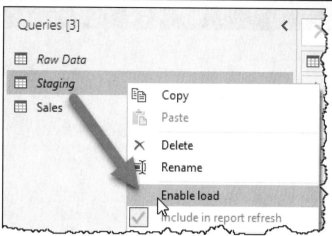

Un-checking the Enable Load option for a query will treat it as a Staging query

Keep in mind that the "Enable load" terminology does not indicate whether the query will be refreshed. When you click Close & Apply (or subsequently choose to refresh the query), the Sales query will call the Staging query, which will call the Raw Data query. But at the end of the process, only the Sales query will show up in the Power BI data model.

Choosing a Load Destination in Excel

While Power BI is quite easy to work with, Excel comes with some choices and a challenge.

The challenge is related to the fact that, unlike Power BI where you can configure each query individually, Excel only allows you to choose one load destination for all queries created in a single Power Query session (since the Power Query Editor was opened). This is unfortunate, as we have three queries, and only want to load one to a worksheet, with the other two being staging queries. Unfortunately, that is not an option as we only get to choose one load destination for all three.

> 🔧 We could have avoided this challenge by creating each query, loading it to the appropriate destination when complete, then creating the next query. The challenge is that this forces you to close the Power Query editor after each query, breaking your mental workflow.

Knowing that we only get to choose one destination, we need to make a smart choice as to what load destination we want to use.

> 🐒 The very worst decision we could make right now would be to simply go to Power Query's Home tab and click the Close & Load button. The reason is that it will then load each new query to a new table on a new worksheet. In other words, we would receive a new worksheet and table for the full contents of the Raw Data, Staging and Sales tables!

To avoid the issue above, we are going to override Power Query's default load behavior:

- Go to Home → click the text (not the image) of the Close & Load button → Close & Load To…

We need THIS Close & Load button!

This will then take you to Excel's Import Data dialog, which will let you choose your load destination:

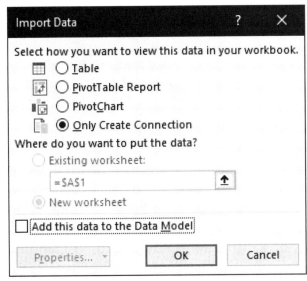

Choosing a Load Destination in Excel

Let's break down our options:

1. **Table**: Would load each of the three queries to a new table on a new worksheet
2. **PivotTable Report**: If you have a single query, this option would load the data into the PivotCache, and create a new PivotTable on a new worksheet. In our case – with three queries in play – it would load all three tables to the Data Model, then create a new PivotTable on a new worksheet.
3. **PivotChart**: Follows a method identical to the PivotTable Report, but creates a PivotChart instead of a PivotTable
4. **Only Create Connection**: Disables the load of each query until we change it (or call one via a reference from another query).

✎ The four options listed above are mutually exclusive, but you can also add the ability to "Add this data to the Data Model" with any of them. Adding this option to the Table choice will load the data to both a worksheet table AND the Data Model (which is not usually recommended), while checking the box with the selection of Only Create Connection will change the behavior of the query to load the data to the Data Model.

It is time to commit the queries:

*   Choose Only Create Connection
*   Click OK

Your queries will all be created as Connection only queries as shown here:

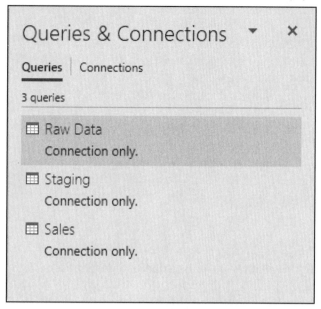

All three queries are loaded as Connection(s) only

So why choose Only Create Connection when you have multiple queries? Consider what would have happened if we had chosen to load all three queries to a worksheet or the Data Model. Not only does each query have to be created, but Excel also needs to build new worksheets or Data Model tables for them. And after those tasks are done, you *still* have to wait for all the data to load… for each of the three queries. Finally, after all the loading is done, you then have to go back, indicate the two tables which should have only been connections, and then wait for Excel to update again as it removes the unnecessary data.

The reason we chose Only Create Connection is purely one of speed. Connection Only queries are created almost instantly. We would rather create all of our queries as Connections quickly, and then update only the ones that do need to load. In fact, we feel so strongly about this that we change our Power Query settings to load new Excel based Power Queries as Connection only by default. Should you wish to do this as well, you can do so via the following steps:

- Go to Get Data → Query Options → Data Load
- Select Specify Custom Default Load Settings
- Unselect Load To Worksheet. You would think there would be a choice here called Only Create Connection, but when you leave both boxes unchecked, you are, in essence, choosing to only create a connection.

> Default Query Load Settings
> ○ Use standard load settings ⓘ
> ● Specify custom default load settings:
>   ☐ Load to worksheet
>   ☐ Load to Data Model

Configuring Default Query Load Settings to load as connection only

☎ Don't forget to un-check the Load to worksheet box! Failure to do so just means you've used a customized setting to replicate the default load settings!

Changing Load Destinations

The challenge we have right now is that our Sales table is loaded as a Connection Only query, but we want to load it to a worksheet. So how do we do that?

The first answer of almost every Excel user we meet is to edit the query and change the load destination from within the Power Query Editor. And they are usually quite confounded when they get to the Close & Load

To... button, only to find that it is greyed out and unavailable. As it turns out, once you have created a Power Query, you cannot change the load destination from within the Power Query editor.

Instead, the method to re-configure the load destination of the Sales (or any other query) is to:

- Go to Excel's Queries & Connections pane
- Right-click the query you wish to change (Sales) → Load To...

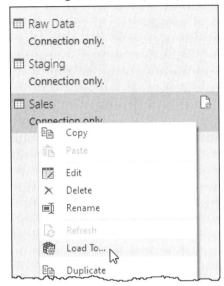

Changing the Load To... destination of an existing query in Excel

You can now select another choice from the Import Data menu. In this case, we'll choose to be consistent with what we did in Chapter 1:

- Select Table
- Click OK

The end result is the same output as we saw in Chapter 1, but using a more robust and scalable query structure:

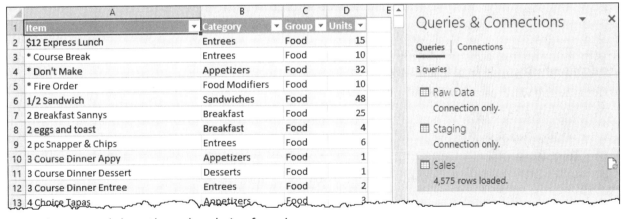

From data to worksheet through a chain of queries

> 🔍 While we showed how to change a load destination from a Connection Only query, be aware that you can change any query from one load destination to another using this functionality.

> 🔍 Pro Tip! Accidentally loaded a query to a Table on a worksheet instead of loading it as Connection Only? Rather than change the load destination and then delete the worksheet, try deleting the worksheet first. When the worksheet is removed, the query will automatically be changed to Connection Only, saving you a step!

Keeping Queries Organized

The more comfortable you get with Power Query and especially the methods explained in this chapter, the more queries you will end up creating. It won't be long before you need a way to keep them organized.

Power Query allows creating folders (and subfolders) in order to group your queries as you need. You'll find this ability in the Query Navigator pane inside the Power Query Editor, as well as in the Queries & Connections pane in Excel.

Creating New Power Query Folders

When creating new folders, you have two different options whether you are in the Query Navigator pane or working with the Queries & Connections pane in Excel.

To create a new (empty) folder:

- Right-click any empty area → New Group...

To move queries to a new group, creating the group on the fly:

- Select the Query (or multiple queries by holding down CTRL as you click them)
- Right-click any selected query → New Group...

You will then be prompted to enter the name of the new group, and (optionally) a description for that group:

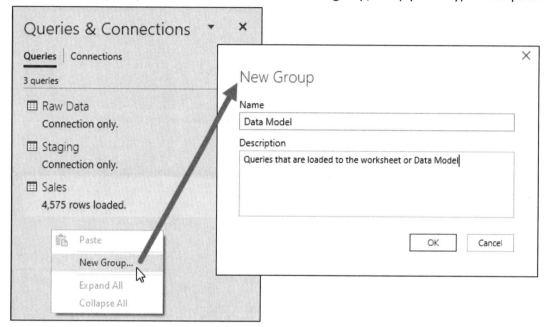

Creating a new group to keep queries organized

In this case, we will create three new groups in all:

- Raw Data Sources
- Staging Queries
- Data Model

Once complete, the Queries & Connections pane would look similar to this:

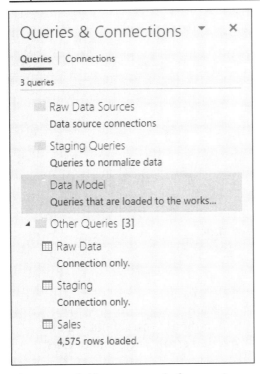

Three new folders are ready for queries

🔍 Inside the Power Query Editor, the group's description shows when hovering the mouse over the group name.

Assigning Queries to Folders

Of course, if you chose to move a query into a specific folder when creating it, they will already be nested within the folder. On the other hand, if you are pre-setting your groups for later use, they will be created in the Other Queries group by default.

Assignment of queries to a group *should* be as easy as dragging and dropping them into the appropriate folder. Unfortunately, while this is the case in the Query Navigator pane inside the Power Query Editor, drag and drop is not supported in the Queries & Connections pane. To assign your queries in this pane, you will need to take the following actions:

- Right-click the query → Move to Group → select the folder you want to hold the query

  🔍 If you are working in Excel, you can easily jump back into the Power Query editor by double clicking any query. Once there, expand the Query Navigator pane, and you'll have full access to drag and drop to make your life easy.

Re-Ordering Queries and Folders

Query groups are displayed vertically in the order you created them. While this has a logic to it, the reality is that you will want to reorganize your queries into another order. Again, like moving folders around, drag and drop is only supported inside the Query Navigator pane in the Power Query Editor. If you are working in the Queries & Connections pane in Excel, the steps you need to take are:

- Right-click the query or group → Move Up (Move Down)
- Repeat this action as many times as needed to get the items in the right order

In this case, we'd like to re-order our folders to put the most important queries at the top, and the least reviewed at the bottom. In other words, we want to see Data Model, Staging Queries and finally Raw Data Sources. And while the above click-steps will work, it just feels so much more natural to use the drag and drop functionality available inside the Power Query Editor:

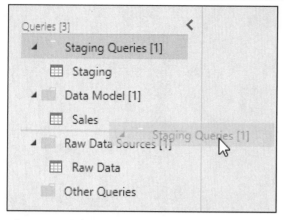

Changing the folder order via drag and drop inside the Power Query Editor

Creating Query Sub-Folders

To create subfolders for grouping your queries, you'll need to:

- Right-click the existing folder → New Group...

  🔧 While queries can be assigned to a new folder that is created on the fly, you cannot create a subfolder hierarchy on the fly and move a query into it. You'll need to create the subfolder first, then move the query afterwards.

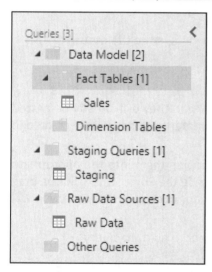

A complete folder structure to hold queries for a dimensional model

Splitting an Existing Query

Of course, many people who just dive-in to Power Query never set their data up using the methods we have outlined in this chapter. In fact, it is much more likely that they would do everything in one query. So how would you fix that? Is it game over? Do you have to rebuild the solution from scratch to get it correct?

Not at all!

Let's consider the query we built in Chapter 1, where the Applied Steps window of the Transactions query ended up with the following steps:

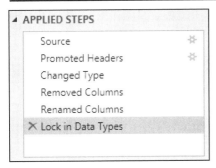

The final Transactions query from Chapter 1

In order to make that query functionally equivalent to the query structure created in this chapter, you would:

- Edit the Transactions query
- Right-click the "Lock in Data Types" step → Extract Previous
- Enter "Staging" as the new query name
- Select the Staging query
- Right-click the "Removed Columns" step → Extract Previous
- Enter "Raw Data" as the new query name

With the end result being a query chain that is almost identical to that constructed earlier:

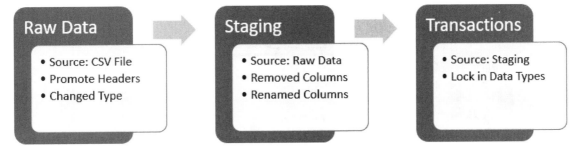

The result of splitting the Chapter 1 solution into three separate queries

The difficult part in this task is really figuring out where to split the queries apart. But the secret is understanding that all the steps prior to the one you select will be split into a new query.

> ✒ The reality is that we don't always recognize when we should stop performing steps in one query and kick off a new query for further transformations via the Reference command. But the good news is that the Extract Previous command will let us do that later when we recognize the need.

Final Thoughts on Query Architecture

Obviously, separating a single task into multiple queries takes more work than doing everything in a single query. Is it worth it, or should you stick to a single query? The answer to this question really depends on your goals with your project.

Ken believes that this provides the ultimate flexibility for reshaping data to feed data models. Miguel prefers to keep the number of queries in his solutions as small as possible. As you work with Power Query, you'll discover the sweet spot that works for you, as this is definitely a style thing. You may decide that one query, two queries or even eight queries per task is the ideal solution. And you may even find that for certain tasks you need to differ from your own chosen style.

In the case of this book, our goal is to focus on the data transformation techniques themselves. For that reason, we will be keeping things simple with a single query in most cases. But when you get into real world solutions, you may want to consider the techniques shown here.

At the end of the day the great news here is that we have options and flexibility to build each solution as we need it in the style that feels most comfortable.

Chapter 3 - Data Types and Errors

This chapter is dedicated to two of the most common issues that face new users to Power Query: understanding that Power Query is about data *types* (not data formats), and how to understand and deal with errors in a Power Query solution.

Data Type vs Formats

One of the common questions we get in live courses, blog comments and forum posts is a variant of, "How do I format my data in Power Query or Power BI?" The short answer is that you don't, but the longer answer is a discussion on data types vs formats.

Formats

To illustrate the issue, let's take a quick look at some sample data in an Excel table in the following workbook:

`Ch03 Examples\Data Types vs Formats.xlsx`

Precision	Whole	Currency	Decimal
0	9,553.000000	1,603.000000	1,330.000000
2	3,940.950000	348.920000	1,571.810000
4	9,350.095000	7,703.331800	7,578.778900
6	5,663.684353	2,951.881907	7,028.786416

Sample numeric data in Excel

What you see here is data that has been formatted in Excel. While each of the values shown in the table is rounded to the number of decimals shown in the first column, you'll notice that they have all been *formatted* to show 6 decimal places. The key distinction you need to recognize here is that the first value in the whole number column is a *numeric data type* with a *value* of 9553, which has been *formatted* to be displayed as 9,553.000000.

Why is this important? If you asked someone in Germany to format this data, they wouldn't choose to display the value the same way. Instead, they would present the value with a *format* of 9.553,000000. The value hasn't changed, but the way it is displayed has.

> ✎ A Format controls how data is displayed without affecting the underlying value or precision in any way.

Data Types

While this is starting to change in Microsoft 365, Excel has treated data types and formatting as very similar things in its history. If you take a look at the true data types that Excel manifests, it is a short list:

- Numbers
- Text
- Blanks
- Errors
- Boolean (True/False)

Dates are actually *numeric values* representing the number of days since Jan 1, 1900, *formatted* to show as a date that we recognize. Times are also *decimal values* (fractions of a day), *formatted* to show in our time format.

Power Query has five major classifications of data types including:

- Numeric
- Dates & Times
- Text
- Boolean (True/False)
- Binary (files)

But within the first two categories, there are also additional data subtypes. The other thing to be aware of is that each of these data types is distinct, which will have an impact on how you convert from one data type to another.

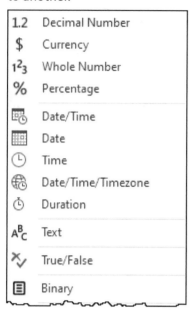

1.2	Decimal Number
$	Currency
1²3	Whole Number
%	Percentage
	Date/Time
	Date
	Time
	Date/Time/Timezone
	Duration
A^BC	Text
	True/False
	Binary

Power Query data types

At this point, the important piece to realize here is that these data types are all about defining the *type* of data, not how it is formatted. Let's prove that by having a look at what happens when we import the sample data table into Power Query.

- Display the Queries & Connections Pane (Data → Queries & Connections)
- Double click the DataTypes query
- Select the cell in the third row of the "Whole" column

There are a few things worth noticing about the query at this point:

1. The Data Type indicator in the top left of the columns all show as "ABC123": a data type that wasn't included in the previous list. This data type has an official name of "any" and indicates that a data type either hasn't been determined for this column, or that there may be a mixture of data types in the column.

2. The cell you selected contains a value of 9350.095. Despite the other values on this row carrying four decimals, only three are needed to show the true value, so that is what Power Query gives you.

3. By selecting a single data cell, Power Query triggers a preview of the data point in the bottom left corner of the windows. This is super handy, as it has much more room to show longer text strings, and even contains selectable text (allowing you to discover if there are leading/trailing spaces on a value).

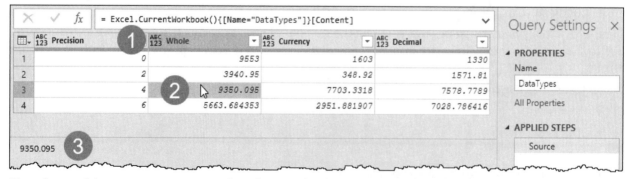

How do you drive an accountant crazy? Make sure the decimals aren't lined up!

What we want to recognize here is that Power Query is showing us the raw data, without any data types defined. Let's define the data types of the columns, starting with the first two:

- Click the ABC123 on the Precision column → Whole Number
- Change the data type of the Whole column (using the same steps)
- Select the same cell you selected previously

Notice anything different? Like the fact that the value of 9350.095 has actually been changed to 9350, not just in the top column, but in the data preview down the bottom of the window?

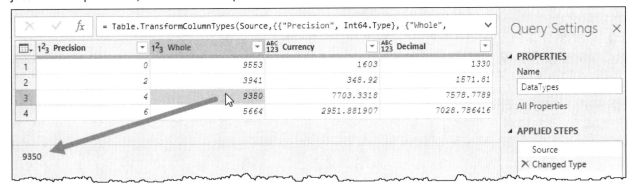

This number has been rounded to zero decimals

By setting the data type to Whole Number, Power Query has changed some of the data points by rounding them to a whole value. If you intended this, then no problem. But if you still need the decimal precision in order to receive correct aggregate values later, and were only doing this for formatting, you have a problem on your hands, as these values have lost that precision.

Next, let's set the data type on the Currency column:

- Click the ABC123 → Currency (Fixed Decimal Number in Power BI)
- Select the cell in the last rows of the Currency column

There are a few things to recognize about this column's output, starting with the very first value. The first thing that you'll notice is that the *formatting* in the column – while it may not appear exactly as shown in the image captured here – is consistent down the entire column, showing two decimal places.

> 🔨 Interestingly, in Power Query's early implementations the Currency (Fixed Decimal) data type did not include a formatting component. In other words, the value of 1603 would have been shown without the decimals. Due to feedback from the user community, Microsoft changed this to not only apply the data type, but also added the Currency formatting based on the settings in your Windows Control Panel.

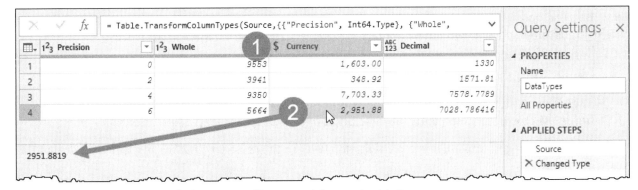

The Currency (Fixed Decimal) data type affects precision and adds formats

The important thing to recognize about this data type is that – as a data type – its primary job is to deal with the precision of the values – something that you can see in the final row of the Currency column. If you check the value preview in the bottom left, you will see that the true value of the data point is 2951.8819, while the column's format shows 2,951.88. Comparing that to the original value of 2951.881907 shows that this value has been rounded off to four decimals.

⚓ Despite the fact that the Currency (Fixed Decimal) data type also includes a format to display two decimal places, it rounds the data point to four decimal places. If this seems odd, think of foreign currency exchange rates which are carried to four decimal places.

The final numeric data type we will explore at this point is the Decimal data type, which we will apply to the Decimal column:

- Click the ABC123 (on the Decimal column) → Decimal
- Select the cell in the last row of the Decimal column

In this case you'll notice that the values are displayed to their full precision, with no rounding and no extra formatting at all. Any trailing decimals of zero are suppressed showing only the number of characters required to display the value. This can be proven by checking the preview for each value and recognizing that the values you see in each cell of the Decimal column match the value preview that appears when you select the given cell.

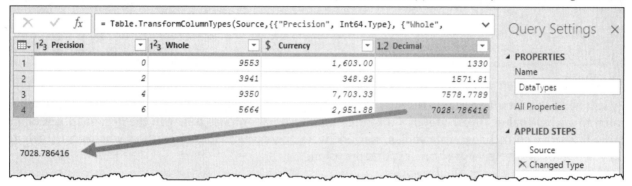

The Decimal data type preserves all decimal values

The big thing to be aware of here is that data types and formats are not at all the same thing:

- **Formats**: Control how a number is displayed, without affecting the underlying precision in any way.
- **Data Types**: Control the type of data and will change the precision of the value to become consistent with the type of data you have declared.

This is obviously a very important distinction that you should be aware of. Setting a data type can (and often does) change the underlying value in some way, while formatting never does.

So How Do You Set Formats in Power Query?

In short, you don't.

In the data types vs formats battle, the Query Editor is all about setting the *type* of data, not the formatting. Why? Because no one is going to read your data in the Query Editor anyway. This tool is about getting the data right, not presenting it. Ultimately, we're going to load the data into one of two places:

- **Excel**: A worksheet table or the Power Pivot data model
- **Power BI**: The data model

⚓ Remember that this book is focused on Excel and Power BI. If you are using Power Query in a different Microsoft product, you may have additional or different load destinations.

The formatting then gets applied in the presentation layer of the solution. That means one (or more) of the following places:

- Worksheet cells. Whether landed to a table, PivotTable or CUBE function, if it lives in the Excel grid, you can apply a number style to the data.
- Measure signatures (if the data is landed to the data model). In Excel this can be controlled by setting the default number format when creating your Measure, and in Power BI it is configured by selecting the measure then setting the format on the Modeling tab.
- Charts or Visuals. In Excel you can force the number format to appear as you want on your chart, and you have similar options in the Power BI visuals formatting tools.

The Order of Application Matters

Since data type changes can affect precision of the values, it is very important to realize that the order of your Changed Type steps matter. To demonstrate this:

- Make sure you still have the Changed Type step selected in the Applied Steps pane
- Click the 123 (on the Whole column) → Decimal
- When prompted, choose to "Add new step" (instead of "Replace current")

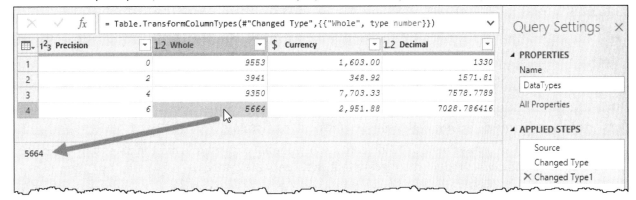

If the Whole column is now a Decimal, what happened to the decimals?

Usually, when applying data types to a column, Power Query just does what you ask without prompting you at all. In the cases where you have a Changed Type step selected **and** attempt to change the data type on a column that is already contained in the step, you will be given a choice to either replace the configuration of the current step or to add a new step. This choice will yield very different results.

When you choose to add a new step, the results of the previous Changed Type are calculated first, and then your new data type is applied based on those values. Based on the steps taken above, we effectively connected to the data and rounded the values in the Whole column to whole numbers, removing all decimals. We then changed the data type on the column to accept decimal values. The issue is that the decimals no longer exist, as the values have already been rounded.

By contrast, if we had selected the "Replace current" instead of "Add new step", the results would have been quite different. Instead of applying the Whole number data type in the original Changed Type, it would have updated the step to use Decimal, and the decimal precision would have been preserved.

> 🐵 The thing we want you to remember is that the step order very much matters, and it is a good reason to review any Changed Type step that Power Query automatically applies when you originally import your data. By default, Power Query only previews the first 1000 rows when setting your data types, meaning that if the first decimal value in your data set shows up at line 1001, Power Query will choose a Whole Number format, rounding all rows in that column upon import. Even if you correct the data type in a new step later in the query, the values have already been rounded!

> 🔦 You may be wondering why Power Query doesn't just override the previous step without asking. The answer is there are data types that must be converted to one format before being converted to another. An example of this would be where you want to convert a text-based date with a time to just the date. You cannot convert 2012-12-23 12:05 PM to a date without converting it to a datetime first, and then converting the datetime to a date.

The Importance of Defining Data Types

Since you have to format your data in Excel or Power BI anyway, and incorrectly choosing data types can affect data precision, can you just avoid setting data types in Power Query?

The answer is absolutely not.

The first reason you need to declare your data types is that all Power Query functions require inputs of *specific* data types, and – unlike Excel – Power Query does not implicitly convert from one data type to another for you. If you have a column formatted with a numeric data type and try to use a command that requires a text input, you will receive an error.

The second reason is that an undefined data type of "any" (which is shown with the ABC123 icon) allows the program to make its best guess when being used. While this can work in some cases it is extremely dangerous to load your data to a worksheet or the data model with the data types still (un)defined as an "any" data type. Why? Let's have a look at a query, and what happens when the data is loaded with an undefined column.

Query	Undefined Dates
1	2020-01-01
2	2020-01-12
3	2020-01-13
4	2020-01-24

Worksheet	Undefined Dates
	43831
	43842
	43843
	43854

Data Model	Undefined Dates
	2020-01-01
	2020-01-12
	2020-01-13
	2020-01-24

Data can be interpreted differently depending on the load destination

As you can see, the Query has the ABC123 indicator of an undefined data type, but the dates look like dates. They are even in italics, which seems to indicate that they really are dates.

But then the data gets loaded to a worksheet. Without a data type defined, Power Query gets to make its best guess as to what you need, so it returns a column of values. (These represent the date serial number for the given date.)

Now here's where things get REALLY dangerous… the query's load destination is pointed to the data model (originally or via modifying the original query). The output now looks great, doesn't it? The problem that you can see in the Excel grid is that the data is left aligned, and the reason is that these are not dates, they are text. And indeed, if you were to check the data model, you could confirm that these dates have indeed been loaded as text.

> ⚒ Power BI is not exempt from this issue. It leverages the data model to store its data, so it will load an undefined date as text, just like Excel's data model.

This is the real danger of leaving your data types undefined. Power Query still applies a *format* to a column defined with an "any" data type, but it doesn't mean the data type is defined. No matter which version you look at above, it is not what we want, and to make matters worse, merely changing the load destination can impact what you get at output.

> ⚒ Later in this book we will get in to playing with transformations such as appending or merging tables. These can combine data from different data sets into the same column. If the data is of different types, you will find that the column will revert to an "any" data type at that point.

> 🐵 Don't get burned! Always make sure that the final step of any query that loads to a worksheet or the data model redefines the data types!

Common Error Types

There are two types of errors in Power Query, and they manifest in different ways:

- **Step Level Errors**: These errors occur at the step level, preventing not only the specific step from being executed, but any subsequent steps as well. You will know you have a step level error in your query when your query will not load at all.
- **Value Errors**: These errors occur at a cell level. The query will still load, but the error values will be replaced with blank values in the end data source.

To understand how these errors manifest, as well as work through how to fix them, open the following sample file:

```
Ch03 Examples\Error Types.xlsx
```

There is a nice table in the worksheet, and so far everything looks like it is working just fine.

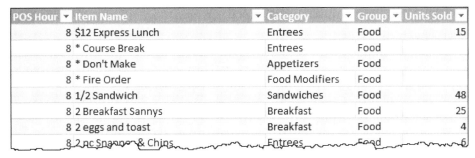

POS Hour	Item Name	Category	Group	Units Sold
8	$12 Express Lunch	Entrees	Food	15
8	* Course Break	Entrees	Food	
8	* Don't Make	Appetizers	Food	
8	* Fire Order	Food Modifiers	Food	
8	1/2 Sandwich	Sandwiches	Food	48
8	2 Breakfast Sannys	Breakfast	Food	25
8	2 eggs and toast	Breakfast	Food	4
8	2 pc Snapper & Chips	Entrees	Food	6

The output table based on the ErrorData query

So far so good, but it is time to cause some problems:

- Go to Data → Refresh All

You'll immediately be prompted with an error letting you know that the source data file cannot be found.

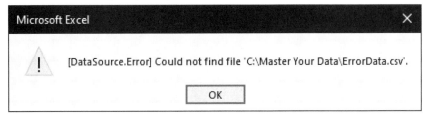

Sorry, but you can't refresh this file...

As it is blocking the file from loading, we know that we are dealing with a Step Level error.

Step Level Errors

The two most common Step Level errors are triggered when Power Query:

- Cannot find the data source
- Cannot find a column name

To get the refresh working we will need to edit the query, find the step that is exhibiting this issue, and figure out which error type we have in front of us. Only then will we be able to fix it.

- Display the Queries & Connections pane (if it isn't already showing)
- Edit the ErrorData query

🖎 When debugging queries, it is a good idea to always click the Refresh Preview button on the home tab of the Power Query Editor. This will ensure you are not working with a cached version of the preview that doesn't show the error you are hunting!

Dealing with Data Source Errors

By default, when you edit a query, the very last step will be selected for you. Step Level errors become very obvious at this point as, if one is present in your query, Power Query will display a big yellow message in the main preview area in place of the data.

Houston, we have a problem – and it's Step Level!

There are a few things to notice about this error message:

- It begins with the specific error type. In this case we have a DataSource.Error indicating that Power Query could not find the data source file.
- It provides a Details area which indicates the specific item that caused the error. In this case it is the full file path to the missing file.

- There is a Go To Error button. This button shows up when the current step is NOT the source of the error.

In most cases, when you click the Go To Error button, you will be taken directly to the step that caused the error. In this case, however, you are taken to the Promoted Headers step instead. And when you attempt to click the gear icon to reconfigure the step, it tells you that there are errors in previous steps.

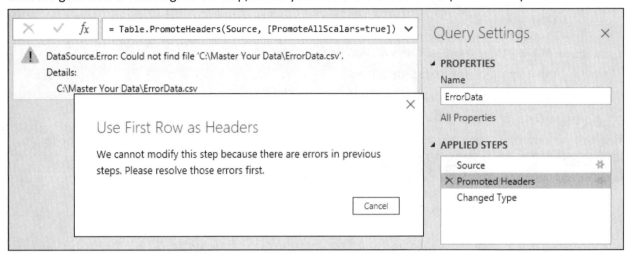

Reconfiguring a step is not possible if a previous step contains a Step Level error

With any luck, this will be classed as a bug, and will be fixed by the time you get this book. Should this happen to you, however, you need to know how to deal with it. The answer is fairly straightforward – just keep clicking the previous step until you find out which step caused the error, or until you get to the very first step of the query.

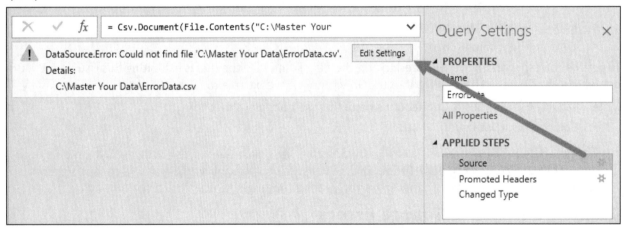

The first step of our query shows that it is causing the error

This type of error is incredibly common, especially when sharing Power Query solutions with colleagues since file paths are always hard-coded. Personalized folders like Desktop and Downloads contain your username in the file path, and even network drives can be mapped to different letters for different people. In fact, every completed example file for this book will present you with this issue, as you won't be storing your data files in the same place we do!

You actually have three different options for updating the file path:

1. Click the gear icon next to the Source step,
2. Click the Edit Settings button in the error message, or
3. Go to Home → Data Source Settings → select the missing data source → Change Source

> ☜ The Data Source Settings dialog can actually be accessed without entering the Power Query Editor. In Excel you'll find it near the bottom of the Get Data menu on the Data tab. In Power BI it is found on the Transform Data menu on the Home tab.

No matter which you choose, you'll be taken to the window to browse and update the file path. Do that now, locating and selecting the data file shown here:

```
Ch03 Examples\ErrorData.csv
```

Once you have made the change, you should now see the preview populated with values.

☎ While the first two methods will update the data source for the selected query only, the last method has a benefit in that it will change ALL instances of the data source, even if it is used in multiple queries. Having said that, you will also need to click Refresh Preview in order to make the editor recognize that you have updated the data source.

"Column x Wasn't Found" Errors

At this point, let's trigger another Step Level error:

- Select the Promoted Headers step
- Double click the Item Name column and rename it to "Item"
- Confirm that you want to insert a new step
- Select the Changed Type step

Notice how, once again, we lost our data preview and are staring at an error? This is a step level error, and once again it will prevent our data from loading. This time however the cause of the error is slightly different.

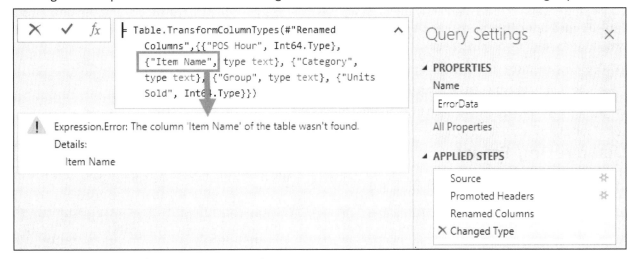

An Expression Error indicating a missing column

In many ways, this error is even more common than the file path error shown earlier. No matter how it was caused, it indicates that one of the columns referred to in this step was no longer present in the previous step. In this case, Power Query is trying to set the data type on the Item Name column, but that column no longer exists, as it was renamed in the previous step to something different.

While this kind of error can show up in many places, by far the most common place you'll see it is in a Changed Type step. The reason for this is because the Changed Type step hard codes the names of columns into its formula. If anything happens earlier in the query that causes the column to be renamed, removed or just no longer present, you'll end up experiencing this issue on any step that hard codes the column names in it.

So how can we fix this? Again, you have some options:

- Delete the step and re-create it based on the current state of the prior step
- Adjust the previous step to make sure the column name still exists
- Remove any previous step that caused the column to no longer exist
- Adjust the formula to update or remove the column that is no longer present

By the time you finish this book you'll be comfortable with the last option but for now we will keep this easy. This step was only inserted to break the query, so let's get rid of it:

- Click the x next to the Renamed Columns step to remove it
- Select the Changed Type step to verify that your data preview is working

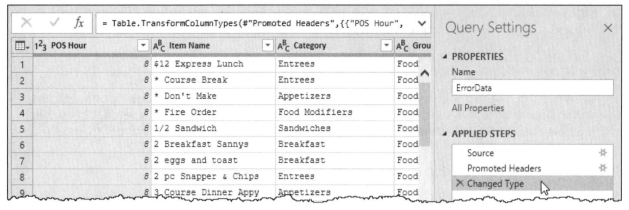

Everything is looking good!

> ✎ In the vast majority of cases, it is safe to remove a Changed Type step that triggers a Step Level error. Ask yourself at that point if you absolutely need to re-apply it where it was, or whether it would be a better option to just re-define all data types at the end of the query.

Value Errors

While Step Level errors are definitely the most egregious errors in Power Query, they aren't the only errors you will encounter. Another common error type is Value errors. These can actually be a bit more sinister as well, as they aren't always obvious.

Value errors are most frequently caused by one of two scenarios:

- Invalid data type conversions, or
- Performing operations with incompatible data types

Let's look at how easy it is to trigger these issues.

Discovering Errors

If you take a look at the Units Sold column of this data, you'll notice that we have some challenges in this column.

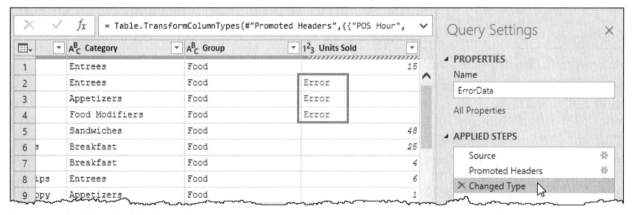

It seems the Units Sold column has some errors…

In this case we can plainly see that rows 2 through 4 contain an Error in the Units Sold column, but the reality is that your erroneous data won't always be showing in the data preview. So how would you identify that an error is present in the column?

If you are using Power BI or Microsoft 365, you'll notice that – immediately under the column header – there is a short red line, followed by a striped bar. This is a visual indicator that there is some kind of error in the column.

In addition, if you'd like to see even more details about your column, you can toggle these settings on the View tab:

- Column Quality

- Column Distribution
- Column Profile

With these settings on, you'll find some quick statistics and charts at the top of your columns which are intended to help you assess your data quality.

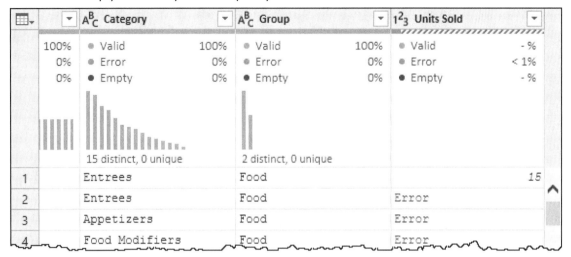

Column quality indicators displayed on our columns

The Column Quality setting provides the first three bullet points, while the Column Distribution provides the charts that show the number of distinct (individual) and unique (only show up on one row) values in the data set. The final setting – Column Profile – provides you a much more detailed view at the bottom of the screen when you select an entire column.

> 🔍 If you check the status bar at the bottom of the Power Query window, you will see that the phrase "Column profiling based on top 1000 rows". It's not immediately obvious, but these words are click-able and will allow you to change the profiling to run over the entire data set instead of the 1000 row default.

You'll notice that some of the statistics and the charts do not show up for the Units Sold column. This is expected since there are errors in the columns. Once we've dealt with them, it will show statistics similar to the other columns.

> 🔍 As these items tend to take a lot of space, we usually work with Column Quality and Distribution off, but Column Profile on. This allows us to see the statistics when we need them by selecting a column but leaves more room in our data preview window for data.

> 🐵 These options were released to Microsoft 365 users after Excel 2019 was released and do not exist in Excel 2019 or earlier. Without these visual indicators, you'll need to scroll down the column to see if any errors are present.

Errors Caused by Invalid Type Conversions

Now that we know we have at least one error in the column, how can we work out the cause?

The answer to this is to select the cell and check the message that comes up in the preview. Before you do, however, you want to be aware that *where* you click will provide you with different functionality:

- If you click the word "Error" in the cell, Power Query will add a new step to the query and drill into that error. While you will still see the error message, this is not what you want to do, as you'll lose all of the other data in the preview window.
- Instead, if you click the whitespace to the side of the Error keyword, Power Query will show you the text of the error message below the preview area. The benefit of this approach is that you won't lose the context of the rest of the query, and don't have any extra steps to manage once you fix the error.

Let's see what caused this error:

- Click the whitespace next to the first Error in the Units Sold column

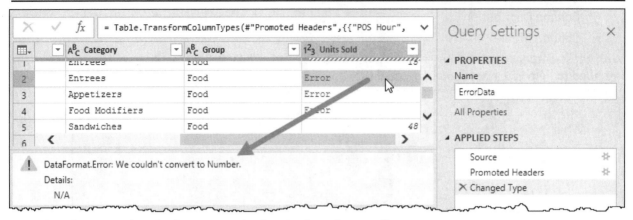

Click the whitespace beside the error to display the "Results Pane"

> 🖋 If you accidentally clicked the Error keyword and created a new step, just delete it to return to the full data preview.

You'll notice that the error message shows up in the Results Pane below the preview and indicates that it is a "DataFormat.Error". This terminology is a bit unfortunate, as it doesn't have anything to do with the format of the data, but rather that the data in these cells was incompatible with the chosen data *type*.

When a Changed Type action is applied, Power Query attempts to take the value provided in the cell and convert it to the data type based on the formats defined for that data type in your Windows Regional Settings. Should it not be able to do so, you'll receive an error that it could not be converted. While it is very rare to see this error arise when setting a column *to* a Text data type, they are very common when changing *from* Text to almost anything else.

If you check the header of the column, you'll see that the data was set to a Whole Number data type (indicated by the 123), but the error was caused as the value in the cell was "N/A". As N/A cannot be represented as a number, Power Query throws an error.

Now that we know the cause, how do we fix it?

One of the beautiful things about Power Query is that we actually have several options. For this data set you could:

- Insert a new step before the Changed Type step to replace N/A with 0
- Insert a new step before the Changed Type step to replace N/A with the null keyword
- Right-click Units Sold → Replace Errors → 0 (or null)
- Select Units Sold then go to Home → Remove Rows → Remove Errors
- Select *all* columns then go to Home → Remove Rows → Remove Errors

> 🐵 Before you leverage functionality to remove rows, you really want to scan your data set to make sure that is the appropriate thing to do. The most cautious approach is to replace errors, and the most heavy-handed approach is to remove rows with errors in any column. Which you will need depends entirely on your data set.

In looking at our data set, it looks like the errors are all being triggered when the Units Sold contains N/A, and these appear to be instructional codes for the kitchen that uses this data set. It looks like we can remove these rows. But let's do that the most cautious way possible, so that we don't accidentally lose any data we may need:

- Select Units Sold then go to Home → Remove Rows → Remove Errors

The result is a nice clean table with no more errors.

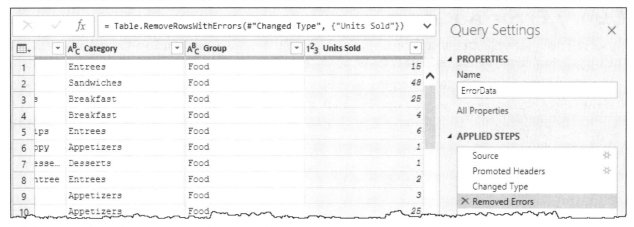

All the errors have been removed from our data set

Errors Caused by Incompatible Data Types

In order to quickly demonstrate the issue with incompatible data types, follow these steps to create a new column which multiplies the Group by the Units Sold:

- Change the data type on the Units Sold column to Text
- Go to Add Column → Custom Column
- Enter the following formula in the formula area

      [Units Sold] * 10

- Click OK

The result is a column that shows errors on every single row.

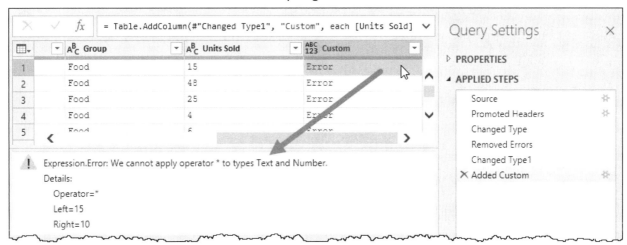

Power Query isn't happy with this formula

The results pane makes reference to an Expression.Error (triggered by an attempted mathematical operation) and informs us that we can't multiply numbers by text. Where Excel might have forgiven you this transgression, and implicitly converted the value in the Units Sold column to a number before multiplying it by 10, Power Query just says, "No, you can't do that."

> ✎ The unfortunate part about this message is that it is not obvious from the error message which of the two inputs (left or right) is textual and not numeric. To figure it out you need to carefully review the formula in the Added Custom step as well as the data types of all columns used in that formula.

While there is a formulaic way to resolve this issue, we'll save that for much later in the book. For right now:

- Delete the Added Custom step
- Delete the Changed Type1 step

The data should now return to show you a nice clean data preview with no errors.

Query Error Auditing

As we've now resolved both the Step Level error related to the missing data source and the Value errors in the Units Sold column, we are now ready to reload the data. So let's do exactly that:

- Click Close & Load (Close & Apply in Power BI)

The data should load except... we get a notification that we have 4572 rows, with 345 errors?

Wait... didn't we fix all of the errors?

Discovering the Source of the Errors

Depending on the color scheme you are using in Excel, it may be impossible to see that the error count is a different color than the count of rows loaded. The reason is that this is actually a hyperlink.

- Click the error count text

Once you do, you'll be launched back into the Power Query Editor, and you'll be looking at a brand new query called "Errors in <your query>".

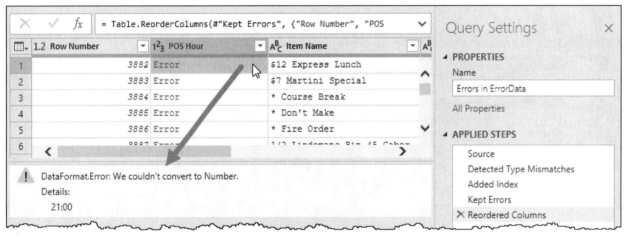

So this is where our errors came from...

Ignoring the exact mechanics of this query for the moment, it basically takes your query, adds a row number for each row of the data set, then filters the query to keep only rows with errors in them. We can now easily see that these errors started at line 3,882 of the file we imported. And that explains why we didn't see them earlier.

In an effort to avoid overly taxing your PC, Power Query limits the amount of data in the preview window and allows you to build your query based on those previews. When you choose to load the data, Power Query then applies the patterns you built to the entire data set. In this way, it avoids the burden of having to load all of the data up front. This is important, as we can use Power Query to connect to massive data sets which would be unworkable if all the data had to be downloaded to our PC before cleaning it up.

The challenge with this approach, however, occurs when there is a difference in the data patterns that happen outside of the preview. Where we were previously alerted to a data problem within the first 1,000 rows of the Units Sold column, the challenges in the POS Hour column don't manifest until row 3,882, so we don't see them until the data is loaded.

Regardless, through the use of this query, we can now determine that the format of the data we are importing has changed from simple whole numbers to numbers in a format of 21:00. Where Power Query could convert 21:00 into a time data type, it cannot convert it to a Whole Number due to the ":" character.

Now that we know the cause of the issue, we can architect a fix for our original import, even if we can't see that issue in the preview window.

Fixing the Original Query

To fix our original query, we need to see it and review the steps. To do this:

- Expand the Query Navigator pane
- Select the ErrorData query

You will then be able to see the original query and review its steps in the Applied Steps window. This is where the tricky part comes in. Where do we fix it?

Let's think about this for a minute…

- We don't want to just remove the rows. Unlike the previous error instances, these errors are on rows that hold valid sales information which we need to keep
- We know that one of the values is showing as 21:00, where the previous values were 8 through 20. What we don't know is what happens after 21:00. Does it revert to 22, or continue with 22:00?
- The actual error is most likely triggered by the Changed Type action

What if – before the query triggers the Changed Type action – it removes ":00" from the values in the column? That should work, so let's apply that.

- Select the Promoted Headers step
- Right-click the POS Hour column → Replace Values… → Insert
- Value to Find: :00
- Replace With: *leave this blank*
- Click OK

🔧 The challenge with fixing errors in this way is that you can't see the effect in the preview window. If this really bothers you, you can always insert a temporary step into your query which will remove the top x rows from your data set. In this case we could choose to remove the top 3,880 rows meaning that our first error would show up in row 2. Just make sure to remove that step before you finalize your query!

At this point, we want to make sure the changes worked. The most reliable way to do this is to re-load our query and hope that those error message counts are gone.

- Go to Home → Close & Load (Close & Apply)

🔧 You could also go back to the Errors query and force a refresh of the preview, but you'll still need to wait for the data set to load, so why not load it to the end destination at the same time?

There are two observations that we can take from the results:

1. We have successfully mitigated the errors, and
2. The Errors query is created as a Connection Only query by default.

The last step is particularly fortunate, as we really wouldn't want to load all of the error rows to a separate worksheet.

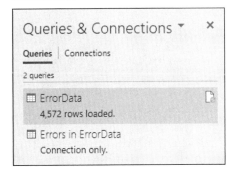

Yay, no more errors!

    ✂ Keep in mind that every data cleanup action is unique and requires understanding the data pattern in play. If some of the new values appeared as 22:01, the above steps would not work. In that case we would need to apply a different set of cleansing steps.

Removing the Errors Query

With the original query fixed, there is no reason to leave the Errors query in the solution. Should we encounter new errors, we will see the count and be able to click on it at that time.

The Errors query can be removed via the following actions in either Excel's Queries & Connections pane or the Query Navigator inside the Power Query Editor:

- Select the query and press the DEL key
- Right-click the query and choose Delete

Final Thoughts on Data Types and Errors

This chapter has been an introduction to the concept of data types in Power Query, as well as identifying, tracing, and handling the most common errors you'll see. These concepts are really important not just for debugging your own real-life solutions, but also for giving you the confidence to try the techniques demonstrated in this book and debug them when your results differ from what is shown. Again, these are only the core concepts. From specific discussions on dealing with dates and currencies through intentionally triggering errors for filtering, there is a lot more to come!

Chapter 4 - Moving Queries Between Excel & Power BI

No matter how much planning you do, there will always be a time where you realize that you need to copy your queries to a different solution. That might mean copying queries from one workbook to another, from Excel to Power BI or even from Power BI to Excel. In this chapter we will explore the steps required in order to quickly port your queries from one solution to another. Keep in mind that – while this book focuses on Excel and Power BI — the steps are virtually identical for any Power Query solution, even if it is contained in another Microsoft product or service.

Copying Queries Between Solutions

In order to show how we can move Power Queries between solutions, we will start with a query chain that was built in Excel using the following structure:

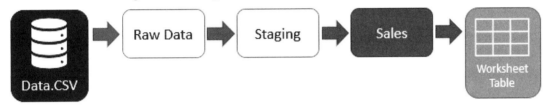

The query workflow in the Simple Query Chain Excel file

Before we dive into this solution, however, we need to ensure that the data source is correctly pointed and saved in the sample file. This will prevent us from encountering any step level errors related to the data source as we explore different options for moving queries between solutions.

To update the sample file:

- Open the following workbook in Excel

        Ch04 Examples\Simple Query Chain.xlsx

- Display the Queries & Connections tab
- Edit the Raw Data query
- Go to Home → Data Source Settings → Select the file path → Edit
- Update the file path to point to the following file:

        Ch01 Example Files\Basic Import.csv

- Close the Data Source Settings dialog
- Go to Home → Close & Load
- Save the workbook

> 🐭 You won't normally need to take the steps above, as you'll most likely have built the queries on your machine with data sources that you have access to. However if you open a solution built by someone else, or a solution whose data sources are no longer in the same location as when it was created, it is a good idea to update the source file path before replicating the queries in another location.

Copying from Excel to a new Excel Workbook

We will begin with the easiest option: Copying a query from one Excel workbook to another.

The first thing you need to do is ensure that Excel's Queries & Connections pane is active, as this is where you will find the list of queries to work with. From there, what users will typically do is select one or more queries that they want to copy.

The Queries & Connections pane supports all of the normal mouse selection methods that you would expect:

- Selecting a single query with a left mouse click
- Selecting a contiguous block of multiple queries by selecting the first query and holding down the SHIFT key as you click the last query you need

- Selecting a non-contiguous set of queries by holding down the CTRL key as you select the ones you need

🔏 One thing that isn't supported is the use of CTRL + A to select multiple queries

While selecting the queries may make sense, what happens if your query has precedent queries and you don't select them (either because you forgot or didn't realize it)? Let's find out:

- Right-click the Sales query → Copy (or select it and press CTRL+C)
- Go to File → New → Blank Workbook

In the new workbook, you will now need to:

- Go to Data → Queries & Connections
- Right-click the empty background of the pane → Paste (or select it and press CTRL + V)

At this point, not only does Power Query paste the copied query, but any precedent queries that made up that query chain. You should also notice that it correctly observes the configured load destinations for each of the queries as well.

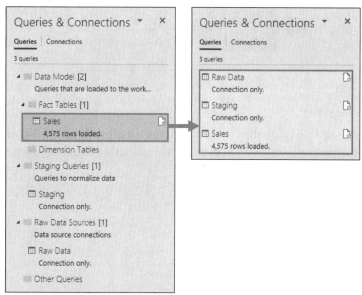

Copy the Sales query (only) to a new Excel Workbook

🔏 This is fantastic when copying from one solution to another, as it means that you can't ever accidentally forget to copy a critical piece of the query infrastructure.

When you are copying an entire chain into a solution (or at least one which doesn't hold any part of this query chain), this works very well. But what happens if part of the chain already exists? For example, we now have the Raw Data and Staging queries in the new workbook. So what will happen if we go back and copy just the Sales query now? Surely it will create a new copy of the Sales query that points to the existing Raw Data and Staging queries in the new workbook, won't it?

- Go back to the original workbook
- Right-click the Sales query → Copy
- Return to the new workbook
- Right-click an empty area of the pane → Paste (or select it and press CTRL + V)

As you will see, rather than integrating and attaching to existing queries, Power Query creates the entire chain of queries all over again. And if the name is already used, it appends numeric characters in parentheses in order to distinguish which queries are related.

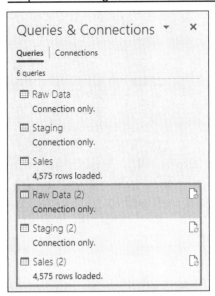

Power Query recreates the query chain, rather than integrating

This can be a little frustrating, as we would much prefer to have an option as to how to mitigate conflicts during a copy and paste. Unfortunately, when using the copy and paste functionality in this way, there is no such option.

Should you end up in this situation and actually needed Sales (2) to re-use the data from Staging - instead of Staging (2) – you would need to "repoint" the source of the Sales (2) query to read from Staging instead of Staging (2). To do this you would:

- Edit the Sales (2) query
- Select the Source step
- Change the formula in the formula bar to refer to the Staging query as follows

  ```
  =Staging
  ```

- Close the Power Query Editor and allow the data to update

At that point you could delete the Raw Data (2) and Staging (2) queries as they would no longer be in use.

> ⚒ It is possible to copy the source code for a query and create it as described above, but it involves working with the Advanced Editor – something that we will explore in the later chapters of this book.

Copying from Excel to Power BI

Now that we know the basics of copying a query from one Excel file to another, let's look at moving from Excel to Power BI. First, let's get set to do this:

- Throw away the new workbook you created for the previous example
- Open Power BI
- Return to the Simple Query Chain workbook in Excel

Now, as you'll see, copying from Excel to Power BI works in a very similar way:

- Right-click the Sales query → Copy (or select it and press CTRL+C)
- Return to the Power BI file
- Go to Home → Transform Data
- Right-click a blank area in the Query Navigator → Paste

Just like in Excel, each query will be created for you.

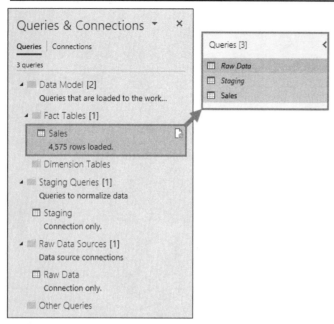

Copying a query from Excel (left) to Power BI (right)

At this point, all that is left to do is click Close & Apply and the data will be loaded for you!

☎ As long as your queries are connecting to external data sources, queries copied in this way will work perfectly well. If your data source is an Excel table, however, you will run into challenges, as Power BI doesn't have worksheets of its own. This will trigger a step level error due to an invalid data source. If you are porting a solution based on Excel tables, you need to Import the queries, as discussed later in this chapter.

Copying from Power BI to Excel

By now, you're getting the idea just how easy it is to move between applications with your Power Query solutions. So what if we have a query in Power BI that we need to re-create in Excel for some reason? No problem!

- Open the Power BI solution
- Edit the queries
- Copy the one you want
- Switch to Excel and display the Queries & Connections pane
- Paste the query

Copying queries from Power BI to Excel is just as easy as going the other way, *providing* that you haven't used a data source connector that isn't available in Power Query for Excel.

The reality is that Power BI contains a great deal more connectors than Excel does (many of which are in beta). In addition – unlike Excel – Power BI also supports custom connectors.

So what will happen if you copy a solution to Excel that relies on a connector that isn't available in Excel? You'll get a step level Expression error like this one:

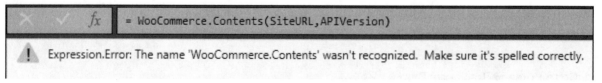

The custom WooCommerce connector is not available in Excel

🔨 Unfortunately, until the Power Query team adds support for the given connector in Excel or provides a way to use Custom Connectors in Excel, there is no way to resolve this issue. All solutions built on these kinds of connectors will only work in Power BI.

Copying from Power BI to a new Power BI Solution

The good news is that copying from one instance of Power BI to another is fairly straightforward. In fact, for most users, since they will only have one version of Power BI Desktop on their PC, a direct copy of a query that works in one Power BI file will certainly work in another.

🐵 If you happen to be one of those users who is running multiple versions of the Power BI installer (a combination of the Windows Store, direct download and Power BI Report server versions), then you may run into an issue copying and pasting from a newer version into an older version of Power BI Desktop. Issues of this type generally only surface when you build a solution against a new or upgraded connector, then copy it back to an older version of the Power BI application. Should this happen you will almost certainly be provided a step level error that a parameter or the entire connector cannot be resolved.

Importing Excel Queries to Power BI

While copying and pasting queries is certainly a valid way to move from Excel to Power BI, we also have the ability to import them as well. So why use one method over the other?

Let's compare the different methods and what they are capable of doing:

	Copy/Paste	Import
Original Excel workbook	Must be *open*	Must be *closed*
Copy/Import specific queries	Yes	No
Copy/Import all queries	Yes	Yes
Imports Data Model Structure	No	Yes
Imports Measures	No	Yes
Modifies connect to Excel Table data sources	No	Yes

Table comparing methods when importing Power Query from Excel to Power BI.

If you don't work with the Power Pivot Data model in Excel, then the biggest benefit you'll see is the auto-adjusting of data sources which refer to the table in the original workbook. As mentioned earlier in this chapter, copying and pasting these queries from Excel to Power BI will cause a step level error as Power BI doesn't understand this data source. When using the Import feature, Power BI gives you a choice as to how you'd like to change the connector to deal with these tables.

If you are using the Excel data model, then you'll immediately see the benefit of importing not only the queries, but also the relationships, sorting hierarchies and measures along with your queries.

We will look at three different scenarios in this section, showing how different data sources can affect the import process.

External Data Sources Only

To begin with, we will explore what happens when you import an Excel file to Power BI where the Excel solution relies only on data sources external to the Excel workbook.

- Open a new Power BI Desktop file
- Go to File → Import → Power Query, Power Pivot, Power View
- Browse to the Excel file we copied our queries from for the earlier examples

  `Ch04 Examples\Simple Query Chain.xlsx`

- Click Start

At this point, Power BI will begin the process of importing the data from the file, letting you know when it is complete:

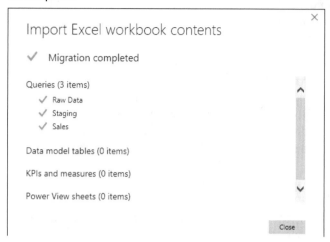

The Excel file has been successfully imported

Oddly, where this would lead you to believe that everything has been finished, you still have a couple of clicks to make:

- Close (to close the dialog shown above)
- Apply Changes (to actually load the data)

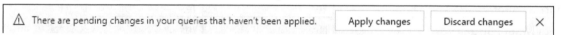

Your import is not complete until you tell Power BI to Apply changes

At this point, the queries will be executed. Your data will load to the data model tables and you'll be ready to build your reports. Except that… in this case… that did not happen. No tables were created at all, despite the fact that we clicked the Apply changes button. What is going on?

The challenge we see here is that Power BI doesn't see Excel workbooks as valid reports. Even though the worksheet may contain PivotTables, PivotCharts and other business intelligence based on the results of the Power Query, it won't change a thing as far as Power BI is concerned. Any Excel query that is not loaded to the Power Pivot data model will be set up as a connection only in Power BI.

To fix this issue, you need to edit the Enable Load setting of the query:

- Go to Home → Transform Data
- Right-click the Sales query → make sure the Enable load is checked
- Go to Home → Close & Apply

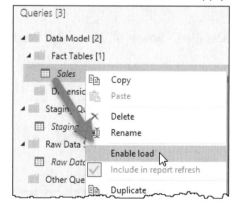

Queries loaded to worksheets show up with their load disabled

This time the table will be loaded to the data model with all of its data, and you'll be ready to build reports to summarize it.

Importing an Excel Data Model to Power BI

It is now time to import a solution that contains a data model and which also sources its data from tables in the host Excel workbook. A view of the query dependency chain of the Excel workbook is shown here:

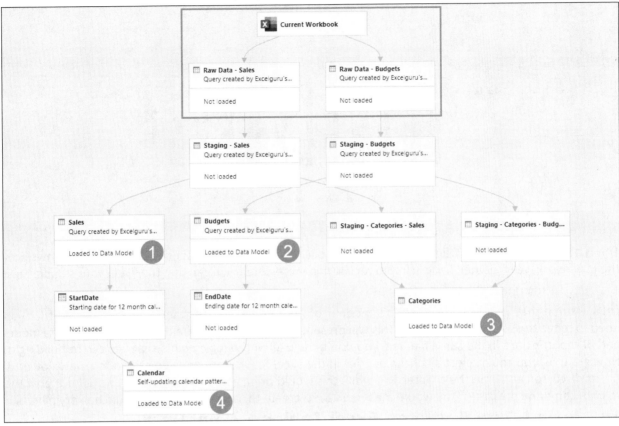

Two Excel tables and twelve queries result in four tables loaded to Excel's data model

While it is not important to understand how these queries work, it is important to realize that the two tables are stored in the "current workbook", referring to the fact that the data and the solution all live in the same file.

You should also be aware that the Power Query structure in this file acts as the ETL layer to serve the following Power Pivot data model which includes the four indicated tables, four relationships and two measures (Sales and Budget).

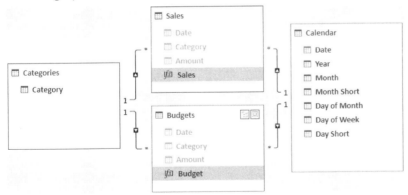

The data model shown here is derived from the Power Query structure

Finally, there is a worksheet in the file called "Report", which contains the following PivotChart and slicer, based on the data model:

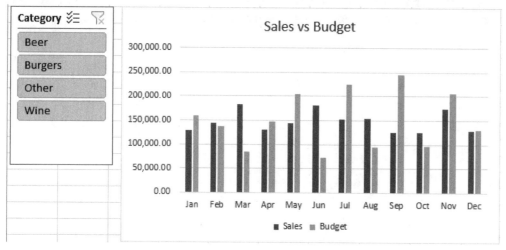

The Excel based report contained in Simple Model.xlsx

This is a fairly simple Power Query and Power Pivot based solution that a user could build which shows how the tools work well together. If you'd like to review it in more detail, you can find the file in your sample files:

        Ch04 Examples\Simple Model.xlsx

Let's assume that you have inherited this model from the original author, and you then decide that you need to move the solution to Power BI. This will present a challenge: all of the data, the queries, data model and BI reporting are in the same file, and you don't know all of the logic points that went in to building it. Now granted, you could select all of the queries in the Excel file at once and copy them to a new Power BI file as discussed earlier in the chapter. But while this would bring across the queries, it would not port the relationships and measures. You would then need to re-create that manually, which could be very painful.

Importing Data Based on Excel Tables – Copy Data

Based on the complexity of the previously discussed model, we want to ensure we move it from Excel to Power BI as easily as possible.

Power BI's Import function is built to handle exactly this scenario, so let's explore how it works. We will import the content from the following Excel file:

To do this:

- Open a new instance of Power BI Desktop
- Go to File → Import → Power Query, Power Pivot, Power View
- Browse to the file in the following location:
        Ch04 Examples\Simple Model.xlsx
- Select the file → Open

> 🐾 Ironically, the ability to import from an Excel workbook doesn't make any reference to the Excel program in any way!

Once you click the Start option on the dialog that comes up, you will be given a choice:

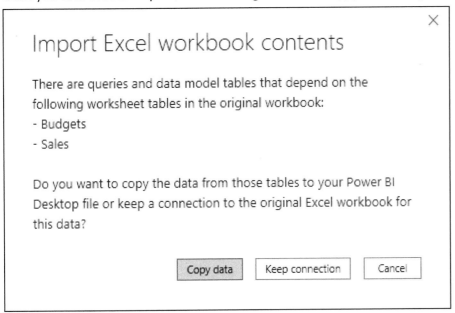

How would you like to import your Power BI data?

For now, let's go with the default option to "Copy Data", which will kick off the import of the queries and data model components.

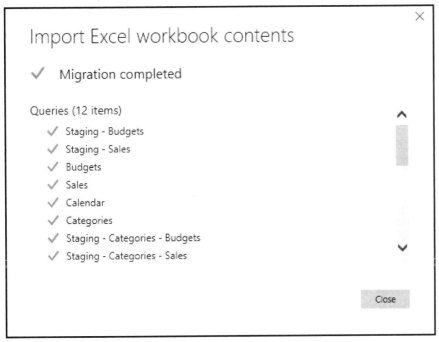

Power BI has successfully imported our queries, data model and measures

So far, all appears well. In fact, if you click the Model button on the left side of the Power BI Desktop window, you'll see that the data model structure including relationships, measures and even the visible/hidden status of fields has been imported correctly.

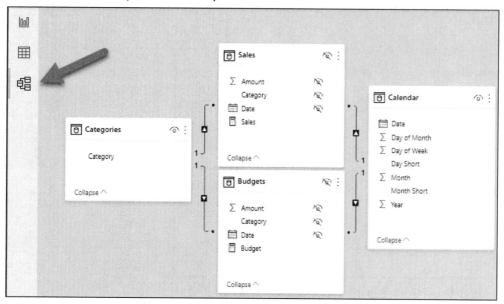

The Excel data model has all been imported to Power BI

If we flip over to the Report page, you'll even see that we can replicate the Excel chart with ease:

- Select the Report page on the left side of the Power BI window
- Go to the Visualizations pane → Clustered Column Chart
- Go to the Fields list → expand Sales → check the Sales measure
- Go to the Fields list → expand Budgets → check the Budget measure
- Go to the Fields list → expand Calendar → check the Month Short field

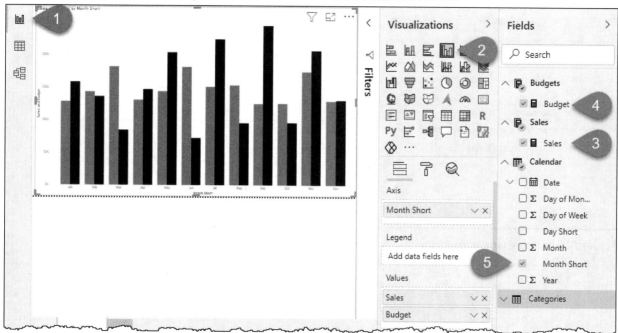

While hard to see in the image, the dates are even sorted in the correct order!

This is pretty amazing as everything looks good. At least, it does until you refresh the solution:

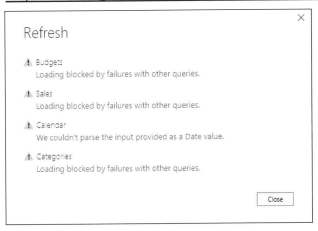

What is going on here?

> 🖎 If your table refreshed without issue, things may look a little bit different for you here, but we still recommend you follow through this section...

To troubleshoot this issue, we need to edit the queries. We'll start by looking at one of the Raw Data queries to see how Power BI replicated the Excel table:

- Go to Home → Transform Data
- Select the Raw Data - Budgets query

You'll see immediately that something is not correct:

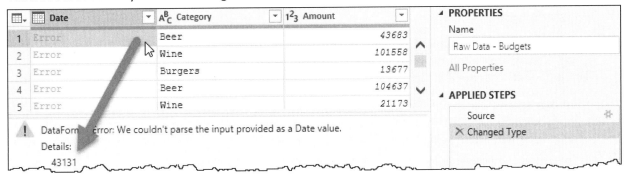

Why are all the dates shown as errors?

In reading the error message, we can see that the column is trying to set 43131 to a date. But where did that number come from?

- Select the Source step and click the gear icon

What you see here is the table that Power BI has created in the file as a result of copying the data from Excel. Interestingly, it contains no dates in the dates column, but rather a column of values:

	Date	Category	Amount	
1	43131	Beer	43683	
2	43131	Wine	101558	
3	43131	Burgers	13677	
4	43159	Beer	104637	
5	43159	Wine	21173	

What's with all the values instead of dates?

There are three things that we want to make sure that you are aware of in this particular step:

1. This table is wholly contained in Power BI and must be updated here if you need to make any changes to the source data. (Updates made to the Excel file will NOT flow into this file upon refresh.)

2. All dates get copied over as date serial numbers (the number of days since Jan 1, 1900), not recognizable dates.

3. There is a limit to how much data Power BI will show you in this step. If you exceed that limit, Power BI will not let you edit the table and – since the table is created using a compressed JSON format — it is virtually impossible to simply edit the Power Query formula to add values if you exceed that limit.

While the last point is certainly concerning from a maintenance standpoint, it is not actually our issue in this case. We can recognize this as the source step shows no errors in the data table.

After closing this dialog and returning to the Changed Type step, we are still presented with the error which complains that couldn't set the value of 43131 as a date. So let's override the Changed Type step and replace it with something that it should be able to work with.

- Select the Date column and click the Calendar data type icon
- Change the data type to Whole Number
- Select Replace (not add new step)

The result will be that the errors disappear and we now see a column full of whole numbers (which represent the date serial numbers).

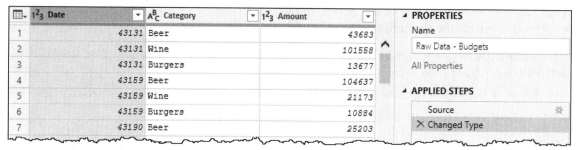

We have our date serial numbers

> 🐟 One strange nuance is that the error bar at the top of the Date column may continue to show as red. Should that happen either ignore it for now or select another query and return to Raw Data – Budgets to force it to update.

So this is progress but still not ideal, obviously, as we'd still prefer to set our data types as dates. But here's the challenge: if you change the Date column to use a Date data type and replace the existing data type included in the Changed Type step, you'll be right back where you started with errors. Instead, what we need to do is this:

- Select the Date column and click the Whole Number data type icon
- Change the data type to Date
- Select Add new step (not replace)

And the results will be exactly what we need:

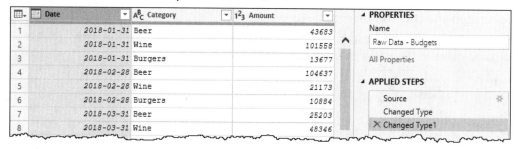

Remember – as described in Chapter 3 on Data Types and Errors – once you have changed a data type, any subsequent changes are based upon that output. While we couldn't change a text-based value to a date, we can change from text to a value, and then from a value to a date.

Now that this has been done, we'll need to take the same steps with the Raw Data – Sales query as well. To do this:

- Select the Raw Data – Sales query
- Select the Date column and click the Calendar data type icon
- Change the data type to Whole Number

- Select Replace (not add new step)
- Select the Date column (again) and click the Whole Number data type icon
- Change the data type to Date
- Select Add new step (not replace)

Once this has been completed you can finalize the queries by going to Home → Close & Apply and let Power BI apply the changes. The data will then be loaded without issue.

🐵 Power BI's method to import Excel tables and convert them to JSON tables has a bug specifically related to the import of date columns. Until this bug is fixed, any time you have a column of dates that you import to Power BI, you'll need to make the adjustments described above.

Notwithstanding the bug around the data types, this feature works very well for importing a data model from Excel to Power BI. And like the original Excel solution, which was entirely contained in a single file, the Power BI solution is just the same, making it very easy to share with someone else, without ever having to worry about updating file paths to the data source.

Having said that there are a couple of potential dangers around using this method as well. Keep in mind that – when complete – any updates you need to make to the source data require editing the query and updating the Source step. This can make things awkward, as you have to not only edit and navigate the query structure to edit the source data, but it tends to be slow as you have to wait for query previews to update as you do. But even those issues are not the true killer – once your table crosses a certain size, Power BI will just refuse to let you make any further changes, instead telling you that the table exceeds the size limit:

Sorry, but you are not fixing the incorrect record you discovered in the Raw Data – Sales query!

🥾 The fact is that these tables were never meant to be used as a database and lack not only the required size but the tools to work with them effectively. For this reason, we would advise you to only use this feature sparingly. Ultimately it is a recommended practice to import the data from an external file (be that an Excel workbook, database or any other source), rather than store it in the same solution.

Excel Tables – Keep Connection

The previous example imported a data model from Excel by copying the data into the file, but it was one of two different options. The other is where we don't copy the data from Excel to the Power BI file, but rather make a connection to the Excel file that holds the data.

While this does create the risk that you'll have to update a path to an external file, it avoids the errors related to dates, as well as the risk that you won't be able to add rows to or modify records in your data source. The data will continue to live in the Excel file, meaning that any additions, deletions or updates made in the Excel file are simply a refresh away.

Let's re-do the previous example, but this time choosing to create a connection to the Excel file, rather than copying the data. The steps to do this are:

- Open a new instance of Power BI Desktop
- Go to File → Import → Power Query, Power Pivot, Power View
- Browse to the file in the following location:

      Ch04 Examples\Simple Model.xlsx

- Select the file → Open
- Click Start → **Keep Connection**

🥾 It is unfortunate that Copy Data is highlighted as the suggested choice here, as we very much feel that Keep Connection creates a better solution overall.

Once again, Power BI will import the data and create the data model, relationships and measures. And once again, we can quickly build the column chart that we built for the previous example:

- Select the Report page on the left side of the Power BI window
- Go to the Visualizations pane → Clustered Column Chart
- Go to the Fields list → expand Sales → check the Sales measure
- Go to the Fields list → expand Budgets → check the Budget measure
- Go to the Fields list → expand Calendar → check the Month Short field

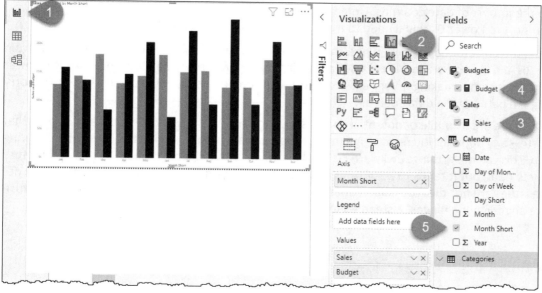

This looks pretty familiar...

At this point you would be forgiven for thinking that everything is the same as the results in the previous example. The only difference is that – in this case – the data still lives in the Excel file, and we are importing it from there, not copying it and storing the data inside the Power BI document. So now, if the Excel file moves, you'll need to update the data source by editing the query, or by changing the data source via:

- Home → Transform Data → Data Source Settings

A bug in Power BI might leave Data Source Settings greyed out. If so, use the Advanced Editor.

Actually, there is one really big difference with this specific solution. The adjustment Power BI applies to point the query to the Excel file results in a query that refreshes without any modifications needed:

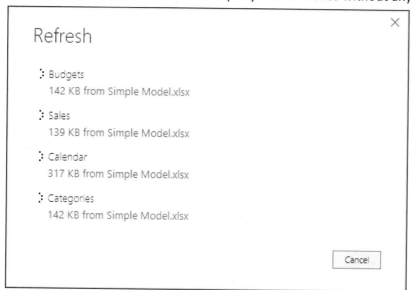

That's the kind of progress we wanted from our copy!

Final Thoughts on Moving Queries Between Solutions

By now you have a good understanding of the options for easily moving queries between instances of Excel and Power BI. The general rule of thumb is:

- If you want specific queries or groups of queries and aren't concerned with data model components, then just copy and paste.
- If you want to move the entire solution from Excel to Power BI, import it (preferably choosing to Keep the Connection to the Excel file)

The one solution that we did not cover is a method to import from Power BI back to Excel. Unfortunately, due to the fact that Power BI's data model is a version newer than Excel's and supports many new features, Microsoft does not provide a way to do this. At first glance, this means that to take a solution from Power BI back to Excel, your only method is to copy and paste the queries, and then rebuild the data model manually.

Ken's Monkey Tools add-in does contain a feature to import a Power BI model back into Excel. While it obviously can't create items that Excel's data model doesn't support, it can rebuild the query structure, many to one relationships and measures. And it even provides a list of what failed to import properly. Whether you want to extract and import only the queries, or the entire data model, Monkey Tools will make this easy for you.

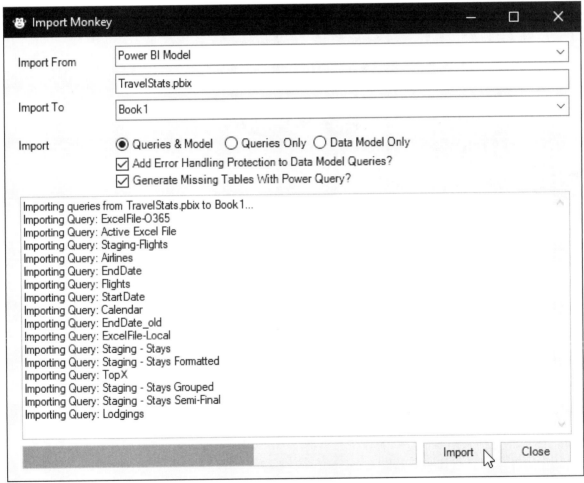

Importing a Power BI model to Excel using Monkey Tools

✎ You can learn more about this add-in, and download a free trial at Ken's website: https://xlguru.ca/monkeytools

Chapter 5 - Importing from Flat Files

As a data pro, it is highly likely that your life is all about importing, manipulating and transforming data before you can use it. And sadly, many of us don't have access to big databases with curated data. Instead, we are fed a steady diet of TXT or CSV files and have to go through the process of importing them into our Excel or Power BI solutions before we can start our analysis. For us, critical business information is often stored or sent to us in the following formats:

- Text files (delimited by characters)
- CSV files (delimited by commas)

Historically, this meant a lot of manual import and cleanup, but Power Query changes that game forever.

Understanding How Systems Import Data

TXT and CSV files are what we refer to as "flat" files – so named because they lack a layer of metadata called a Schema that describes the contents of the file. This is critically important to us, as it means that the data must be interpreted when it is imported to another program like Excel or Power BI. To truly master data importing with Power Query, we need to be clear what happens by default, and how (and when) we should take control and override the default settings.

> 🔦 While TXT and CSV files are certainly not the only flat file formats that exist, they are by far the most common we see. As a rule of thumb, any file that presents a single "sheet" of data is typically a flat file.

Determining Your System Defaults

The first thing we need to understand is that the output we receive when importing data from a flat file is directly related to the settings that are contained in the Windows control panel. To determine (and change) your regional settings, you'll need to dig through a few layers of the Windows user interface to get to the correct settings:

- Press the Win key → type Control Panel → click Control Panel
- If the Control Panel shows in category view click Change date, time or number formats
- If the Control Panel shows in icon view, click Region

This will launch the Region panel where you can review (and change) your system defaults:

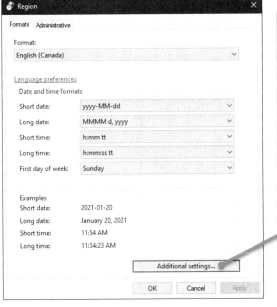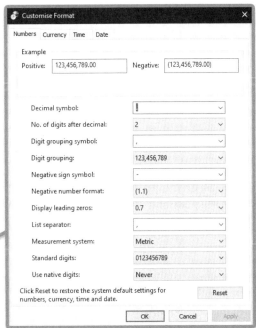

The Region area of the Windows Control Panel

If you've ever wanted to change your default date formats or the way negative numbers are displayed by default – in any Windows application – you've come to the right place!

The main thing we want you to discover about your system is the defaults that YOU use. You'll see here that our system is set to display valid dates in the ISO format of yyyy-MM-dd, not the standard dd-MM-yyyy that Canada would default to, or the MM-dd-yyyy that is the default in the USA. In addition, we have customized settings for the negative number format as well. In Europe, the decimal – where we use the comma – would be shown as a period.

🐵 Unlike Excel, Power Query is case-sensitive. MM is used for months and mm for minutes.

The important thing to recognize here is that these settings are specific to your PC, and what you are going to see when you declare a *data type* for a column in Power Query is that the *format* will be based on *your* control panel settings. This is true even if you build the solution and send it to someone else; they will see the formats from *their* system.

Now that we know where these settings are controlled, let's look at why this is important when working with Power Query.

How a Program Interprets Flat Data

The challenge that a program has when interpreting data is that it really needs to know three things:

1. Are data points separated by a single character, pattern of characters or consistent width,
2. What character or series of characters separates one complete record from another, and
3. What is the data type associated with each individual data point.

The problem with a flat file is that there is no schema contained within the document that defines these things. The importing program, therefore, has to make some assumptions in order to try and get this correct. While most programs do a good job of dealing with the first two points, inferring the data type is frequently problematic.

For example, consider this data point: 1/8/18

It's probably fair to assume that this is a date, but which date is it? Is it Jan 8, 2018, Aug 1, 2018, Aug 18, 2001, or even something else? The answer completely depends on what the program exported to the file, based on how the engineer who coded the export function wrote it. If the programmer was American, it is almost certainly Jan 8, 2018. But if they were European it very well could be Aug 1, 2018. And if the programmer decided to read the preferred date format from your Windows regional settings, it could be almost anything!

The reason that this is super important is that there is no metadata in the file to tell you which format this truly is, so the program makes a guess when it imports the data. And the default it will attempt to apply is that which you've set in your Windows regional settings.

> 🔧 Ask yourself: Have you ever opened a csv or text file in Excel, and half the dates were correct, and the other half were shown as text? No, you haven't. If you answered yes to this question, you have actually seen data where half the dates were *wrong* and the other half were text. There are only twelve days per year that could be correct in this case… 1/1, 2/2, 3/3, etc…

Let's look at a specific example of a data set import where the following assumptions are in play:

* The data set was exported to a text file and uses an MM/dd/yy format
* The users control panel regional settings use a short date format of dd/MM/yyyy
* The users control panel regional settings use a decimal separator of '.' and digit grouping of ','

As a quick summary, for each data point in the file, the program will attempt to apply the data type, and then format it as per the defaults defined in the Control Panel's regional settings.

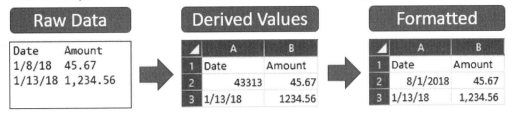

From text file to Excel, messing up the dates all the way

The true algorithm behind the scenes is obviously going to be much more complicated than what is described here, but you can assume that it follows this general process:

- The program attempts to convert 1/8/18 into a date using the dd/MM/yyyy format defined in the control panel. This works, generating a date serial number of 43313 (the number of days since Jan 1, 1900.) In Excel, this value would then be placed into a cell.
- The program attempts to convert 1/13/18 into a date using the dd/MM/yyyy format, but since there aren't 13 months, it assumes that this cannot be a date. It therefore treats the data as text and lands it to a cell as such.
- The program attempts to convert 45.67 to a value. When this succeeds, the value is placed in a cell. (If not, it would be treated as text.)
- The process repeats for each data point in the file

Once all of the data points have been landed as values, the program will apply *formats* to the data, displaying it based on your preferences as defined in the Control Panel's regional settings.

What's the issue? The Jan 8, 2018 value, exported to the file as 1/8/18 using the MM/dd/yy format defined by the programmer gets interpreted incorrectly by the program as the Control Panel believes that this date string should be Aug 1, 2018.

And the worst part? Once it has been interpreted and stored in your program as a value, it's too late to change it. This has always been the challenge with importing TXT and CSV files into Excel. It was far too easy to get this data wrong, and people wouldn't even recognize it.

Dates are particularly problematic in this area. As many popular database software were written by American software engineers, they very commonly export data in a MM/dd/yy format, despite the fact that the USA is the only country in the world that follows this date standard. This can cause issues for any country that follows a different standard, but it is incredibly problematic in Canada. We joke that we have two types of IT pros: the proudly patriotic who set everyone's date settings to dd/MM/yy, and those who have just given up and leave our default settings as US English and MM/dd/yy. The big challenge for us is that that these two IT people can work at the same company, meaning that there is a mix of settings across the organization!

It is also important to realize that this is not solely an issue that affects dates. It affects numbers and currencies as well, as different countries in the world use different currency indicators and delimiters. And as the world economies become increasingly global, inconsistent data formats are hitting more and more data sets that we have to interpret.

The good news is that Power Query allows us to control what happens during the import process. While it will provide defaults based on the same classic import logic, it does allow us to reconfigure these steps and tell it exactly how to interpret the data correctly. It does this not by applying a Change Type step, but rather an explicit Change Type with Locale that allows us to define the locale of origin of the data.

Importing Delimited Files

The process of importing a delimited file such as a CSV or tab delimited TXT file is fairly straightforward, and follows the basic ETL process of Extract, Transform and Load the data. Indeed, you've already seen this in Chapter 1, but this time we'll import a file that has data which is a bit more challenging.

The Source Data File

We will start by importing a delimited file called Ch05-Delimited.CSV. The data inside the file, as shown in Notepad ++, looks like this:

```
Date,Account, Amount
12/01/08,12500, $353.82
12/01/08,12100, $324.48
12/01/08,14400, $(955.82)
12/01/08,11900, $346.24
12/01/08,15000, $(305.44)
12/01/08,14400, $498.03
12/01/08,13900, $164.56
12/01/08,10100, $110.42
```

Our comma delimited source data

The first question you have to ask yourself is what formats these dates are in. For this example, we'll assume that they are in the MM/dd/yy format. How do we know for sure? Power Query will scan the top 1000 rows of the data set to see what it can figure out. Beyond that, we need to go back to the program that exports the data and run some tests to figure it out. The good news is that once you've done this once, you can usually rely on the fact that the system will do the same thing every time you run a report using the same options.

You'll notice that the file also contains numeric formats that are going to be challenging for anyone in Europe. Not only do they contain a $ character, but the values use the comma for thousands separators and periods for decimals.

Extracting the Data

Let's get started. In a new workbook:

- Create a new query → From File → From CSV or Text
- Browse to the Ch05 Examples\Ch05-Delimited.csv file and double click it
- Click Transform Data to be taken to the Power Query editor

Our data preview should then be showing something similar to the following:

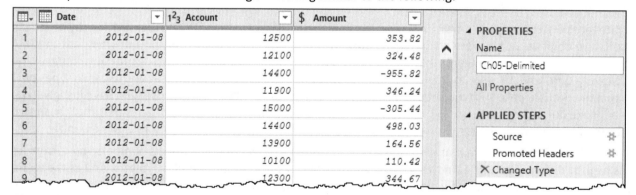

The power query editor with an imported delimited file

> 🖎 Remember that Power Query attempts to set the data type and then displays those data points using the settings from the Control Panel's regional settings. Your data and values may not look as shown here.

Now how did this show up on your system? Did it work? Is the first date showing up as Dec 1, 2008, or something else? Do the values in the Amount column show up as values, text, or errors? Welcome to the challenge of dealing with data in Power Query, as the answer will be different for different people depending on the settings in your Control Panel!

The Problem

In the case of the preview shown above, you can see that the dates have been interpreted as dates and are showing in the yyyy-MM-dd format as per my control panel settings. That is great, but the dates were not interpreted correctly. There are no errors, they're just wrong as Dec 1, 2008 was interpreted as Jan 8, 2012.

In order to fix this, we need to take explicit control over the Changed Type step. Let's remove what is there and re-create it from scratch so that it will work for anyone in the world, no matter their settings.

- Delete the Changed Type step (click the x on the left side of the step name)

🐵 Remember, once the Changed Type step has been applied, the data types have already been set and won't be retroactively changed. In order to override a Changed Type step to force a locale on the import, you must either delete the step, or insert a new step before the existing Changed Type step.

The data will now revert to the state it was in after applying the Promoted Headers step, but before any data types were defined for the columns:

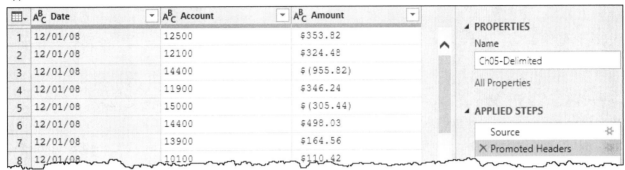

Everything is text, so we can see what we are dealing with

Using Locale to Correctly Set Data Types

At this point we want to take explicit control over the Date column, telling Power Query how to interpret and convert the dates into the proper date serial numbers. To do this we will change the data type while defining the "locale of origin" of the data. (In other words, tell me the format that was used to generate this data.)

- Click the ABC data type icon at the top of the Date column
- Choose Using Locale... (at the bottom of the menu)

You will then be prompted with the dialog to Change Type with Locale, where you can instruct Power Query as to the original source and format of the data:

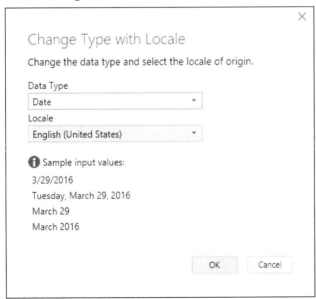

This is a column of dates encoded in the US standard

While the first drop-down is fairly self-explicit, the confusing part of this dialog is that the Locale always leads with language first and country second. Whether you choose English-UK or English-Australia will still interpret dates in the d/M/y format, so don't worry if you don't get the country perfect. Instead, worry that the sample input value that appears after you make your choice will interpret the data properly.

In the case of this data sample, the choice is easy. We need English (United States), as this is the only country that follows the M/d/y standard.

🔍 The list of English locales is massive, as virtually every country in the world has some form of English. To get to English US quickly, type F. That will take you to Faroese, which is only a few lines away from English US!

Once you click OK on the choice, notice how the data preview now interprets the dates properly:

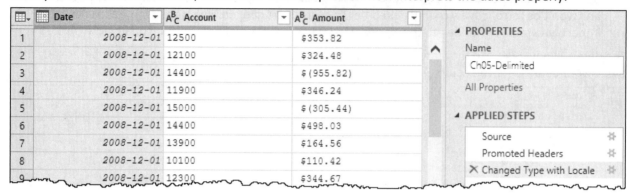

Those dates look a lot more like Dec 2008

Next, we want to ensure that the file interprets the Amount column correctly when refreshed by someone in Europe. This will again require converting the column while setting the locale.

- Change the data type of the Amount column → Using Locale
- Set the data type to a Currency
- Set the locale to English (Canada)
- Click OK

At this point the currency indicators are cleared (remember this is about data types – you can format the results when you land the data to the end destination), and the values get aligned to the right side of the Power Query cells.

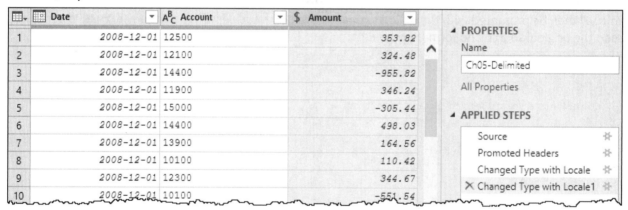

The data after applying a second Changed Type with Locale step

There are three important points to realize based on what has just happened.

1. Every time we add a step that changes with Locale, we will get a distinct step in the Applied Steps list. They are never combined into a single step.

2. The Amount column was set using a different country than the date. The reason we can do this is that there is no difference between choosing Canadian or US dollars in this case. This action does not add currency metadata, but rather tells Power Query how to read a value like $1,000.00 and convert it into a value.

3. Each column in the data set can be set using different Locales, allowing you a huge amount of flexibility when importing multi-region data.

🔍 Remember, the entire goal of converting with Locale is to tell Power Query how to interpret a text-based value and change from text into the correct data type.

👀 If you work in a culture or company where date and numeric formats can be inconsistent, we highly recommend that you always set your date and currency data types using locale. It won't hurt anything for a user who has Control Panel settings which line up perfectly with the data, but it is critical when the user does not!

At this point there is only one column left to deal with, and that is the Account column. We'll set it to a whole number, and update the query name:

- Change the data type of the Account column → Whole Number
- Change the query name to Transactions

As you can see, we end up with a total of three Changed Type steps in this query, where the first two specifically define the locale of each column.

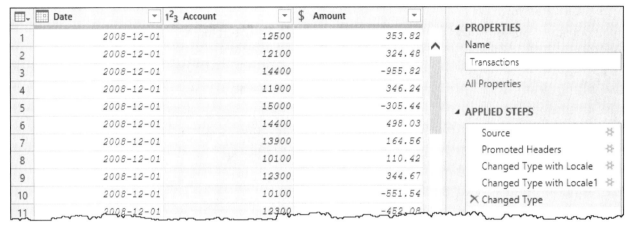

This query will load for anyone!

At this point, anyone in the world will be able to refresh this query – at least – they will once they reconfigure the Source step to update the path to the Ch05-Delimited.csv file.

The final step is to close and load the data to the destination of your choice.

🐒 If you need to override your regional settings, you have an option to do this in your Excel workbook or Power BI file. In Excel, go to Get Data → Query Options → Current Workbook → Regional Settings and define your locale there. All new connections will be created using that locale as a default. In Power BI Desktop you need to go to File → Options → Options and Settings. Power BI has a Regional Settings tab at both a Global or project level, depending on your preference.

Importing Non-Delimited Text Files

Once you get used to handling locale settings, the process of importing delimited files is fairly straightforward. Granted, sometimes the data can be dirty, but at least it is already separated nicely into columns for you.

On the other hand, if you've ever had to import and clean non-delimited text files, you know how painful it can be. They typically arrive with some default name like ASCII.TXT, and are essentially a character by character representation of what the output should look like when printed. This means that they embody all kinds of crazy issues including (but not limited to) the following:

- Characters aligned by position, instead of delimited by a character
- Inconsistent alignment
- Non-printing characters (such as control codes)
- Repeating header rows

For many Excel pros, a major part of their job is taking this information, importing it into Excel and cleaning it. And all of this **before** they can actually get to the analysis that actually adds business value.

If you've been there, you know the process follows this general flow:

- Import the file into Excel via Data → From Text
- Working in a postage stamp sized window, you try to work out how the columns are delimited and which to skip

- The result gets dumped into a worksheet, and needs to be turned into a table
- The table needs to be sorted and filtered to remove garbage rows
- Text in columns needs to be cleaned and trimmed

And the best part is that next month, when you get the updated data file, you get to relive the exciting process **all over again**. Wouldn't it be nice if there were a better way? Great news! There is, and you've found it.

Connecting to the File

Connecting to a non-delimited text file is performed in the same manner as any other text file:

- Create a new query → From File → From Text
- Browse to Ch05 Examples → GL Jan-Mar.TXT
- Click Transform Data

Upon doing so, you'll see that Power Query lands the data in a single column:

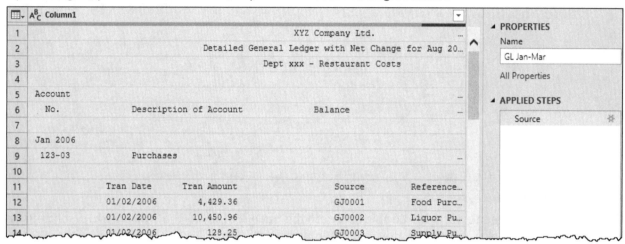

The Power Query view of a non-delimited text file

> ✎ Notice the ... at the end of some of the rows? That indicates that there is more text than fits in the cell. If your column is too narrow, just mouse over the right side of the column header, left-click and drag it wider.

> ✎ If your text is all smashed together, go to the View tab and make sure the boxes for Monospace and Show Whitespace are both checked. You'll want those on when cleaning up a file like this.

As you scan the preview window, you'll notice that the file is not delimited with any consistent delimiters and – because of that – Power Query has not made any guesses about your data or added any steps in the Applied steps window beyond the Source step. Instead, it has left the entire process to you. Given the state of this file, this is probably not a bad thing.

Before we dig into this, it should be noted that there are **many** ways to approach this task, and none of them are right or wrong. The example in this chapter has been architected to show a great deal of transformations via the user interface, as well as the typical route an Excel Pro might approach this task. With more experience you'll find that quicker routes to the end goal are almost certainly possible.

Cleaning Non-Delimited Files

The general goal when starting to clean up a non-delimited file is to try and get the data into a semblance of columnar data as quickly as possible. In this case, the top 10 rows don't seem to add much value, while the 11th row looks like it may be column headers.

- Go to Home → Remove Rows → Remove top Rows → 10

The rows disappear and will not be imported into the end solution.

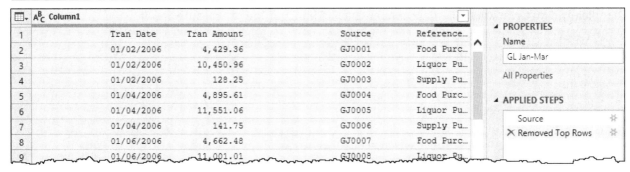

Top rows removed, bringing our headers closer to the top

Next, we need to choose a direction to break into this data. We could try breaking in from the left or right, but currently we've got a ton of extra leading spaces and duplicated spaces in the middle. It would be nice to get rid of those.

In Excel it is a standard practice to run textual data through the TRIM() and CLEAN() functions in order to remove all leading, trailing and duplicate spaces, as well as remove all non-printing characters. Power Query also has this functionality, so we'll apply that now:

- Right-click Column1 → Transform → Trim
- Right-click Column1 → Transform → Clean

And the data looks a bit better:

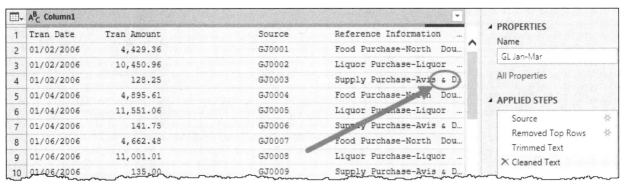

Data trimmed and cleaned

At this point you may notice that Power Query's trim functionality doesn't work quite the same as Excel's. While Excel's TRIM() function removes all leading and trailing spaces and replaces any duplicate spaces in the middle of the data with a single space, Power Query's doesn't do that last part. Instead, it only trims off the leading and trailing spaces.

The CLEAN() function in Power Query does line up with Excel's however, although it's more difficult to see. Non-printing characters are rendered as a little question mark in a box within the Excel user interface. In Power Query they show as a space. Regardless, if you step back and forth between the Trimmed Text and Cleaned Text steps, you'll see that the spaces around Avis & Davis have been cleaned away by the Cleaned Text step.

Splitting Columns by Position

The next step is to start splitting apart the columns. The basic approach at this point is to split by the number of characters, making an educated guess as to how many you need, then refining that guess. Since the number of characters in the date is 10 characters, let's try 12 for a first go:

- Go to Home → Split Column → By number of characters → 12 → Repeatedly → OK

That plainly didn't work out! The date column may be fine, but the others sure aren't.

	A^B_C Column1.1	A^B_C Column1.2	A^B_C Column1.3	A^B_C Column1.4		PROPERTIES
1	Tran Date	Tran Amou	nt	Sou		Name
2	01/02/2006	4,429.	36	GJ0		GL Jan-Mar
3	01/02/2006	10,450.	96	GJ0		
4	01/02/2006	128.	25	GJ0		All Properties
5	01/04/2006	4,895.	61	GJ0		
6	01/04/2006	11,551.	06	GJ0		APPLIED STEPS
7	01/04/2006	141.	75	GJ0		Source
8	01/06/2006	4,662.	48	GJ0		Removed Top Rows
9	01/06/2006	11,001.	01	GJ0		Trimmed Text
10	01/06/2006	135.	00	GJ0		Cleaned Text
11	01/09/2006	3,276.	19	GJ0		Split Column by Position
12	01/09/2006	12,773.	43	GJ0		× Changed Type

Data which didn't split as well as we'd intended

This is not an issue. We'll just try again:

- Remove the Changed Type step
- Click the gear beside the Split Column by Position step
- Change it to 15 → OK

This is much better!

	A^B_C Column1.1	A^B_C Column1.2	A^B_C Column1.3	A^B_C Column1.4		PROPERTIES
1	Tran Date	Tran Amount		Source		Name
2	01/02/2006	4,429.36		GJ0001		GL Jan-Mar
3	01/02/2006	10,450.96		GJ0002		
4	01/02/2006	128.25		GJ0003		All Properties
5	01/04/2006	4,895.61		GJ0004		
6	01/04/2006	11,551.06		GJ0005		APPLIED STEPS
7	01/04/2006	141.75		GJ0006		Source
8	01/06/2006	4,662.48		GJ0007		Removed Top Rows
9	01/06/2006	11,001.01		GJ0008		Trimmed Text
10	01/06/2006	135.00		GJ0009		Cleaned Text
11	01/09/2006	3,276.19		GJ0010		Split Column by Position
12	01/09/2006	12,773.43		GJ0011		× Changed Type

A much more inspiring view of our data

> ⚒ It is also worth mentioning that there is nothing forcing you to choose the "Repeatedly" setting in the options when splitting columns. If the document is inconsistent, you can choose to split once from the left/right side. This allows you very granular control on a column-by-column basis.

We can now make two more changes.

Since the Changed Type step just declares all of the columns as text, (which they won't be when we're done), we can remove the Changed Type step as it's irrelevant. We can then promote the first row to column headers.

- Remove the Changed Type step
- Go to the Transform tab → Use First Row as Headers

The Beauty of Errors in Power Query

Our data is now starting to look somewhat cleaned, even if we'd like to change some of the column headers as we go along. At this point, it is typically recommended to work from left to right cleaning up as much of the columnar data as we can, making sure it's all valid.

If you scroll down at this point, you'll find that there are a lot of garbage rows in this data, mostly from the repeating page headers and section breaks that were included in the document. The first block of these issues occurs at row 40 and introduces a bunch of ugliness:

	AᴮC Tran Date		AᴮC Tran Amount		AᴮC		AᴮC Source
39	01/30/2006		122.14				GJ0039
40		null		null		null	
41	Feb 2006			null		null	
42	123-03		Purchases				
43		null		null		null	
44	Tran Date		Tran Amount				Source
45	02/01/2006		4,395.03				GJ0040
46		null		null		null	

Irrelevant rows mixed in with real data

The question is how to deal with these. Some are dates, some are text, some are nulls. Try this:

- Change the type of the Tran Date column → Using Locale → Date → English (US)

Immediately, we can see a red bar pop up in the header of the Tran Date column and scrolling down our preview window reveals that we have a bunch of errors in the Tran Date column.

	Tran Date		AᴮC Tran Amount		AᴮC		AᴮC Source
39	2006-01-30		122.14				GJ0039
40		null		null		null	
41	2006-02-01			null		null	
42	0123-03-01		Purchases				
43		null		null		null	
44	Error		Tran Amount				Source
45	2006-02-01		4,395.03				GJ0040
46		null		null		null	

Errors as a result of trying to convert to dates

In Chapter 3 we covered how to fix errors, under the silent assumption that all errors are bad. But what we didn't mention is that unlike any other program, errors are truly exciting in Power Query! The reason is that we can control them and react to them.

If you look carefully at this data, you'll see that errors were only caused in rows that happen to be part of the rows that we want to filter out anyway. In addition, every row that has a null in the TranDate column holds values in the subsequent columns that are also not part of the transactional data that we want to keep. So let's get rid of both of those:

- Select the Tran Date column → Home tab → Remove Rows → Remove Errors
- Filter the Tran Date column → uncheck (null)

The results are quite encouraging, and we've now got a TranDate column with valid dates from top to bottom:

	Tran Date		AᴮC Tran Amount		AᴮC		AᴮC Source
39	2006-01-30		122.14				GJ0039
40	2006-02-01			null		null	
41	0123-03-01		Purchases				
42	2006-02-01		4,395.03				GJ0040
43	2009-03-20		2:08pm				
44	2006-02-01		12,834.54				GJ0041

The Tran Date column showing valid dates from top to bottom

☎ If your data ends with a row full of errors in row 42, it is because you applied the last two steps in the reverse order. It is critically important to handle errors in a column before you try to filter it. If you apply a filter to a column that contains an error, it will truncate the data set.

Despite the fact that we have made progress, we still appear to have some rows which aren't very useful. The challenge is that we don't really want to filter out those dates as some of them might be valid one day (hey, Power Query is pretty useful... do you think it will wrap the four digit year clock and last until Mar 1, 10123?).

Let's move on to the next column and see if we can fix these issues there.

- Double click the Tran Date column → Rename → Date
- Double click the Tran Amount column → Rename → Amount
- Change the data type on the Amount column → Using Locale → Currency → English (US)

You'll now see that Power Query attempts to set all the entries to values, and again triggers some errors (this time in the Amount column). After reviewing that they are all rows that we don't need:

- Select the Amount column → Home → Remove Errors
- Filter the Amount column → uncheck (null)

And if you check the data set around row 40 (and further), you'll see that all the garbage rows are completely gone.

Removing Garbage Columns

Removing extra columns is very simple, you just want to follow a process when doing so to make sure that they are truly empty. That process is simply this:

- Filter the column
- Ensure that all the values shown in the filter list are blank or null

Alternately, if you have the Column Quality and Column Distribution features turned on via the View tab, you'll get a good indicator in the header of the column. If there is one distinct value, you can be assured that what you see in the preview is what you'll get were you to load the data.

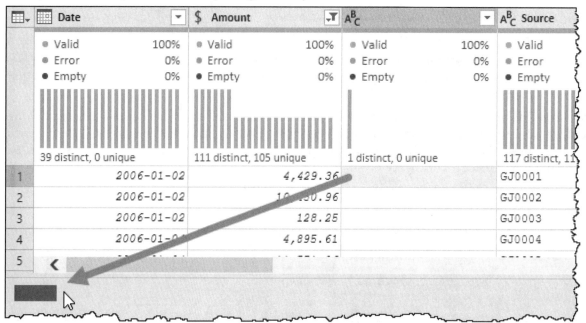

One distinct value, but no Empty values... is that right?

In the case of this column you can see that – while there is only one value – it is not populated with empty cells. As this file was full of spaces and was split based on width, each cell contains 15 spaces (which you can confirm by clicking in the cell and selecting characters in the value preview at the bottom left). It's not truly empty, but it is consistent and unneeded.

Checking each of the columns in the data set, you can see that the 3rd column (with a blank header) only appears to hold blank values. That column can be removed.

Likewise, if you scroll all the way over to the right side of the window, Column9 holds only (null) values. Those columns can also be removed.

- Select the 3rd column → press the DEL key
- Select Column9
- Press the DEL key

Merging Columns

At this point it becomes fairly clear that our initial splitting of the columns was a bit aggressive. It seems that we have four columns that were broken apart incorrectly.

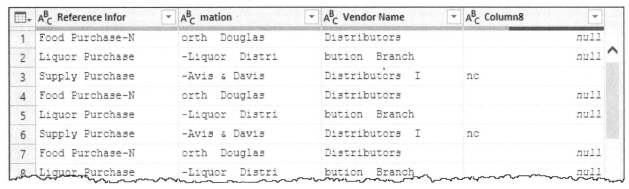

Columns split apart in error

Fortunately, all is not lost here, and we certainly don't need to go back and start over. We just need to put them back together again.

- Select the "Reference Infor" column → hold down SHIFT → select Column8
- Right-click one of the column headers → Merge Columns

You're then given the option of using a separator and providing a new name for the (new) column. In this case we don't need a separator of any kind. And since we're going to split this column up differently in a second anyway, the name really isn't important to us.

- Click OK

And your columns are put back together:

Humpty Dumpty WISHES he had Power Query!

Splitting Columns by Delimiter

Based on the re-aggregated data, it becomes very clear that the new column is delimited by the – character. So let's break that apart into its components. One thing we want to take into consideration is that we don't know if there is a vendor who uses a hyphen in their company name, so we don't want to go too aggressive with our split.

- Right-click the Merged column → Split Column → By Delimiter
- Choose a Custom delimiter and enter a – (minus sign)
- Choose to split "At the left-most delimiter"

> 🔧 You are not limited to delimiters of a single character when splitting by delimiter. In fact, if you want to split by an entire word, you can enter that word as your delimiter.

The data is then split into 2 separate columns: Merged.1 and Merged.2. Let's rename those to something more sensible:

- Change the name of Merged.1 → Category
- Change the name of Merged.2 → Vendor

This results in a data set that is almost perfect:

		Source		Category		Vendor	
1	.36	GJ0001		Food Purchase		North Douglas Distributors	
2	.96	GJ0002		Liquor Purchase		Liquor Distribution Branch	
3	.25	GJ0003		Supply Purchase		Avis & Davis Distributors Inc	
4	.61	GJ0004		Food Purchase		North Douglas Distributors	
5	.06	GJ0005		Liquor Purchase		Liquor Distribution Branch	
6	.75	GJ0006		Supply Purchase		Avis & Davis Distributors Inc	
7	.48	GJ0007		Food Purchase		North Douglas Distributors	
8	.01	GJ0008		Liquor Purchase		Liquor Distribution Branch	

The data set is now almost perfect…

Trimming Duplicate Spaces

The last thing needed in this data set is to deal with the duplicate spaces that have been left between words in the Vendor column. Since we can't rely on Power Query's trim function, it looks like we're going to have to take care of this ourselves.

- Right-click Vendor → Replace Values
- Set the Value To Find equal to 2 spaces
- Set the Replace With value to 1 space

And you now have a completely clean data set that can be loaded into a table.

> 🔧 Unfortunately, there is no easy function to remove internal "whitespace" from a text string. If you suspect that you have some instances which have more than two spaces, you may have to run this trim process a couple more times in order to completely clean the data.

We are finally at the point where we can finalize our query and actually build a report from it. Naturally, we'll do that by creating a PivotTable

- Change the Query name to Transactions
- Go to Home → Close & Load To… → New Worksheet

Power Query's Moment to Shine

At this point we should pause and recognize something important. Your data is clean. Unlike loading data using Excel's standard method to import from a text file, no further cleanup is necessary. The data was loaded, cleaned and transformed in one user interface dedicated to the process. You're now sitting in a position where the data can actually be used.

Click anywhere in the table and choose to insert a new PivotTable, placing it in G2 of the current worksheet. Configure it as follows:

- Date on rows, grouped by Month
- Vendor on rows, under group
- Category on Columns
- Amount on Values

At the end of the process, your PivotTable should look as follows:

Sum of Amount	Column Labels			
Row Labels	Food Purchase	Liquor Purchase	Supply Purchase	Grand Total
⊟ Jan	54904.19	158292.64	1664.94	214861.77
Avis & Davis Distributors Inc			1664.94	1664.94
Liquor Distribution Branch		158292.64		158292.64
North Douglas Distributors	54904.19			54904.19
⊟ Feb	67719.29	186132.13	1848.72	255700.14
Avis & Davis Distributors Inc			1848.72	1848.72
Liquor Distribution Branch		186132.13		186132.13
North Douglas Distributors	67719.29			67719.29
⊟ Mar	104769.36	242315.79	3383.58	350468.73
Avis & Davis Distributors Inc			3383.58	3383.58
Liquor Distribution Branch		242315.79		242315.79
North Douglas Distributors	104769.36			104769.36
Grand Total	227392.84	586740.56	6897.24	821030.64

A PivotTable built from our text file

But let's face it. Everything accomplished in this chapter so far is entirely possible with just standard Excel. So why do we need Power Query? Is it the full sized window? That's cool, but not critical.

The reason Power Query is so critical is when dealing with the final part of the equation. Next quarter comes along and we get a new data file. In the Excel Pros world, that means another tedious afternoon of importing, cleaning and reformatting. But armed with Power Query this all changes.

- Go to Get Data → Data Source Settings
- Select the data source → Change Source → Browse
- Update the file path to Ch05 Examples\GL Apr-Jun.TXT
- Click OK → Close
- Go to Data → Refresh All

The query's output will update the table, but we have to force the PivotTable to update. So you'll need to do that last step again.

- Go to Data → Refresh All

   🖎 Data landed to the data model (in Excel or Power BI) only needs a single update to update the data as well as all pivots/visuals created against the data model.

There is the benefit of using Power Query:

Sum of Amount	Column Labels			
Row Labels	Food Purchase	Liquor Purchase	Supply Purchase	Grand Total
⊟ Apr	55196.09	191992.54	1660.94	248849.57
Avis & Davis Distributors Inc			1660.94	1660.94
Liquor Distribution Branch		191992.54		191992.54
North Douglas Distributors	55196.09			55196.09
⊟ May	68516.29	177125.03	1841.22	247482.54
Avis & Davis Distributors Inc			261.07	261.07
Liquor Distribution Branch		177125.03		177125.03
North Douglas Distributors	62668.47			62668.47
ACME&Co Supply Haus LLC			1580.15	1580.15
Sysco	5847.82			5847.82
⊟ Jun	102759.26	226607.59	3376.48	332743.33
Liquor Distribution Branch		226607.59		226607.59
ACME&Co Supply Haus LLC			3376.48	3376.48
Sysco	102759.26			102759.26
Grand Total	226471.64	595725.16	6878.64	829075.44

The PivotTable updated for the next quarter

New vendors, new transactions, new dates, all working with no issues. It's revolutionary, and you're going to wonder how you ever did your job without it.

   🖎 If you'd just saved the new file over the old one, you wouldn't even have had to edit the Source step to update the file path. Instead you'd simply go to Data → Refresh All (twice) to update the solution.

Chapter 6 - Importing Data from Excel

Without question, one of the easiest ways for someone to start tracking information in a tabular format is to open Excel and start logging the data in a worksheet. While Excel isn't really intended to act as a database, this is exactly what happens and for that reason, Power Query treats Excel files and data as valid data sources.

Unlike flat files, where all data is stored in a single "sheet", Excel is a bit more nuanced. Not only does a file contain multiple sheets, but there are also different ways to refer to the data within those sheets, either via the entire worksheet, a defined table, or a named range.

When working with Excel data, there are two general approaches:

- Connecting to data housed within the active workbook
- Connecting to data stored in an external workbook

In this chapter we will explore each of these nuances, as what you can access actually varies depending on the connector you use.

Data Within the Active Workbook

The first scenario we are going to explore is where the data is stored within the active workbook.

> ✎ The example in this section must be run from Excel, as Power BI doesn't have its own work-sheets, so doesn't support the required function to import data in this way. Despite this, we recommend that Power BI readers follow through this section, as there are options exposed in this connector that Power BI cannot access.

When importing data from within the active workbook, Power Query can only read from a few locations:

- Excel Tables
- Named Ranges (including dynamic Named Ranges)

Rather than connecting to an official Excel table, we will start by connecting to data that is in a tabular format, but with no table style yet applied. The data we will use for this is located in the Ch06 Examples\Excel Data. xlsx, which contains four worksheets with the same data on each:

- Table (where the data is pre-formatted in a table called Sales)
- Unformatted
- NamedRange
- Dynamic (which also contains a formula in H2)

We will use these four worksheets to demonstrate exactly how Power Query handles the different options available for connecting to our data.

Connecting to Excel Tables

Let's start by looking at the easiest data source to import: The Excel Table.

- Open the Ch06 Examples\Excel Data.xlsx file
- Go to the Table worksheet

You'll be presented with the data already formatted as a nice Excel table as shown here:

	A	B	C	D	E	F
1			Fred's Pet Store			
2			Sales Listing For Month of:			
3			2014-06-30			
4						
5	Date	Inventory Item	Sold By	Cost	Price	Commission
6	2014-06-26	Tubby Turtle	Fred	8.00	30.00	0.90
7	2014-06-26	Talkative Parrot	Jane	17.00	32.00	0.96
8	2014-06-20	Rambunctious Puppy	Fred	9.00	30.00	0.90
9	2014-06-21	Lovable Kitten	John	12.00	45.00	1.35
10	2014-06-28	Cranky Crocodile	Fred	10.00	35.00	1.05

Data in a nice Excel table called "Sales"

To pull this data into Power Query

- Click any cell inside the table
- Create a new query → From Other Sources → From Sheet

> 🥿 The From Sheet button was called From Table/Range in versions of Excel prior to Microsoft 365. Regardless of the name, it can also be found on the Data tab near the Get Data button, saving you a couple of clicks!

Unlike many other data connectors, you'll be launched into the Power Query editor immediately, skipping the preview window. This makes sense, as you were already looking at the data you wanted to import.

	Date	Inventory Item	Sold By	Cost	Pi
1	2014-06-26 12:00:00 ...	Tubby Turtle	Fred	8	
2	2014-06-26 12:00:00 ...	Talkative Parrot	Jane	17	
3	2014-06-20 12:00:00 ...	Rambunctious Puppy	Fred	9	
4	2014-06-21 12:00:00 ...	Lovable Kitten	John	12	
5	2014-06-28 12:00:00 ...	Cranky Crocodile	Fred	10	
6	2014-06-14 12:00:00 ...	Slithering Snake	Fred	13	
7	2014-06-02 12:00:00 ...	Talkative Parrot	Fred	17	
8	2014-06-23 12:00:00 ...	Cranky Crocodile	Mary	10	
9	2014-06-09 12:00:00 ...	Rambunctious Puppy	Mary	9	

PROPERTIES
Name
Sales
All Properties

APPLIED STEPS
Source
X Changed Type

The data is imported directly into Power Query, skipping the preview window

> 🥿 If you were to compare the steps that Power Query has recorded in the Applied Steps window to those of a CSV file, you'll notice that there is no Promoted Headers step when importing from a Table. This is because the metadata of an Excel table includes the header information in its schema, so the Source step already knows what the headers are.

As with any data source, when importing from an Excel table, Power Query will get the data and then attempt to set the data types for each column. You should be aware that the formatting of the data from the Excel worksheet is ignored in this process. If it looks like a number, Power Query will apply a Decimal or Whole Number data type. This isn't usually much of an issue, but when it comes to dates, Power Query *always* sets these to a DateTime data type, even if the underlying date serial numbers are rounded to 0 decimals. That implies a level of precision that does not exist, so we are going to change that (as well as override the final three columns with a Currency data type.)

- Change the data type on the Date column → Date → Replace current
- Select the Cost column → hold down SHIFT → select the Commission column
- Right-click one of the selected column headers → Change Type → Currency → Replace

At this point the data is ready for any further cleansing or reshaping that you may wish to do. As the goal of this example was to demonstrate the connector, we will skip that, but we do need to be concerned about the name of the query.

The query automatically inherits the name of the data source: Sales. The challenge is that – when you load a query to a worksheet – the created table will be named after the query: Sales. Since table names must be unique in a worksheet, this will create a conflict. As Power Query never changes the data source, the new table name would be changed to a name that doesn't conflict, creating a table called Sales_2.

☎ When Power Query creates a new table and renames the output table due to a conflict, it does not update the name of the query to match. This can make it difficult to trace your queries later!

To avoid the potential naming conflict, let's change the name of this query before loading it to a worksheet:

- Change the name of the query to "FromTable"
- Click Close and Load to load the table to a new worksheet

🔧 There is very little reason to create a duplicate of your table without performing any transformations in the process. This process is shown merely to illustrate how to connect and load from an Excel table.

Connecting to Tabular Ranges

The next variation we want to explore is where the data is in a tabular shape, but not formatted as an official Excel table. You'll find an example of this on the Unformatted worksheet:

◢	A	B	C	D	E	F
1			**Fred's Pet Store**			
2			**Sales Listing For Month of:**			
3			**2014-06-30**			
4						
5	Date	Inventory Item	Sold By	Cost	Price	Commission
6	2014-06-26	Tubby Turtle	Fred	8.00	30.00	0.90
7	2014-06-26	Talkative Parrot	Jane	17.00	32.00	0.96
8	2014-06-20	Rambunctious Puppy	Fred	9.00	30.00	0.90
9	2014-06-21	Lovable Kitten	John	12.00	45.00	1.35
10	2014-06-28	Cranky Crocodile	Fred	10.00	25.00	1.05

The data is identical to the first example, but without a Table style applied

To import this data, we'll do the same thing as we did previously:

- Click any (single) cell inside the data range
- Create a new query → From Other Sources → From Sheet

At this point, Excel will kick off the process of creating an official Excel table for you, prompting you to confirm the table boundaries and whether the data set includes headers.

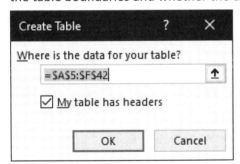

If Power Query offers you this, click Cancel!

☎ If you click OK, Excel will turn the data into a table, but it picks a default name (like Table1) for the table then launches you in to Power Query immediately without giving you a chance to update the table name to something more logical/descriptive. The challenge is that the original name gets hard-coded into the query and – when you change the table name later – the query breaks. That leaves you in a state where you have to manually edit the formula in the Source step of the query to update the name. As helpful as this appears, our advice to you is – until Microsoft gives us the ability to define the table name in this dialog – click Cancel immediately and set up your table yourself.

If you accidentally clicked OK, close the Power Query editor and discard the query. We want to set you up for long term success here, so are going to format this as a table before loading it to Power Query.

- Click any (single) cell inside the data range
- Go to Home → Format as Table → choose a color style (or press CTRL + T if you are okay with the default of blue)
- Go to the Table Design tab
- Change the name (on the far left) to SalesData (with no space)

Why do this? Because the table name is an important part of the navigation structure for your workbook. Each table and named range is selectable from the Name Box beside the formula bar and will jump you directly to that data in the workbook. Consider how much less useful this would be when populated with Table1, Table2, Table3, etc... Name your tables appropriately and this becomes a VERY useful feature for quickly jumping to key ranges inside your solution:

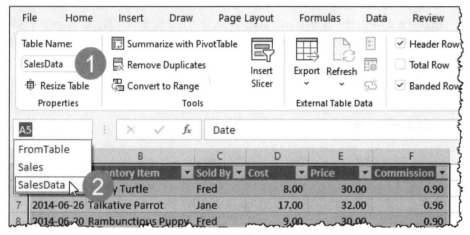

The Name Box is already populated with three items

Now, with the table set up, this is as easy as creating a query using the From Table route that we used previously. For completeness, we'll do that now:

- Go to the Name Box → select SalesData (which will select the entire table)
- Create a new query → From Other Sources → From Sheet
- Change the data type on the Date column → Date → Replace current
- Select the Cost column → hold down SHIFT → select the Commission column
- Right-click one of the selected column headers → Change Type → Currency → Replace
- Change the name of the query to "FromRange"
- Click Close and Load to load the table to a new worksheet

As nice and helpful as this functionality is, it is also a bit frustrating, as it forces a table style on the data. But doesn't the feature "From Sheet" indicate that you should be able to pull data from other Excel objects as well?

Connecting to Named Ranges

Pulling data from Excel tables is by far the easiest way to pull Excel data into Power Query, but it isn't the only method.

The challenge with applying a table style is that it locks column headers in place (breaking dynamic table headers driven by formulas), applies color banding and makes other stylistic changes to your worksheet that you may not want. Consider a scenario where you've spent a large amount of time building an analysis, and you don't want a table style applied to the data range.

The good news is that we *can* also connect to Excel ranges, we just need to do a bit of work to make it possible. The secret is to define a named range over the data. Let's explore that now using another instance of the same data.

To begin:

- Go to the NamedRange worksheet

- Select cells A5:F42
- Go to the Name Box → enter the name "Data" → Press Enter

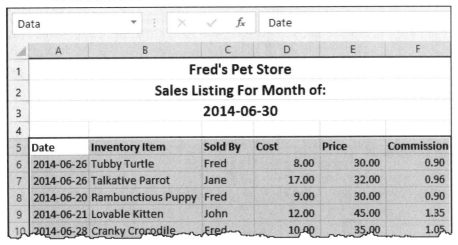

Creating a named range

🔨 Once committed, you can select this name using the drop-down arrow on the left. No matter where you are in your workbook it will jump you to this worksheet and select the data in the named range.

The next steps are key:

- Go to the Name Box → select Data
- Create a new query From Sheet

🔨 If the Named Range is selected and showing in the Name Box when you use the From Sheet command, Power Query will avoid forcing a table style on your data and will instead refer directly to the data in the named range.

This time the Power Query interface resembles the import of delimited files more than the connection to an Excel table:

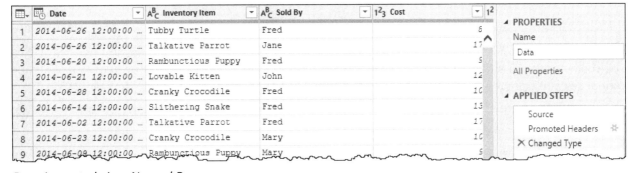

Data imported via a Named Range

One of the features of Excel tables is a pre-defined header row. Since that doesn't exist with a Named Range, Power Query has to connect to the raw data source and run its analysis to figure out how to treat the data. Similar to the way it works with flat files, it identified a row that appears to be headers, promoted them, then makes an attempt to apply data types to the columns.

To make this data consistent with the previous examples and then load it to a new table, we would then:

- Change the data type on the Date column → Date → Replace current
- Select the Cost column → hold down SHIFT → select the Commission column
- Right-click one of the selected column headers → Change Type → Currency → Replace
- Change the name of the query to "FromNamedRange"
- Click Close and Load to load the table to a new worksheet

Dynamic Named Ranges

One of the great features of Excel tables is the fact that they automatically expand both vertically and horizontally as new data is added. But again, the challenge is that they carry a bunch of formatting with them. Yet using named ranges lacks the automatic expansion ability that is so fantastic with Excel tables. The workaround for this is to create a dynamic named range which will automatically expand as the data grows.

This method isn't available via button clicks and requires setting up a dynamic name before we can even get started, so let's do that now.

- Select the Dynamic worksheet
- Go to the Formulas tab → Name Manager → New
- Change the name to "DynamicRange"
- Set the formula as shown below:

      `=Dynamic!$A$5:INDEX(Dynamic!$F:$F,MATCH(99^99,Dynamic!$A:$A))`

- Click OK

🕵 If you'd rather not type the entire formula, you'll find it in H2 of the Dynamic worksheet. Just make sure not to copy the ' character at the beginning of the cell contents.

The named range should now be contained in the Name Manager's name list:

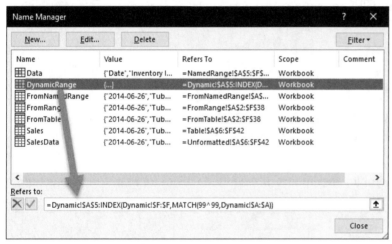

The new DynamicRange has now been created

The challenge we have now is that we can refer to this named range in formulas, but since it is dynamic, we cannot select it from the Name Box. So if we can't select it, how can we attach to it with Power Query?

The secret is to create a blank query and tell Power Query which range we want to connect to.

- Create a new query → From Other Sources → Blank Query
- In the formula bar, type the following:

      `=Excel.CurrentWorkbook()`

🕵 If you don't see the formula bar between the Power Query ribbon and data area, go to the View tab and click the "Formula Bar" checkbox.

Upon pressing Enter, you'll see a table that lists all of the Excel objects in this workbook which you can connect to:

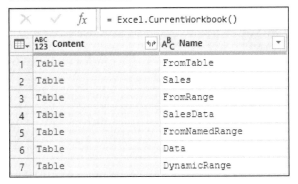

A listing of all of the objects Power Query sees in the current Excel workbook

And there at the bottom is the DynamicRange object we just created. Click the green text in the Content column that reads "Table" (to the left of DynamicRange) and it will drill into the range:

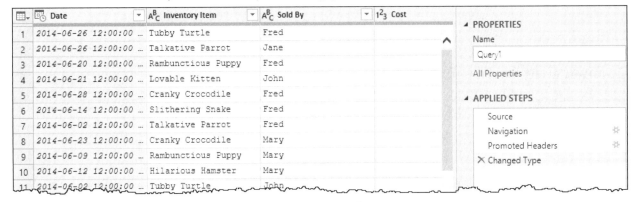

Reading the steps in the applied steps window, we can see that we:

- Connected to the Source of our data (the Excel workbook)
- Navigated into the DynamicRange table

At this point, Power Query again made some assumptions about the data for us and took the liberty of applying a few more steps to promote column headers and set the data types. All that is left for us to do at this point is to update the data types and load the data to a worksheet:

- Change the data type on the Date column → Date → Replace current
- Select the Cost column → hold down SHIFT → select the Commission column
- Right-click one of the selected column headers → Change Type → Currency → Replace
- Change the name of the query to "FromDynamicRange"
- Click Close and Load to load the table to a new worksheet

Connecting to Excel Worksheets from the Host Workbook

Unfortunately, there is no connector to connect to an entire worksheet from within the same workbook. You can engineer a workaround, however, by defining a Print_Area over the majority of the worksheet. As a Print_Area is a named range, you'll then be able to select it via the Name Box and read from it using the steps outlined in the section on Connecting to Named Ranges.

Data From Other Workbooks

While all of the techniques above are helpful for building solutions that are wholly contained in Excel, what if our data shows up in a new Excel file on a monthly basis, or we are using Power BI for our reporting? In both of these cases we want to connect to that file and use it as a data source, rather than build the solution inside the same workbook.

For this example, we will be connecting to Ch06 Examples\External Workbook.xlsx, which contains two worksheets (Table and Unstructured). While each sheet contains identical sales information, the data on the Table worksheet has been converted to a table called Sales. The Unstructured worksheet contains a static Named Range, a dynamic Named Range, as well as a Print Area.

If we were to open this workbook in Excel, we could see each of these items defined in the Name Manager:

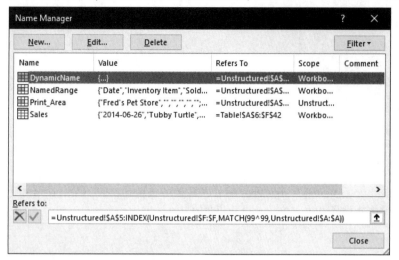

The named items present in the External Workbook.xlsx file

Connecting to the Excel File

To begin with, let's see what is exposed when we connect to an external Excel file. In a new workbook (or Power BI file):

- Make sure External Workbook.xlsx is closed
- Create a new query → From File → From Workbook

🙈 Power Query will not read data from an open workbook. Make sure you close it before you try to connect to it or you'll receive an error!

A query Navigator window will pop up, allowing you to choose what you'd like to import:

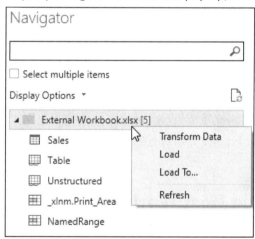

The available components of the External Workbook.xlsx file

You'll notice that you have the ability to connect to each of the following objects:

- **Tables**: (Sales)
- **Worksheets**: (Table and Unstructured)
- **Named Ranges**: (the Print_Area and NamedRange)

But what you don't see is the dynamic named range (DynamicName). While you gain the ability to connect to an unformatted worksheet via this connector, you unfortunately lose the ability to read from dynamic named ranges in an external file.

At this point, if you select any one item, Power Query will launch the Power Query Editor and drill into that object for you. But what if you want multiple items?

It is very tempting to check the checkbox next to Select Multiple Items. Indeed, this will work, and you'll get a distinct query for each item you select. The challenge is that this creates a connection to the data source for each query. While you can update them all at once via the Data Source settings dialog, you may prefer to take the approach of building a single connection to the data source, and then referencing that to pull out any additional data you need. This way you can update the data source via the Data Source settings dialog or by editing the Source step in the original data source query.

For this example, we will take the latter approach and build a query that connects to the file, then reference that table to drill into a table, a worksheet and a named range. To begin:

- Right-click the file name → click Transform Data
- Change the name of the new query to Excel File

You'll now be looking at a table that represents the contents of the file:

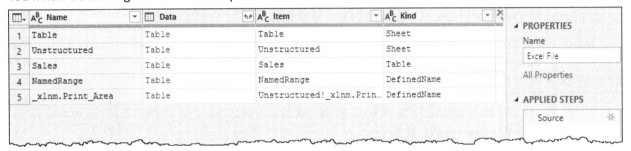

The contents of the External Workbook.xlsx file

There are a few things to remark on in this preview:

- The first column shows the names of the objects per Excel
- The second column holds a Table that holds the contents of the specific objects we retrieve
- The Item column shows a more qualified representation of the object name (including the worksheet name in the case of the Print Area)
- The Kind column tells us what kind of object the Table in the Data column contains
- The Hidden column (not shown) tells us if the object is visible or not

The other thing you should be aware of is that the Table objects shown in the Data column are in a different color than the rest of the preview data. This indicates that these items are clickable, and that we can drill down into them.

Connecting to Tables

Why don't we start by looking at what we see when we connect to a table in another workbook? Let's set up a new query to do that which refers to our "Excel File" query:

- Expand the Query Navigator pane on the left (click the > button above Queries)
- Right-click the Excel File query → Reference
- Double click the Excel File (2) query in the Navigator → rename it to Table
- Click the Table keyword for the Sales table (3rd row of the Data column)

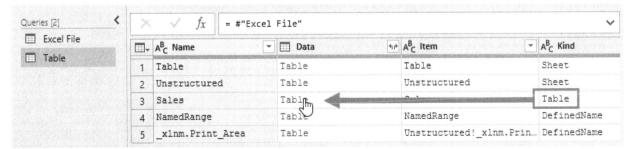

Drilling into the Sales table

The result is that you can now see that a table imported from an external workbook is treated quite similar to one imported from within the same workbook:

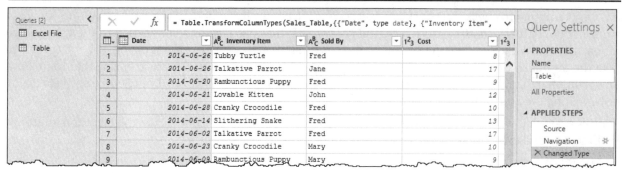

Connecting to a table in an External workbook

> 🐭 Interestingly, the data type algorithm for an external workbook appears to be better, as it shows our dates as Date data type, not a DateTime.

One thing to be aware of is that the steps in the Applied steps window would be identical if you had just selected this single table from the original data preview screen, or if you had selected multiple queries. When connecting to an external workbook, Power Query always connects to the root of the workbook, navigates into the object you choose, and then performs its regular algorithms. The one difference that would be in play is that the Source step would point directly at the file, instead of pointing at the Excel File query.

Connecting to Named Ranges

Let's take a look at a Named Range now.

- Go to the Query Navigator → right-click the Excel File query → Reference
- Double click the Excel File (2) query in the Navigator → rename it to Named Range
- Click the Table keyword for the NamedRange name (4th row of the Data column)

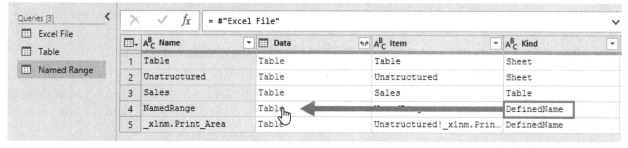

Drilling in to the NamedRange Named Range

The results shouldn't be much of a surprise at this point. Since the named range contains the headers and data of records on the unstructured worksheet, but is not formatted as an official Excel table, Power Query navigates into the object, makes the assumption that the first row is headers, and then sets the data types. There is virtually no difference from what would happen if the data were in the same workbook, except that the Date column is set as a Date data type:

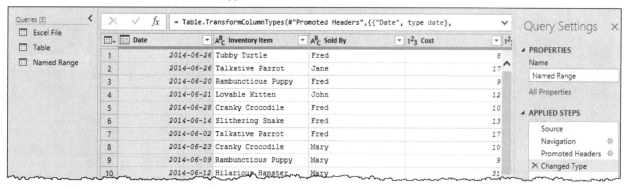

Importing from a Named Range in an external workbook

Connecting to Worksheets

Now let's take a quick look at importing the contents of an entire worksheet; something that cannot be done from within the host workbook.

- Go to the Query Navigator → right-click the Excel File query → Reference
- Double click the Excel File (2) query in the Navigator → rename it as Worksheet
- Click the Table keyword for the Unstructured worksheet (2nd row of the Data column)

This time, the results don't look quite as stellar:

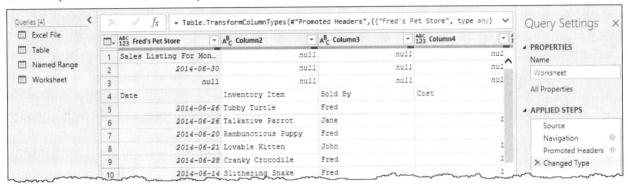

What is with all the nulls?

Unlike retrieving data from an Excel table or named range, connecting to the worksheet brings you the entire *used range* of the worksheet. This contains rows 1 through the last used row, and column A through the last used column. Each blank cell in that range will be filled with the keyword *null*.

You'll notice here that the connector has connected to the Excel file, navigated into the worksheet and then promoted headers. This has resulted in the value in A1 becoming our header row, which isn't really what we need here. So let's take control of this and clean up the data the way we'd like to see it.

- Delete the Changed Type step
- Delete the Promoted Headers step
- Go to Home → Remove Rows → Remove Top Rows → 4
- Go to Home → Use First Row as Headers

When done, our data should look much cleaner:

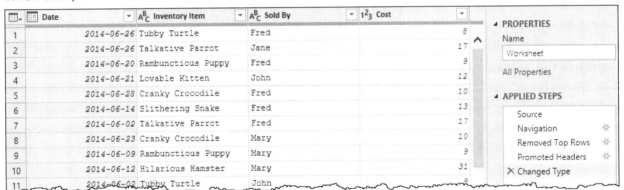

That's more like it!

The only problem? If you scroll all the way to the right side of the data preview, you'll find a Column7, full of *null* values. It was not included in the named range, but when reading from the worksheet, it shows up. No problem, right? If the column is full of *null* values, we can just select the column and delete it... or can we?

At this point, it is worth having a discussion around future proofing the solution and avoiding step level errors caused by the Changed Type step in future.

Notice that when we promoted headers, Power Query automatically added a data type for that column, hard coding the column name into the step as shown here:

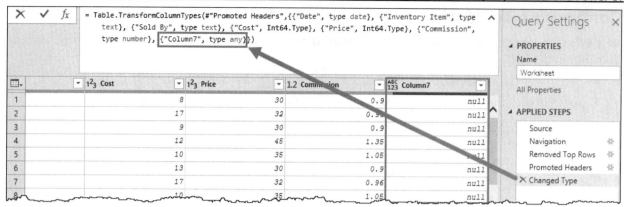

Why is Column7 a problem? Can't we just delete it?

This could present us with some potential issues, depending on what happens in future when someone:

- Creates a "Profit" column next to commission. In that case, Profit would appear as the column header, not Column7.
- Deletes the extraneous data that exists in that column of the spreadsheet. In that case Column7 wouldn't appear at all.
- Resets Excel's *used range* by deleting all extra columns and rows in the data set. If this was an issue triggered by Excel reporting extra cells in its *used range* property, then Column7 would no longer appear.

In any of these cases, our query would trigger a step level error, as Column7 – which was hard-coded in the Changed Type step – will no longer exist.

> It is also very important to realize that we have explained this based on the used range in Excel which – to be fair – is usually fairly reliable. But this same issue can be triggered if your reporting system exports to Excel and has a habit of changing the number of columns in the report!

Instead of leaving things to chance, we can future proof this to reduce the chance of a step level error in future. To do this, we'll work very hard to make sure that we keep only the named columns we need, and that Column7 never gets recorded in a Power Query step.

- Delete the Changed Type
- Select the Date column → hold down SHIFT → click the Commission column
- Right-click any of the selected column headers → Remove Other columns
- Re-select all the columns if they don't remain selected
- Go to Transform → Detect Data Type

By using Remove Other Columns instead of deleting a specified column we ensure that we are keeping only the columns we know will exist in future, and never hard code a column that may change or disappear.

The last thing you may want to check is if there are a vast number of blank rows below your data set. Should this happen you can get rid of them via the following actions:

- Select all the columns in the data set
- Go to Home → Remove Rows → Remove Blank Rows

The final caveat on this solution is: if the user created a new "Profit" column in the spreadsheet, our future proofing steps mean that it would not show up, as it would be removed during the Remove Other Columns step. So while these steps would prevent invalid data from messing up your query, they could also prevent new valid data from being imported. (This is one reason to prefer tables over worksheets when you have the choice.)

> Should you have control over your data set and know that the number of columns will never shrink, then these steps are not required. It's only when you have a data set that changes shape horizontally that you have to be concerned.

With a sample of each type of connection built, we can now load all of these queries to the worksheet (or Power BI model). Unfortunately, having built all of them in one session of Power Query, we only get to choose one load destination in Excel. Since we want the majority of them to land in the worksheet, we can take care of it as follows:

- Choose to Close & Load to a Table on a New Worksheet
- Right-click the "Excel File" worksheet tab → Delete → Delete

The queries will now each be loaded to their own worksheet, with the "Excel File" query set to load as a Connection Only.

> ✎ If you are working in Power BI, simply uncheck the Enable Load property on the Excel File query prior to choosing Close & Apply.

Final Thoughts on Connecting to Excel Data

Where possible it is preferable to build your solutions against Excel tables rather than named ranges or worksheets. They are easier to set up than the alternatives, are easier to maintain, and are quite transparent about where the data is stored. Of course, there are situations – like where a file is created via automation – where tables cannot be used. In these cases, you do have the option to use other techniques.

The other thing you want to consider when building a solution in an Excel file is where you should store your data. Should the queries live in the same file as the data, or should you keep the source data in a separate Excel file and connect to it as a data source?

In many of the examples in this book, we are building the queries in the same file where the data resides. This is purely for convenience and portability of the solution, as it avoids having you update the data source for every completed example file you open. Having said this, it makes sharing and co-authoring solutions much more difficult in the real world.

Some of the benefits of keeping your Excel data source in a separate file include:

- Having the ability to have multiple users updating the data (even simultaneously when using co-authoring)
- An easy ability to upgrade the solution when the data grows to where it should be in a database (move the data, and update the query to point to the new source)
- The ability to build multiple reporting solutions off the same Excel data source
- The ability to read data directly from a worksheet

On the other hand, the drawbacks of separating your file may include:

- The lack of ability to read from dynamic named ranges
- A requirement to manage and update the file path for different users
- Blocking the ability to use co-authoring when editing your Power Queries

Ultimately, your needs will dictate the solution that is best for you. As a rule of thumb, however, we prefer to keep our data source separate from the business logic unless we have a specific reason to do otherwise.

Chapter 7 - Simple Transformation Techniques

One of the big issues facing data pros is that no matter where we get our data from, it doesn't always arrive in a useful state. So not only do we waste time getting the data into our solution to begin with, we then have to spend even more time cleaning it up and changing its layout in order to work with it.

Un-Pivoting the Curse of Pivoted Data

Consider the classic Excel scenario where a user has started tracking their sales on a daily basis and they send it to you in the format shown below:

Sales Category	Sales in Units							
	2014-01-01	2014-01-02	2014-01-03	2014-01-04	2014-01-05	2014-01-06	2014-01-07	Total
Beer	103	243	101	137	103	185	111	983
Wine	175	223	138	57	66	199	83	941
Liquor	162	207	103	179	150	147	180	1,128
Total	440	673	342	373	319	531	374	3,052

The dreaded pivoted data set

Naturally, after tracking their sales in this way for days or weeks they bring it to you and ask you to build a variety of different reports from it. The answer to this dilemma is, of course, to build PivotTables against the data source. But the issue is that this data set is already pivoted.

This is probably one of the biggest issues facing data pros with data collected by users. PivotTables were built to quickly take tables of data and turn them into a report that the user wanted to be able to consume. The challenge is that users think in this kind of output format, not a tabular format, so tend to build their data in the format a PivotTable produces, not one that they consume.

Many users immediately think that a simple transposing of the data set will work, but that only changes the look of the data, it doesn't truly convert it into a format that PivotTables are ready to consume.

This data is still pivoted...			
Category	Beer	Wine	Liquor
2014-01-01	103	175	162
2014-01-02	243	223	207
2014-01-03	101	138	103
2014-01-04	137	57	179
2014-01-05	103	66	150
2014-01-06	185	199	147
2014-01-07	111	83	180

This is data is <u>unpivoted</u>		
Category	Date	Units
Beer	2014-01-01	103
Beer	2014-01-02	243
Beer	2014-01-03	101
Beer	2014-01-04	137
Beer	2014-01-05	103
Beer	2014-01-06	185
Beer	2014-01-07	111

Transposed data (on the left) vs properly un-pivoted data (on the right)

The worst part about this issue was that there was no tool to easily convert the data back from pivoted to un-pivoted, resulting in a huge amount of labor in order to pull this off... at least... until now.

Let's take a look at how our lives truly change with Power Query. Open the Ch07 Examples\UnPivot.xlsx file, and let's un-pivot the data set within.

Preparing the Data

You'll find that the data inside the file is already stored in a nice clean table called SalesData, making it very easy to connect to whether you are in the same workbook, a different workbook, or Power BI.

> ⚓ In order to make it easy to demonstrate how this solution survives updates, we will demonstrate this in Excel, but be aware that these concepts apply to the Unpivot Process and are the same no matter which program you are using to drive the process.

Let's pull the data into Power Query

- Create a new query → From Sheet

The data lands in Power Query and creates a query with two steps: Source and Changed Type.

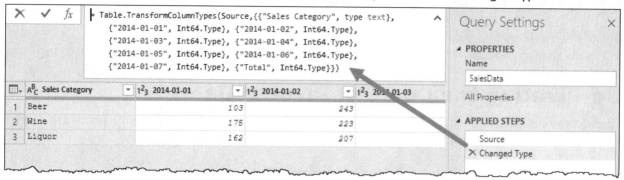

The query automatically adds a Changed Type step for us...

When you are building any solution it is important to think about what will happen when this data is updated in future. But when you are building an UnPivot solution, this is critical. Ask yourself what will happen next month... will we still have columns for Jan 1, or will we restart on Feb 1? What about next year? We may still have Jan 1, but will it still be 2014, or will it move to a new year?

The reason this question is so important is that the Changed Type step has hard-coded the current column names into the solution. If those columns aren't present in future, you'll end up receiving a step level error that blocks loading and needs to be resolved. In our experience, people build UnPivot solutions to last beyond one period, so this becomes a big issue. Our advice? Unless you specifically need to set your data types prior to unpivoting your data, delete any preceding Changed Type steps that hard code column names that may not exist in future. It will save you headaches later.

Our overall goal here is to un-pivot the data, but there is also a column we really don't need. The totals column that was imported from the original data source can be removed since we can simply rebuild that with a PivotTable (or Matrix in Power BI). Let's clean up this data and make sure we won't run into issues in future:

- Delete the Changed Type step
- Select the Total column (not shown) → press the DEL key on your keyboard

We're now left with just our key data: The Sales Category column and a column for each day.

Un-pivoting Other Columns

It is now time to show the magic behind the un-pivot ability.

- Right-click the Sales Category column → Unpivot Other Columns

> ✎ For this data set, we only need the Sales Category to be repeated on each row, but you should be aware that you can select multiple columns before unpivoting your data. Simply hold down SHIFT or CTRL to select the columns you want on every row of the output before choosing to Unpivot Other Columns.

The results are simply astounding; it's done.

Sales Category	Attribute	Value
1 Beer	2014-01-01	103
2 Beer	2014-01-02	243
3 Beer	2014-01-03	101
4 Beer	2014-01-04	137
5 Beer	2014-01-05	103
6 Beer	2014-01-06	185
7 Beer	2014-01-07	111
8 Wine	2014-01-01	175
9 Wine	2014-01-02	223

PROPERTIES

Name

SalesData

All Properties

APPLIED STEPS

Source

Removed Columns

✕ Unpivoted Other Columns

Un-pivoting magic in action

Can you believe how easy that is?

We only have a couple more changes to make here, and our data set can be finalized:

- Change the name of the Attribute and Value columns to Date and Units respectively
- Set the data types for Sales Category, Date and Units to Text, Date and Whole Number
- Rename the query to Sales

👠 Notice that there is no need to use Change Type with Locale in this instance. Since the data already resides inside Excel, Power Query will recognize this data correctly no matter what your regional settings are.

When complete, the data should look like this:

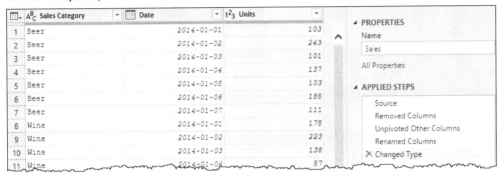

Seriously, how easy was that?

Re-Pivoting via a PivotTable

Since the data is now perfectly clean and ready for use, let's do exactly that. We'll load it and then build a couple of PivotTables based on the data.

- Load the table to a new worksheet
- Select a cell in the table → Insert PivotTable
- Insert the PivotTable in F1 of the same worksheet
- Place Sales Category on rows, Date on Columns and Units on Values

And next, we can build an alternate view from the same data set:

- Select a cell in the table → Insert PivotTable
- Insert the PivotTable in F11 of the same worksheet
- Place Sales Category on rows, Date on Rows and Units on Values
- Right-click F12 → Expand/Collapse → Collapse Entire Field

We've now got two completely different summaries based on a single set of un-pivoted data.

	A	B	C	D	E	F	G	H	
1	Sales Category	Date	Units			Sum of Units	Column Lal		
2	Beer	2014-01-01	103			Row Labels	2014-01-01	2014-01-02	201
3	Beer	2014-01-02	243			Beer	103	243	
4	Beer	2014-01-03	101			Liquor	162	207	
5	Beer	2014-01-04	137			Wine	175	223	
6	Beer	2014-01-05	103			Grand Total	440	673	
7	Beer	2014-01-06	185						
8	Beer	2014-01-07	111						
9	Wine	2014-01-01	175						
10	Wine	2014-01-02	223						
11	Wine	2014-01-03	138			Row Labels	Sum of Units		
12	Wine	2014-01-04	57			⊞ Beer	983		
13	Wine	2014-01-05	66			⊞ Liquor	1128		
14	Wine	2014-01-06	199			⊞ Wine	941		
15	Wine	2014-01-07	83			Grand Total	3052		
16	Liquor	2014-01-01	162						

Two PivotTables built from an un-pivoted data set

Surviving an Update

At this point, you'd probably be fairly comfortable saving the file, returning it to the user, and letting them continue to update it. After all, Power Query solutions can be refreshed at any time.

Naturally you do so, and the users make their updates, then send it back to you. Upon opening the file you see that they've done things that only an end-user could think of as acceptable:

Sales Category	2014-01-01	2014-01-02	2014-01-03	2014-01-04	2014-01-05	2014-01-06	2014-01-07	Total	2014-01-08
Beer	103	243	101	137	103	185	111	983	34
Wine	175	223	138	57	66	199	83	941	86
Cider						78	92	170	47
Liquor	162	207	103	179	150	147	180	1,128	23
Total	440	673	342	373	319	609	466	3,222	

The table, as returned by the end-user

Looking through the changes, you're astounded to see the following issues:

- The new day is added **after** the total column
- A new sales category has been injected with retroactive data
- The user didn't complete the total on the new column

The question is, how will the refresh fare given these changes? Let's find out. Go to the Sales worksheet and click the Refresh All button two times (once for the Query and once for the PivotTables).

The results are nothing short of amazing, and shown below:

Sum of Units	Column Labels								
Row Labels	2014-01-01	2014-01-02	2014-01-03	2014-01-04	2014-01-05	2014-01-06	2014-01-07	2014-01-08	Grand Total
Beer	103	243	101	137	103	185	111	34	1017
Liquor	162	207	103	179	150	147	180	23	1151
Wine	175	223	138	57	66	199	83	86	1027
Cider						78	92	47	217
Grand Total	440	673	342	373	319	609	466	190	3412

Row Labels	Sum of Units
⊞ Beer	1017
⊞ Liquor	1151
⊞ Wine	1027
⊟ Cider	217
2014-01-06	78
2014-01-07	92
2014-01-08	47
Grand Total	3412

Not only does our data all show up, but it shows up in the correct places!

Every issue that your user threw at you was handled. The totals are there, the data is in the right order and the historical values have been updated.

The Difference Between Unpivot, Unpivot Other & Unpivot Selected Columns

There are actually three un-pivot functions on the right-click menu in Power Query; Unpivot Columns, Unpivot Other Columns, and Unpivot Only Selected Columns.

Based on the terminology of the user interface, what would you expect to happen if you originally took these actions?

- Selecting the Jan 1 through Jan 7 columns
- Use the UnPivot Columns command

The answer is that you'll get a new step called "Unpivoted Columns", which provide identical results as when we used the Unpivot Other Columns command on the Sales Category column. But if you use this command, would you expect it to refresh properly when you added the data for Jan 8?

As it turns out, it would have. While you might think that Power Query would record a step that says "unpivot the columns you selected", this is not the case. What Power Query *actually* does is look at all the columns in the data set and determine that there was (at least) one column which was not selected. Rather than build you a specific "unpivot these columns" command, it will actually build an Unpivot Other Columns step based on the column(s) you did not select.

The good news is that this makes it very difficult to make a mistake and build a scenario that blows up when new daily data columns are added to the data source. Essentially – whether you use Unpivot Columns or Unpivot Other Columns – you will get a solution that is future proofed and assumes that unnamed columns will always be unpivoted.

But what if you want to lock in a specific "unpivot this column only" command so that a new column added to the data set will not be unpivoted? That is exactly what the Unpivot Only Selected Columns command is for. Instead of a Table.UnpivotOtherColumns() command, it will record a Table.Unpivot() command which specifies the only columns to unpivot in future.

> ⚒ Our recommendation is to use the Unpivot Other Columns or Unpivot Only Selected Columns commands. You don't lose any functionality, but you do get an explicit step name in the Applied Steps window that is much easier to read when you are reviewing the data transformation process later.

Pivoting Data

Whether to drive a PivotTable, Matrix or other visualization, most data sets require their data served up in an unpivoted format. But there are also times where – to get your data into that unpivoted format – you need to actually pivot the data. Have a look at the following data sample which you'll find in the Ch07 Examples\ Pivot.xlsx file:

Category	Date	Measure	Units
Beer	2021-01-01	Actual	200
Beer	2021-01-01	Budget	150
Beer	2021-01-02	Actual	50
Beer	2021-01-02	Budget	200
Beer	2021-01-03	Actual	100
Beer	2021-01-03	Budget	0
Wine	2021-01-01	Actual	200
Wine	2021-01-01	Budget	200

Completely unpivoted data

This data is fully unpivoted. But what if you wanted to get it into a format that had distinct columns for Actual and Budget? That's where the Pivot function comes in. Let's explore that.

- Create a new query → From Sheet
- Change the data type on the Dates column → Date → Replace
- Update the query name to Sales

With the pre-work all done, it is now time to switch it up so that we get distinct columns for the Actual and Budget values:

- Select the Measure column
- Go to Transform → Pivot Column

You'll then be prompted with the Pivot Column dialog:

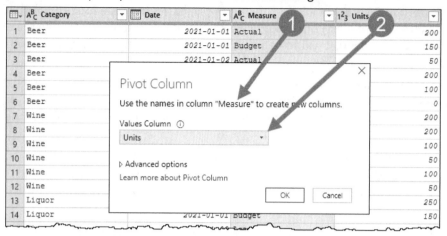

Configuring the output desired when Pivoting a column

When Pivoting a column, it is important to make sure you select the column you wish to use for the pivoted column headers before launching the command, as you cannot change that within the dialog. Once inside the dialog, you'll then be prompted to select the column that contains the values you would like to aggregate based on the column headers.

> 🐵 The Values column in the Pivot Column dialog will always default to the first column in the data set, which is seldom what you need. Don't forget to change this!

> 🔧 If you click the little triangle to the left of Advanced Options, you'll find that you can also change how the values are aggregated. Just like in an Excel PivotTable, you'll find that the defaults are Sum for numeric columns and Count for text-based columns. But unlike Excel, you'll also find a "Do not aggregate option" that we will make use of in later chapters.

To finish the Pivot operation:

- Configure the Values Column to Units
- Click OK

And the results are that we've now extracted the Actual and Budget values into separate columns:

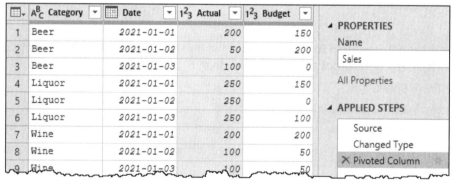

We now have separate columns for Actual and Budget

At this point, the data can be further transformed if necessary, or loaded for use.

Splitting Columns

Another common task, especially when importing from flat files, is the ability to split data points out of a single column based on some kind of delimiter or pattern. Fortunately, Power Query offers us some different options, depending on the output we need from the end product.

For this example, we are going to look at a rather odd data export – one that we wished we'd never seen in the real world. The data file is contained in the Ch07 Examples\Splitting Data.txt file, and when imported via the "From Text/CSV" connector into the Power Query editor, will look like this:

	A^B_C Column1		A^B_C Column2		A^B_C Column3		A^B_C Column4		A^B_C Column5	
1	Start		End		Days		Cooks: Grill/Prep/Li...		Hours	
2	5:30 AM		1:00 PM		Mon		Don/Romona/Tisa		7.50	
					Tue					
					Wed					
					Thu					
					Fri					
3	5:30 AM		1:00 PM		Sat		Ta/Kaitlin/Eldridge		7.50	
					Sun					
4	11:30 AM		6:00 PM		Mon		Trang/Jerrell/Chanell		6.50	
					Tue					
					Wed					
					Thu					
					Fri					

Yuck. How do you normalize this?

There are two issues in this file that we need to take into account:

- The Grill cook, Prep cook and Line cook positions are contained in a single column, separated by the / character
- There are multiple days of the week contained in the Days column

Why someone would set their data up this way is above our pay grade but the reality is that it's left to us to clean it up. Our goal is to build a table with one row per day (inheriting the appropriate Start and End times, as well as the hours). In addition, the specification we've been asked for is to split the cooks into individual columns.

Splitting Columns to Other Columns

We'll start with the cooks, as this looks to be fairly straightforward:

- Right-click the Cooks column → Split Column → Split by Delimiter

The key part of the dialog is shown here:

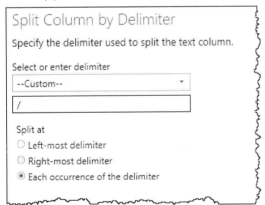

Splitting to multiple columns based on a delimiter

There are a few things to be aware of when looking at this dialog:

1. Power Query scans looking for what it believes is the delimiter and – in most cases – gets this correct. Should it make a poor choice, however, you can simply change it. (For our purposes, the / is perfect.)

2. The drop-down box gives you several common delimiters, but a custom option if the delimiter found or needed isn't in that list. As the / character is not as common as things like a comma or a tab, Power Query has set it to Custom in this case

3. The option for the Custom delimiter is not restricted to a single character. Indeed, you can use entire words, if that is what is necessary in your data set.

Underneath the delimiter option, you'll find that you also have the choice to apply how aggressive the splitting action is. You can split by only one instance of the delimiter (from left or right), or by each occurrence. In our case, we want to split by each as we have three positions in one cell.

After confirming the default, and renaming the newly split columns to Grill, Prep and Line, the output will look like this:

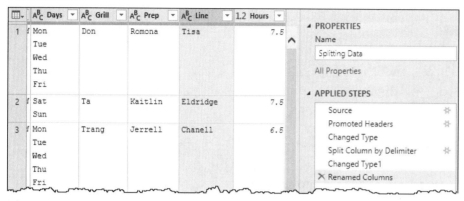

The cooks have now been split into individual columns

Of course, this still leaves us with an issue in the Days column, so let's deal with that next.

Splitting Columns to Rows

The next step we want to take is to split the Days column to separate those components. One method to do this would be to split the days into new columns, and then unpivot those columns. But we can also take advantage of one of the Split Column options to do this in a single step.

- Right-click the Days column → Split Columns → By Delimiter

This time, we need to take a little bit more control over the Split Column options:

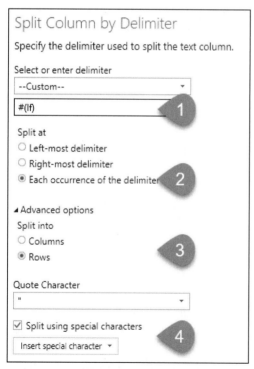

This time the dialog opens with the Advanced Options section open

Working from top to bottom of this dialog:

1. The delimiter is a line feed, which requires a special character code to enact. Fortunately, Power Query has put that character code set in the dialog for us.

2. We will still be splitting by each occurrence of the delimiter. Notice that unlike the cooks, which always had three items, the days column sometimes holds two values, and sometimes five.

3. By default, the Split Column by Delimiter function will split into columns. We have overridden the default choice here to force Power Query to split the data into rows instead of splitting it into columns.

4. The option to Split using special characters is checked (due to the presence of the line feeds). Should you ever identify that you need a special character – such as a Tab, Carriage Return, Line Feed or non-breaking space – you can insert them into the delimiter string by checking this box and choosing the special character from the drop-down list.

✎ The first thing you'll notice here is that the dialog has opened with the Advanced Options area open. The reason for this is actually wholly based on the delimiter that Power Query identified for this data: the line feed (hard return) character. Had this been a simple comma, you would have had to open the Advanced Options section yourself.

☺ Working with special characters can be painful, as it may not be immediately obvious which you need and – in the case of Carriage Returns and Line Feeds – you may need the correct character or a combination of characters. If Power Query doesn't provide the correct delimiters initially, the only way to deal with this is via trial and error by reconfiguring this dialog when things don't work the way you expect.

Overall, the only change we need to make to the default Power Query presented us with is to change the Split Into section to split into Rows instead of Columns. Once we've done that, the data splits nicely into new rows:

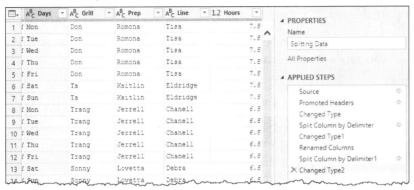

We've got cooks for days!

If these were truly the requirements, we could load our data at this point, and be done.

Split and Unpivot vs Splitting to Rows

Let's look at a little variance from the original requirements and say that we've decided that our cooks really should be unpivoted as well. To do that in as few clicks as possible, we could:

- Select the Grill column → hold down Shift → Select the Line column
- Right-click one of the selected columns → Unpivot Columns
- Rename the Attribute column → Cook
- Rename the Values column → Employee

And the result would look like this:

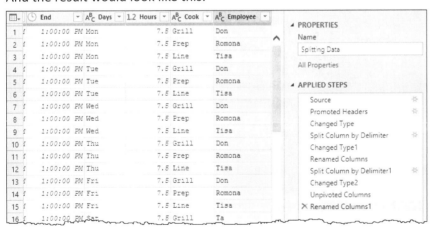

Truly unpivoted data set

So... could we have saved ourselves a bunch of clicks in this process? Rather than splitting our cooks into columns which had to be renamed, then unpivoting the results and renaming the columns again, we could have just split the original cooks column into new rows?

We could have, except that we would be missing one critical piece of information: the type of cook. The reason? The position was only included in the column header, and not the data itself:

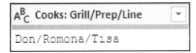

Remember that we only know Don is a Grill cook based on the header...

While splitting the Cooks column would have put the employees into their own rows, the fact is that the type of cook doesn't exist in the record, so would have been lost. Splitting to columns was critical in this case, as it allowed us to change the header to the type of cook, which we then brought into our data via the unpivot option.

> ⚒ Of course, the steps above assume that the cooks are always entered in the correct order. Should that not be the case, we would need to approach this differently. The most likely approach at that point would be to split the employees to rows, and then retrieve the position via a merge against another table – something we'll learn about in Chapter 10.

The good news is that we have multiple ways to get to our end goal, where sometimes we do need to perform some extra steps in order to generate all the data we need for our solution.

Filtering and Sorting

For the most part, filtering comes fairly naturally to users of Power Query, as the filter structure is quite familiar to anyone who has used Excel or other office programs. For this section, we are going to explore some of the different options (and potential gotchas) in both filtering and sorting in Power Query.

To get started, we need to import the data from Ch07 Examples\FilterSort.csv. As this file contains dates and values written in a US format, we should also make sure that both the Date and Sales columns specifically define the data types using Locale. The initial import is therefore performed as follows:

- Create a new Query → From File → From Text/CSV
- Delete the default Changed Type step
- Change the data type on the Date column → Using Locale → Date → English (US)
- Change the data type on the Sales column → Using Locale → Currency → English (US)
- Change the data type on the Quantity column → Whole Number

The results of the initial import should now look as shown here:

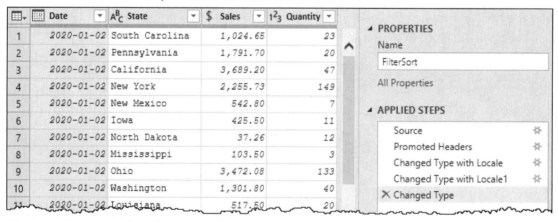

The initial import of the FilterSort.csv file

At least... the first 11 rows of the data are shown here. As it turns out, this file spans from Jan 1, 2020 through May 31, 2026, and contains over 53,500 rows, much more data than we actually need for our purpose.

Filtering Specific Values

Filtering for specific values is relatively straightforward. Simply click the drop-down arrow at the top of the column, uncheck the items you don't want to keep, or uncheck select all and check the ones you do want. There is even a handy search box which will allow you to put in part of the item to filter the list down for you:

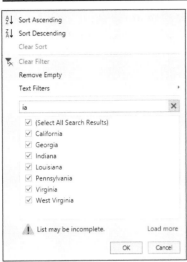

Filtering the results of the State column to only states containing "ia"

This search is obviously pretty handy, as you can quickly cut down the list to only a fraction of the items, uncheck Select All, then check just the items you want to keep.

> 🔧 If you were to commit the filter pictured, Power Query would add a new step that includes any state containing the letters "ia".

> 🐵 Be aware that this search box applies a filter to show any value containing the character pattern you enter. Wildcards and mathematical operators are not accepted.

One challenge you will run into is when working with data sets that have more than 1,000 rows in the column. As Power Query only scans the data in the preview by default, you will occasionally see the message that the List may be incomplete, with an option to click Load More. Clicking this option asks Power Query to scan more data, and it will do so, until it reaches a maximum of 1,000 unique values, as this is the maximum that can be displayed in the drop-down list. At that point you will see a footnote that a limit of 1,000 values was reached.

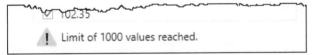

The Sales column has more than 1,000 unique values...

The challenge that can occur here is when the value you need to filter for is outside of not only the top 1,000 rows of the preview, but when it is outside of the top 1,000 unique values in the column. At that point you cannot get it to show up in the filter search area, making it impossible to select via the filter pane.

Should this happen, don't lose hope. You just need to create your filters manually. Even though our data set doesn't exhibit this issue, let's pretend that it does, and we need to set a manual filter:

- Filter the State column → Text Filters → Contains

You'll be prompted with this handy dialog that allows you to create the filter manually, even if the data does not exist in the visual filter pane:

Creating a manual filter for "Contains ia"

This view of the Filter Rows dialog is super useful when you cannot see your data in the filter list, or when you need to configure something a bit more complex like an "and" or "or" condition for your filter. And it gets even more useful when you click the Advanced button:

The Advanced view of the Filter Rows dialog

While filters in the Basic view are all applied to the original column you selected, the Advanced view allows you to apply filters to multiple columns at once, add more layers of filters (via the Add Clause button) and mix and match your filters in any way you see fit. Just be aware that "And" filters are additive, where "Or" filters are alternative.

> 🐵 If you need to reconfigure your filter setup to remove or reorder your clauses, this can be done by clicking on the … menu that appears on the right side of the screen when you mouse over the clause.

	Date	AᴮC State	$ Sales	1²₃ Quantity	
1	2020-01-02	Pennsylvania	1,791.70	20	
2	2020-01-02	California	3,689.20	47	
3	2020-01-02	West Virginia	3,662.75	13	
4	2020-01-02	Georgia	1,392.65	51	
5	2020-01-03	California	12,441.39	597	
6	2020-01-03	Pennsylvania	5,928.48	450	
7	2020-01-03	Georgia	1,384.49	255	
8	2020-01-03	West Virginia	2,227.55	79	
9	2020-01-03	Louisiana	14,184.68	555	
10	2020-01-03	Virginia	1,702.23	71	
11	2020-01-04	Virginia	4,250.40	134	
12	2020-01-04	California	2,265.27	126	

PROPERTIES
Name
FilterSort
All Properties

APPLIED STEPS
Source
Promoted Headers
Changed Type with Locale
Changed Type with Locale1
Changed Type
✕ Filtered Rows

The results of applying a filter for States containing "ia" where sales are also >1000

> 🐵 When configuring filters that span multiple columns, a single Applied Step will be created, and only the initial column shows up with an active filter icon when selecting the step. If you are concerned with leaving a clearer audit trail, apply your filters as individual steps instead.

Filtering with Contextual Filters

At first glance, the filter drop-down looks very much the same no matter which column you attempt to filter. The length is consistent, and it also shows selectable values in the filter area. But if you look closely, you'll see that the flyout menu just above the search box gets named depending on the data type of the column and provides filters specific to the context of that data type.

For example:

- For text, you'll see Text Filters, which contains filters for Equals, Begins With, Ends With, Contains, as well as a "does not" version for each of those.

- For numeric data types, the menu becomes Number Filters, and displays the following options: Equals, Greater Than, Greater Than or Equal To, Less Than, Less Than or Equal To, and Between.

While each data type has its own appropriate filter options, we want to focus on one of the biggest: Dates.

So many options for date filtering!

This list looks super impressive, and many of them will do exactly what you'd expect. For example:

- Filtering to January would cut your list down to show only dates where the month is January. Of course, if you have six years of data, you'll have January results from six different years which may – or may not – be what you are after.
- Filtering to Is Earliest, would filter the data set to only rows which match the earliest date in the selected column
- Using a Between filter would allow you to hard code the start and end ranges.

But the tricky part around working with the context sensitive date filters is understanding what "This", "Last", and "Next" actually mean. Unlike every other filter, which is based on *your data*, these filters are *relative to the current date/time on your system*.

Consider a scenario where it is December 1, 2021, and you set a solution that filters the sales database to use This Year (found under the Year submenu).

January 5, 2022, you're back in the office after some time off and open the report to finalize the 2021 numbers... and you watch your report values drop from $6 million to under $10 thousand. Why? Because the report would update to pull for the current year to date – which is now based on 2022, not 2021.

In addition, unlike Excel's default filters that allow you to select Year, Month or Day – even when there is only a single date column in the data set – Power Query's filter doesn't have that hierarchical ability. You also won't find specific numeric years under the Year sub-menu. So how would you filter to only get dates for 2021 in this case? One way is to use a Between filter:

- Filter the Date column → Date Filters → Between
- Set the filters as shown below

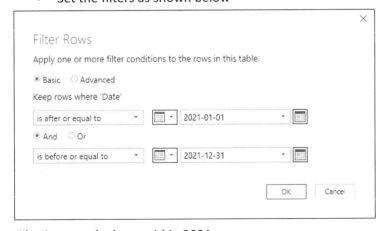

Filtering to only dates within 2021

✎ Alternately, you could always add a new column that extracts the years and then filter that for a specific year. To do this you would select the Date column → Add Column → Date → Year → Year, then filter for just the year you need.

The one knock on setting your filters in this way is that they are not dynamic. When you need to force them to filter for 2022, you'll need to edit the query and change it manually.

Sorting Data

The next-to-last technique we'll explore in this chapter is that of sorting. Carrying on from the previous section, we want to sort our data in ascending order by State. We then want to sort the data by date, but as a sub-sort of the State. In other words, these sorts need to layer on each other, not replace each other.

The steps to do this are:

- Click the Filter arrow on the State column → Sort Ascending
- Click the Filter arrow on the Date column → Sort Ascending

And the results are exactly what we were shooting for:

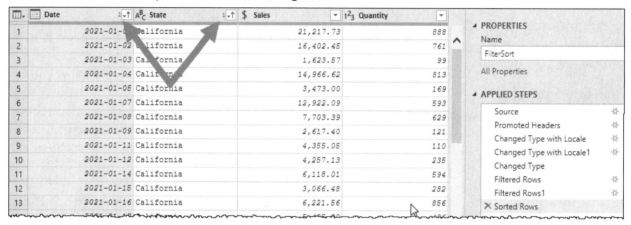

Power Query sorted first by State and then by Date

As you can see, Power Query applies successive sorts by default, unlike Excel. It even puts a subtle indicator next to the filter icon showing the order in which the sorting was applied.

> 🔧 When using Dark Mode in Excel, the sort order icons are barely visible, but they are there!

While sorting can be useful and can give us a great deal of comfort when looking at our raw data, we also need to realize that it does have a performance cost. You should ask yourself if you really need to have your data sorted at all. Sometimes it certainly is required in order to get the data shaped properly. But if the data is going to be fed to a Pivot Table of the data model in Excel or Power BI, sorting your output is needless overhead as the visuals take care of that for you.

Grouping Data

Another challenge that we can run into as data pros is an overwhelming amount of data. Take the previous sample file, for example. It contains 53,513 rows of transactional data covering 7 years and 48 states. What if we only wanted to see the Total Sales and Total Units by Year?

Naturally, we could import all of the source data and feed it into a PivotTable or Matrix visual, but what if we will never need to drill-in to the detail rows? Do we really need to import all that data?

Fortunately, Power Query has a Grouping function that will allow us to group rows during our transformation, allowing us to import the data at the exact granularity that we need. This can be super useful for reducing the file size as it avoids carrying an excess of unneeded detail rows.

Let's use the same raw data file as we used in the last example. In a new workbook/Power BI file:

- Create a new Query → From File → From Text/CSV → Ch07 Examples\FilterSort.csv
- Delete the default Changed Type step
- Change the data type on the Date column → Using Locale → Date → English (US)
- Change the data type on the Sales column → Using Locale → Currency → English (US)
- Change the data type on the Quantity column → Whole Number

Once again, we see the following:

The initial import of the FilterSort.csv file

Our reporting goal this time isn't particularly concerned with analyzing data by day or month, so let's convert that Date column to become years:

- Select the Date column → Transform → Date → Year → Year

That's better, but we still have over 53,000 rows. Let's fix that.

- Select the Date column → Transform → Group By
- Click the Advanced button

At this point you'll be taken to the Group By dialog as shown here:

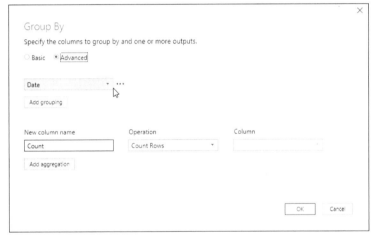

The Group By dialog (in advanced view)

> 🔍 The reason we go straight into Advanced view is that this view gives you the option to add additional grouping and aggregation columns.

As you can see, the column we had selected prior to grouping (Date) has been placed into the "Group By" area. Should we need to, we could change and/or add new grouping levels here as well. For our purposes, grouping by the year will work perfectly.

> 🔍 As you mouse over the fields in this dialog, you'll notice a little ... menu pop up will become visible. This menu hides the ability to move fields up or down, as well as remove grouping/ aggregation levels if you need to get rid of them.

Now that we've configured how we'd like our data grouped, we can look at how we'd like it aggregated. By default, Power Query offers to give you a transaction count by counting the rows of the table. That's not what we are after here, so let's change it to give us the Total Sales $ and Total Quantity by Year and State. In the aggregation section at the bottom of the dialog:

- Change the column name from **Count** to **Total Sales $**
- Change the operation from **Count** to **Sum**
- Change the column from **Date** to **Sales**

- Click Add Aggregation
- Configure it to return **Total Quantity** as a **Sum** of **Quantity**

When complete, the dialog should appear as follows:

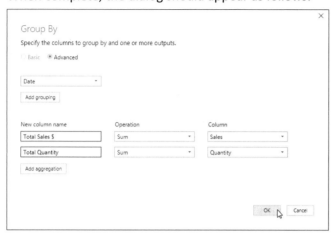

Grouping data by Year (Date) and returning the Sum of Sale and Quantity

Upon clicking the OK button, the data will be summarized immediately, yielding a total of 7 rows of data (for this data set):

1²₃ Date	1.2 Total Sales $	1.2 Total Quantity
2020	51582296.33	2358840
2021	56790122.76	2536553
2022	61269318.83	2702834
2023	76817470.11	3678432
2024	25605823.37	1226144
2025	25605823.37	1226144
2026	25605823.37	1226144

The summarized data set yields a total of 7 rows

This is very cool, but there are a couple of key observations that you should recognize about this feature:

1. Source data columns that were not included in the grouping or aggregation area (State) are dropped. There is no need to remove them before running your Grouping operation.

2. While the columns used in the aggregation area can be defined in the dialog, the grouping levels cannot be renamed there. They must be renamed prior to or post grouping.

3. While we only used the SUM operation in this example, the aggregation operations available to you include generating the Sum, Average, Median, Min or Max of column values, as well as the ability to Count Rows and Count Distinct Rows.

   ✎ There is one more aggregation option available in the grouping dialog: All Rows. This mysterious option will be explored in Chapter 13.

It's now time to finalize this data set and load it to our destination:

- Rename the Date column as Year
- Rename the query as Grouping
- Go to Home → Close & Load to load the data

One of the most common issues we see with self-service BI pros is that they frequently import an abundance of data that they don't need. When you are importing your data, challenge yourself to see if you can reduce the number of columns and rows of detail you are carrying. Remember that you can always go back to the grouping step and remove it (or reconfigure it) if you over-summarize your data! Trust us, you'll thank yourself for reducing your data set size as your solution will be more stable and more performant.

Chapter 8 - Appending Data

One of the jobs that data pros get on a regular basis is appending multiple data sets together. Whether these data sets are all contained within a single Excel workbook or spread across multiple files, the issue is that they need to be stacked into a single table.

A common scenario that illustrates this need is where data – extracted from a central database software on a monthly basis – needs to be consolidated for year-to-date analysis. In February, someone extracts the January information and sends it to the analyst. Then in March the February data is sent to the analyst to add to the solution, and so the cycle continues on a monthly basis through the year.

The classic Excel process to deal with this solution usually boils down to the following initially:

- Import and transform the January file into a tabular format
- Turn the data into an official Excel table
- Build the reporting analysis against the Excel table
- Save the file

And then, on a monthly basis:

- Import and transform the newly received data file
- Copy the new data and paste it at the end of original table
- Refresh the reports and visuals

While this works, the process is plainly not all sunshine and rainbows, and there are some very obvious issues here. This chapter will not solve the issue of a user making a mistake in the transformations (although future chapters will), but it will show you how Power Query can consolidate two or more data sets without ever worrying about a user pasting over the last few rows of data.

Basic Append Operations

The Ch08 Examples folder contains three CSV files; Jan 2008.csv, Feb 2008.csv and Mar 2008.csv. We will walk through the process of importing and appending each file.

Importing the files is fairly straightforward:

- Create a new query → From File → From Text/CSV
- Browse to the Ch08 Examples\Jan 2008.csv → Open → Transform Data

Power Query will open the file, and execute the following steps automatically for this data source:

- Promote the first row to headers, showing Date, Account, Dept and Amount
- Set the data types to Date, Whole Number, Whole Number and Decimal Value

To be safe, we will remove the Changed Type step, and re-create it, forcing our dates to import based on the US standard that they came from.

- Remove the Changed Type step
- Change the data type of the Date column → Using Locale... → Date → English (US)
- Change the data type of the Amount column → Using Locale... → Currency → English (US)
- Change the data type of the Account column → Whole Number
- Change the data type of the Dept column → Whole Number

At this point our query will look as shown below:

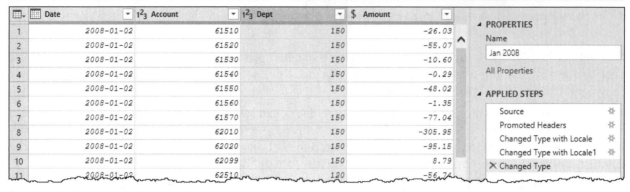

The Jan 2008 query before loading

Since our goal is not to report on *only* January sales, we're going to load this query as a connection only, in preparation for later appending.

> 🔏 Remember, in Power BI, you can right-click the query and un-check the enable load option, while in Excel you need to go to Close & Load To… → Only Create Connection.

We now need to replicate the process with both the Feb 2008.csv and Mar 2008.csv files. The import process uses exactly the same steps, and when complete you should have three new queries in your solution, each of which loads as a connection:

- Jan 2008
- Feb 2008
- Mar 2008

When complete, each query should be visible in the Queries & Connections pane in Excel, or in the Query Navigator pane within the Power Query Editor.

The queries show up in the Queries & Connections pane in Excel (left) and the Query Navigator (right)

Appending Two Tables

The next job is to create the table which will be used to drive our business intelligence, which requires appending the tables together. One route to do this in Excel is to right-click one of the queries in the Queries & Connections pane and choose to Append Queries. This would prompt you with the following dialog box:

The Append queries dialog

While this seems fairly easy we actually recommend that you do not use this feature in order to append tables. Yes, it allows you to append two queries (including appending a query to itself if you ever have the need to do so). It even allows you to switch to the "Three or more" view to append multiple tables all in one go. But it does have a couple of things that we're not fans of:

1. There is no Queries & Connections pane in Power BI, and we'd rather you learn a method to do this which works in multiple programs.

2. This will create a new query called "Append 1" which combines all merged tables into a single step in the Applied Steps window, making it more difficult to audit.

Instead of using this functionality, we would rather you learn to make a reference to the first table, and then perform the append operations inside the Power Query Editor. The major difference between these approaches is that this one will work anywhere you find Power Query, and it will also record a distinct Append step for each table you append to the query. Having distinct steps makes it much easier to audit your query later, rather than have an unknown number of queries all combined into a Source step.

We will choose to use the Jan 2008 query as our base and will start by appending (only) the Feb 2008 query to it.

*   Edit any one of your queries and then expand the Query Navigator pane
*   Right-click the Jan 2008 query → Reference
*   Rename the Jan 2008 query → Transactions
*   Go to Home → Append Queries
*   Append Feb 2008 → OK

The result at this point will look as shown here:

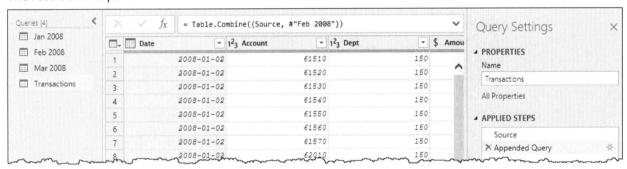

The results of appending Feb 2008 to Jan 2008

> ✎ If you had appended the query directly from the Excel user interface (or selected the Jan 2008 query and chosen to Append As New), you'd have a single step called Source. While the Applied Steps window will have less items, it means that you have to click on the Source step and read the formula bar to recognize what has happened. In this case our audit trail is very clear as the Source step points to the Jan 2008 query, and we can plainly see another query was appended to that data.

At this point you may be tempted to scroll down the query to see if all of your records are actually there. Unfortunately this won't really work as Power Query doesn't actually load all of your data in the initial window, but rather shows a preview of your data. The number of rows it will show you varies with the number of columns you add, but you can see this in the bottom left corner of the Power Query editor:

4 COLUMNS, 999+ ROWS

Power Query shows you how many preview rows it can handle right now

Of course, this leads to a big question: If you can't see all the data, how do you know it worked?

The answer is to finalize the query. So let's load the data to a worksheet and see what we get:

The Queries & Connections pane shows that we have 3,887 records

> ⚲ To see the number of records in Power BI, go to the Data view (on the left side) and select your table in the Fields list. The row count will be shown in the bottom left of the interface.

In order to validate and visualize the output, why not summarize it with a PivotTable at this point?:

- Select any cell in the Transactions table → Insert → PivotTable
- Place the PivotTable in cell F2 of the current worksheet
- Drag Amount to the Values area
- Drag Date to the Rows area
- Right-click cell F3 → Group → by Months (only) → OK

Once done, you'll see that you have a PivotTable that shows that both tables were indeed consolidated into one:

	A	B	C	D	E	F	G	H
1	Date	Account	Dept	Amount				
2	2008-01-02	61510	150	-26.03		Row Labels	Sum of Amount	
3	2008-01-02	61520	150	-55.07		Jan	89790.94	
4	2008-01-02	61530	150	-10.6		Feb	56211.14	
5	2008-01-02	61540	150	-0.29		Grand Total	146002.08	
6	2008-01-02	61550	150	-48.02				

January and February transactions are now in one PivotTable

Appending Additional Tables

At this point we want to add the March records to the query as well. And this is where Excel users who use the Append feature from the Queries & Connections pane get burned. Their natural instinct is to right-click the Transactions query and Append the March data to it. The problem with this approach is that it will create a *new query*, not add the step to the Transactions query. As the PivotTable is based off the results of the Transactions table, we need the new append step in that query, not a new one.

In order to add March's data to our existing Transactions query, we will need to edit the Transactions query. At that point, we need to make a choice. Should we edit the existing Appended Query step, or add a new one? The answer to this really depends on how much data you will be adding to the solution over time vs how clear you want your audit trail to be.

Let's say that you are going to be adding twelve appends over time, and don't want a long list of steps. In that case you would:

- Click the gear next to the Appended Query step → click Three or more Tables
- Select each table you wish to add → Click Add>>

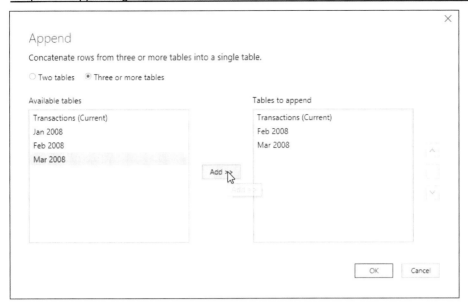

Adding multiple appends in a single step

Alternately, if you prefer to do one query at a time and focus on creating an easy-to-consume audit trail, you would take the following action each time you add a new query to the data source:

- Edit the Transactions query
- Go to Home → Append Queries
- Choose to append the new query

Adding one query at a time to create distinct steps

In fact, if you want to make your audit trail even more clear you can right-click the step name and choose Properties in order to modify the step names and provide notes that show on hover:

Customized step names with tooltip descriptions

To customize step names and add the tooltips, just right-click the step and choose Properties. This will allow you to modify the default step name and add a custom description that shows up when hovering over the information icon.

☎ All steps except Source can be renamed in this way. To rename the Source step you will need to learn to edit the underlying M code of the query.

🌶 There are two schools of thought on editing the default query names. While it can be tempting to edit each step name to make it more descriptive, the challenge for a true Power Query pro is that they will now need to spend more time reviewing each step to understand what the formula actually is. Our advice? Learn how to read and associate the default step names with their actions, but use the Description ability to leave notes about your intent.

No matter which way you decided to append the March table to the data set (via editing the existing step or creating a new one), it is time to load the data and verify that the append of the March data actually worked.

It's now that we revisit an unfortunate issue with our Power Queries when loading to an Excel table. When you look at the worksheet that holds our PivotTable, you can see that the Transactions Query (and therefore the Excel table), does hold all 6,084 rows – the combined totals of the three previous data sets. Yet the PivotTable has not changed:

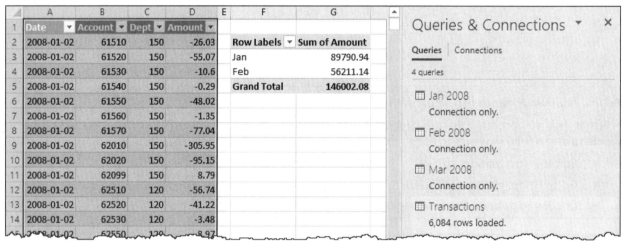

The transactions table has updated, yet the PivotTable has not

This is not a major issue, just a minor inconvenience and a reminder. If you load your data to an Excel table, then feed it to a PivotTable, you'll need to refresh the PivotTable as well in order to have the updated values flow through.

- Right-click the PivotTable → Refresh

And it does indeed update:

January through March records are now showing in a single PivotTable

🌶 Remember, if the query is loaded to the data model in either Excel or Power BI, a single refresh is sufficient to update both the data source and any Pivots or visuals.

Obviously, editing your file on a monthly basis to add and transform the new data source and then append it to the Transactions query is going to get old pretty fast. In Chapter 9, we'll show you a method to make this even easier. But the fact is that appending and editing individual appends as shown here is a vital skill that you must possess in order to master Power Query.

Combining Queries with Differing Headers

When appending queries, so long as the headers of the queries being combined are identical, the second query will just be appended to the first as you'd expect. But what if the columns don't have the same column headers?

In the case of the image below, the name of the Date column changed to TranDate in the Mar 2008 query, and the analyst didn't notice. Everything was fine as the Jan 2008 and Feb 2008 records were appended. But when the analyst went and appended the Mar 2008 records to the table, things broke down:

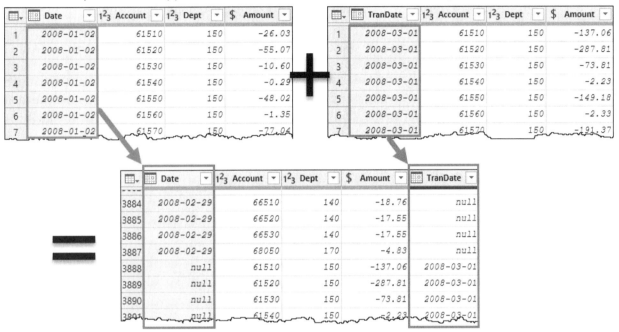

How would Power Query know that the TranDate column values should go into the Date column?

When appending two tables, Power Query loads the data from the first query. It then scans the header row of the second (and subsequent) query(ies). If any of the headers are not present in the results retrieved to date, the new column(s) are added. It then fills the appropriate record into each column for each data set, filling any gaps with *null* values.

In the case of the scenario above, this means that the TranDate column (found in the March query) is filled with *null* values in January and February, since the Jan 2008 query doesn't have a Tran Date column.

On the flipside, because the column name changed in the source file, the Mar 2008 query has no Date column, instead possessing a TranDate column. For this reason, the Date column is filled with *null* values for each March record, while the TranDate column holds the values that were intended to be in the Date column.

The fix for this is to do the following:

- Edit the Mar 2008 query → rename the TranDate column to Date
- Edit the Transactions query
- Go to Home → Refresh Preview

To be fair, the preview should refresh on its own, but the above click steps enforce that.

> 🖊 Want to try this yourself? Edit one of the monthly queries and rename any one of the columns to something different. Return to the Transactions query and you'll see your newly named column!

Appending Tables & Ranges in the Current File

While retrieving and appending data from external files is quite common, Excel users will also use this ability to append data tables from within the same workbook.

When combining a small number of tables you'll just use the method outlined above:

- Create a staging (connection only) query for each data source
- Reference one
- Append the other(s)

But what happens when you want to build a system where Excel is acting like a quasi-database and users are creating a new table on a monthly basis to hold the transactions for that month right inside the workbook? Do you really want to have to manually adjust the query to append a new table on a monthly basis? Not really. Could we set up a solution that automatically includes all new tables when refreshing?

The answer to this question is yes, and it involves leveraging the Excel.CurrentWorkbook() function that we used in Chapter 6 to read from dynamic named ranges.

Let's look at some specific examples, starting with the Ch08 Examples\Append Tables.xlsx.

This particular file holds three tables which contain the gift certificates issued by a spa on a monthly basis. Each worksheet is named for the month and year separated by a space, and each worksheet contains a table listing the certificates. While each table is also named after the month and year, these date portions are separated with the _ character, (Jan_2008, Feb_2008, etc…) as a space is not permitted within a table name. Each month, the bookkeeper diligently creates and names a new worksheet, and sets up and names the table as part of their month-end process. The one thing that they seemed to have missed is putting the issue or expiry dates in the body of the table:

	A	B	C
1	Gift Certificates Issued - Jan 2008		
2			
3	Cert Number ▼	Value ▼	Service ▼
4	1001	459	Massage
5	1002	201	Pedicure
6	1003	291	Pedicure
7	1004	319	Pedicure
8	1005	286	Pedicure

A sample of the January gift certificate information

So how can we build a solution that automatically includes all new tables the bookkeeper adds without having to teach the bookkeeper how to edit the Power Query?

Consolidating Tables

Unfortunately, there is no button in Excel to create a query to the visible objects in the current workbook, so we'll need to go and create this entire query from scratch:

- Create a new query → From Other Sources → Blank Query
- Rename the query as Certificates
- Type the following into the Formula Bar:

```
=Excel.CurrentWorkbook()
```

You'll see your list of tables and – using tricks we learned in previous chapters – we know that we can click in the whitespace beside the words in the Content column to preview the data:

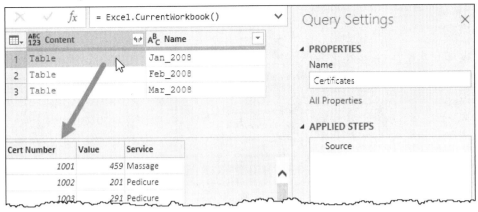

Previewing the records contained in the Jan_2008 table

If you look carefully at the top right corner of the Content column, you'll notice that it has an icon that looks like two arrows going in different directions. This is a cool feature which essentially allows you to expand and append each of these tables, all in one go. This feature is called the Expand operation and the best part is that – since the "Name" is applicable to each row of the table in the content column – it will associate that with every row.

Let's give it a go:

- Click the Expand arrow to expand the Content column
- Uncheck the "Use original column name as prefix" setting → OK

The data expands nicely, keeping the details of our Name column in place, as shown here:

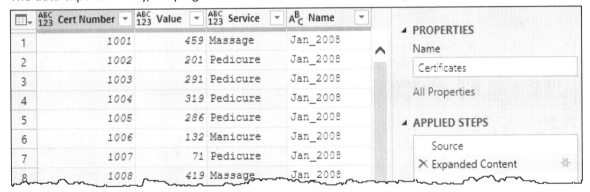

Our sub-tables have been expanded and appended

> ✎ Keep in mind that the column names and data will expand subject to the rules covered in the previous section so – if your columns aren't named consistently – you'll see some columns that appear to have *null* values in them.

The next thing we want to do is to convert that Name column to be a column of valid month-end dates. Since Jan_2008 isn't a valid date, we're going to use a little trick to turn it in to a valid date before changing it to the month-end:

- Right-click the Name column → Replace values
- Replace the _ character with " 1, " (space one comma space)
- Select all the columns → Transform → Detect Data Types
- Select the Name column → go to the Transform tab → Date → Month → End of Month
- Right-click the Name column → Rename → Month End

The completed query will now look as follows:

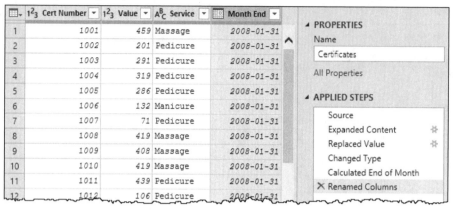

Completed query, ready to go

Everything looks good here, yet when you choose to Close & Load, you'll see that you trigger an error... that's odd. Click the refresh button next to the query, and you'll see that the count of errors changes – increasing to 63 errors!

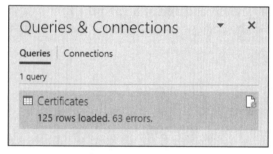

63 errors? But it looked so good!

So what happened? Let's go back and step through the query. But before we do, make sure you move the Certificates worksheet to the end of the workbook as shown here:

The Certificates worksheet is now last in the tab order

> 🔧 Normally we wouldn't bother moving this worksheet, but it will help to ensure you see the errors in the same place as we are showing here.

Once the worksheet has been moved, edit the query and select the Source step.

At this point, you'll notice that you've got one more table listed than you did in the past — the Gift Certificates table that was created as an output from this query!

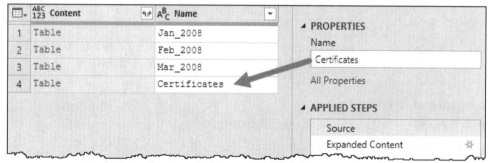

Our new query shows in the list of all workbook queries!

> 🔧 If you don't see the Certificates table when selecting the Source step, it is because Power Query has cached your preview. You can solve this by going to Home → Refresh Preview and indeed you should *always* do this when debugging queries for exactly this reason!

☎ When using =Excel.CurrentWorkbook() to enumerate tables or ranges, remember that the output query will also be recognized upon refresh. To deal with this, some future proofing steps may be required depending on how you built your query.

You should now step through each step of the query, paying attention to what happens.

When you step on to the Replaced Value step, do you notice anything dangerous unfolding here?

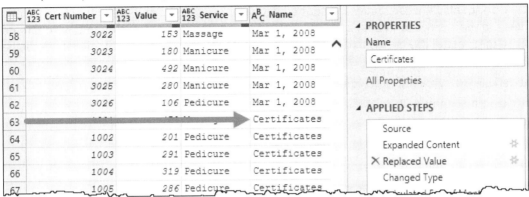

Given that our next step is to convert the Name column to dates...

When the Changed Types step is evaluated next, it tries to convert all data in the Name column to dates, which it obviously can't do for Certificates. Instead, it places an error value in the column for each cell that contained that text:

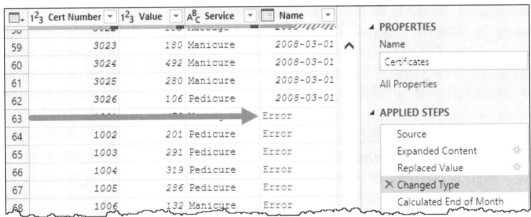

Invalid dates converted into Errors

This issue actually works in our favor, as everything from the Gift Certificates table is a duplication of the data. With those rows throwing errors, we can simply filter them out.

- Make sure the Changed Type step is selected
- Select the Name column → Home → Remove Errors
- Confirm that you'd like to insert a new step into the middle of your query
- Go to Home → Close & Load

With the filtering done, you'll get a positive result from Power Query loading only 62 rows of data with no errors:

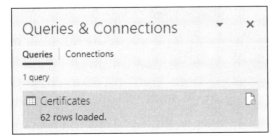

62 rows loaded from 3 tables

This solution should now work well as it is adding in any new tables where the table name follows the Month_Year format, but filtering out any others. The only challenge? We're now relying on our bookkeeper to remember to name those tables correctly. Given that it is not the most visible element, this could be dangerous.

Consolidating Ranges and Worksheets

Now what if the worksheets didn't have tables, but the clerk named the worksheets instead? Could we consolidate all the worksheets? We can, but as mentioned in Chapter 6, there is no built-in function to read from the worksheets in the active workbook. Instead, we have to make use of the ability to talk to named ranges... a specific named range. The trick is to define a Print Area, as that has a dynamic name which can be enumerated via the Excel.CurrentWorkbook() formula.

- Select the Jan 2008 worksheet → go to the Page Layout tab → Print Titles
- In the Print area box enter A:D → OK
- Repeat this process for the Feb 2008 and Mar 2008 worksheets
- Create a new query → From Other Sources → Blank Query
- Rename the query as FromWorksheets
- Enter the following in the Formula Bar:

      =Excel.CurrentWorkbook()

And you'll now see a list of all of the tables and named ranges, including the Print Areas!

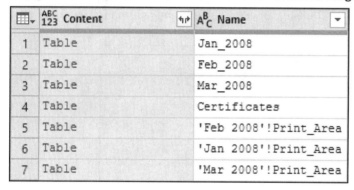

	ABC 123 Content		ABC Name
1	Table		Jan_2008
2	Table		Feb_2008
3	Table		Mar_2008
4	Table		Certificates
5	Table		'Feb 2008'!Print_Area
6	Table		'Jan 2008'!Print_Area
7	Table		'Mar 2008'!Print_Area

Excel.CurrentWorkbook() showing the Print Areas

As we currently have both tables and the print areas, let's filter this down and expand it to see what we get:

- Filter the Name column → Text Filters → Ends With → Print_Area
- Replace the following text on the Name column with nothing: '!Print_Area
- Replace the remaining ' text in the Name column with nothing
- Expand the Content column (unchecking the prefix option)

Notice that things are different here. You have managed to create a hack that reads from the worksheet, reading each column in your print range:

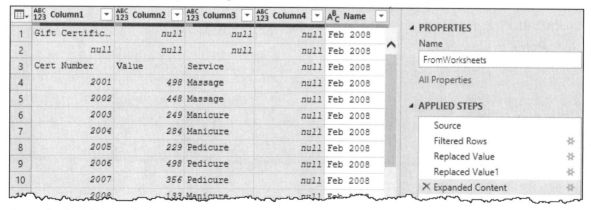

	ABC 123 Column1	ABC 123 Column2	ABC 123 Column3	ABC 123 Column4	ABC Name
1	Gift Certific...	null	null	null	Feb 2008
2	null	null	null	null	Feb 2008
3	Cert Number	Value	Service	null	Feb 2008
4	2001	498	Massage	null	Feb 2008
5	2002	448	Massage	null	Feb 2008
6	2003	249	Manicure	null	Feb 2008
7	2004	284	Manicure	null	Feb 2008
8	2005	229	Pedicure	null	Feb 2008
9	2006	498	Pedicure	null	Feb 2008
10	2007	356	Pedicure	null	Feb 2008
	2008	133	Manicure	null	Feb ...

PROPERTIES
Name
FromWorksheets
All Properties

APPLIED STEPS
Source
Filtered Rows
Replaced Value
Replaced Value1
× Expanded Content

A raw look at the worksheet

This obviously means that more data cleanup will need to be done in order to aggregate these ranges and turn them into clean tables, but the good news is that it can be done.

One tricky consideration with this data set is that it could be very dangerous to promote the first row to headers, as someone could remove the Feb 2008 column if they aren't concerned with maintaining the history. For this reason we will manually rename our columns, trigger errors by setting data types, and then filtering those errors out.

The steps to clean up this particular data set therefore become:

- Remove Column4 (as it is empty)
- Rename the columns as Certificate, Value, Service and Month End
- Right-click the Month End column → Replace → Find a single space → Replace With " 1, "
- Set the data type for the Certificate column → Whole Number
- Set the data type for the Value column → Whole Number
- Set the data type for the Service column → Text
- Set the data type for the Month End column → Date
- Select all columns and go to Home → Remove Errors
- Filter the Certificate column → un-check *null* values
- Select the Month End column → Transform → Date → Month → End of Month
- Go to Home → Close & Load

When complete, you'll notice that it provides the exact same number of rows (and indeed data) as the Certificates query we built previously:

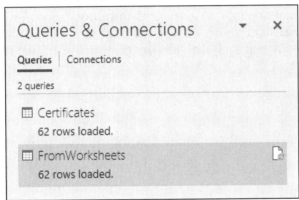

Two approaches, same results!

When working with print areas, it is a good suggestion to try to restrict the print area to only the rows and columns you need for two reasons. The first is that more data points takes longer for Power Query to process. The second is that each column is just referred to as Column# in the expansion window, making it very easy to pull in extraneous columns that just need to be removed later.

Use =Excel.CurrentWorkbook() with Care

The biggest thing to remember about building solutions using the Excel.CurrentWorkbook() function is this function reads all the objects in the current file. Since this affects the calculation chain, we get hit with a recursion effect, meaning that as our new tables are built, Power Query recognizes them and reads them as potential content as well.

The implications of this appear at refresh when the query attempts to load itself, thereby duplicating the data in the output. When working with this method it is important to remember this and guard against it. Strategies to protect against problems here range from filtering errors on key columns to using naming standards for both your input and output columns allowing you to filter out the ones you don't need.

> ✎ Whatever method you choose, make sure to test it through a couple of refreshes before releasing it to production!

Final Thoughts on Append Queries

The implications of this ability are numerous. Consider for a second that you can reach out to three separate files, import them, combine them into a single Transactions table, and build a PivotTable or Power BI visual based on that data. That is one business intelligence solution based on three separate files.

And when we want to refresh the solution, we simply need to click the Refresh All button to update it. Power Query will kick off the refresh of the Transactions table, which will kick off the refresh of the three individual data tables to feed it.

Assume now that this solution was built on files that weren't date specific, instead they were Product 1, Product 2 and Product 3. We've built the solution by loading in the CSV files that hold the pertinent data and built our business intelligence reports against them. And then the next month comes along... and IT sends us replacement files with new transactions for each product.

You save the new Product 1 file over the old one and do the same for products 2 and 3. And then you click Refresh All. And you're done.

Seriously, let that sink in for a moment. You're done.

It should not be lost, however, that the process of appending queries is not specific to working with external files, although it certainly sings there. As you've also seen it is entirely possible to set up a solution that combines all tables or print areas in the host workbook to create one master list for analysis.

In both cases, the time has been cut to a fraction of the previous process, and there is no risk of having users accidentally paste over existing data, as Power Query doesn't work using cut and paste. It simply appends one set to the other, removing the duplicated headers. You have the best of both speed and consistency in a single solution.

But let's be honest... we have explored setting up manual appends of external data sources, as well as self-updating systems for data within a workbook. Is it possible to combine these and create a system which can combine all files in a folder without having to manually add each file in Power Query? The answer is definitely yes, and something that we will cover in Chapter 9.

Chapter 9 - Combining Files

The classic methods for combining data sets from multiple files can only be described as incredibly tedious and error-prone. Each file needs to be imported, transformed, copied and pasted into the master table. Depending on how big and complex the transformations are, how many files there are, and how long the solutions have been running, this can be a terrifying situation to rely on.

We've already seen that Power Query can eliminate the copying/pasting dangers, but as great as the ability is to import and append files on a one-by-one basis, this still leaves some pretty serious issues on the table.

- Manually importing multiple files is tedious
- Manually repeating complex transformation steps is error-prone

The good news is that Power Query has a way to deal with both of these issues as well.

Sample Case Background

In this chapter, we are going to look at importing, unpivoting, and appending a series of quarterly part requirements for a manufacturing company. The production divisions submit a report named for their division each quarter, which get stored in a folder structure as shown here:

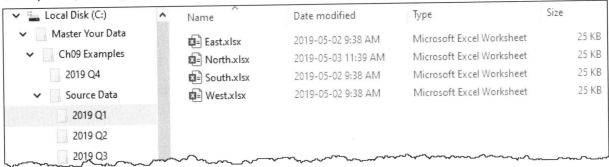

Four files per quarter contained in the Ch09 Examples\Source Data folder

Within each workbook is a worksheet called Forecast, which contains the following pivoted data structure. The big gotcha here is that this data is *formatted* like an Excel table, but it is actually just a range of data – although a different table called Parts does exist in the file as well:

Production Forecast
For the quarter ending Mar 31, 2019

Units to Produce	1,797	1,781	1,790	1,410	1,287	1,353	6,778

Parts needed by product

Part Nbr	Product A	Product B	Product C	Product D	Product E	Product F	Total
Part 1	-	-	-	4,230	2,574	1,353	4,230
Part 2	3,594	1,781	-	7,050	5,148	6,765	12,425
Part 3	3,594	8,905	-	4,230	6,435	-	16,729
Part 4	-	5,343	3,580	5,640	-	-	14,563
Part 5	3,594	8,905	8,950	1,410	2,574	-	22,859
Part 6	1,797	8,905	5,370	4,230	1,287	-	20,302
Total	12,579	33,839	17,900	26,790	18,018	8,118	91,108

The data from the Forecast worksheet of the 2019 Q1\East.xlsx workbook

Our goal is to create a refreshable solution that returns data in the following format:

Name ▼	Year ▼	Quarter ▼	Products ▼	Part ▼	Units ▼
East	2019	Q1	Product A	Part 2	2
East	2019	Q1	Product A	Part 3	2
East	2019	Q1	Product A	Part 5	2
East	2019	Q1	Product A	Part 6	1
East	2019	Q1	Product B	Part 2	1
East	2019	Q1	Product B	Part 3	5
East	2019	Q1	Product B	Part 4	3

The table we've been asked to generate

This is going to be tricky, as we have the following issues:

- The files are all stored in subfolders of the Ch09 Examples\Source Files folder
- The contents of each file need to be unpivoted before being appended
- Not all divisions produce the same Products, so the number of columns varies by file
- The division name from the file name must be preserved
- We need to keep the dates formats from the subfolder names
- We need to be able to refresh the solution when we add a new subfolder to it later

And yet, even with all these challenges, you'll see that Power Query is up to the task.

Process Overview

Before we dive into the mechanics of building the solution, we need to show a quick overview of how Power Query approaches this task.

Recipe for Combining Files

The process of combining files follows a five-step recipe pattern:

- Step 0: Connect to the Folder
- Step 1: Filter and future proof
- Step 2: Combine the files
- Step 3: Data shaping via the Sample Transform
- Step 4: Data shaping via the Master Query

In this chapter we will walk through each portion of this recipe, showing you how it works, as well as why these steps matter to you. Before we do, however, it's important to understand the architecture of what you are about to build.

Query Architecture Related to Combining Files

One of the things that intimidates many users is that Power Query doesn't just combine files by using a single query. Instead, when you click the Combine Files button, it asks you to choose a sample data file, then creates four new queries to get the job done. That can be a bit overwhelming if you're not expecting it!

Assuming that you've created a specific query called Files List to show the files you want to combine, and a Master Query to contain the results of the combined files (as we'll discuss later in this chapter), the query architecture will end up looking like this:

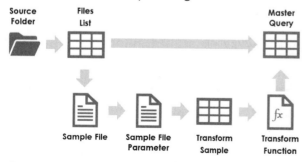

Four new queries (shown in the lower half) get created when you Combine Files

While each of the new queries is a key component of the process, three of them will be placed in a "helper" folder, and you'll never touch them. They are easy to identify as:

1. They will be stored in a folder called "Helper Queries, and
2. They are denoted with an icon that doesn't look like a table

If you look at the diagram above you'll notice that three of the queries we list show a table icon:

- **The File Listing.** This query – originally created by the author – contains the list of only the files you wish to combine. As you'll learn later, this can be a stand-alone query, or part of the Master Query (at your choice). Regardless of which approach you take this is the trigger point for combining files.

- **The Transform Sample.** During the Combine step, you'll be asked to choose a file to act as the sample, and this query refers to that sample showing you the contents of the file you chose. Its purpose is to let you perform data transformations on a single file, before the files are all appended into a single table. (The steps you perform here are automatically rolled up in the Transform function so that they can be applied to all files in the folder).

- **The Master Query.** The purpose of this query is to take each file contained in the FilesList (step or query), pass it to the Transform Function (based on the steps taken in the Transform Sample) and return the reshaped result of each file. It then expands the tables, appending them in to one long data table and allows you to make further transformations if necessary.

It might sound a bit complicated, but as you'll see, it offers incredible flexibility and is actually pretty easy to use once you understand how it is put together. The great thing is that this setup allows:

- Data Transformations *before* the tables are appended
- Data Transformations *after* the tables are appended
- Preservation of file properties including names or dates

👠 This method doesn't only work for Excel files. It works for any other file type with a connector in Power Query (CSV, TXT, PDF files and more!)

Let's get started and apply this overview to our sample data.

Step 0: Connect to the Folder

The first thing we need to do is connect to the data folder. If you recall from Chapter 1, each time you connect to a data source, Power Query goes through four distinct steps:

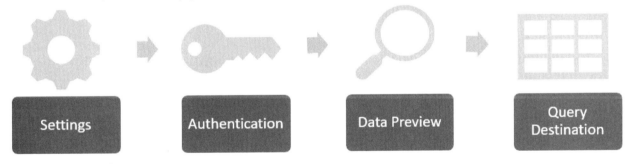

Connecting to a data source

We start with Settings, which is where we choose and configure the connector we want to use to connect to the appropriate folder. Next, Power Query checks if you need to authenticate to the data sources (and prompts you for authentication if required). After it is verified that you can access the data source, you'll be given the initial preview window, at which point you can choose whether you would like to load the data or go to the Power Query Editor to reshape the data before loading.

The reason we mention this again, and the whole reason there is a Step 0 of this recipe is that there are actually multiple different connectors that can be used to read from a folder, depending on the system that hosts your files. While the entry point is different depending on the type of system (Windows, SharePoint, Azure), solutions built to combine files all leverage the same schema once you get to the data preview, as shown here:

Column	Contains
Content	A reference to the actual file
Name	The name of the given file
Extension	The file type
Date accessed	The date the file was last accessed
Date modified	The date the file was last modified
Date created	The date the file was created
Attributes	A record containing such items as the file size, visibility state, etc...
Folder Path	The full path to the file

The schema behind any "From Folder" style solution

So once you get through the configuration and authentication steps for the specific data source, you'll find that the steps shown in this chapter can be applied to a variety of different data sources.

Connecting to a Local/Network Folder

By far the easiest "From Folder" scenario to create is where we want to combine files that live in a folder on your local PC or a mapped network drive. As Windows has already authenticated your folder access, you won't be prompted to fill in any credentials.

For this chapter, we will use this method to connect to the Ch09 Examples\Source Data folder. To do this:

- Create a new query → From File → From Folder
- Browse and Select your Folder (Ch09 Examples\Source Data)

At this point, you'll be prompted with the preview window showing you all the files in not only the folder you selected, but any subfolders as well:

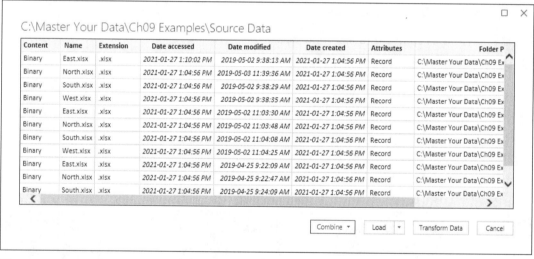

The preview window showing all files in the folder (and subfolders)

The important thing to recognize is that this view follows the schema shown earlier, with all the listed columns in exactly the same order.

As far as connecting to a local folder, that's it. The only choice left is determining where you'd like to load the data. As we want to control the output, we're going to choose to edit the query via the Transform Data button.

> ✎ The From Folder connector can be used to read from local folders on your PC, mapped network drives, or even UNC file paths.

Connecting to a SharePoint Folder

If you store your data in a SharePoint site, you should know that you have two options for connecting to your data:

1. If you sync the folder to your computer, you can use the Local Folder connector described earlier, or

2. If you want to connect to the cloud hosted version of the SharePoint folder, you can do that with a SharePoint specific connector.

The SharePoint connector does run slower than connecting to a locally synced version of the folder, because the files need to be downloaded during the execution of the query, but doesn't require having the files stored locally on the PC. To set it up:

- Create a new query → From File → From SharePoint Folder
- Enter the URL to **the root of the site** (not a library or folder)

The challenge is that – unlike working with a local folder – you cannot connect directly to a sub-folder. You must connect to the root, then filter down to find the folder you need. So how do you find that URL?

The easiest way is to log in to your SharePoint site via your favorite web browser, and then inspect the URL. Look for the second "/" to the left of the word "Forms" and keep everything to the left:

```
https://<SharePointDomain>/sites/projects/rockets/Forms/AllItems.aspx

<---------- connect to this ----------->|<---- ignore all this ---->
```

Extracting the root URL for your SharePoint site

So if our domain was https://monkey.sharepoint.com, then we would connect to:

```
https://monkey.sharepoint.com/sites/projects
```

> 🔍 If your company uses Microsoft 365, your SharePoint domain will be in the format of <tenant>.sharepoint.com. If your SharePoint is managed by your own IT department, it could be anything.

Once you confirm the URL, you'll get prompted to authenticate if you've never connected to the domain previously. At this point, you will need to sign in with the appropriate credentials:

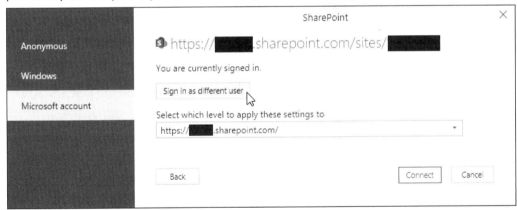

Connecting to SharePoint on Office365

The key to successfully navigating this dialog is to make sure you pick the correct type of account to sign in with. As SharePoint can be configured in different ways, we can't completely predict which authentication you'll need to use for certain, but the following should help in increasing the odds of choosing the correct method the first time.

- If your SharePoint is hosted on Office365, you must choose Microsoft Account and log in with the email you use for Office365.
- If your SharePoint is hosted by your IT department, and you never have to login in to access your content, you may want to try using Anonymous access. If that doesn't work, then you'll need to log in using Windows credentials.

> 🔍 Don't know if your company is using Office365? Does the domain end in sharepoint.com? If so, choose Microsoft account, and enter your regular work email credentials.

> ☎ Credentials get stored in a file on your computer, so choosing the wrong one can get you into a state where the wrong credentials are cached. To manage or change your credentials go to Data Source Settings → Global Permissions. Find the domain, select it and choose Clear Permissions. You'll then be prompted again the next time you try to connect.

Once your credentials have been validated, Power Query will attempt to connect to the folder. If you entered a valid URL, it will take you to the preview window. But if you didn't – either by providing an incorrect root site or adding a subfolder to the URL – you'll get an error message and will need to try again.

> 🔑 There is one additional nuance to connecting to SharePoint, and that is that people can actually store documents in the root of the SharePoint domain as well. To connect to these files, you would still use the From SharePoint Folder connector, but you would enter a URL of https://<SharePoint-Domain> (with no trailing folders). Be aware that this does not enumerate the individual sites.

Connecting to OneDrive for Business

The big secret around OneDrive for Business is that it is actually a personal site that lives on SharePoint. The implication of this is that you have the same options of connecting to OneDrive for Business folders as you do for a SharePoint site: either via the From Folder option (if it is synced to your desktop), or via the From SharePoint Folder (if it isn't).

The trick is understanding the correct URL to connect to, as it is different from the SharePoint site URL. When connecting via the From SharePoint Folder option the URL you need to enter is in the following format:

```
https://<SharePointDomain>/personal/<email>
```

You should also be aware that each instance of the "." and "@" characters in your email address will be replaced with the underscore character.

> 🔑 If your company uses Microsoft 365, your SharePoint domain will be in the format of <tenant>-my.sharepoint.com, but if your SharePoint is managed by your IT department it could be anything. By far the easiest way to get the correct URL is to log in to OneDrive for Business in your web browser and copy everything up to the end of your email address, as this will contain the correct URL for you.

Connecting to Other File Systems

While we have covered the most common connectors, there are also other connectors that return the same folder schema upon connection including (but not limited to) Blob Storage, Azure Data Lake Gen 1 and Azure Data Lake Gen2. Each will require connecting via its own specific URL and require authentication, but once done will take you to an identical experience as those listed earlier.

But what if you store your files in a different online storage system? Maybe you keep your files in Google Drive, DropBox, Box, Onedrive (Personal), or any of dozens of alternate solutions that exist. Even if no specific connector to that file system exists – so long as the vendor provides an application which can sync the files to a local copy on your PC – you can connect to these files via the From Folder connector!

Step 1: Filtering and Future Proofing

After choosing the appropriate Step 0 and connecting to the data folder, we will be looking at a list of all files in the folder and any subfolders. The challenge here is that *any* file stored in this folder will be included, but Power Query can only combine one type of file at a time.

In order to prevent errors that arise from combining multiple file types, we need to make sure we restrict the files list to a single file type. Even if you only see one type of the file in the folder, you should do this, as you just never know when Joey from accounting will decide to store his MP3 collection in the same folder as the Excel files you want to combine! To make things more challenging, Power Query is also case-sensitive, so if you restrict the list to only ".xlsx" files, when Joey gets his caps lock key stuck and starts saving the files as ".XLSX", they'll be filtered out. We need methods that will future proof our solution, just in case Joey gets assigned to our division.

Step 1 Recipe

Step 1 is all about filtering to the files you want to combine, and future proofing the solution against irrelevant files in future. It can be distilled into a recipe that looks like this:

- Filter to the appropriate subfolder level (if necessary)
- Convert the Extension to lowercase
- Filter the Extension to one file type

- Filter the Name to exclude temp files (file names starting with ~)
- Perform any additional filtering required
- Optional: Rename the query as FilesList and load it as a connection only

Let's explore this in a little more detail.

Applying Step 1 to the Sample Scenario

When connecting to a folder using the local From Folder connector, we are able to connect directly to a specific subfolder. This is super handy, as we usually end up right where we want to be. On the other hand, if you're using a connector that pulls from SharePoint or Azure, you won't be so lucky, and will need to filter down to the appropriate subfolder. This can be done by filtering the "Folder Path" column, but there is a bit of a challenge here: the *entire* folder path to each file is contained in these cells. While it's easy to read on a local file system, in a SharePoint solution every file name is prefaced with the entire site URL. To deal with this, we recommended you take the following approach to filtering your files list down to just the required subfolder.

- Right-click the Folder Path → Replace Values
- Value to Find → <original folder path or site url> plus the folder separator
- Replace with → nothing

So in the case of the local folder solution where we attached to...

```
C:\Master Your Data\Ch09 Examples\Source Data
```

... we would replace the following with nothing:

```
C:\Master Your Data\Ch09 Examples\Source Data\
```

		Date modified		Date created		Attributes		Folder Path
1	7 PM	2019-05-02 9:38:13 AM	2021-01-27 1:04:56 PM	Record				2019 Q1\
2	4 PM	2019-05-03 11:39:36 …	2021-01-27 1:04:56 PM	Record				2019 Q1\
3	4 PM	2019-05-02 9:38:29 AM	2021-01-27 1:04:56 PM	Record				2019 Q1\
4	4 PM	2019-05-02 9:38:35 AM	2021-01-27 1:04:56 PM	Record				2019 Q1\
5	4 PM	2019-05-02 11:03:30 …	2021-01-27 1:04:56 PM	Record				2019 Q2\
6	4 PM	2019-05-02 11:03:48 …	2021-01-27 1:04:56 PM	Record				2019 Q2\

The Folder Path column now shows the subfolder names only

If you are connecting to a local folder and are able to connect at the subfolder level, no worries, you won't need to do this at all. But if you are working through SharePoint, OneDrive, or Azure, this trick can make it much easier to see and filter into the appropriate subfolder structure. In fact, for deeper file paths or scenarios where there are a huge number of files, you may want to iterate this process a few times in order to get to the subfolder you need:

1. Replace the "current" folder path with nothing
2. Filter to the next subfolder level
3. Go to 1 as many times as needed to get to the correct folder

Once we've drilled down to the specific folder or subfolder that contains our intended files, we need to make sure that we are restricting the list to only a single file type. During this process we need to make sure we'll never get burned by case sensitivity issues, and it is also a good practice to filter out temp files – particularly if you are aggregating Excel files. To do this:

- Right-click the Extension column → Transform → lowercase
- Filter the Extension column → Text Filters → Equals
- Click Advanced and set the filter as follows:
- Extension → equals → .xlsx
- Name → Does not begin with → ~

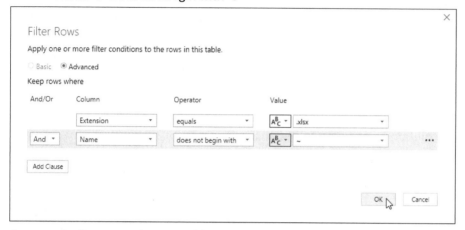

Future proofing our solution by restricting to only valid xlsx files

🔖 When an Excel file is opened on your local hard drive, a second copy prefaced by the ~ character is created in the folder. That file should disappear when Excel is closed, but in cases of crashes that isn't always true. By filtering to remove files that begin with ~, we avoid these files. If you aren't combining Excel files you can skip this step but it won't hurt or cause any problems if you include it anyway.

At this point, you should carefully review the files that remain in your list. In order to combine the files, not only do they need to be of the same file type, but they must have a consistent internal structure. If you still have a mixture of files (like sales reports, financial statements and budget prep files, etc…) you may need to do some additional filtering at this stage to restrict the list to only those files with consistent structures that you want to combine.

🔖 Remember that you can filter based on file names, folders or even dates as needed. By far the easiest way to ensure that only relevant files are included however is to set up a clear folder structure in advance, which collects the files in a predictable and filterable way.

For our scenario, we are in a good space now, looking at a list of Excel files. Even though the files are still within subfolders of the main Source Data folder, we are okay with this and can move forward.

The final step of this section is optional:

- Rename the query as FilesList
- Load the query as a Connection Only query

These steps are the way Ken prefers to build his "From Folder" scenarios as it offers the following two benefits:

1. It builds a very obvious place where you can go to review which files are being combined without having to navigate part way through a query to determine the details
2. It only hard codes the file path into the solution once

While the solution will be illustrated using this method, be aware that you can skip it, continue on with the next section and everything will work just fine anyway.

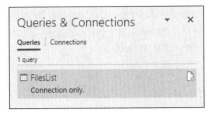

We have elected to load the FilesList query as a "Staging" query

Step 2: Combining the Files

With the list of files curated, it is now time to trigger the combination of the files themselves.

Step 2 Recipe

Step 2 of the process involves the following actions:

- Optional: Reference the FilesList query to create the Master Query
- Rename the Master Query
- Click the Combine Files button
- Choose the Sample file

At this point, Power Query will go and perform its magic, creating four new queries and adding a bunch of steps in your Master Query.

Applying Step 2 to the Sample Scenario

It is highly recommended that you always rename your Master Query *before* triggering the Combine process, as the name of the Master Query gets incorporated into the name of some of the created folders and queries. (This just makes things easier to trace later if you end up with multiple routines that combine different folders in the same solution.) The key here is to provide a descriptive name that is not too long and is something that you'd be happy loading to your worksheet or data model. In the case of our sample scenario, we are trying to come up with a list of parts that we need to order, so a name like "Parts Required" or "Parts Order" might make sense. For this example we'll keep things short and clean and call our Master Query "Orders".

So which query is the Master Query anyway? This depends on whether you decided to use the optional step of creating the dedicated FilesList staging query:

- If you loaded the FilesList query as a staging query, the Master Query will be called FilesList (2) and is created by referencing the FilesList query (right-click → reference)
- If you did not load the FilesList query as a staging query, then the FilesList query is your Master Query

Once you've identified which query is your Master Query, we can begin the process of combining the files:

- Select the Master Query and rename it as "Orders"
- Click the Combine Files (double arrow) button at the top of the Content column

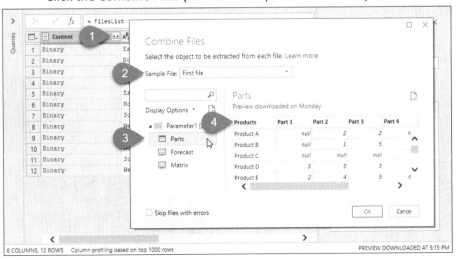

Combining a folder of Excel files

Once clicking the Combine Files button (#1 in the image above), you'll see a preview that pops up. In this preview you'll be asked to choose the file to use as a Sample (#2). Once you choose a file, you'll also see any components of the sample file (#3) and a preview of the data (#4) for any object you select.

> 🔧 The one drawback of using a separate FilesList query is that you can only choose the First File as an option for the preview here. If you skip that optional step, any of the files in the folder would be available. This might seem like a big loss until you realize that you can still use any file, you just need to return to the FilesList query and sort or filter it to get the file you want as the first row, and it will then be available here.

In this case of these workbooks, you'll notice that they hold a table called Parts, as well as a Forecast and Matrix worksheet. Unfortunately, while the parts table is nice and clean, this actually serves as a lookup table for the data range contained on the Forecast sheet. So it looks like we're going to need to import the less perfect layout that is the Forecast worksheet, and perform some manual cleanup. Let's do that now:

- Select the Forecast worksheet → OK

Power Query will think for a moment, and then combine the files, resulting in the following:

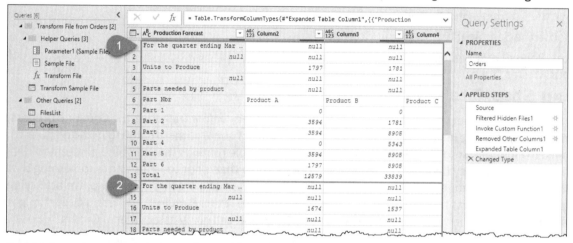

Suddenly we have four new queries and five new steps in our Master Query

There is a lot to take in here...

Effectively, what has happened here is that Power Query has created a collection of "Helper Queries", and then added steps in the Master Query to leverage them. On the left, you'll see a folder called "Helper Queries" which contains a Parameter, Sample File and the Transform File function. And under that, the very important Transform Sample File.

You should also be aware that the query preview is still focused on the Master Query – the query you had in focus when you elected to combine the files. We will review the steps on the right side when we get to Step 4, but the important thing you want to recognize is that Power Query has essentially extracted the contents of the Forecast for each file and appended them. Now if the data was already in good shape to be stacked, this would be great, but if you look at the first and second files shown in the image, you'll notice that Power Query has stacked two pivoted data sets, and that they have different headers for each data set.

Once you've had a chance to read and master the contents of this entire book, you'll realize that it IS possible to deal with a data set like this in a single query. Having said that, it is also complicated to do so. Wouldn't it be nice if we could unpivot this data *before* appending it, avoiding that kind of a headache? The good news is that we can. The better news is that it is super easy when leveraging one of these helper queries.

> 🔧 Pro Tip: While it may look like you can only access a single object from each file in the Combine step, that isn't actually true. If you need to combine multiple worksheets from multiple workbooks or maybe the 2nd worksheet in each workbook, you can do so. Just right-click the Folder listed in the preview and choose Transform Data. That will extract a table that lists all of the workbook objects, similar to the CurrentWorkbook() examples shown in Chapters 6 and 8!

Step 3: Data Shaping via the Transform Sample File

After triggering the original combination, the next thing we want to do is clean up our data. The general goals of this step are to do the following to create a normalized data set:

- Split the data into columns
- Remove garbage rows and columns from the data set
- Clean the data for analysis

Of course every data set is different in the way this needs to be approached, but the end game is the same: reshape it into a data set with descriptive headers and one data point per row and column intersection.

Why Should I Use the Transform Sample File?

While the "how" is obviously an important question, the "where" needs to be answered first as in this expanded collection of queries, there are two places you can reshape your data:

1. The Transform Sample File, or
2. The Master Query (Orders)

We would encourage you to do as much data cleanup as you can in the Transform Sample, rather than the Master Query. The main benefit of the Transform Sample is that you can build your query against a *single* sample file, making data cleanup much easier. You completely avoid the confusion or challenges of an appended data set overcomplicating things, as your transformations get applied to the data set *before* the data is appended. In the case of operations like pivoting, unpivoting or grouping, this can have a massive impact on complexity.

What's even better is that – as you perform your data cleanup in the Transform Sample – the steps are all synced to the Transform File function. This function is then invoked against all of the other files in the files list before appending, and it happens auto-magically.

> 🔪 Our rule of thumb: Use the Transform Sample wherever possible.

Using the Transform Sample File

So let's go and leverage the Transform Sample File to clean up one of these worksheets. Click the Transform Sample File query in the Query Navigator pane, and you'll be taken to the following view:

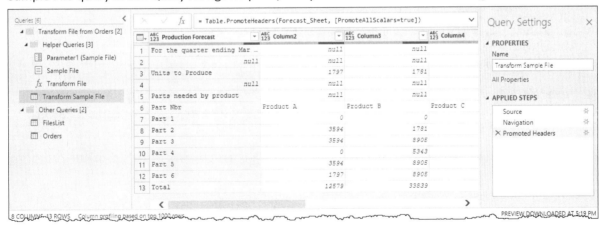

All 13 rows of the Transform Sample File based on the first file from the FilesList query

When you reach the Transform Sample File for the first time, it is important to review the steps that Power Query automatically coded for you. In this case the Applied Steps contain:

- **Source**, which contains the original table of all objects available in the Excel file
- **Navigation**, drills in to the Table representing the Forecast worksheet
- **Promoted Headers**, which lifts the first row to headers

In looking carefully at the data, the row that was promoted to headers doesn't appear to hold much value, nor do the next five rows of data. The headers we want are really contained in the seventh row of the file (assuming the first row wasn't promoted to headers in the first place). Let's fix that:

- Delete the Promoted Headers step
- Go to Home → Remove Rows → Remove Top Rows → 6
- Go to Home → Use First Row as Headers

At this point, Power Query helpfully does something very dangerous. Can you spot it?

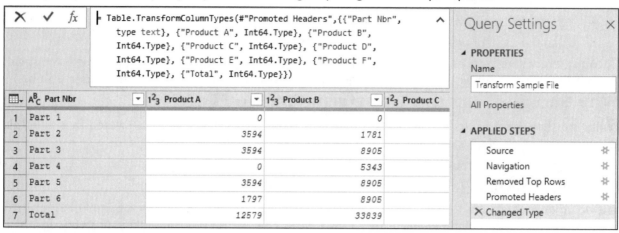

Which step didn't you create yourself?

Every time a row is promoted to headers, Power Query helpfully declares the data types. While this can be useful, it also hard codes the names of the columns into the step. The problem? We casually mentioned this in the case background at the beginning of the chapter:

- Not all divisions produce the same Products, so the number of columns varies by file

So what happens when you encounter another division which doesn't produce – say – Products A, B or C, like the North division shown below? Boom! Step level error.

Part Nbr	Product E	Product F	Product G	Total
Part 1	3,348	1,537	-	4,885
Part 2	6,696	7,685	2,118	16,499
Part 3	8,370	-	1,059	9,429
Part 4	-	-	-	-
Part 5	3,348	-	3,177	6,525
Part 6	1,674	-	-	1,674
Total	23,436	9,222	6,354	39,012

Knowing your data will help you anticipate and avoid issues when you are combining files…

> 🔧 Be careful when making changes in the Sample Transform File, particularly where column names may vary between files. Do everything you can to make sure that only the column names you know will exist in all cases get hard-coded!

Truthfully, at this stage, we don't really need to declare our data types anyway, so let's continue preparing our data for unpivoting, but in a safe way:

- Delete the Changed Type step
- Filter the Part Nbr column → Uncheck Total
- Locate the Total column and delete it
- Right-click the Part Nbr column → Unpivot Other columns

The results are shown here:

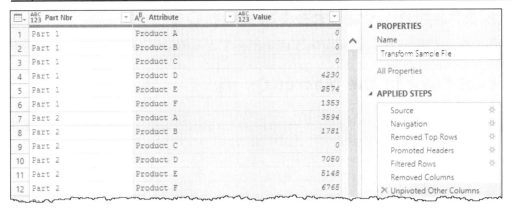

The unpivoted data set

> 🦶 Wait a minute... Didn't we just hard code the name of the "Total" column when we removed it? Indeed, we did. But is that safe? The answer is a bit more nuanced here, but since it appears to show up in both the East and North data ranges, then we can probably assume that it will show up in all the data sets. If it didn't, we could work around the issue by leaving it in the data, unpivoting, and then filtering Total out of the Attribute column as that would not produce any errors if Total was not found.

With the data nicely unpivoted, we can change the column names, set the data types, and we are done.

- Rename the Attribute column → Product
- Rename the Value column → Units
- Select all columns → Transform → Detect Data Type

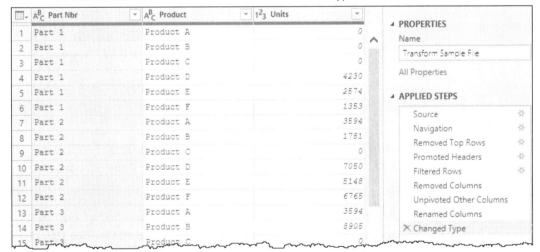

A portion of the 36-row final output generated for the Sample File

Overlooking the challenge of anticipating a potential issue with a hard-coded header, this is a fairly straight-forward unpivot job when keeping it to the context of a single file. Trying to do this in the Master Query would have been *much* more complicated!

> ☎ What happens if you fail to anticipate an issue and get a step level error in one of the files when you run the Combine? You will need to debug it, of course! Go back to the FilesList and insert temporary steps to keep the top x rows or remove top x rows until you discover which file causes the error. Once you have it as the first file in the FilesList, you can then debug it in the Transform Sample Query to see what went wrong.

Step 4: Data Shaping via the Master Query

We can now return to the Master Query to see the effects of our work. And when you do, you'll be greeted with a lovely step level error...

Fix the Step Level Error in the Master Query

Unfortunately, this will look familiar...

> ⚠ Expression.Error: The column 'Production Forecast' of the table wasn't found.
> Details:
>   Production Forecast

What the heck?

The root cause of this error is the Changed Type step of the Master Query. Remember that first row that Power Query promoted to headers? That generated header columns of "Production Forecast", "Column 2", etc... And since Power Query also hard-coded a Changed Type step in the Master Query, those column names were recorded there. Why is that a problem? We got rid of that column name and promoted others instead!

This error is incredibly common and can easily be fixed by just deleting the Changed Type step in the Master Query and re-applying it.

ABC 123 Part Nbr	ABC 123 Product	ABC 123 Units		
1	Part 1	Product A	0	**PROPERTIES**
2	Part 1	Product B	0	Name
3	Part 1	Product C	0	Orders
4	Part 1	Product D	4230	
5	Part 1	Product E	2574	All Properties
6	Part 1	Product F	1353	
7	Part 2	Product A	3594	**APPLIED STEPS**
8	Part 2	Product B	1781	Source
9	Part 2	Product C	0	Filtered Hidden Files1
10	Part 2	Product D	7050	Invoke Custom Function1
11	Part 2	Product E	5148	Removed Other Columns1
				✕ Expanded Table Column1

Bye, bye step level error, hello data!

> 🔧 **Pro Tip:** If you know you are going to be renaming columns in the Transform Sample File, you can even delete the Changed Type step of the Master Query before you leave it in the first place.

Preserving File Properties

While the Transform Sample File contained a preview of 36 rows at the end, the preview window here displays 288 rows, indicating that it applied the data transformation pattern to each of the files in the Files List, then appended them into one long table. That is fantastic, but there is still an issue.

Each of the files submitted was for a different division, but the division name wasn't contained within the file itself. Instead, the file was saved using the name of the division. The challenge is that we seem to have lost that somewhere during the process. In addition, while the files did actually contain the quarter end dates, that data was held within the top few rows that we removed via the Transform Sample File. We were able to take that approach with these files since each division was stored in a subfolder which was named in the yyyy-qq format. But again, we seem to have lost the folder name along the way as well. So how do we get that information back?

At this point it is helpful to review the steps that Power Query generated for us in the Master Query when we combined the files, the first of which is the "Filtered Hidden Files1" step.

> 🔧 The Filtered Hidden Files 1 step will be the second step if you opted to create a separate FilesList query. If you elected to skip that step it will appear further down the query but will be immediately after the point where you triggered the Combine Files process.

Here are what the subsequent steps do:

- **Filtered Hidden Files1**: Adds a filter to remove any hidden files from the list of files. (Yes, Power Query lists hidden and system files which are stored in the folders as well.)
- **Invoke Custom Function1**: Adds a new column which leverages the Transform File function that was generated based on the actions you took in the Transform Sample File. The effect of this step is to create a column which holds a table object representing the transformed data of each file.
- **Removed Other Columns1**: This step removes all columns except for the column that was created via the Invoke Custom Function1 step. *It is this step where our File Name and Folder Names disappear.*
- **Expanded Table Column1**: This step expands the results of the column added via the Invoke Custom Function1 step. The results are that each table is appended into one long table.

Understanding that, we know that we simply need to modify the Removed Other Columns1 step in order to preserve any of the file properties that Power Query assumed we didn't need.

- Select the Removed Other Columns1 step → Click the gear icon
- Check the boxes next to Name and Folder Path → OK

At this point, as shown in the image below, we will have now restored the Name and Folder Path columns to our data set.

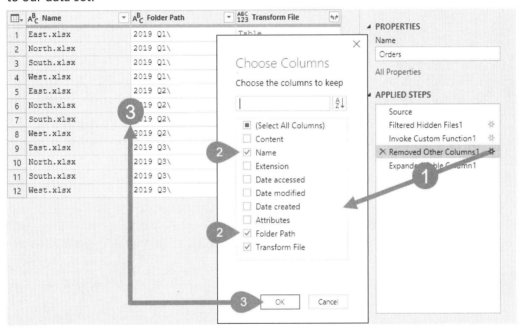

Modifying the Removed Other Columns1 step to bring back key columns

Adding More Steps

At this point we can now make further modifications to the query for actions that need to be applied to all files. The specific actions we will take are as follows:

- Select the Expanded Table Column1 step (only so we don't get prompted to insert a new step on each of the following actions)
- Rename the Name column to Division
- Right-click the Division column → Replace Values → Find ".xlsx" → Replace with nothing
- Right-click the Folder Path column → Split Columns → By Delimiter → left most Space

☎ When splitting columns, Power Query will automatically add a Changed Type step. You should think about whether this is necessary or not. If it may cause issues in future, then delete it and apply your data types as the final step before you load it to the eventual destination.

As the Changed Type doesn't really seem necessary here, we will get rid of it, even though it shouldn't cause any issues.

- Delete the Changed Type step
- Rename the Folder Path.1 column to Year

- Rename the Folder Path.2 column to Quarter
- Right-click the Quarter column → Replace Values → Find \ → Replace with nothing
- Select all columns → Transform → Detect Data Type

At this point the Master Query has been completed, unpivoting and appending the data while preserving portions of the file name and folder path to add key elements required for our analysis:

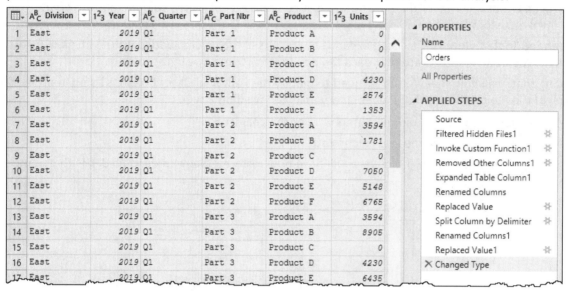

The first four columns of our unpivoted data set were driven from Folder and File names

☎ Data types are never carried over from Sample Transform. Always make sure you set them as the final step of your query before loading it to a worksheet or the data model!

As the data has been successfully transformed, we'll now load it out so that we can use it for reporting. This time we'll load it to the data model:

- In Power BI simply click Close & Apply
- In Excel go to Home → Close & Load To... → check Only Create Connection AND Add this data to the Data Model

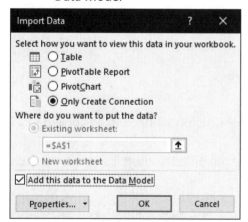

Loading the data to the data model

What you'll notice is that – despite creating multiple queries in one session – only the Master Query gets loaded to the destination. All of the helper queries, including the Transform Sample File, are loaded as staging queries by default.

Updating Your Solution

With the data loaded, we are now at a point where we can build some reusable business intelligence.

Leveraging the Data

To demonstrate the complete cycle from import through refresh, we need to build a quick report using a matrix or PivotTable. The steps to create this object will depend on which application you are using:

If you are using Power BI:

- On the Report page → go to the Visualizations pane → Matrix

If you are using Excel:

- Select B3 on a blank worksheet → go to Insert → PivotTable
- Confirm that you want to use the workbook's Data Model → OK

Once you've created the object, drag the following columns from the Orders table on the right into the field areas as follows:

- Values: Units
- Rows: Part Nbr
- Columns: Year, Quarter

The results (in both Excel and Power BI) are shown below, assuming you have clicked the indicated "Expand" button in Power BI to show the quarterly data

Sum of Units	Column Labels ▼			Grand Total
	= 2019			
Row Labels ▼	Q1	Q2	Q3	
Part 1	32577	37021	36415	106013
Part 2	64475	69373	68647	202495
Part 3	54568	56851	54715	166134
Part 4	42019	44117	44117	130253
Part 5	58306	63370	62305	183981
Part 6	52367	53309	52898	158574
Grand Total	304312	324041	319097	947450

Year	2019				Total
Part Nbr	Q1	Q2	Q3	Total	
Part 1	32577	37021	3641	106013	106013
Part 2	64475	69373	68647	202495	202495
Part 3	54568	56851	54715	166134	166134
Part 4	42019	44117	44117	130253	130253
Part 5	58306	63370	62305	183981	183981
Part 6	52367	53309	52898	158574	158574
Total	304312	324041	319097	947450	947450

Comparing the Excel and Power BI results

Adding New Files

It's time to explore what happens when we add new data to our solution.

If you open the Ch09 Examples folder in your Windows explorer, you'll find that it doesn't only contain the Sample Data folder we connected to; there is also a 2019 Q4 folder which contains updated data for the different divisions. Drag that folder in to the Source Data folder so that we now have four quarterly folders in the folder that drives our solution:

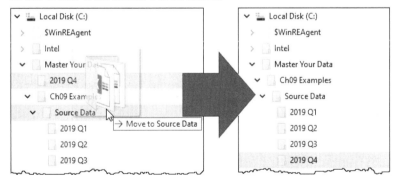

It is time to add some new data to our solution...

Once you've moved the folder, return to the solution and force an update:

- Power BI: Go to Home → Refresh
- Excel: Go to Data → Refresh All

A few seconds later, you can see that we've got Q4 included:

Sum of Units	Column Labels					
	2019				Grand Total	
Row Labels	Q1	Q2	Q3	Q4		
Part 1	32577	37021	36415	33502	139515	
Part 2	64475	69373	68647	65198	267693	
Part 3	54568	56851	54715	52745	218879	
Part 4	42019	44117	44117	41923	172176	
Part 5	58306	63370	62305	59113	243094	
Part 6	52367	53309	52898	50602	209176	
Grand Total	304312	324041	319097	303083	1250533	

Year	2019				Total	
Part Nbr	Q1	Q2	Q3	Q4	Total	
Part 1	32577	37021	36415	33502	139515	139515
Part 2	64475	69373	68647	65198	267693	267693
Part 3	54568	56851	54715	52745	218879	218879
Part 4	42019	44117	44117	41923	172176	172176
Part 5	58306	63370	62305	59113	243094	243094
Part 6	52367	53309	52898	50602	209176	209176
Total	304312	324041	319097	303083	1250533	1250533

3-2-1 Data updated!

How incredibly cool is that? Not only is it easy to append multiple files, but we've just created a refreshable business intelligence platform that can be updated with a couple of clicks as we get new data!

The thing you really want to recognize here is that you have options to build and update your solution depending on the way you receive your data. Consider the following chart which shows the flexibility and update methods available to you when updating solutions built on external files:

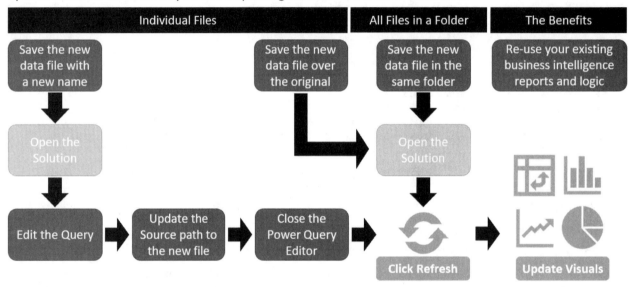

Updating solutions that connect to external files

Whether you receive a replacement file that you can save over the previous version, get a new version of data that you need to use instead, or want to build an ever growing (or rolling) solution, Power Query has you covered!

Mitigating Speed with Last x Files

As amazing as the "From Folder" solution is, you have to think that it will end up slowing down if you just perpetually add new files to the source data folder. It only makes sense that it would take longer to process a hundred files than it would ten. Especially given that Power Query cannot be configured to only update files that are new or have been changed. Each time you hit the refresh button Power Query reloads ALL the data from ALL of the files in your folder.

Imagine that we take the solution we built previously and keep it running for 10 years. With 16 data files per year (4 divisions x 4 quarters), you'll be processing over 176 files by the time 2030 ends. Now to be fair, these files are pretty small, but what if each file took 5 seconds to refresh? We're now in excess of 14 minutes to refresh the solution, which feels like forever.

The first question you have to ask yourself when building these solutions is whether you really need all of this data. In 2030, will you really care about the data from 2019? If you're comparing against data from the prior year, you probably need a maximum of 32 files. So why not limit the solution to do that?

The secret to limiting your files is to return to the files list portion of your query and:

- Sort the files in descending order by date
- Use the Keep Top Rows to keep the top x files you need

The trick is really to figure out *which* field to use for your date sorting. In the case of this example, we could use the Folder Path, as the users name these in a logical order. If we don't have a structure like that, then we may want to rely on one of the Date Created or Date Modified fields.

🔧 Keep in mind that the number of files you keep could vary between one and any number that you reasonably need. We've built many solutions that kept only the last 24 rolling months of data!

🐵 If you are just copying and pasting new data files into a folder, the Date Created property *should* be safe to use when sorting however... be aware that the Date Created field may be newer than the Date Modified. The reason for this is that a file created via a copy and paste will be "created" when pasted, even though it will have been "modified" the last time the source file was modified. Relying on the "Last modified" date can also be dangerous, as merely opening certain file types can trigger that date to be updated.

©2014 WALTER MOORE
14 OCT 14

Chapter 10 - Merging Data

One of the classic issues that has presented itself to data pros for years is combining two separate data tables into one in order to serve a PivotTable. While this was easy for SQL pros in many cases via different styles of Joins, in Excel the route was to use a VLOOKUP() or INDEX(MATCH()) combination – functions that are terrifying to many users – in order to read data from one table into the other.

When Power Query hit the scene, it introduced yet another method to combine two tables together; one that didn't involve learning SQL joins, Excel formulas, or learning how to build a relational database structure.

Merging Basics

For this example, we'll look at a scenario where we have two separate data sources; a table of sales transactions (Sales), and another that contains product details (Inventory). They happen to be stored in tables in an Excel worksheet, but the only real relevance of that detail is that it will drive our choice of connector to get to each data source.

The challenge with these data sources is that the Sales table holds the Date, SKU (stock number), Brand and number of Units sold, but it doesn't hold any information about the price or cost of the products. That information (and more) is, however, held in the Inventory table.

Date	SKU	Brand	Units
2021-03-12	510007	Budweiser	64
2021-03-12	510010	Canadian	45
2021-03-12	510014	Canterbury	62
2021-03-12	510019	Corona Extra	64
2021-03-14	510019	Corona Extra	24
2021-03-12	510021	Corona Grande	38
2021-03-14	510021	Corona Grande	31
2021-03-12	510032	Granville Island	24

SKU	Brand	Type	Unit	Pack Size	Price	Cost	Margin
510007	Budweiser	Lager	Cans	15	29.5	24.4	5.1
510010	Canadian	Lager	Cans	6	12	9.95	2.05
510014	Canterbury	Ale	Cans	6	11.5	9.5	2
510019	Corona Extra	Lager	Bottles	6	13.5	11.25	2.25
510021	Corona Grande	Lager	Bottles	1	4.5	3.7	0.8
510032	Granville Island	Ale	Bottles	6	13	10.95	2.05
510037	Guinness	Stout	Cans	4	13	10.99	2.01
510038	Heineken	Lager	Bottles	6	14.5	11.95	2.55

The 'Sales' and 'Inventory' tables

We'd like to merge the two tables together in order to get a comprehensive list of products with their finer details.

Creating Staging Queries

Whether you choose to open the Ch10 Examples\Merging Basics.xlsx file to perform this task within the same Excel workbook, connect to it from Excel as an external data source or use Power BI to read from the Excel tables is completely up to you. What we need to do is create a staging query for each of the two data tables.

- Create a new query that connects to each table in the Ch10 Examples\Merging Basics.xlsx file
- Save each query as a staging query (disable the load or set to Connection Only)

  ✎ In order to merge or append queries together in Excel, the queries must exist. Just having a table in the Excel workbook isn't good enough as there is no Power Query component associated with a table until it is explicitly created.

When complete, you should have the two simple queries ready to use:

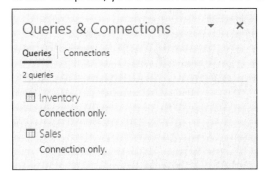

The Sales and Inventory queries are now available for merging

Performing the Merge

Like appending queries, Excel users have the option to Merge queries by right-clicking one of the queries in the Queries & Connections pane. Again, as with appending queries, this will result in a single step called Source in the Power Query user interface which merges the two queries. As this can be hard to quickly read, we will choose to right-click and Reference the query so that we can see each step as a distinct line item in the query.

- Right-click the Sales query → Reference
- Rename the query as "Transactions"
- Go to Home → Merge Queries → Merge Queries (not Merge Queries as New)

  ⚓ The Merge Queries as New command will replicate the process we see from Excel's Queries & Connections pane, creating a new query and performing the merge in the first step.

At this point, you'll be taken to Merge dialog, where you can choose which table you would like to merge with the one you started from.

In this dialog, the current state of the active query (in our case Transactions – sourced from the Sales query) will also be shown at the top of the form. Underneath the data preview of this query you'll see a drop-down that lets you select any query in the solution, which indicates the table you wish to merge against the current data.

  ⚓ Interestingly, this dialog allows you to merge a query against itself – an advanced technique that we will see in Chapter 14.

Since the current state of our query is based on the Sales query's data, we will choose to merge against the Inventory table.

- Choose the Inventory table from the drop-down
- Leave the default Join Kind as "Left Outer"
- Leave the Fuzzy Matching checkbox unchecked

Oddly, after making all of our configuration choices, the OK button does not light up:

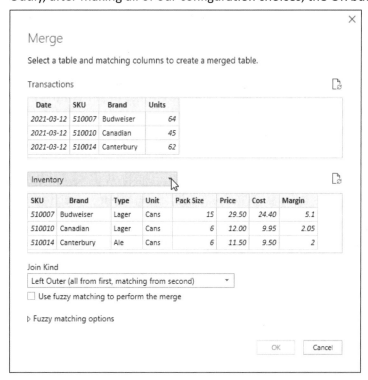

We've chosen tables, but why can't we proceed?

The issue at hand is that Power Query doesn't know which fields you want to use to perform your merge.

In order to perform a merge, you ideally want to have a column that contains unique values in one table but has repeating records in the other table. This is called a one-to-many structure and is the best way to ensure that you end up with results that match what you'd expect.

   ✎ Power Query does support one-to-one and many-to-many joins, as you'll see shortly.

In this case, the SKU Number column contains unique products in the Inventory table, and repeats many times in the Sales table, so we'll use those.

- Click the SKU Number header in each table
- Click OK

You'll now be launched into the Power Query editor, and you'll see a nice new column of tables on the right side of your Sales table:

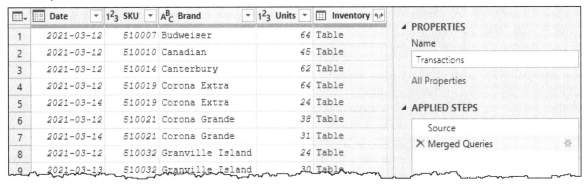

A new column of tables, containing the matching Inventory records

We know what to do with a column of tables — expand them! The only question here is which columns we need. As the SKU Number and Brand already exist in the sales table, we don't need those, so let's make sure that we exclude them during the expansion.

- Click the Expand icon (top right of the Inventory column header)
- Uncheck the SKU Number and Brand columns
- Uncheck the column prefix option → OK

And, as you can see, you've now got the product details merged into the sales table:

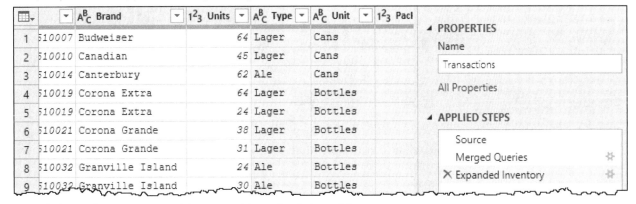

Details from the Inventory table merged into the Sales table

You'll find that you have 20 records, one for each transaction in the original sales Transaction table, exactly replicating Excel's VLOOKUP Exact Match or SQL Left Outer Join scenario.

Join Types

One of the things that SQL pros have known for years is that there are actually multiple different ways to join your data. Sadly, this fact has been somewhat hidden from Excel Pros over the years, as we have typically only seen examples of the Left Outer Join (VLOOKUP). In Power Query, however, there are now many different Join Types supported via the Merge dialog. These Join Types can allow us to find not only matching data, but also mis-matched data: something very important to anyone trying to match or reconcile records.

Consider these two tables:

Transactions			
Account	**Dept**	**Date**	**Amount**
64010	150	2015-12-15	8,975
64020	150	2015-12-15	13,708
64030	150	2015-12-15	32,555
64010	250	2015-12-15	22,752
64015	150	2015-12-15	34,147
64030	250	2015-12-15	19,733
64040	250	2015-12-15	33,438
64010	350	2015-12-15	45,876

Chart of Accounts		
Account	**Dept**	**Name**
64010	150	18 Holes
64020	150	9 Holes
64030	150	Twilight
64040	150	Special
64010	250	Power Cart
64020	250	Pull Cart
64030	250	Clubs
64040	250	Golf Balls

Can we match these records?

The data between these tables is related, but there are a couple of interesting nuances to it.

The first nuance that we need to look at is the Chart of Accounts table on the right. This listing provides a distinct list of all accounts in the system but requires combining the Account and Dept fields in order to generate the unique identifier. If you look carefully, you'll see that the values in the first four rows of the Account column repeat on the next four rows, so there are plainly duplicates. Likewise, the first four rows of the Dept column all contain the value 150, and the next four contain the value 250. Put them together with a delimiter, however, and there is only one instance of 64010-150, 64020-150, 64010-250, etc... You can also see this same pattern in the Transactions table on the left.

What this means is that we can match the data from the Transactions table to get the account name from the Chart of the Accounts table, provided that we can make a match based on the "composite key" between the two tables:

Transactions				
Account	**Dept**	**Date**	**Amount**	**Name**
64010	150	2015-12-15	8,975	18 Holes
64020	150	2015-12-15	13,708	9 Holes
64030	150	2015-12-15	32,555	Twilight
64010	250	2015-12-15	22,752	Power Cart
64015	150	2015-12-15	34,147	???
64030	250	2015-12-15	19,733	Clubs
64040	250	2015-12-15	33,438	Golf Balls
64010	350	2015-12-15	45,876	???

Chart of Accounts		
Account	**Dept**	**Name**
64010	150	18 Holes
64020	150	9 Holes
64030	150	Twilight
64040	150	Special
64010	250	Power Cart
64020	250	Pull Cart
64030	250	Clubs
64040	250	Golf Balls

The goal is to match the Account Name based on the Account – Dept combination

The second nuance we want to call out here are the shaded rows. In the image above, you can see that there was no entry in the Chart of Accounts table for the 64015-150 or 64010-350 combinations. As it happens, there are also no entries in the Transactions table for the "Special" or "Pull Cart" accounts either.

In the case of this specific data, these mismatches carry varying levels of concern. The Chart of Accounts is a table that holds accounts that transactions CAN be posted to. So, if an account exists that is never used, it's not really a big issue. But on the other side, if a transaction is posted to an account-dept combination that does not exist? That is a BIG problem!

> 🖂 This problem is not limited to accounting data. It exists any time you need to match, compare or reconcile between two lists. Customers vs credit limits? Sales vs orders? Parts vs prices? The possibilities are limitless!

We are now going to look at seven specific configurations of joins that we can make between these two tables to combine the data, or extract portions of interest.

🔍 Keep in mind that data types are SUPER important when merging data. Before you perform a merge, you should always ensure that the columns being used for the join have been defined using the correct data types, and are consistent between the columns to be joined.

By now you should be feeling fairly comfortable creating "Connection Only" staging queries, so we won't walk through that process in detail. You can follow along by opening to the Ch10 Examples\Join Types.xlsx file which already contains staging queries for the Transactions and COA (Chart of Accounts) tables.

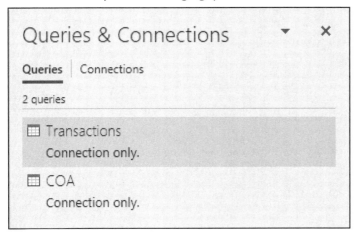

The Transactions and COA queries

Left Outer Join

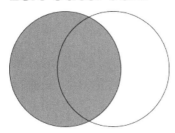

Left Outer Join: All records from left, matches from right

The first join type we will explore is the default join type: the Left Outer Join. This join works by returning all records from the Left (top) table, and any matching records from the Right (bottom) table. Items in the right (bottom) table without a match are simply ignored.

To create this join type:

- Determine which table you'd like to be the "left" side (we will use Transactions)
- Right-click the "left" query → Reference
- Rename the query to "Left Outer"
- Go to Home → Merge Queries
- Choose the "right" table (COA)

At this point, we have to pause and deal with that first nuance that we discussed earlier. Our merge needs to be based on a combination of the Account and Dept fields. While we could create those columns in our data set by merging them using a delimiter, there is actually no need to do so. Simply click the Account column, hold down CTRL and select the Dept column for each table:

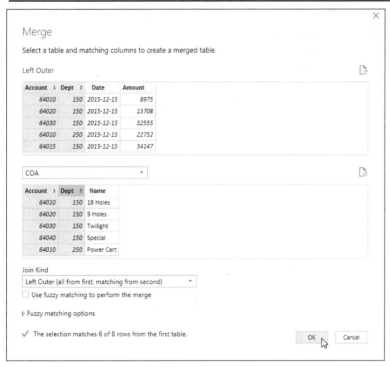

Merging tables using Composite Key joins

The order of the join columns will be indicated with a 1, 2, etc... in the order you selected them. Keep in mind that the data columns don't need to be in the same order between the queries, as long as the selection order is consistent.

> 🐾 While it never creates it visually, the columns are joined using an implied delimiter. This is important as Power Query will join the data properly if you had – say – products 1 to 11 and department 1 to 11. The implied delimiter avoids ambiguous joins based on a key of 111, instead treating the values as 1-11 or 11-1.

> 🐵 The indicator at the bottom of the preview tells you how many matches Power Query estimates *based on Power Query's data previews*. While this number is correct in our case – there are only 6 of 8 items in the left table with matches in the right table, it is important to remember that the previews may be limited to 1,000 (or less) rows for each table. This means that it is entirely possible you'll see an indicator of a poor match which actually matches perfectly when executed in full.

At this point, we can click OK to confirm the join, resulting in a new column called COA (named for the table we chose as the "right" table for our join). For illustration, we will then expand the column as follows:

- Click the Expand icon on the COA column → check the box to use the column prefix → OK

The results are shown here:

	Account	Dept	Date	Amount	COA.Account	COA.Dept	COA.Name
1	64010	150	2015-12-15	8975	64010	150	18 Holes
2	64020	150	2015-12-15	13708	64020	150	9 Holes
3	64030	150	2015-12-15	32555	64030	150	Twilight
4	64010	250	2015-12-15	22752	64010	250	Power Cart
5	64030	250	2015-12-15	19733	64030	250	Clubs
6	64040	250	2015-12-15	33438	64040	250	Golf Balls
7	64015	150	2015-12-15	34147	null	null	null
8	64010	350	2015-12-15	45876	null	null	null

The results of the Left Outer Join

The key things to notice here are these:

- The first 6 rows contain the results from the left (Transactions) table, and their matching details from the right (COA) table
- Rows 7 and 8 show results from the Transactions table, but show null for matches from the COA table
- When the data is loaded to a worksheet or the data model, all nulls will load as empty values

In a normal world, you probably wouldn't expand the Account and Dept columns from the right table. In this case we did specifically to call out the fact that these columns do not contain values, as no matching record was found in the COA table.

Right Outer Join

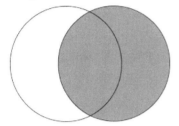

Right Outer Join: All records from right, matches from left

As mentioned previously, the Left Outer Join is the default. Now let's look at the Right Outer Join.

For this join, we are going to use almost exactly the same steps as the Left Outer Join:

- Determine which table you'd like to be the "left" side (we will use Transactions)
- Right-click the "left" query → Reference
- Rename the query to "Right Outer"
- Go to Home → Merge Queries
- Choose the "right" table (COA)
- Hold down CTRL → select the Account & Dept columns in each table
- Change the Join Kind to **Right Outer** → OK

At this point it is worth calling out one potentially weird thing that may happen: one of the rows of your data may show *null* values for all columns except the one that holds the Table objects representing the matches from the "right" table:

	1^2_3 Account	1^2_3 Dept	Date	1^2_3 Amount	COA
1	64010	150	2015-12-15	8975	Table
2	64020	150	2015-12-15	13708	Table
3	64030	150	2015-12-15	32555	Table
4	64010	250	2015-12-15	22752	Table
5	null	null	null	null	Table
6	64030	250	2015-12-15	19733	Table
7	64040	250	2015-12-15	33438	Table

Row 5 shows a bunch of null values before our table...

Although it may look odd, this is entirely predictable. It simply means that we have items in the right table that have no match in the left table. Let's expand the table to review them:

- Click the Expand icon on the COA column → check the box to use the column prefix → OK

This time, the results look as follows:

	1²₃ Account	1²₃ Dept	Date	1²₃ Amount	1²₃ COA.Account	1²₃ COA.Dept	A⁸C COA.Name
1	64010	150	2015-12-15	8975	64010	150	18 Holes
2	64020	150	2015-12-15	13708	64020	150	9 Holes
3	64030	150	2015-12-15	32555	64030	150	Twilight
4	64010	250	2015-12-15	22752	64010	250	Power Cart
5	null	null	null	null	64040	150	Special
6	64030	250	2015-12-15	19733	64030	250	Clubs
7	null	null	null	null	64020	250	Pull Cart
8	64040	250	2015-12-15	33438	64040	250	Golf Balls

The results of the Right Outer Join

This time the COA columns are all populated with values but, since Special and Pull Cart (shown on rows 5 and 7) have no transactions posted to them, the first columns show null values.

Full Outer Join

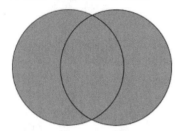

Full Outer Join: All records from both tables

Let's look at what we get when we use the Full Outer Join type on the same data. Once again, we'll use the same steps, changing only the join type:

- Determine which table you'd like to be the "left" side (we will use Transactions)
- Right-click the "left" query → Reference
- Rename the query to "Full Outer"
- Go to Home → Merge Queries
- Choose the "right" table (COA)
- Hold down CTRL → select the Account & Dept columns in each table
- Change the Join Kind to **Full Outer** → OK
- Click the Expand icon on the COA column → check the box to use the column prefix → OK

The output of the Full Outer Join looks as follows:

	1²₃ Account	1²₃ Dept	Date	1²₃ Amount	1²₃ COA.Account	1²₃ COA.Dept	A⁸C COA.Name
1	64010	150	2015-12-15	8975	64010	150	18 Holes
2	64020	150	2015-12-15	13708	64020	150	9 Holes
3	64030	150	2015-12-15	32555	64030	150	Twilight
4	64010	250	2015-12-15	22752	64010	250	Power Cart
5	null	null	null	null	64040	150	Special
6	64030	250	2015-12-15	19733	64030	250	Clubs
7	null	null	null	null	64020	250	Pull Cart
8	64040	250	2015-12-15	33438	64040	250	Golf Balls
9	64015	150	2015-12-15	34147	null	null	null
10	64010	350	2015-12-15	45876	null	null	null

The results of the Full Outer Join

In this case, notice that not only do you have the records that match between the tables, you also have all the mis-matched results that get exposed via the Left Outer Join (rows 9 and 10), as well as those exposed by the Right Outer Join (rows 5 and 7). This join can be super handy when you are trying to get an overview of your two lists, working out which data did not line up.

> 🔎 This join type also brings to light why, when comparing two lists, you often want to expand the columns from the right table that the join is based on. If there is no match with the left table, the only place the keys show up is in the results of the right side of the join!

Inner Join

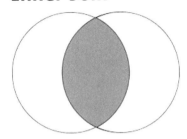

Inner Join: Only records with matches in both tables

For this join, we will use the same steps as the previous queries but electing for an Inner Join. The results of this are shown here:

	1^2_3 Account	1^2_3 Dept	Date	1^2_3 Amount	1^2_3 COA.Account	1^2_3 COA.Dept	A^B_C COA.Name
1	64010	150	2015-12-15	8975	64010	150	18 Holes
2	64020	150	2015-12-15	13708	64020	150	9 Holes
3	64030	150	2015-12-15	32555	64030	150	Twilight
4	64010	250	2015-12-15	22752	64010	250	Power Cart
5	64030	250	2015-12-15	19733	64030	250	Clubs
6	64040	250	2015-12-15	33438	64040	250	Golf Balls

The results of the Inner Join

This join obviously yields much less data than the joins we have looked at previously. The reason is simple: it only returns results where records can be matched between the two tables.

Left Anti Join

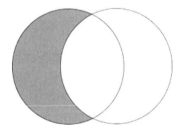

Left Anti Join: Records from left table with no match in right

The joins we have explored to date have primarily been about targeting data that matches. When reconciling two lists of data for differences, we actually care more about mismatches than matches. (Ironically, in the accounting world we spend a ton of time trying to identify matches for the sole purpose of eliminating them – it is the mis-matched leftovers we really care about!)

The results shown below were produced by following the exact same steps we've been using for each join type, but choosing the Left Anti Join:

	1^2_3 Account	1^2_3 Dept	Date	1^2_3 Amount	1^2_3 COA.Account	1^2_3 COA.Dept	A^B_C COA.Name
1	64015	150	2015-12-15	34147	null	null	null
2	64010	350	2015-12-15	45876	null	null	null

The results of the Left Anti Join

You'll notice that there are only two records: the two transactions that didn't have an appropriate account-dept combination in the Chart of Accounts table.

🐾 If your sole goal is to identify the records in the left table that don't have matches in the right table, there is no need to expand the results of the merge. Instead, you can simply delete the resulting column as every record will return null values anyway!

Right Anti Join

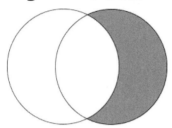

Right Anti Join: Records from right table with no match in left

Using the same pattern we've been using to date, but choosing a Right Anti Join yields the results shown here:

	1^2_3 Account	1^2_3 Dept	Date	1^2_3 Amount	1^2_3 COA.Account	1^2_3 COA.Dept	A^B_C COA.Name
1	null	null	null	null	64040	150	Special
2	null	null	null	null	64020	250	Pull Cart

The results of the Right Anti Join

As you can see, only the Special and Pull Cart accounts exist, as these are the only two items from the COA table which didn't have a transaction posted against them.

🐾 Be aware that every time you create a Right Anti Join, the result of the join will show a single row of *null* values, and a nested table in the final column. This is to be expected, as there are no matches from the left table, resulting in the *null* values for each column. If you are only after the items that have no matches, you can right-click the column that holds the results of the merge and choose Remove Other Columns prior to expanding it.

Full Anti Join

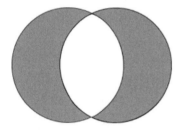

Full Anti Join: All records without a match

Another very useful join type, especially if you are trying to identify items that do not match between two lists, is the Full Anti Join. The bad news is that this is not a default join type available via the user interface. But the good news is that it is easy to create:

- Create the Left Anti Join query
- Create the Right Anti Join query
- Reference the Left Anti Join query to create a new query
- Go to Home → Append Queries → Append the Right Anti Join query → OK

The result is the complete opposite of the Inner Join (which only shows items that match perfectly), in that the Full Anti Join shows all items that do not match between the two tables:

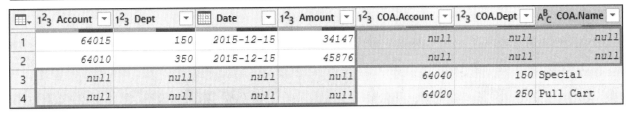

1²₃ Account ▼	1²₃ Dept ▼	Date ▼	1²₃ Amount ▼	1²₃ COA.Account ▼	1²₃ COA.Dept ▼	A᛫C COA.Name ▼
1	64015	150	2015-12-15	34147	null	null	null
2	64010	350	2015-12-15	45876	null	null	null
3	null	null	null	null	64040	150	Special
4	null	null	null	null	64020	250	Pull Cart

The Full Anti Join, showing the data that couldn't be matched

As you can see, rows 1 and 2 show the results of the Left Anti Join query, indicating the records in the left table with no matches in the right table. Stacked below them in rows 3 and 4, we see the items from the Right Anti Join, indicating the records in the right table with no matches in the left. This join is extremely useful, as it is your complete exception listing for all unreconciled items!

> 🔨 Remember: When you append queries, columns in the appended query that don't exist in the primary query will be added and filled with null values. If you deleted the empty columns in the Left Anti and Right Anti joins, this pattern still works, providing that the names in the Right Anti Join are unique from those produced by the Left Anti Join.

Cartesian Products (Cross Joins)

Whether you call it a cross join, many to many join or by its official name of Cartesian Product, this join type consists of taking the individual values from two lists and creating a set of ordered pairs where all possible combinations are represented. A simple example of this type of join is shown here, where we need a list of all products and the colors in which we can produce them:

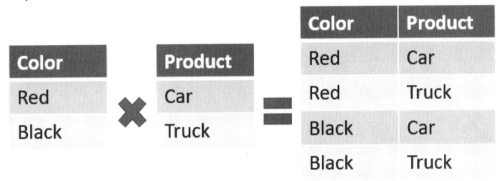

The results of a Cartesian join between the Color and Product tables

Recipe

Creating a Cartesian Product in Power Query can be done via a simple recipe, as detailed here:

- In each of the tables to be merged
  - Connect to the data source and perform any required cleanup
  - Go to Add Column → Custom Column
  - Name the column MergeKey with a formula of =1
- Right-click one of the tables → Reference
- Merge against the other table using a Left Outer Join based on the MergeKey column
- Remove the MergeKey column
- Expand all columns except the MergeKey from newly created column

> 🔨 It is possible to skip the addition of the MergeKey column in each of the tables to be merged by adding a Custom Column where the formula is equal to the name of the other table. While this works, using the MergeKey approaches runs faster. (Our tests yielded a 30% reduction in time based on joining via the MergeKey.)

Example

Armed with the recipe above, lets walk through this using the data found in Ch10 Examples\Cartesian Products. xlsx. The goal of this example will be to take a table containing fixed monthly expenses and create a straight-line budget for each month of the year.

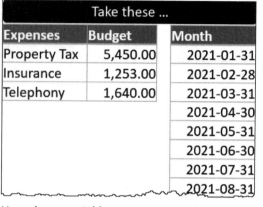

How do we quickly create a straight-line budget?

Using the recipe above, we would start by preparing our individual data. Beginning with the "Expenses" table (shown on the left in the image above), we would:

- Connect to the data table
- Go to Add Column → Custom Column
- Set the column name as MergeKey with a formula of =1
- Load the query as a Connection Only query

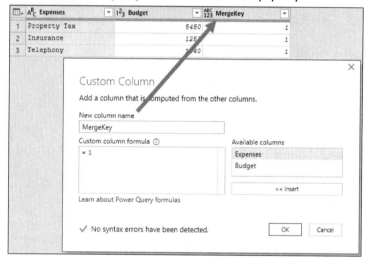

Creating the MergeKey column in the Expenses query

We would then perform the same steps to set up the "Months" table – adding the MergeKey column – and then also loading it as a Connection Only query as well:

Month	MergeKey
1	2021-01-31	1
2	2021-02-28	1
3	2021-03-31	1
4	2021-04-30	1

The Months table is properly prepared for merging

At this point, we simply need to decide which table we want to use as the left table (which columns would you like on the left in the output) and perform the merge. We will put the Expenses table on the left in order to replicate the originally pictured goal. To do that:

- Right-click the Expenses query → Reference
- Go to Home → Merge Queries
- Choose to Merge to the Months query → select the MergeKey column in each table → OK
- Remove the MergeKey column
- Expand all columns *except* the MergeKey column from the Months column

And that's it! We now have a complete table where the expense category is recoded for each month in the Months table:

	ABC Expenses	123 Budget	Month
1	Property Tax	5450	2021-01-31
2	Property Tax	5450	2021-02-28
3	Property Tax	5450	2021-03-31
4	Property Tax	5450	2021-04-30
5	Insurance	1253	2021-01-31
6	Insurance	1253	2021-02-28
7	Insurance	1253	2021-03-31
8	Insurance	1253	2021-04-30
9	Telephony	1640	2021-01-31
10	Telephony	1640	2021-02-28

Our straight line budget is now complete

At this point, any time someone adds a new month to the Months table or adds a new budget category and amount to the Expenses table, it can be updated with a single refresh.

> 🖉 This technique works very well provided that the values in the Expense table are consistent for each month. When budgeting in the real world, we also have many expenses that do not fit this structure, but it isn't a problem. We can create a separate query (or queries) to normalize them into the same column structure, and then append them into one master table.

Accidental Cartesian Products

The previous example showed where the deliberate use of a Cartesian Product can be very helpful. Unfortunately, it is actually quite easy to create an accidental Cartesian Product as well. Consider a scenario where someone adds January 2021 into the Months table twice. Upon refresh, we would end up with two Jan 2021 results for Property Tax, two for Insurance and two for Telephony, as each date would be combined with each item in the Expenses table.

The answer to safeguard against this problem is fairly straightforward in this case: in the Months table, just right-click the Month column and choose to Remove Duplicates. It should be safe to do, as we shouldn't ever be forecasting the same month twice.

Removing duplicates prior to merging should also be done with caution, however. In the case of the very first example in this chapter, attempting to merge the Sales and Inventory tables based on the Brand column (which exists in both tables), would create a Cartesian Product, resulting in duplicated sales data rows in the output. The reason for this is that – while we expect duplicate rows in the Sales table – there are also duplicated items in the Brand column in the Inventory table as shown here:

Unlike SKU, the Brand column will create a Cartesian Product during a merge

As you can see, de-duplicating the brand column in the Inventory table is not an option, as doing so would cause us to lose one of the two products from this vendor. And naturally, de-duplicating the Sales table would cause similar problems.

To avoid accidental Cartesian Products, it is a good idea to use the Column Profiling tools to check that the Distinct and Unique statistics match. If they do (like SKU), then the column can be safely used for the key of the "right" table in the join without the risk of triggering a Cartesian Product. If they don't match (like Brand) – then the danger is real – a value in the "left" table's column matches that in the "right" table's column will yield a Cartesian Product.

Approximate Match Joins

While Power Query provides a variety of joins that can replicate an "exact match" scenario, one join type that does not exist is the ability to perform an approximate match. Keep in mind this is not a "fuzzy" match – which we will talk about later – but rather where we want to look up and return a value equal to or between two data points. Excel users will know this as the VLOOKUP() approximate match scenario seen here:

Source Table		Lookup Table		Desired Output		
Order ID	**Units**	**Quantity**	**Unit Price**	**Order ID**	**Units**	**Unit Price**
1	75	1	5.95	1	75	5.95
2	2,755	1,000	5.75	2	2,755	5.65
3	5,919	2,500	5.65	3	5,919	5.55
4	1,000	5,000	5.55	4	1,000	5.75
5	14,169	10,000	5.45	5	14,169	5.45
ID	Key	Key	Return	ID	Key	Return

We need to look up the closest price without going over...

In the case shown above, a purchaser earns a better price the larger the order they place. The problem is that we do not have a data point in our lookup table for 2755 units, so we need the proper price for that order quantity – a quantity that falls between 2500 and 5000 units. As the customer hasn't reached the 5000 unit price point, we therefore need to return the $5.65 price for reaching the 2500 unit price tier.

> ✎ You will also notice in the image above, that we have carefully labelled each column below the data. Identifying the Key and Return columns is usually fairly straightforward, as they are usually the only columns in your Lookup table. But one additional wrinkle is that you may have multiple ID columns depending on the width of the Source table.

Recipe

Most users would immediately attempt to leverage one of Power Query's join algorithms to merge these tables together. Interestingly, this is not how we solve this issue. The recipe to solve an approximate match in Power Query is:

- **Step 1**: Connect to the Source and Lookup tables
    - Connect to and clean your data as normal
- **Step 2**: Prepare Lookup table
    - Rename the [Key] columns to ensure they match in both tables
- **Step 3**: Perform the match
    - Reference the Source table
    - Go to Home → Append → Lookup table
    - Filter the [Key] column → Sort Ascending
    - Filter the [ID] column(s) → Sort Ascending
    - Right-click the [Return] column → Fill → Down
    - Filter the [ID] column → uncheck null

It is a short recipe, overall, but trust us – that is all it takes to perform an Approximate Match in Power Query.

Example

The data for this example can be found in Ch10 Examples\Approximate Match.xlsx and is shown in the image below. Our goal is to create the table shown on the far right by using an Approximate Match, and we will walk through the above recipe to do so.

Take these ...						... and create this ...			
Units	**Price Per**	**Order ID**	**Quantity**			**Order ID**	**Quantity**	**Price Per**	**Revenue**
1	5.95	TX000987	75			TX000987	75	5.95	446.25
250	5.85	TX000988	2,755			TX000990	1000	5.75	5,750.00
1000	5.75	TX000989	5,919			TX000988	2755	5.65	15,565.75
2500	5.65	TX000990	1,000			TX000989	5919	5.55	32,850.45
5000	5.55	TX000991	14,169			TX000992	10670	5.45	58,151.50
10000	5.45	TX000992	10,670			TX000991	14169	5.45	77,221.05

The source data and output goal

The first step of the process is to create individual queries to connect to both the Prices and the Orders tables. The real goal here is to get your data into a clean tabular format, making sure the columns are well named and complete. As that is already the case here, simply connecting to the data is sufficient.

With our queries in place, we can move to Step 2, which involves making sure the *Key* columns are consistently named between the two tables. In order to do that, lets carefully identify all the recipe components:

- **Source table**: This will be the Orders table (shown in the middle of the above image), as it contains the bulk of the information that we wish to enrich. The *ID* column for our pattern will be the **Order ID** column, and the Source's *Key* column will be the **Quantity** column.
- **Lookup table**: This will be the Prices table, shown on the left, as it is the table that holds the value we wish to return (or merge) into the Source table. Specifically, we want to *Return* the **Price Per** column and – to do this – we need to work out the correct value by comparing the *Source Key* (**Quantity**) against the *Lookup Key* (**Units**), when looking for our match.

Since the names of the *Key* columns are inconsistent, we need to fix that. As we never want to compromise our source data, we will make that change in Power Query.

- Edit the Prices query
- Select the Units column → rename → Quantity

▦ ▾	1²₃ Quantity	▾	$ Price Per	▾
1	1		5.95	
2	250		5.85	
3	1000		5.75	
4	2500		5.65	
5	5000		5.55	
6	10000		5.45	

The updated Lookup table (Prices)

🐒 While we chose to rename the Key column in the Lookup table, you could rename the Key column in the Source table if you prefer to do so. The end goal is simply to make sure that the column names are the same in each table.

With the data now fully prepared, we can move to Step 3, where we actually create the match.

- Right-click the Source table (Orders) → Reference
- Go to Home → Append Queries → Append the Prices Query

The results – if you scroll to the bottom of the preview – should now look like this:

▦ ▾	AᵇC Order ID	▾	1²₃ Quantity	▾	$ Price Per	▾
20	TX001006		4247		null	
21	TX001007		10826		null	
22	TX001008		3481		null	
23	TX001009		6062		null	
24	TX001010		4089		null	
25	null		1		5.95	
26	null		250		5.85	
27	null		1000		5.75	
28	null		2500		5.65	
29	null		5000		5.55	
30	null		10000		5.45	

Appending the Source and Lookup tables

As we already know, when appending two tables, columns with the same name get stacked, where columns with new names get added to the table. This was why it was so important to make sure that the *Key* column was consistent between the two tables. You'll also notice that for each order from the Source table, the price currently shows as *null*, while the Order ID for all the rows from the Prices table also show as *null*.

🐒 The reason we started with the Source table is solely because we usually want those columns on the left of the output when complete, and this saves reordering the columns later. If you want to start from the Lookup table and append the Source table, the recipe will still work.

☎ If your Source table is over 1000 rows long, you may not even be able to see the Lookup table in your data preview. Don't worry about this, just follow the recipe steps. Even though it might not show up properly via the preview, the steps will get executed to the entire data set at load time, and the recipe will work!

We are now going to take the steps that yield the magic in this pattern:

- Filter the Quantity column → Sort Ascending
- Filter the Order ID column → Sort Ascending

At this point the data will look like this, with each row of the Prices table showing up above the relevant rows from the Orders table:

	ABc Order ID 2↕↑	123 Quantity 1↕↑	$ Price Per ▾
1	null	1	5.95
2	TX000987	75	null
3	TX001003	76	null
4	null	250	5.85
5	TX000996	817	null
6	TX001004	955	null
7	null	1000	5.75
8	TX000990	1000	null
9	TX000998	2365	null

Our approximate match is almost complete!

The magic of this pattern comes from the sorting that is applied to the *Key* column (Quantity), as this mixes all the pricing rows in with the original data in ascending order. By then applying the second sort of the ID column (or columns if you have multiple sorting criteria), we can ensure that the rows from the Prices table always come before the rows from the Orders table. (In the case of tied values like the 1000 shown on rows 7 and 8, this will ensure that the Lookup row is always above the Source row.)

We are now just two steps away from the finish:

- Right-click the Price Per column → Fill Down
- Filter the Order ID column → uncheck null
- Select the Quantity and Price Per columns → Add Column → Standard → Multiply
- Rename the Multiplication column as Revenue

And that's it. The rows from the Prices table are no longer present, but the prices for the order quantities are, as are the Revenues that were part of the desired output table:

	ABc Order ID ▾	123 Quantity ▾	$ Price Per ▾	$ Revenue ▾
1	TX000987	75	5.95	446.25
2	TX001003	76	5.95	452.20
3	TX000996	817	5.85	4,779.45
4	TX001004	955	5.85	5,586.75
5	TX000990	1000	5.75	5,750.00
6	TX000998	2365	5.75	13,598.75
7	TX000988	2755	5.65	15,565.75
8	TX001008	3481	5.65	19,667.65

We have successfully replicated Excel's VLOOKUP() with an Approximate Match!

Fuzzy Matching

Each of the joins illustrated in this chapter so far requires the data between the two tables to have some sort of consistency. The data points either need to match exactly, or they need to follow an ordered logic. So long as you're working with computer-generated data, this usually isn't far from what you'll encounter. But what happens when you are trying to match human-entered data against your computer-generated data?

Spelling mistakes, casing, abbreviations, punctuation and alternate terms are just some of the things that you'll find lead to inconsistencies between the data sets being matched. Since Power Query's default joins only join data that matches exactly, it can significantly impact your ability to compare two lists.

Take these ...					
Employee	**Quantity**	**Item**		**Product**	**Price**
Donald A	5	Laptops		Laptop	1,399
Mary	2	Monitor		Monitor	159
Bob	1	laptop		Mouse	29
Ron	2	Mice		Keyboard	49
Don B	7	Keyboards			
Cheryl	1	Screen			

... and create this ...			
Employee	**Quantity**	**Item**	**Price**
Donald A	5	Laptops	1,399
Mary	2	Monitor	159
Bob	1	laptop	1,399
Ron	2	Mice	29
Don B	7	Keyboards	49
Cheryl	1	Screen	159

The Products table (left) is completed manually and compared to the Pricing table (right)

The source data for this example can be found in Ch10 Examples\Fuzzy Match.xlsx.

Everything looks fine at first glance, but upon performing a standard Left Outer Join in Power Query, based on matching the Products[Item] and Pricing[Item] columns, only one item yields the proper price:

	A^B_C Employee	1^2_3 Quantity	A^B_C Item	1^2_3 Price
1	Donald A	5	Laptops	null
2	Mary	2	Monitor	159
3	Bob	1	laptop	null
4	Ron	2	Mice	null
5	Don B	7	Keyboards	null
6	Cheryl	1	Screen	null

This is a bit of a disaster as only Mary's Monitor has a price!

As you can see from the image above, this is just not going to work. From items with an extra s at the end (indicating that they are plural), to "laptop" in lowercase that doesn't match the proper case "Laptop" in the pricing table, to "Screen", which is an alternate for "Monitor", we have almost no matches at all.

In many tools, the only answer would be to go back and clean up the Products table manually. But with Power Query, we have a method to be able to deal with some of this ambiguity: it is called Fuzzy Matching.

> ✎ If you are collecting data based on user input, it is ALWAYS better to put data validation rules in place to stop users from entering mis-matched data to begin with, rather than trying to fix it via a fuzzy match. Unfortunately, we don't always have that kind of control, and that is where this tool can become very useful.

Basic Fuzzy Matches

Creating a basic Fuzzy Match is actually fairly easy; as you are creating your regular join, simply click the checkbox next to "Use fuzzy matching to perform the merge":

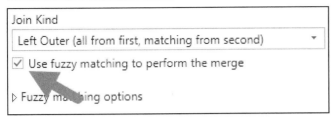

Turning a regular match into a "fuzzy" match

That single step changes the output drastically, resulting in the following result when merging Products[Item] and Pricing[Item] as shown earlier:

	A^B_C Employee	1²₃ Quantity	A^B_C Item	1²₃ Price
1	Donald A	5	Laptops	1399
2	Mary	2	Monitor	159
3	Bob	1	laptop	1399
4	Ron	2	Mice	null
5	Don B	7	Keyboards	49
6	Cheryl	1	Screen	null

Leveraging Power Query's basic Fuzzy Match

In this case shown here, Power Query has increased our matches to four of six entries, simply by checking the Fuzzy Match checkbox. But why?

Power Query leverages the Jaccard similarity algorithm to measure the similarity between pairs of instances, and flags anything that scores 80% similar or above as a match. In this case, the algorithm scores both "Laptops" and "laptop" as similar enough to "Laptop", despite one having an extra character, and one using a character in a lower versus upper case. Things like transposed characters (friend vs freind), and light punctuation (mrs vs mrs.) will also be matched where a standard join would not do so.

When working with Fuzzy Matching, it is helpful to realize that generally, the longer words are, and the more similar characters they possess, the more likely they will return an accurate match. To understand this, consider how confident you are that the following two words are the same:

- Dogs vs Cogs
- Bookkeeperz vs Bookkeepers

Both words have only one letter different, but with less characters in play, we can't be as confident that they are a mistake.

> 🔨 Fuzzy matching is only supported on merge operations over text columns. If you need to perform a fuzzy match with columns that use a different data type for any reason, you'll need to convert them to text first.

Transformation (Translation) Tables

While the basic Fuzzy Match solves some of our issues, we can also see from the previous image that two of our records still don't yield a match: Mice (which we'd like to match to Mouse) and Screen (which we need to match to Monitor). These words just simply aren't close enough based on the Jaccard similarity algorithm to be flagged as a match. So how do we work through this issue?

The secret is to create a special table to translate one term from another, as shown here:

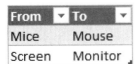

A simple Translation table

> 🔨 While the name of this table isn't important, it must contain a 'From' column and a 'To' column in order to map the terms properly.

In this case of the example file, this table is called Translations, as we'll load it to Power Query as a Connection Only query. After doing so, the process to create a Fuzzy Match that *also* leverages this table is to take the following steps:

- Create a query that joins your data
- Check the option to "Use fuzzy matching..."
- Click the triangle to expand the Fuzzy Join options
- Scroll down and select the Translation table as the "Transformation Table"

As you can see, upon expanding the results of the merge, we now have all of our data points matched up nicely:

	A^B_C Employee ▾	1^2_3 Quantity ▾	A^B_C Item ▾	1^2_3 Price ▾
1	Donald A	5	Laptops	1399
2	Mary	2	Monitor	159
3	Bob	1	laptop	1399
4	Ron	2	Mice	29
5	Don B	7	Keyboards	49
6	Cheryl	1	Screen	159

We've finally matched up all of our data!

> 🖋 Again, it is a better idea to enforce some data validation to ensure that the end-users are entering valid Item names up front, but at least we now have a method to deal with it if they don't; add the term they entered in the 'From' column, and the correct value in the 'To' column.

Reducing Similarity Thresholds

As mentioned earlier, Power Query leverages the Jaccard similarity algorithm to measure the similarity between pairs of instances, and flags anything that scores 80% similar or above as a match. It also provides you the option to tighten or relax that similarity score as well. The higher the number, the more certain the match needs to be. In other words, setting this to 1 (100%) would then exhibit the Exact match requirement of the Join type you have selected.

While you'd never set a Fuzzy match's Similarity threshold to 1, you may be tempted to go the other way and loosen the restriction. Before you do so, however, we'd like to make sure that you are familiar with the potential downsides.

Assume you need to match the Employees between the Products and Depts tables shown here:

Take these ...				Employee	Dept
Employee	**Quantity**	**Item**		Don A	Accounting
Donald A	5	Laptops		Don B	Billing
Mary	2	Monitor		Mary	Finance
Bob	1	laptop		Bob	Finance
Ron	2	Mice		Ron	Finance
Don B	7	Keyboards		Cheryl	Finance
Cheryl	1	Screen			

... and create this ...			
Employee	**Quantity**	**Item**	**Dept**
Donald A	5	Laptops	Accounting
Mary	2	Monitor	Finance
Bob	1	laptop	Finance
Ron	2	Mice	Finance
Don B	7	Keyboards	Billing
Cheryl	1	Screen	Finance

The Products (left) and Dept (right) tables

The challenge here is that the clerk recording sales has decided to use Donald A's full name, where the Human Resources department knows him as "Don A" (not Donald.) How well is this match going to work? As it turns out, even using a basic Fuzzy Match, not well:

	AᴮC Employee	1²3 Quantity	AᴮC Item	AᴮC Depts.Employee	AᴮC Depts.Dept
1	Donald A	5	Laptops	null	null
2	Mary	2	Monitor	Mary	Finance
3	Bob	1	laptop	Bob	Finance
4	Ron	2	Mice	Ron	Finance
5	Don B	7	Keyboards	Don B	Billing
6	Cheryl	1	Screen	Cheryl	Finance

Wait… Donald who?

As it turns out, the similarity between Don A and Donald A scores somewhere between 50% and 59% similar. Given that this is less than the default of 80%, they do not get matched up.

Now we already know that we could solve this issue by creating a separate table to hold Don's aliases. We all love having options though, so let's see if we can solve this by just adjusting the similarity threshold and avoid adding another table.

The option to do this – like providing a Translation table – is contained under the little triangle that hides the Fuzzy Matching options:

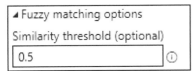

Relaxing the Jaccard Similarity threshold

In the case of the example data, relaxing this value to 0.6 (60% similarity) will have no effect on the output. But knocking it down to 50% finds Donald a match:

	AᴮC Employee	1²3 Quantity	AᴮC Item	AᴮC Depts.Employee	AᴮC Depts.Dept
1	Donald A	5	Laptops	Don A ✓	Accounting
2	Mary	2	Monitor	Mary	Finance
3	Bob	1	laptop	Bob	Finance
4	Ron	2	Mice	Ron	Finance
5	Don B	7	Keyboards	Don B	Billing
6	Don B	7	Keyboards	Ron !	Finance
7	Cheryl	1	Screen	Cheryl	Finance

We've finally matched Donald to his accounting alter-ego

At first glance, this is pretty great. We've managed to match Donald to Don without having to add another table to our solution. But as we look closer, we can see that something isn't quite right…

Prior to relaxing the similarity threshold, we were matching six sales records to six employees, and returning six rows. Why do we now have seven?

If you look carefully at rows 4 and 5, we can see that Ron and Don B have been matched to the correct employee codes in the Depts table. But then, on row 6, Don B has also been flagged as a match for Ron!

What we are seeing in action here is a match tolerance that has been set too low and is flagging a false positive. In addition, it has created an accidental (fuzzy) Cartesian product!

> 🐵 Avoid relying on a reduced Similarity Threshold unless absolutely necessary. This is a dangerous tool that can lead to mismatched data and accidental cartesian products.

While a basic fuzzy match can lead to false positives in the matches, (it is matching to 80% similarity after all), the Power Query team provided a default value that limits the amount of false positives while still providing fuzzy matching capabilities. You should only change this tolerance if you know the implications and should always review the results of your matches after doing so.

Strategies for Maintaining Fuzzy Matching

Naturally, the big question here is "How do I maintain a solution that relies on fuzzy matching?" It can seem intimidating, especially if you are refreshing a relatively new solution and keep coming up with issues.

In order to set up a maintainable system that relies on Fuzzy Matching, we'd recommend that you take the following actions:

- Before merging your data, perform replacements of frequently occurring character terms or patterns that you know need to be fixed. I.e., If you know that your computer-generated lookup table never includes the # sign in front of an address, but your source table may contain an address written this way, just right-click the column and replace all # signs on the column with nothing.

- Leverage one of the Anti-Join patterns discussed earlier in the chapter to land a table of Exceptions (unknown terms) for you to review after each refresh.

- Create an Excel or DAX formula to count the number of unknown items (rows) in the Exceptions table and return it to a report page for easy visibility. (At each refresh, you'll then be able to see if the count of unknown items is 0, or that your translation list needs to have additional items added to it.)

Upon refresh, you then have a mechanism to not only alert you as to whether any unknown items exist, that same solution can also list exactly what the unknown items are!

In the case where you do have unknown items, you'll then enter them in your translation table along with the terms they map to. (We highly recommend using copy/paste from your Exceptions table to your Translation table wherever possible in order to ensure that the spelling is correct.) Provided that you entered all of the missing terms correctly, a full refresh should then match everything up properly.

Depending on how clean or dirty your data is, and how often you refresh it, you should see the number of mismatches decrease at each refresh. The reason for this is simple: you're building a dictionary of terms that is getting more robust every time you encounter an issue.

> ✎ The Fuzzy Matching algorithm is not only present in the Merge operations but is also implemented in other experiences such as the **Group by** feature and the most recent new feature called **Cluster Values**. While – at the time of printing – these experiences were only available inside the Power Query Online experience, the goal of the Power Query team is to have parity between all versions of Power Query so we are hoping that in the near future you'll see these features in your favorite Power Query product integration.

Chapter 11 - Web Based Data Sources

One of the really interesting use cases for Power Query is when we can leverage it to pull data relevant to our business from the web and use it to enrich our own corporate data sources.

Data generally is stored on the web in one of two different ways:

1. A file that is stored in a website repository, or
2. An HTML based web page.

Provided that the first is stored in a format that Power Query understands (CSV, XLSX, etc…), extracting data from them is fairly easy. The latter, however, can be more challenging as the page may or may not contain a consistent structure. The Power Query team has been working on this feature and – at the time of writing – had released a preview of a new "web table inference" feature in Power BI to deal with this issue.

Connecting to Web-Hosted Data Files

Assume you've found the following file on the web and would like to connect to it directly:

```
https://data.cityofnewyork.us/api/views/c3uy-2p5r/files/fb52d9bb-0a7c-4cc4-824e-1930c818e5d1?download=true&filename=NYCCAS_Air_Quality_Indicators_Open_Data.xlsx
```

Despite the fact that this is an xlsx file, you would not use the Excel connector to extract it, as it is stored on the web, not a local folder on your computer. Instead, you would use the "From Web" connector as follows:

- Create a new Query -> From Other Sources -> From Web
- Enter the file path in the URL field and click OK

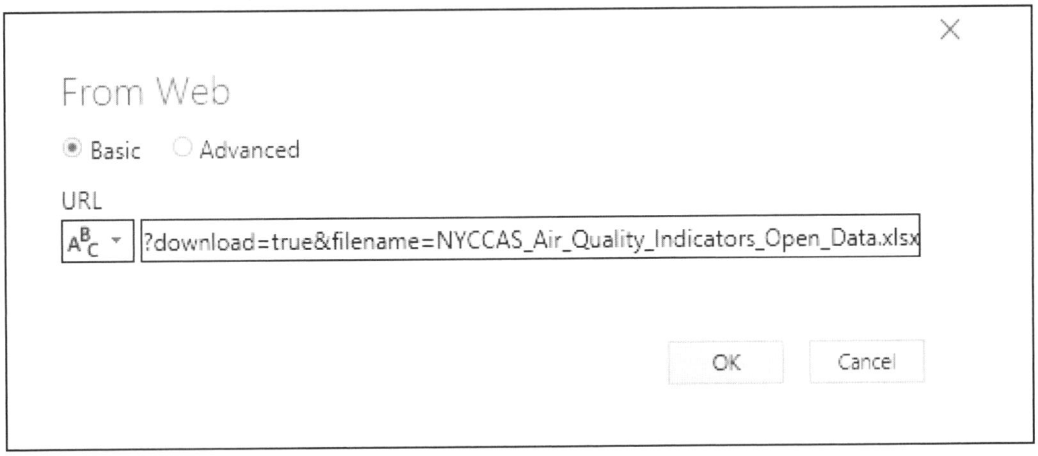

Connecting to an Excel file hosted on the web

If you haven't connected to the site before, you'll then be prompted to choose the appropriate authentication method.

> The cityofnewyork.us site provides a large amount of open data that can be read without authentication. Choose Anonymous when connecting to this source.

After clearing the authentication method, you'll see that the experience is exactly the same as connecting to a local Excel file:

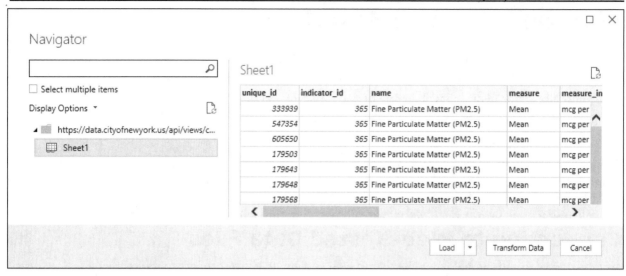

Excel from… does it matter?

This is the beautiful thing about the way the Power Query team has designed this software. While the connector is different, the rest of the process is identical to working with a locally stored file. For this reason, we won't actually perform any transformations on this data set – the important thing is that you realize that it's easy to connect to and import data from a file stored on the web.

Connecting to HTML Web Pages

Assume for this scenario, that you'd like to pull a list from the New York City website of all of their open datasets. The URL you discover to find this information is:

```
https://data.cityofnewyork.us/browse?limitTo=datasets
```

> 🔧 Note: As we do not control this website, there is a chance that the page format may change or the URL may be deprecated between the time the book is released and you read this chapter. Should this happen we have saved a copy of the page in the example files. Just double click on the NYC Open Data.html file, copy the path from your web browser, and use it in place of the URL above.

The page itself appears to contain a table of the datasets, with some pertinent information about each:

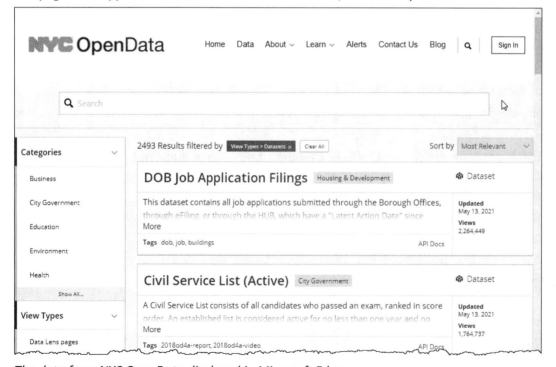

The data from NYC OpenData displayed in Microsoft Edge

Connecting to the Web Page

🔧 At the time of writing, the "New web table inference" feature was still a preview feature in Power BI Desktop and hadn't been released in Excel at all. Should your Navigator screen look different than what is shown below, you haven't yet received this update. In this case you'll be presented with the interface shown in the "Connecting to Pages Without Tables" section of this chapter.

To begin, we connect to the web page in the same manner as we connected to a web-hosted file:

- Get Data → From Web → OK
- Choose Anonymous authentication (for this data set) if prompted

Once again, you'll be taken to a preview window, but this time you'll notice that we have some more options to play with:

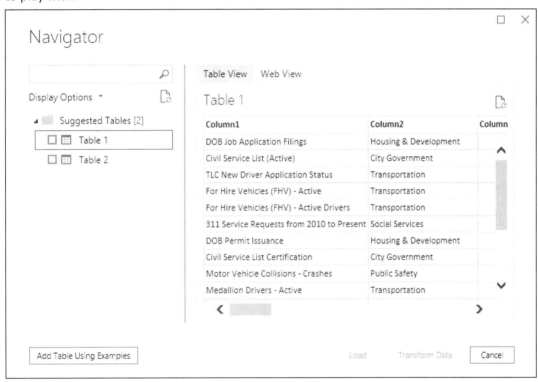

Connecting to an HTML web page with Power Query

Natural and Suggested Tables

One of the things that we can recognize about this web page immediately is that it doesn't actually contain any defined tables. If it did, we would see those listed in the left-hand pane of the Navigator window under the heading "HTML Tables". Instead, all we see are two "Suggested Tables" – tables that the Power Query engine has inferred from the CSS of the HTML document.

After selecting Table 1 in the Navigator list, Power Query helpfully shows a preview of the table that it has defined. If we like it, we can simply check the box and choose if we'd like to Load the data or modify it before doing so.

You also have the ability to switch into a web-based preview of the data, allowing you to compare the fully formatted web page against the tabular inference that Power Query has made. To do so, click Web View above the preview area:

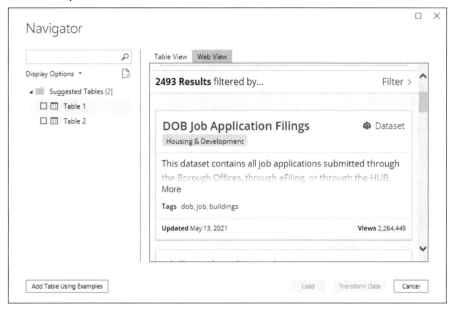

Previewing a web page in the From Web Navigator

Typically, you'll use this view to quickly compare data from an inferred or official table against the human friendly web view, and not much more. Be aware that selecting a table in the navigator does not highlight or change the web view in any way, so you'll most likely change back to Table View before committing to loading or modifying the query.

Add Table Using Examples

But what if you want more control over how the data is interpreted? This is where the "Add Table Using Examples" can become very useful. Clicking that button will take you to a new user interface that shows a data preview at the top, and an empty column at the bottom. The intent here is that you'll select the first cell in Column 1, type in what you want to extract for the first record, and Power Query will do the rest:

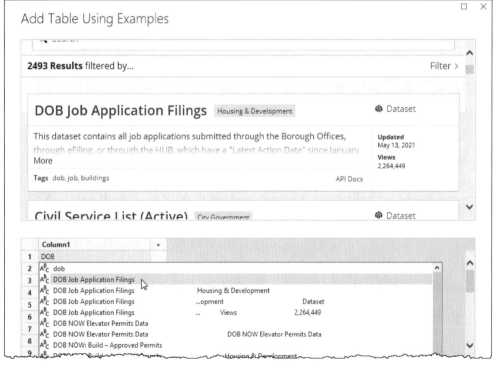

Extracting the dataset titles via Table Using Examples

When working with this feature, we find that "less is more" is definitely true. Type part of the data you wish to extract and then either double click or highlight and press Enter on the text that matches your intended value. After a short delay, the column should populate with the other items that Power Query has inferred from the data. Should one of the entries be incorrect, simply type over it to refine the list.

> 🐵 If your suggestions result in a large amount of *null* values being displayed, it means that Power Query couldn't determine the proper logic to extract your values.

Once you have finished with your first column, double click to rename it, then click the + icon if you'd like to add any more columns. In the view below, we have constructed a table with Data Set, Views and Last Update columns based on the values that appear for the first record in the data set:

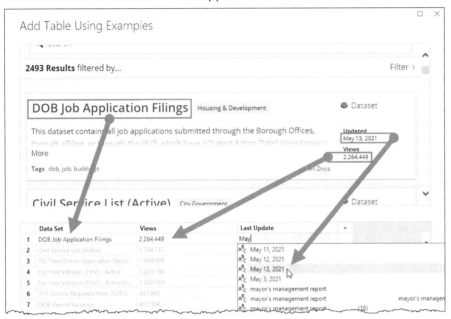

Extracting data via Table Using Examples

Once complete, you can access your Custom Table by clicking OK, and then choosing to Load or Transform the data further:

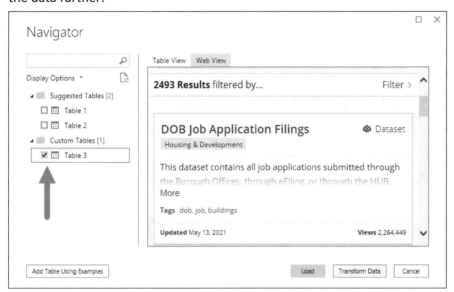

Your custom table is automatically selected for import

Connecting to Pages Without Tables

While we are hopeful that the Table Using Examples feature will be released in Excel before the book goes to print, there is definitely the potential that this may not happen. If that is the case, and the web page doesn't contain defined table tags, you're left with a horrendous experience of trying to drill into the HTML elements. This experience is about as much fun as navigating a subterranean labyrinth using a candle for light where every signpost simply says, "This way out".

The best route for help you have is to open your web browser, turn on the developer tools, and try to find the element you want to extract. For this example, we will consider the following web page:

> https://data.cityofnewyork.us/Housing-Development/DOB-Job-Application-
> Filings/ic3t-wcy2

> ✎ Note: A local copy of this web page has been saved in the Example Files under the name DOB Job Application Filings.html in case the page format has been changed or deprecated.

Our goal is to extract the data in this table from the web page:

This table doesn't show in the preview window

> ✎ While this table is identified in Power BI's new web table inference feature, the data did not show up in Excel's connector at the time of writing. As it is possible that – even with the new connector – you may end up in a similar scenario, we need to explore how to navigate an HTML document structure via Power Query. Just be warned... it's not for the faint of heart!

So how do you know that you're going to get stuck going down this rabbit hole? Both of the following are true:

1.   The table you are after does not show up (either as a natural HTML Table or a Suggested Table), and

2.   You cannot create the table using the Table Using Examples feature.

This scenario was quite easy for us to replicate in Excel since we don't currently have the new interface. Connecting to the web page yields the following preview:

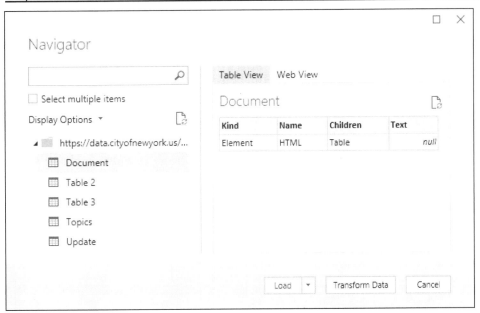

Only four HTML tables are present, and the one we want is missing

To find the path to the elements we want, in Microsoft Edge or Chrome, we need to go to the page and press F12 to expand the Developer Tools.

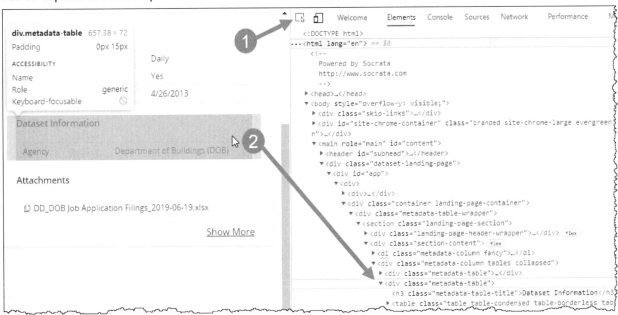

Navigating HTML hell

The trick to finding your element is then to:

- Click the Element Inspector button (at the top left of the Developer Tools window) or press Ctrl + Shift + C
- Mouse over the page to highlight the element you want
- Left-click it to select that element in the Elements window

Once you have done this you can begin the painful second portion; replicating the navigation in Power Query.

- Create a new query → From Other Sources → From Web → Enter the URL

  ```
  https://data.cityofnewyork.us/Housing-Development/DOB-Job-Application-
  Filings/ic3t-wcy2
  ```

- Click OK → select Document → Transform Data

You'll now be looking at this rather unfriendly view in the Power Query editor:

⊞▾	A^B_C Kind	▾	A^B_C Name	▾	⊞ Children	⇊	A^B_C Text	▾
1	Element		HTML		Table		*null*	

A most uninspiring view

Now you need to very carefully replicate the steps you took in the web developer interface, drilling into Power Query's corresponding Table element. There are some parallels between the two programs to help, but even so, it is easy to get lost.

The trick to navigating this process is to recognize that the Name field in Power Query contains the element shown in the web developer tools. In this case, we have HTML, and in the browser we saw *<html class* at the top. These two items are the same.

- Click the Table in the Children column to drill into it

⊞▾	A^B_C Kind	▾	A^B_C Name	▾	⊞ Children	⇊	A^B_C Text	▾
1	Element		HEAD		Table		*null*	
2	Text		*null*		*null*			
3	Element		BODY		Table		*null*	

Children of the HTML element

We now see the HEAD and BODY tags. Based on the HTML we expanded, we need to drill into the Body tag. We'd click the Table there and keep going.

The killer with this process is that in the HTML the tags all have names, yet in Power Query we don't see them, making it very easy to get lost. In addition, the Applied steps window doesn't trace our route, it just keeps combining steps together, giving us no way to back up one level. Should that happen, your only recourse is to start over again from the beginning.

And as if that wasn't the worst part of the issue, at the end of this navigation process, one column of the table is displayed as raw text, where the other is wrapped in a <span> element, meaning that there is additional manipulation needed:

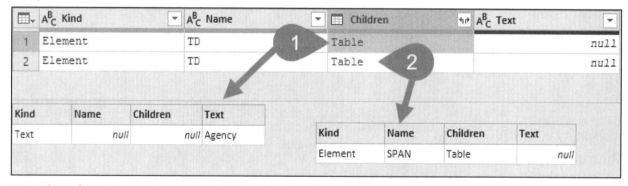

It just doesn't get any easier – even the table column formats are inconsistent!

As the steps to get this into a nice clean table are out of the scope of this chapter, we are going to abandon this approach at this point. The steps to complete this process have, however, been saved in the completed example, which can be found at Ch11 Examples\From Web – The Hard Way.xlsx. This particular query has been saved as "TheHardWay". Even with that query to review, you'll need to recognize that the Navigation step was generated as documented below.

Starting from the initial table:

⊞▾	A^B_C Kind	▾	A^B_C Name	▾	⊞ Children	⇊	A^B_C Text	▾
1	Element		HTML		Table		*null*	

Drill into the Children Table for

- HTML (row 1)
- Body (row 3)
- Main (row 6)
- DIV (row 4)
- DIV (row 2)
- DIV (row 1)
- DIV (row 2)
- DIV (row 1)
- SECTION (row 1)
- DIV (row 2)
- DIV (row 2)
- DIV (row 2)
- TABLE (row 2)
- TBODY (row 1)
- TR (row 1)

If you follow the above carefully, you'll have drilled into the exact same place as displayed in the Navigation step of the TheHardWay query and can follow the rest of the steps through to the end.

We should recognize that the job of drilling into the HTML document can be done, which is better than the alternative. Having said that, it is not for the faint of heart, and can be an incredibly frustrating process.

Caveats and Frustrations with the Web Experience

The From Web experience has certainly been a weakness in Power Query's otherwise incredible arsenal of tools. The good news is that – based on the preview we've displayed in Power BI – things are going to get better. (And hopefully we will even see that interface in Excel by the time you read this book!)

It is important, however to realize that even with better connectors there are still some things to watch out for as you develop solutions based on web data.

None of the discussions below should be seen as reasons not to develop solutions based on website data. Instead, they are intended to make sure you go into this area with both eyes open, seeing not only the benefits, but also the risks of relying on web-sourced data you don't control.

The Collecting Data Experience

Building solutions against web data can be a very painful experience in Power Query. As we showed in the Power BI example earlier, the tool can work well if there are table tags or well designed CSS behind the document. At that point you'll be presented natural or suggested tables, and things are easy. If not, however, all bets are off, and you're sent down the HTML-hell path. Unfortunately though, it's not even as simple as table tags or CSS… settings to optimize web page delivery such as lazy loading of content can mean that Power Query doesn't even see the complete page, as it picks up the page structure before it is completely loaded.

Our hope is that the Power Query team will continue to work on this area, adding user interface options to enhance the experience, and hopefully never send someone into HTML-hell again.

Data Integrity

Another major concern with web data is the source and integrity. Be cautious of connecting and importing data from sites such as Wikipedia, or other sites that you don't have a business relationship with.

While demos love to use Wikipedia as a great example, the reality is that this site can be dangerous to rely on. The content is curated, but changeable by users. Although the site makes a great effort to curate data, the information on the site is far from perfect, and may contain data that is not entirely factual.

The other issue is how readily the data is updated. Imagine investing in the time to build a complicated query against a web page, only to find out that the owner/curator doesn't update it on a timely basis. You need to be assured that when you refresh the data that the routine isn't merely refreshing out of date data, but rather current data. Here you've invested a significant amount of time and make business decisions assuming that the last refresh you did pulled the most recent data.

Solution Stability

There is another very real concern when building your business logic against web sources that you do not own or control. Like your company, each company that surfaces these feeds and pages wants to better serve their customers. Unfortunately for us, that doesn't mean that they are interested in putting out a consistent experience that never changes, in fact quite the opposite. They are also trying to update things, changing the web pages to add new bells or whistles, or make the sites more attractive to the human eye. This has the very real side effect of blowing your query apart, usually without notice, and often times when you don't have time to fix it.

Chapter 12 - Relational Data Sources

If you work in an organization where you are granted direct access to the company databases, this is by far the ideal source from which to get your data. Not only are you guaranteed to get access to the most up to date data but loading from databases is generally more efficient than loading from files.

Connecting to Databases

Power Query supports connecting to a large variety of databases without the need to install any additional drivers. The connections available can be found in three separate areas in the Excel or Power BI user interfaces.

- Get Data → From Database
- Get Data → From Azure
- Get Data → From Other Sources

If you can't find the one you need, all hope is not lost. Providing you install the vendor's ODBC driver you should be able to connect to your database via the From Other Sources → ODBC connector.

Connecting to a Database

Since the experience for connecting to most databases is very similar, we are going to connect to a Microsoft Access database. This is a SQL database hosted on Microsoft's Azure web services, which means that no matter where in the world you are, you can connect and explore the data within it.

For this example, we'll connect to the AdventureWorks database, and analyze the total sales by year by region for their company.

> 🔧 In an effort to make sure you don't cause yourself issues when making your initial database connection, we highly recommend reading the steps below (up to the "Managing Connections" section) before attempting to make your connection.

To get started, you'll need to go through the following steps:

- Create a new query → From Azure → From Microsoft Azure SQL Database

Connect to the following database:

- Server: xlgdemos.database.windows.net
- Database: AdventureWorks

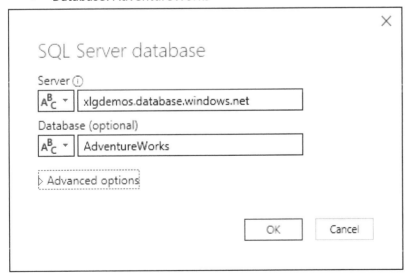

Connecting to the Azure database

> 👹 Buried under the Advanced Options section there is the ability to provide a custom SQL statement and other connector specific options. Avoid these unless you are a SQL ninja and can write deadly efficient code or you were provided explicit instructions to connect to the database by the database administrator.

At this point you will be prompted to enter the credentials in order to connect to the database. You'll notice that you have a few options here.

The default option is to use the Windows credentials that you used to log on to your computer. If you are working on a database that is within your organization and the IT department has allowed Windows authentication, this will most likely work for you. However, the best course of action is to always reach out to your IT team so they can give you all the server, database, and access level information that you need in order to connect to your data source.

You are also able, on the same tab, to provide an alternate set of Windows credentials. This is useful if you need to connect to the database using a different set of user credentials.

To connect to our database, however, you'll need to flip to the Database tab of the dialog, as we've used database security, not Windows security when creating our user ID's. On that tab you need to take 3 actions:

1. Choose Database Security
2. Enter the Username: `DataMaster`
3. Enter the Password: `D4t4M@ster!`

Once you have the credentials correctly as shown below, click the Connect button:

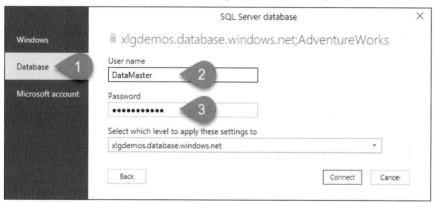

Connecting to the database using Database security credentials

> 🦋 The user credentials you used are cached in an encrypted file that resides within your local user settings. This means that the username and password do not (and cannot currently be set to) travel with the solution when it is emailed or even opened by another user. This is a security feature to ensure that each user actually has the proper credentials in order to access and refresh the data.

Managing Credentials

If you mistype the name of your connection, database, user ID or password, and need to modify them, you can do so by going through the following steps:

*   Excel: Data → Get Data → Data Source Settings
*   Power BI: Home → Transform Data → Data Source Settings

You'll be launched into the Data Source Settings box:

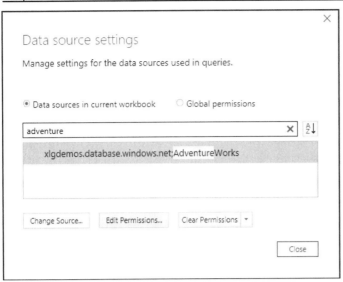

The Data Source Settings interface, filtered for the term "adventure"

While the current workbook (project) view contains only the sources in the current workbook, the Global Permissions view can become **very** crowded over time, so it's very handy that you can filter it by using the search pane. In the image above, we've filtered to find the term "adventure", as we know that it was part of the URL to the Azure database.

From here we have three options:

- **Change Source**. This option is helpful if we mistyped the URL and need to correct it or if we simply want to point our queries to a new database or server.
- **Edit Permissions**. This option allows us to change the username and password, as well as review or update the credentials type used to access the database.
- **Clear Permissions**. This is a good option if we want to remove the data source from our cached connections, forcing us to re-authenticate next time we connect to it. This is also a great option if we have messed up our initial connection and want to start over.

Clicking the Edit Permissions button will allow us to see the credentials type:

Data Source Settings for the Azure database

We can also trigger the window to update/replace the username and password by clicking the Edit button in the credentials section if needed.

Can't Connect to our Database?

We have specifically chosen to host our database on Windows Azure so that it is running as close to 100% uptime as possible, and have been doing so since we published the first version of this book. During this time we have received a number of support requests from users who were not able to connect to the database. The most frequent causes of these issues are – in this order:

- Forgetting to choose Database security credentials,
- Mis-typing the username or password,
- A corporate firewall or VPN that blocks access to our database.

> ⚒ Of course, you could assume that our database could also go offline as well. While this in entirely possible, since the first edition of M is for Data Monkey was published, every support request we have received was caused by one of the three issues listed above.

Should you run into a situation where your access to our database is blocked, we have also included a Microsoft Access version of the AdventureWorks database in the sample files. Instead of using the SQL Azure connector, just use the Access Database connector. You'll find that the experience is almost identical.

Using the Navigator

Once Power Query has connected to the database, you'll find yourself launched into the Navigator interface, which will allow you to select the table(s) that you'd like to connect to. In this case, we'd like to pull some data from the SalesOrders table. Since there are so many tables, let's use the search feature to narrow down the list:

- Enter salesorder into the search area
- Click on the SalesLT.SalesOrderHeader table

The preview pane will reach out to the database, and give us a glimpse into the data that is stored within that table.

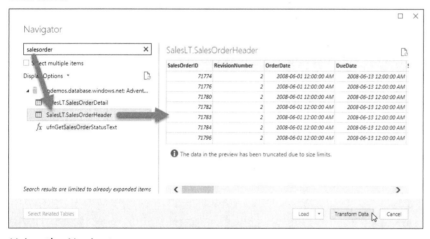

Using the Navigator

The data in here looks fairly useful, so let's click Transform Data and see what useful information we can glean from it.

Exploring the Data

The first thing you'll notice here is that there are two steps in the Applied Steps window: Source and Navigation. If you select the Source step, you'll see that it goes back to the raw schema of the database, allowing you to see what other tables, views and objects exist in the database. The Navigation step then drills into the table you selected.

The second thing you'll notice is that there is a **lot** of data here. Let's thin it down a bit. Select the following columns:

- OrderDate, SalesOrderNumber, SubTotal, TaxAmt, Freight, SalesLT.Customer and SalesLT. SalesOrderDetail
- Right-click one of the headers → Remove Other Columns

- Right-click the OrderDate column → Transform → Year
- Right-click the OrderDate column → Rename → Year
- Right-click the SalesOrderNumber column → Rename → Order#

The query is now a lot more compact and focused.

	1²₃ Year	AᵇC Order #	$ SubTotal	$ TaxAmt	$ Freight	SalesLT.Customer	SalesLT.SalesOrderDetail
1	2008	SO71774	880.35	70.43	22.01	Value	Table
2	2008	SO71776	78.81	6.30	1.97	Value	Table
3	2008	SO71780	38,418.69	3,073.50	960.47	Value	Table
4	2008	SO71782	39,785.33	3,182.83	994.63	Value	Table
5	2008	SO71783	83,858.43	6,708.67	2,096.46	Value	Table
6	2008	SO71784	108,561.83	8,684.95	2,714.05	Value	Table
7	2008	SO71796	57,634.63	4,610.77	1,440.87	Value	Table

Trimming down the SalesOrderHeader table

Most of the column headers make perfect sense, but there is something significant about the last two columns. Those columns aren't showing values from the SalesOrderHeader table, they are showing related values from other tables in the database!

This is one of the great things about connecting to databases: most databases support automatic relationship detection, allowing you to browse through the related records without having to set up a relationship yourself, or perform any merges at all. But why is SalesLT.Customer showing "Value", where SalesLT.SalesOrderDetail is showing "Table"?

If you were to examine the actual database structure, you'd find that the Customers table has a one-to-many relationship defined between the Customer and SalesOrderHeader tables. (While a customer may have many sales orders, each sales order can only have one customer.) The "Value" you see is actually a record from the Customer table that holds all of the related fields for that single Customer:

	1²₃ Year	AᵇC Order #	$ SubTotal	$ TaxAmt	$ Freight	SalesLT.Customer	SalesLT.SalesOrderDetail
1	2008	SO71774	880.35	70.43	22.01	Value	Table
2	2008	SO71776	78.81	6.30	1.97	Value	Table
3	2008	SO71780	38,418.69	3,073.5	960.47	Value	Table
4	2008	SO71782	39,785.33	3,182.83	994.63	Value	Table
5	2008	SO71783	83,858.43	6,708.67	2,096.46	Value	Table

CustomerID	29847
NameStyle	FALSE
Title	Mr.
FirstName	David
MiddleName	null

The SalesLT.Customer column contains the single related record for each order header

By contrast, if we preview the first Table of the SalesOrderDetail column, we can see that there are multiple order details for the given transaction:

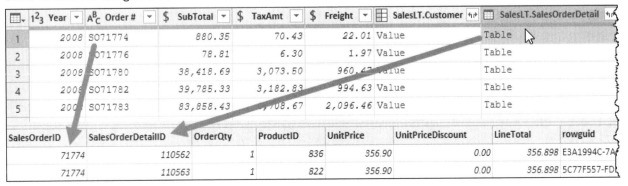

	1²₃ Year	AᵇC Order #	$ SubTotal	$ TaxAmt	$ Freight	SalesLT.Customer	SalesLT.SalesOrderDetail
1	2008	SO71774	880.35	70.43	22.01	Value	Table
2	2008	SO71776	78.81	6.30	1.97	Value	Table
3	2008	SO71780	38,418.69	3,073.50	960.47	Value	Table
4	2008	SO71782	39,785.33	3,182.83	994.63	Value	Table
5	2008	SO71783	83,858.43	708.67	2,096.46	Value	Table

SalesOrderID	SalesOrderDetailID	OrderQty	ProductID	UnitPrice	UnitPriceDiscount	LineTotal	rowguid
71774	110562	1	836	356.90	0.00	356.898	E3A1994C-7A
71774	110563	1	822	356.90	0.00	356.898	5C77F557-FD

Sales order 71774 has multiple line items representing different products

While the relationship between the SalesOrderHeader and SalesOrderDetail tables is also one-to-many, in this case the unique value is found on the SalesOrderHeader table that we connected to.

> 🔨 Why do you care about this? It allows you to use the relationships in the database to perform some basic joins between tables without using the Join techniques shown in Chapter 10.

Let's narrow down our data and do a bit more data cleanup:

- Select the SalesLT.SalesOrderDetail column → Delete it
- Click the double-headed arrow at the top right of the SalesLT.Customer column
- Choose to extract the SalesPerson (only) and click OK
- Right-click the SalesPerson column → Replace Values
- Replace "adventure-works\" with nothing

Your data will now look like this:

	123 Year	ABC Order #	$ SubTotal	$ TaxAmt	$ Freight	ABC SalesPerson
1	2008	SO71782	39,785.33	3,182.83	994.63	linda3
2	2008	SO71935	6,634.30	530.74	165.86	linda3
3	2008	SO71938	88,812.86	7,105.03	2,220.32	jae0
4	2008	SO71899	2,415.67	193.25	60.39	shu0
5	2008	SO71895	246.74	19.74	6.17	shu0
6	2008	SO71885	550.39	44.03	13.76	jae0
7	2008	SO71915	2,137.23	170.98	53.43	linda3

We just joined data from multiple tables without creating a Join!?!

> 🔨 While we only retrieved one related column from another table, we could certainly have done more, even drilling down into related tables of related tables!

It's now time to finalize this query and report on the data. As we are working with Excel, we will:

- Rename the query as "OrdersBySalesPerson"
- Select all columns → Transform → Detect Data Types
- Close & Load To → New Worksheet

With the data loaded we will build a quick PivotTable to summarize the data:

- Select a cell in the table → Insert → PivotTable
- Place the table on the same worksheet, starting in cell H2

And we will configure the PivotTable as follows:

- Rows: SalesPerson, Order #
- Values: SubTotal, Tax Amt, Freight
- Set each column to show in an Accounting style with no decimals or symbols

The result is a nice PivotTable that we can update at any time:

Row Labels ▾	Sum of SubTotal	Sum of TaxAmt	Sum of Freight
⊟ jae0	518,096.43	41,447.71	12,952.41
SO71776	78.81	6.30	1.97
SO71780	38,418.69	3,073.50	960.47
SO71784	108,561.83	8,684.95	2,714.05
SO71797	78,029.69	6,242.38	1,950.74
SO71831	2,016.34	161.31	50.41
SO71832	35,775.21	2,862.02	894.38
SO71846	2,453.76	196.30	61.34
SO71867	1,059.31	84.74	26.48
SO71885	550.39	44.03	13.76
SO71898	63,980.99	5,118.48	1,599.52
SO71917	40.90	3.27	1.02
SO71936	98,278.69	7,862.30	2,456.97
SO71938	88,812.86	7,105.03	2,220.32
SO71946	38.95	3.12	0.97
⊟ linda3	209,219.83	16,737.59	5,230.50
SO71774	880.35	70.43	22.01
SO71782	39,785.33	3,182.83	994.63
SO71783	83,858.42	6,708.67	2,096.46

The PivotTable created from a Windows Azure SQL Database

The beauty of this solution is that we could also add slicers, PivotCharts and other items to the worksheet to display the data as we wanted. But the best part is that with a simple Data → Refresh All, we can refresh the data from the online database at any time, updating the solution as needed.

Query Folding

One of the great features that databases offer is the ability to take advantage of query folding to optimize query performance. While the technology is built-in and will work by default for us when we build solutions using Power Query's user interface, we can also accidentally shut it down, causing our queries to be processed by Excel alone. To understand how to avoid this mistake, we need to understand what query folding is, and how it works at a rudimentary level.

What is Query Folding?

We don't really tend to always think about what is happening behind the scenes as we're clicking the various commands to select, filter, sort and group our data. As you're aware by now, each of these steps is recorded in the Applied Steps window, letting us build a sequential macro. What you may not be aware of, however, is that Power Query is also translating as many of those commands as it can into the native query language of our database (SQL) and sending those to the database.

What is even more amazing is that a server that has Query Folding capabilities will accept those individual queries, and then attempt to fold them into a more efficient query. The impact of this shows when issuing subsequent commands such as "Select all records in the table" followed by "Filter to exclude all departments except 150".

In layman's terms, instead of loading all 1,000,000 records, then filtering down to the 1,500 for that department, the server instead takes the queries to build a more efficient one that reads:

```
Select * From tblTransactions WHERE Dept = '150'
```

The impact of this is massive, as it saves the processing time to deal with 998,500 records.

While not all commands can be folded, a great many can, pushing the processing workload to the server.

So how do you know if it's working? Returning to the previous query, you'll notice that on the right-click menu for each step there is an option to "View Native Query". Shown here is the view for the "Removed Other Columns" step:

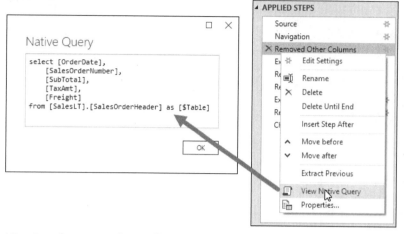

Viewing the query that will get sent to the SQL Database

Of course, this is relatively early in the transformations we performed, but we can see that query folding has continued all the way up to and including the Replaced Value step:

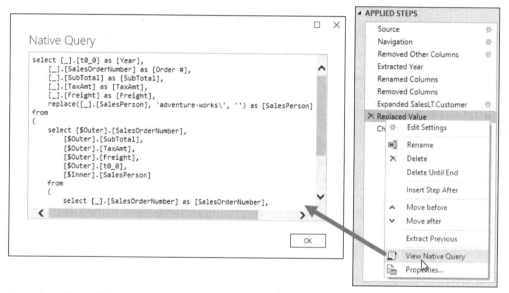

User interface driven steps are still being "folded" into a consolidated SQL statement...

As long as the View Native Query command is available, you can be assured that query folding is still taking place. But look at what happens on the Changed Type step:

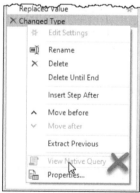

View Native Query is greyed out

At this point the View Native Query option is greyed out, indicating that this step might not be folded into a SQL Statement. When Power Query executes its refresh, it will retrieve the SQL statement from the previous step, then continue the rest of the remaining steps using local processor and RAM.

🐒 The absence of the View Native Query button might not always mean that a query step isn't folding but it is the only indicator that we currently have in the Excel and Power BI Desktop user interfaces.

👹 It is important to realize that – once you have broken query folding – no subsequent steps will fold. For this reason, you want to keep your query folding alive as long as possible!

One new feature that we cannot wait to see in Excel and Power BI Desktop is query folding indicators. The image below is taken from Power Query online, and shows query folding indicators next to steps in a (different) query which is targeting an Azure database:

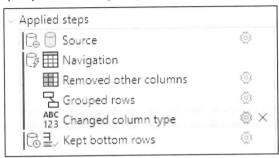

Upcoming query folding indicators

These indicators are much more discoverable than the current method of mousing over steps, and immediately show us that the Navigation through Changed column type steps are folding, but the Kept bottom rows step broke the query folding chain.

What Technologies Support Query Folding?

As the list of Power Query connectors is always growing, we can't really provide a comprehensive list of connectors that do or don't support query folding. Having said that, the one important thing to realize about query folding is that it is a technology that effectively offloads the processing to the data source, meaning that a compute engine is needed at the source for it to work. This is why you will most commonly see Query Folding working for databases which have both a storage and a compute engine. While it would be nice to have this functionality for TXT, CSV and Excel files, these do not contain a compute engine. As a general rule of thumb, "files won't fold". I.e. if you are connecting to a file, query folding will not be available. On the other hand, if you are connecting to a database, then query folding **may** be available.

One of the notable exceptions to the "files won't fold" rule is Microsoft Access. Access – despite being a file – does support query folding. Having said this, since the file is typically hosted on your local PC, the performance gains may not be as noticeable as folding against a full-blown database on a server.

You should also be aware that not all databases support query folding. If the database you are connecting to does not, then Power Query will just download the full set of data and perform the requested steps using its own engine to process them. Everything will still work – eventually – but it may be horribly inefficient.

It is also worth understanding that not all database connectors are created equal. One particularly problematic data connector is ODBC. While ODBC is absolutely great if you have no other option, an ODBC connector is essentially a "one size fits all" connector. This means that it has not been optimized for your specific data set and could break query folding very easily. Only ever use ODBC to connect to a database if there isn't a native (or custom) connector available and watch your query folding (via the View Native Query activity) very carefully.

Common Database/Query Folding Myths

Based on our experience, there seems to be some common confusion around efficiently pulling data from databases, as well as the query folding technology. Let's look at some of them:

Myth 1: The most efficient way to pull data from a database is to generate a single SQL query that does all the work in a single Power Query step.

It is actually deeply saddening to see this in practice in the real world, but it happens. In one case we saw a solution where the consultant had taken this approach, building a very complicated SQL statement, and hard coding it in the connector using the Advanced Options window. Did it work? Yes, in fact the query worked very quickly. Could the consultant write better more efficient SQL than Power Query? Almost certainly!

But then the client needed to modify it due to a change in business need. Of course, the reason the client hired the consultant was because they didn't have SQL knowledge. Based upon the consultant's advice, the client now has to either consume more billable hours or learn to modify the SQL themselves. (As it turns out, they spent several hours of their time to do the latter.)

Now, could the client just have made the modification to the logic via the user interface as a new step? Yes, but given that the query started with a custom SQL step, query folding was broken immediately, which could have had big performance impacts.

So, what if the consultant had built the query through the user interface to begin with? It would have taken the client a few minutes to make the needed change, and they could have got back to business as usual much more quickly.

Myth 2: A step that breaks query folding will always break query folding. Unfortunately (or maybe fortunately), things aren't as black and white as that. The reality is that Power Query is using an algorithm to generate the SQL code, and sometimes the order of the steps can lead Power Query to a place where it cannot create a valid SQL statement. In that case, query folding will obviously break.

When query folding breaks, don't give up immediately. Try changing the order of your steps to see if it has any effect. (To do this, right-click the applied step and choose Move Before or Move After.) There are occasions where the step order can get query folding to light up again.

Myth 3: Someone must maintain a super-secret list of what steps will fold? This is a really common misconception. Folks, we're sorry to tell you but no such list exists, and probably won't. Why? It is because the commands that will fold are dependent on the Power Query connector, as well as potentially the order of the steps being executed. The more you work with your own databases, you will start to understand which items break query folding in your configuration, but there isn't a master list that covers all scenarios.

Myth 4: Query folding doesn't persist through a chain of queries. This is just patently untrue. (If it were, it would cast some serious doubt on the query structuring we outlined in Chapter 2!) If you'd like to prove that query folding can persist across multiple queries, it is very easy to do so:

- Return to the example from this chapter (or open the Ch12 Examples\AdventureWorks-Complete file)
- Edit the query
- Right-click the Removed Other Columns step → Extract Previous
- Call the new query "Database"

You've now created a two step query chain that goes from Database to OrdersBySalesPerson. Go to the OrdersBySalesPerson and right-click the Replaced Value step. View Native Query is still available!

Myth 5: As long as I can connect, it doesn't matter what connector I use. This little myth just about killed one of our client's BI projects. Their IT department taught them to connect to their SQL database by using an ODBC connector, rather that Power Query's built-in SQL Server connector.

At first, all was great. The client connected to the database, immediately filtered to retrieve the ~1 million rows of data from the previous week and built the solution that answered all of their problems. They were loving Power Query and living the good life. But as time progressed, the solution got slower and slower to the point where it wouldn't even refresh in a full 8 hour workday.

The issue – as it turns out – was that the IT department taught the user to connect Power Query to the Microsoft SQL Server via an ODBC connector that they had installed and configured. The reason that this was such a huge issue is that this combination of technologies results in query folding breaking when you filter rows. It was a huge shock to us, as this seemed like a step that should definitely work, but with it – a refresh was downloading the entire multi-million row database into Excel's memory, then trying to reduce the data.

The solution? Repointing the query to use the SQL Database connector instead of ODBC. That's it. We changed the connector and left the rest of the query intact. Last we heard, the query was still refreshing in just a few minutes.

Data Privacy Levels

Depending on how far you are into your Power Query journey, you may have run across prompts to declare the Privacy Levels of your data source. So, what are they, and why do they matter? As it happens, these are very closely related to query folding and how it works.

A common misconception about query folding is that each native query that you can see gets sent to the database. This is not true, it is only the final valid native query that gets submitted. Having said that, each query sends two submissions to the database.

While this may not be technically perfect, you can look at the purpose of the first submission as sending any parameters to the database, as well as retrieving a preview that might drive current variables like "most recent date", "first customer name", etc... Power Query will then update, fold and compile its query, and send it to the database for retrieval.

The reason this is important to understand is that – depending on how you've built your query – it is possible that some of your data may be sent to the data source. This obviously can raise some concerns, as we don't want to accidentally leak sensitive data, particularly if it is going outside of our controlled network.

The Power Query team's answer to this concern was to provide the ability to declare the Privacy Level of each of your data sources as one of the following types:

- **Private**: A Private data source is completely isolated from other data sources. Contains sensitive or confidential information.
- **Organizational**: An Organizational data source is isolated from all Public data sources, but it is visible to other Organizational data sources.
- **Public**: A Public data source gives everyone visibility to the data contained in the data source.

In an ideal world, you'd mark all of your data sources correctly so that this system can protect you from sending crucial and sensitive information to a data source that should not know about it, accidentally leaking or exposing confidential data to a source you don't control.

The way the privacy levels work is – whenever you try to combine data sources – the privacy levels of each data source are checked for compatibility where:

- Public data can be *sent* to Public or Organizational sources.
- Organizational data can be *sent* to Organizational sources (but not Private or Public sources).
- Private data can't be sent anywhere (even to other Private sources).

In theory, if you have an Excel spreadsheet marked as Organizational, you would not be able to send data from the spreadsheet to a Public website. On the other hand, if your spreadsheet was marked as public, and you were sending it to a corporate database declared as organizational, that would be fine as data can be sent from a Public source to an Organizational source.

In practicality, working with privacy levels can be very challenging. And if you get it incorrect, you'll be hit with a frustrating message about the Formula.Firewall:

> ! Formula.Firewall: Query 'Events' (step 'Added Custom') is accessing
> data sources that have privacy levels which cannot be used together.
> Please rebuild this data combination.

There is nothing more frustrating than this error in Power Query

 We will explore Formula.Firewall errors in greater detail in Chapter 19.

Declaring Data Privacy Levels

Setting privacy levels isn't difficult. As soon as you need to do so, Power Query will prompt you:

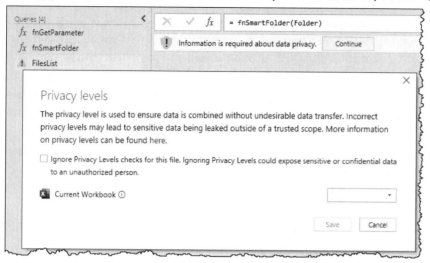

This query has been prompted to provide Privacy information

It is important to realize that Privacy settings aren't restricted to working with databases, either. It is a mechanism to protect you from accidentally leaking data between any data source. The image above is actually using a function to connect the FilesList query to SharePoint, which triggers the yellow prompt to declare the privacy levels. Clicking continue takes you to the dialog where you can set the privacy levels for each data source in the workbook.

> 🐵 When a workbook is opened, Power Query checks if the user has changed since the last save. If so, the privacy settings are discarded and need to be re-declared. If you are working in Excel and anticipate this becoming an issue for you, the following blog post provides a VBA based solution to at least remind the user what they need to do in order to fix the issue: `https://bit.ly/3cjNIhP`

Managing Data Privacy Levels

If you need to review or modify your data privacy levels, you can do this in the same location as managing the solution's credentials. As a reminder, you can find these settings via:

* Data Source Settings → Select your data source → Edit Permissions

At this point you have the ability to change the Privacy Level for your specific connection.

Managing the Privacy Level of the Azure database

Privacy vs Performance

While the goal of the privacy levels method is good (who wants to accidentally leak data?), the implementation can be very frustrating to work with. In the best-case scenario, the privacy engine has a serious impact on performance, and in the worst case, it leads to "Formula.Firewall" errors, preventing data from being combined at all.

Consider the following chart which displays the average of 5 refresh operations for two queries:

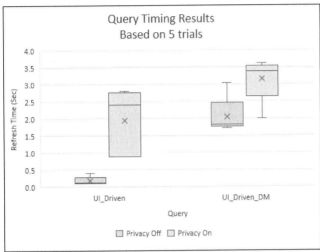

Comparing the refresh times of two Excel based queries

The important thing to realize about these queries is that they are both manipulating source data from Excel tables within the same workbook that stores the queries. In other words, there is absolutely no reason that we should need to check the privacy on these data sources when combining them, as the data all lives within the same file. If we were reaching out to combine this data with a database, then maybe we would need these checks. But with the data all coming from the same source, this is adding no value to us.

Despite this, you can see the results are fairly clear that refreshes with the privacy engine disabled are always faster, and sometimes significantly so.

> ✎ This performance chart was created in Excel using Ken's Monkey Tools add-in. Learn more about this add-in, and download a free trial at Ken's website:
> `https://xlguru.ca/monkeytools`

Disabling the Privacy Engine

Before disabling the privacy engine, it is important that you consider both the pros and cons of doing so:

Pros	Cons
Faster refreshes	Potential data leakage
Disables Formula.Firewall errors	May block scheduled Power BI refreshes

Pros and Cons of disabling Power Query's privacy engine

If you are combining with web-hosted or external data sources that your company doesn't control, you may be exposing your data to risk. In addition, if your intent is to publish your Power BI model and schedule the refresh, you are quite likely to find that the Power BI service will not let you override your privacy settings.

On the other hand, if you are building solutions that are 100% contained within your corporate network, disabling the privacy engine may yield a couple of pretty important benefits. The first is an easier time of developing solutions as you don't have to worry about the formula firewall (which we will discuss later in the book), and the second is a performance increase.

Privacy settings are controlled via the Query Options dialog which can be accessed via the following click-path:

- Excel: Data → Get Data → Query Options
- Power BI: File → Options & Settings → Options

You'll also find that there are two Privacy tabs within this interface: one in the "Global" area, and the other in the section for the Current Workbook/File. Let's look at the Global area first:

Reviewing the Global Privacy options in Excel

As you can see, there are 3 options here.

1. **Always combine data according to your Privacy Level settings for each source**. This will inherit the Privacy Level setting for each data source based on the level configured in the Credentials area.

2. **Combine data according to each file's Privacy Level settings.** This is the default setting, and what we would recommend you stick with.

3. **Always ignore Privacy Level settings.** This setting excites a lot of users, but we actually recommend that you don't select this option.

The reason we are not fans of the last option is that it sets you up to accidentally leak private data to a public source with no warning. (It's similar to turning off VBA macro security back in Excel 2003 and earlier to avoid being nagged. It works, but you leave yourself totally exposed.) We don't want to see anyone making career shortening moves just to get a bit better performance from Power Query.

Instead of turning off privacy at a global level, we advocate turning privacy off on a solution-by-solution basis as needed. This keeps your data protected and forces you to evaluate each data source before changing the setting. You can do this via the Privacy tab under the Current Workbook (File) area:

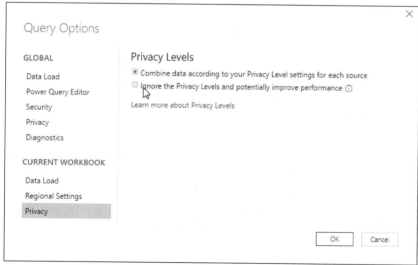

The correct place to suppress Privacy Levels

The first option in this window is the default behavior which will prompt you to declare Privacy Levels for all unspecified data sources. It will also enforce privacy checks when combining data (whether you feel you need them or not.)

The second option allows you to disable Privacy Levels for the specific solution and is the route that we would advocate you use when suppressing privacy levels.

Optimization

Power Query can be slow – particularly if you must leave your privacy checks enabled. It's an unfortunate fact, and one that Microsoft is keenly aware of and trying to improve on a constant basis. Given this, it is important that we have some strategies to try and maximize our performance where we can.

1. Never use an ODBC connector if there is a specific database connector available to you. You have a much higher likelihood of breaking query folding with an ODBC connector than you do a connector that is custom built (and optimized) for your data source.

2. Avoid providing a custom SQL statement when setting up your initial query. The only exception to this rule is if you are a SQL ninja and are confident that you can provide a more efficient query than the query folding steps can build for you. By providing a custom SQL statement, you immediately break the query folding capabilities for any subsequent steps, potentially hurting your long-term performance.

🐵 Query folding often breaks when executed against any line that contains a custom M or SQL statement. Even worse, it can stop any further query folding from taking place.

3. Push as much work to the database as possible. If the database supports Query Folding, this pushes the workload to the server, rather than being performed using Power Query on the local workstation. As databases are designed to process data efficiently, this will help with performance.

4. Do as much work as possible in your initial query design using the Power Query user interface commands, rather than reaching to custom M code. While it will be tempting to inject parameters dynamically to control filters, (especially after you learn how to use dynamic parameter tables later in this book), you should be aware that this will break the query folding capability.

🦮 Remember, Power Query was not built as a replacement for SQL Server Management Studio (SSMS) or any other tool that helps you manage your database. It was built as a tool to help self-service BI pros, who generally know very little – if any – SQL syntax, to extract, filter, sort, and manipulate data. Power Query's job is to build your SQL code for you.

Chapter 13 - Reshaping Tabular Data

One of the great things about Power Query is its ability to clean and reshape data from a non-tabular format into the tabular format that is used to drive data model and Excel tables. But sometimes data arrives in a tabular format that isn't conducive to our end goal, and it still needs to be reshaped. While you saw some of these techniques showcased in Chapter 7, this chapter will focus on patterns to help you perform some transformations that may be a bit daunting at the outset.

One of the biggest challenges we struggle with related to our data transformation patterns is actually naming them, as there aren't really defined search terms that we feel are consistent. Instead, we often name the patterns based on the tools they use to reshape them. For this reason, we have provided before and after images of the data patterns we are working with and the desired results. Our hope is that this will allow you to quickly scan the chapter and refer to the appropriate data recipe that you need at any given time.

Complex Pivoting Patterns

No matter the name or goal of these patterns, each of the patterns in this section involve leveraging Power Query's Pivot feature in order to unwind the data into the desired format.

Pivoting Stacked Data

The first data pattern we want to introduce is arguably one of the most important – not only because it is a common data shape that you'll see in the real world – but because this pattern is also used by other data transformations. We call this pattern Pivoting Stacked Data, and the goal of this pattern is to take a single column output and pivot it into a tabular format as shown here:

How would you reshape the data on the left into the table on the right?

Before we dive into this example however, we need to take a very careful look at this data to be transformed, as it has some key characteristics. While this is based on a download of credit card transactions, this pattern shows up in many different data sets. Look at the following sample very carefully:

The first few rows of our Stacked Data

Notice that – excepting the first row which appears to be a header – the data follows a very consistent pattern. It appears to be "Date", "Vendor", "Amount", <blank>. After that, the same pattern is evident for the second record, the third and so on. Ignoring the header, this is a consistent block of stacked records, where each record is four rows long, and this four-row pattern repeats throughout the entire data file.

🐵 That consistent repeating pattern is the key that we need in order to leverage the pattern we are about to see. While the pattern doesn't need to be four rows every time, it must be consistent from record to record. If there is even one record in the data set which contains a different number of rows, this pattern will not work.

Providing that you see this repeating pattern in your data, the recipe to unwind it into a tabular format can be summarized as follows:

Step 1: Add columns for transaction and line IDs

- Add Column → Index Column → From 0
- Select the Index column → Add Column → Standard → Integer-Divide → *the divisor*
- Select the Index column → Transform → Standard → Modulo → *the divisor*

Step 2: Pivot the data

- Select the Index column → Transform → Pivot Column
- Set the Values field to your data column
- Expand the Advanced options and choose "Don't Aggregate"

Step 3: Cleanup

- Right-click the Integer-Division column → Remove
- Rename the newly created columns
- Set your data types

🖊 Each step of this pattern can be consistently applied between data sets, but the divisor you will need depends on how many rows are in each record.

Let's walk through applying this pattern to a data set.

To begin, we will import our data set into a new workbook, then begin with Step 1 of the recipe:

- Create a new Query → From Text/CSV → Ch13 Examples\Stacked Data.txt
- Add Column → Index Column → From 0

This newly created Index column now provides us with a unique "file line ID" for each line in the file.

The next two steps of this process involve performing a bit of math on the values of the Index column. We don't plan on covering a full math lesson here, but for those of us who haven't done long division since the early days of our elementary school careers, it may be helpful to translate long division terms into the terms used by Power Query:

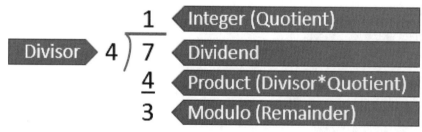

Remember long division? Those values each have (sometimes more than) one name!

We are actually going to calculate both an Integer and a Modulo in our recipe. The Dividend is pretty easy to get – it is the value in the Index column, but that leaves us missing one crucial piece: the Divisor. Using the appropriate divisor is the secret to making this whole recipe work, so it is critically important that we get it correct.

The value we need to use for our divisor is the value from the newly added Index column, which represents the first row of the second record in the data set. In this case, our divisor is equal to 4:

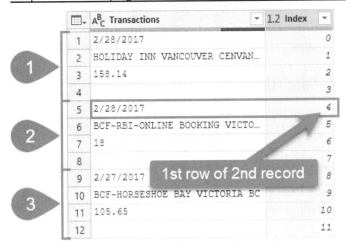

Determining the first row of the second record

> 🐵 It is critically important to retrieve this value from the Index column, and not to pick up the base 1 row number displayed on the left side of the preview window, as the pattern we are about to use requires performing its mathematics against a base 0 value. This also means that it is important to always start your Index column from 0 for this recipe, as opposed to starting from 1.

Armed with our divisor, we can now complete Step 1 of the recipe:

- Select the Index column → **Add Column** → Standard → Integer-Divide → 4
- Select the Index column → **Transform** → Standard → Modulo → 4

If you have followed these steps correctly, the data should now look like this:

	Transactions	Index	Integer-Division
1	2/28/2017	0	0
2	HOLIDAY INN VANCOUVER CENVAN…	1	0
3	158.14	2	0
4		3	0
5	2/28/2017	0	1
6	BCF-RBI-ONLINE BOOKING VICTO…	1	1
7	18	2	1
8		3	1
9	2/27/2017	0	2
10	BCF-HORSESHOE BAY VICTORIA BC	1	2
11	105.65	2	2
12		3	2

Successful application of Step 1 of the Pivoting Stacked Data recipe

Notice how the Integer-Division column now contains 0 for each of the first four rows, increments to 1 for the next four rows and continues this pattern? The column returns the integer from the long division pattern and represents the Record ID for each record in the data set.

We also modified the Index column to return the modulo from the long division pattern. The net effect of this is that we no longer display the file's Line ID, but rather the Line ID of each individual record. These values will always range from 0 to one less than the divisor you used for the Modulo calculation. The key thing to recognize about them is that – in our case – 0 lines up with a Date, 1 lines up with the Vendor, 2 with the Amount, and 3 with the blank value.

Now that our data is ready, we can move to step 2:

- Select the Index column → Transform → Pivot Column
- Set the Values field to Transactions
- Expand the Advanced options and choose "Don't Aggregate"

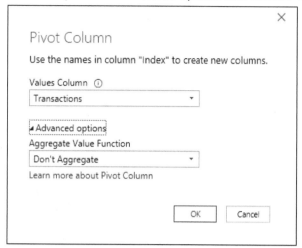

Pivoting our data

The view, once you click OK is nothing short of magic:

	1²₃ Integer-Division	Aᴮc 0	Aᴮc 1	Aᴮc 2	Aᴮc 3
1	0	2/28/2017	HOLIDAY INN VANCOUVER CENVAN...	158.14	
2	1	2/28/2017	BCF-RBI-ONLINE BOOKING VICTO...	18	
3	2	2/27/2017	BCF-HORSESHOE BAY VICTORIA BC	105.65	
4	3	2/25/2017	WESTIN GRAND HOTEL VANCOUVER...	117	
5	4	2/23/2017	ORIGINAL JOES RESTAURANT VAN...	57.96	
6	5	2/22/2017	JOEY BENTALL ONE VANCOUVER BC	185.93	
7	6	2/21/2017	SUTTON PLACE HOTEL VAN VANCO...	458.96	
8	7	2/20/2017	SPICY & FINE INDIAN CUISIVAN...	27.72	

Just... wow!

If you look carefully, you can see where all of the pieces went:

- The Index column (our record line IDs) are in the column headers,
- The Integer-Division column (our record IDs) are in the first column, and
- The Transactions data points are nicely distributed in a matrix format.

How cool is that? The only thing left to do is move on to Step 3 and clean up the data set:

- Remove the Integer-Division Column
- Remove any other columns that you no longer require (we will remove '3')
- Rename the columns appropriately (Date, Vendor, Amount)
- Set your data types (in our case, we will set the date column using Locale since the format is in US English)

Once complete, our data looks perfect:

	Date ▼	A B C Vendor ▼	$ Amount ▼
1	2017-02-28	HOLIDAY INN VANCOUVER CENVAN...	158.14
2	2017-02-28	BCF-RBI-ONLINE BOOKING VICTO...	18.00
3	2017-02-27	BCF-HORSESHOE BAY VICTORIA BC	105.65
4	2017-02-25	WESTIN GRAND HOTEL VANCOUVER...	117.00
5	2017-02-23	ORIGINAL JOES RESTAURANT VAN...	57.96
6	2017-02-22	JOEY BENTALL ONE VANCOUVER BC	185.93
7	2017-02-21	SUTTON PLACE HOTEL VAN VANCO...	458.96

Our data is perfectly transformed

This has to be one of our favorite data patterns that we demonstrate. Partly because it looks so magical, but partly because it is super useful in other patterns. As soon as you recognize a consistent repeating pattern, your data may be a candidate to use the Pivoting Stacked Data recipe.

Before we leave this, however, there are a couple of points that we should mention:

- If your first record contains the headers for your data set, you'll be able to promote those immediately after pivoting. We didn't have that luxury here, since the headers weren't included.
- This data set contained a repeating set of blank rows. Many users are tempted to filter these out of the data set before running the pivot operation. While this may work, it can potentially have consequences if one of the valid data points contains a blank. (For example, assume that one of the vendor names was blank.) Should this happen, you will end up removing a critical line, shifting the pattern and causing it to return incorrectly assigned values after the pivot. For this reason, we recommend that you remove blanks AFTER the pivot operation.

Pivoting Vertically Stacked Sets

The next technique we are going to look at is the concept of vertically stacked sets of data. In the case of the data sample below – like our previous example – we still have blocks of multiple records stacked upon each other. Unlike the previous example however, this time each set has multiple columns in each layer:

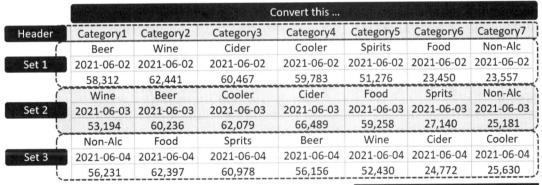

	Convert this ...						
Header	Category1	Category2	Category3	Category4	Category5	Category6	Category7
	Beer	Wine	Cider	Cooler	Spirits	Food	Non-Alc
Set 1	2021-06-02	2021-06-02	2021-06-02	2021-06-02	2021-06-02	2021-06-02	2021-06-02
	58,312	62,441	60,467	59,783	51,276	23,450	23,557
	Wine	Beer	Cooler	Cider	Food	Sprits	Non-Alc
Set 2	2021-06-03	2021-06-03	2021-06-03	2021-06-03	2021-06-03	2021-06-03	2021-06-03
	53,194	60,236	62,079	66,489	59,258	27,140	25,181
	Non-Alc	Food	Sprits	Beer	Wine	Cider	Cooler
Set 3	2021-06-04	2021-06-04	2021-06-04	2021-06-04	2021-06-04	2021-06-04	2021-06-04
	56,231	62,397	60,978	56,156	52,430	24,772	25,630

... to this ...		
Category	Date	Amount
Beer	2021-06-02	58312
Wine	2021-06-03	53194
Non-Alc	2021-06-04	56231
Wine	2021-06-02	62441
Beer	2021-06-03	60236
Food	2021-06-04	62397

Vertically stacked sets of records

Let's see how we can unwind a multi-column stacked set of data:

- Open (or connect to) the Ch13 Examples\Vertical Sets – Begin.xlsx workbook
- Create a new Query against the (blue) Data table

There are a variety of ways to accomplish this goal, but for now we are going to stick to a method that we can do by clicking user interface buttons. The secret in this one is all about the very first three steps:

- Go to Transform → Transpose
- Add an Index Column from 0
- Right-click the Index column → Unpivot Other Columns

The result of these transformations looks like this:

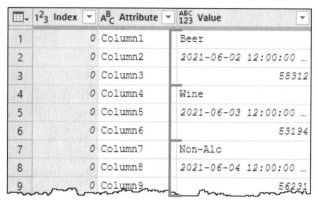

Something interesting is going on in that Value column…

The big trick here was transposing the data before unpivoting it. The result yields a single column of stacked values – something that we already know how to deal with. Let's bust out the previously demonstrated Pivoting Stacked Data pattern to finish this off:

- Right-click [Value] → Remove Other Columns
- Add Column → Index Column → From 0
- Select the Index column → Add Column → Standard → Integer-Divide → *3*
- Select the Index column → Transform → Standard → Modulo → *3*
- Select the Index column → Transform → Pivot Column
- Set the Values field to **Value** and set the Advanced option to Don't Aggregate
- Right-click the Integer-Division column → Remove
- Rename the columns so they are named "Category", "Date" and "Amount"
- Set the data types to Text, Date and Whole Number

> 🥿 The divisor we used for this example was 3. While not pictured here, this value represents the number of rows in each block of records and can be found after adding the Index number from 0. (Remember it is the first row of the second record.)

At this point your data is ready to be loaded and analyzed:

	ABC Category	Date	123 Amount
1	Beer	2021-06-02	58312
2	Wine	2021-06-03	53194
3	Non-Alc	2021-06-04	56231
4	Wine	2021-06-02	62441
5	Beer	2021-06-03	60236
6	Food	2021-06-04	62397
7	Cider	2021-06-02	60467
8	Cooler	2021-06-03	62079
9	Sprits	2021-06-04	60978
10	Cooler	2021-06-02	59783

The results of unpivoting our data set

The trick with Power Query, as you apply different data transformations, is to recognize key characteristics of other patterns you might use. Any time you see this stacking of records within a single column, your solution is only a few steps away.

Pivoting Horizontally Stacked Sets

Now what if the data is stacked horizontally instead of vertically? Something like this:

Convert this ...								
Course	Title	Date	Instructor	Date	Instructor	Date	Instructor
Intro to Excel	Beginner	01-Jan	Joe Blogs	01-Feb	Mark Lanu	25-Feb	Mary Smith
Pivot Table Magic	Intermediate	15-Jan	John Doe	28-Jan	Joe Blogs	25-Feb	Ann Alyst
Mastering Power Pivot	Expert	03-Jan	Mark Lanu				
Row IDs		Set 1		Set 2		Set 3	

... to this ...			
Course	Title	Date	Instructor
Intro to Excel	Beginner	01-Jan	Joe Blogs
Intro to Excel	Beginner	01-Feb	Mark Lanu
Intro to Excel	Beginner	25-Feb	Mary Smith
Pivot Table Magic	Intermediate	15-Jan	John Doe

How do we pivot horizontally stacked sets?

🖎 To be fair, this is a pretty horrible data format that doesn't even meet normalization rules. If you tried to add a table style to the original data in Excel, it would modify your column headers to Date, Date1, Date2, etc... as each column must have a unique name in a table. The same issue would be present if you pulled the data into Power Query and promoted the first row to headers.

This particular recipe is summarized here, but has some different steps depending on the shape of your original data set.

Step 1: Prepare the data
- Pull the data set into Power Query (avoid promoting the header row if possible)
- Does your data have Row ID columns(s)?
  - Yes: Select the Row ID column(s) → right-click → Unpivot Other Columns
  - No: Select all column(s) → right-click → Unpivot Columns
- Remove the Attribute column

Step 2: Run the Pivoting Stacked Data recipe, aggregating the **[Value]** column

Step 3: Cleanup
- If your "header" rows were promoted to Headers
  - Rename the numeric columns appropriately
- If your "header" rows were left in your data (not promoted to headers) originally
- Promote the first row to Headers
  - Remove top rows → the same divisor used for the Pivoting Stacked Data recipe
  - Perform any remaining cleanup required

🖎 If you memorize one Power Query recipe pattern, the Pivoting Stacked Data pattern is a good one to choose!

Let's see this recipe in action, beginning with Step 1. In a new workbook or Power BI file:
- Create a new Query → From Text/CSV → Ch13 Examples\CourseSchedule.csv
- Delete the Changed Type and Promoted Headers steps
- Select the first 2 columns (our Row ID columns) → right-click → Unpivot Other Columns

- Select the Attribute column → press DEL

At this point, the data should now look as follows:

	ABC Column1	ABC Column2	ABC Value
1	Course	Title	Date
2	Course	Title	Instructor
3	Course	Title	Date
4	Course	Title	Instructor
5	Course	Title	Date
6	Course	Title	Instructor
7	Intro to Excel	Beginner	01-Jan
8	Intro to Excel	Beginner	Joe Blogs
9	Intro to Excel	Beginner	01-Feb
10	Intro to Excel	Beginner	Mark Lanu
11	Intro to Excel	Beginner	25-Feb

Step 1 of pivoting horizontally stacked sets – with the headers nested in the data

With the data correctly prepared, we can move on to Step 2 of the recipe, which will use a ***divisor*** value of 2:

- Add Column → Index Column → From 0
- Select the Index column → Add Column → Standard → Integer-Divide → *2*
- Select the Index column → Transform → Standard → Modulo → *2*
- Select the Index column → Transform → Pivot Column
- Set the Values field to **Value** and set the Advanced option to Don't Aggregate
- Right-click the Integer-Division column → Remove

At this stage, the data should now look as shown here:

	ABC Column1	ABC Column2	ABC 0	ABC 1
1	Course	Title	Date	Instructor
2	Course	Title	Date	Instructor
3	Course	Title	Date	Instructor
4	Intro to Excel	Beginner	01-Jan	Joe Blogs
5	Intro to Excel	Beginner	01-Feb	Mark Lanu
6	Intro to Excel	Beginner	25-Feb	Mary Smith
7	Mastering Power Pivot	Expert	03-Jan	Mark Lanu
8	Mastering Power Pivot	Expert		
9	Mastering Power Pivot	Expert		

Our data has now been successfully pivoted

We are now at Step 3 of the recipe – the cleanup stage. This is where we will promote the headers and perform any other data cleanup. But before we continue, it is worth reviewing a choice that we made when importing our data.

When we imported the data, we specifically deleted the Changed Type and Promoted Headers steps that would have promoted the header rows on the table. Had we left those, we would still have our two columns (0 and 1) at this point, but the first data row would contain the Intro to Excel course, not the Course header. (Those headers would have been pivoted into the attribute column which we deleted at the end of Step 1.) What this means is that – had we left the headers promoted – we would have to rename columns 0 and 1 manually. It is not a huge issue, but something you should be aware of.

Since we removed the Promoted Headers step, the headers remained in our data, giving rise to the three rows of headers that we now see in our data. Since we did this, we can follow this branch of the recipe to automatically promote our headers at this point:

- Home → Use First Row as Headers → Use Headers as First Row

- Home → Remove Rows → Remove Top Rows → 2

🔦 The great thing about this recipe is that it uses the same value as the divisor of the Pivoting Stacked Data recipe, so you only need to work out one value for the entire pattern.

No matter whether you manually renamed the columns or used the branch of the recipe that we illustrated, the data should now appear as follows:

	Course	Title	Date	Instructor
1	Intro to Excel	Beginner	01-Jan	Joe Blogs
2	Intro to Excel	Beginner	01-Feb	Mark Lanu
3	Intro to Excel	Beginner	25-Feb	Mary Smith
4	Mastering Power Pivot	Expert	03-Jan	Mark Lanu
5	Mastering Power Pivot	Expert		
6	Mastering Power Pivot	Expert		
7	Pivot Table Magic	Intermediate	15-Jan	John Doe
8	Pivot Table Magic	Intermediate	28-Jan	Joe Blogs
9	Pivot Table Magic	Intermediate	25-Feb	Ann Alyst

Our data reshaping is almost done!

The final steps to complete this cleanup are to filter the blanks out of the Date column, set your data types, rename the query and load it to our intended destination. And the beauty of it is... even if someone expands the data source to add more sets to it, they will automatically be picked up in a refresh!

🔦 Depending on the data source being imported, you may not see the two blank rows shown in the image above. In this case, Power Query interpreted the blank records as empty text strings, so preserves them during the Pivot operation. If the values were interpreted as *null* during the initial import, they would have been suppressed during the Pivot operation.

The steps of the example illustrated in this chapter are saved in the "HeadersInData" query contained in the Ch13 Examples\Horizontal Sets – Complete file. For completeness, we have also included a "HeadersPromoted" query that shows the version of the recipe if the headers were promoted during Step 1.

Complex Unpivoting Patterns

Each of the previous examples of unpivoting illustrated in this book have been relatively simple as they have each only had one level of headings. In this section we will look at something more complex; pivoting data with multiple levels of headings. We will start by first looking at the method, and then adding some complexity to make the operation run more efficiently.

Unpivoting Subcategorized Data Overview

When we refer to subcategorized data, we are referring to any data set that has multiple heading rows, as shown in the image below:

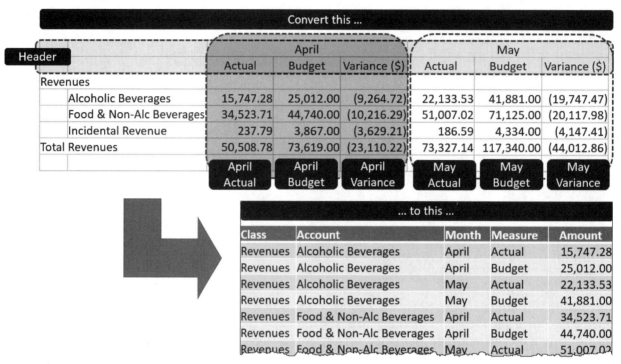

Data with multiple header rows per column

The tricky part about this data set is that Power Query only supports one header row. Not only do we have two header rows in this data set, but we also somehow need to assign the values of April and May to three columns each in the next row.

The recipe we are providing for unpivoting subcategorized data will work with any number of subheadings, and follows a numbered set of steps as outlined here:

1. Demote the headers into the data (if required)
2. Transpose the dataset
3. Fill up/down columns where needed
4. Merge the original "headers" with a delimiter (see note below)
5. Transpose the data (back to original form)
6. For columns where row 1 shows only the delimiter, replace values with text to be used as column headers
7. Promote row 1 to headers
8. Perform any other cleanup that can be done before unpivoting
9. Unpivot columns
10. Split the **Attribute** column by the delimiter used above
11. Perform any final data cleanup

> 🔧 The most important part of this pattern to remember is to use a delimiter that does not exist in your data set.

Let's dive in to working with this pattern, connecting to an Excel file called "Financial Statement.xlsx". In a new workbook or Power BI file:

- Create a new Query → (Excel) Workbook → Ch13 Examples\Financial Statement.xlsx
- Select the Pivoted worksheet → Transform Data

At this point it is a good idea to pause and look very carefully at your data:

UnPivot Data With Sub Categories	Column2	Column3	Column4	Column5	Column6	Column7
1	null	null	null	null	null	null	null
2	null	null April	null	null May	null
3	null	null Actual	Budget	Variance ($) Actual	Budget	null
4 Revenues	null	null	null	null	null	null
5	null Alcoholic Bev...	15747.28	25012	(9264.72)	22133.53	41881
6	null Food & Non-Al...	34523.71	44740	(10216.29)	51007.02	71125
7	null Incidental Re...	237.79	3867	(3629.21)	186.59	4334
8 Total Revenues	null	50508.78	73619	(23110.22)	73327.14	117341
9	null	null	null	null	null	null
10 Expenses	null	null	null	null	null	null
11	null Cost of Sales	21977.81	24296	2318.19	23442.63	40289

Stopping for a quick check before unpivoting our subcategorized data

Step 1 of the recipe is all about reviewing your data to ensure that every header row of your data set is in the data preview area, not in the column headers (and taking action to correct this issue if necessary.) Power Query is famous for automatically promoting headers. While this is normally a great feature, it is an absolute killer here. Why? Because during the recipe execution we will lose the column headers.

In the case of a fresh import from Excel, Power Query automatically promoted the first row to headers here, resulting in the first column being named "UnPivot Data with Sub Categories" instead of Column1. This truly isn't a big deal, but why let Power Query promote the header at all?

To clean this up we are going to:

- Delete the automatically generated Changed Type and Promoted Headers steps
- Go to Home → Remove Rows → Remove Top Rows → 2

This removes the two blank rows that existed at the top of the data set, but leaves our first header in the first row where we need it, and the subsequent header row(s) immediately below:

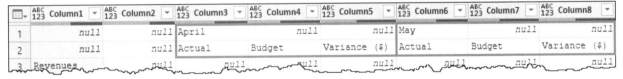

Column1	Column2	Column3	Column4	Column5	Column6	Column7	Column8
1	null	null April	null	null May	null	null
2	null	null Actual	Budget	Variance ($) Actual	Budget	Variance ($)
3 Revenues	null	null	null	null	null	null

Now we can see our header rows (and issues)

> 🔧 If you are working with a data set that includes headers as part of the schema, Power Query will inherit the column names without the need to promote the header row. Should this happen to you and you need to "Demote" the headers into the data, you can do so by going to Home → Use First Row as Headers → Use Headers as First Row.

The header format you see here is extremely common with subcategorized data. Whether the cells were originally merged, centered across selected Excel cells or just entered above the "Actual" header, they will all take this form: the data point followed by *null* values as you look across the data set.

Ultimately, what we need to do here is fill the April and May values across into those *null* cells, then merge rows 1 and 2 together. If we could do that, then we would be able to promote the merged rows to act as a header which we could then unpivot. It sounds easy – except that Power Query has no ability to fill across, and merging can only be done across columns, not rows. So how do we do it? We continue with Step 2 of the recipe!

Step 2: We now need to transpose the data:

- Go to Data → Transform → Transpose

The results are that our data is rotated 90 degrees, effectively meaning that every row has become a column and every column has become a row:

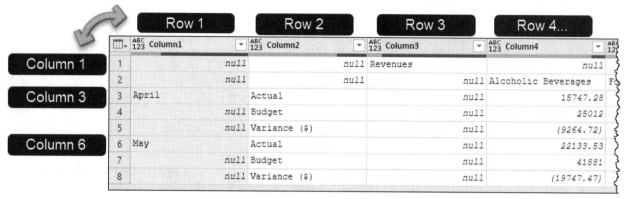

Transposing data rotates rows into columns and vice versa

This might seem a bit odd, but it actually gives us the flexibility to do what we couldn't when the data was in the original form: build a single header row. Let's continue…

Step 3: We need April to be placed into rows 3 through 5 of Column1, and May to be placed in rows 6 through 8. As it turns out this is *super* easy to do in Power Query:

- Right-click Column1 → Fill → Down

This will fill the values April and May into the *null* cells below, yielding the following result:

	ABC 123 Column1	ABC 123 Column2	AB 12
1	null	null	R
2	null	null	
3	April	Actual	
4	April	Budget	
5	April	Variance ($)	
6	May	Actual	
7	May	Budget	
8	May	Variance ($)	

April and May on the correct rows with 2 clicks!

> ✎ The Fill command can be used to fill up or down, but only works when filling into *null* values. If your cell appears blank, you'll need to replace (nothing) with the keyword *null* before running the Fill command.

Step 4: We now need to merge the original "headers" with a delimiter, but not just any delimiter will do. It is critically important that you pick a character (or series of characters) that does not occur naturally in the data set. The reason is that we are going to look for this delimiter later, and don't want to trigger a false positive with it.

A great character to use as a delimiter is often the | (pipe) character, which can be found by typing SHIFT + \ on your keyboard as this character seldom appears in normal data. On the other hand, if it does, either choose another character, or build a pattern that you know won't appear naturally. (We have often used something like -||- in the past if the pipe character was used.)

Let's merge our headers into a single column now:

- Select Column1 and Column2 → Transform → Merge Columns
- Use a Custom delimiter → | → OK

As you can see, we have a new column called "Merged" which combines the data points, separating them with our custom delimiter. And for any cells that remained as *null* value prior to merging them, only the delimiter is present:

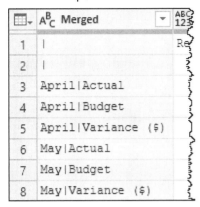

This is exactly what we need

We've managed to make a great candidate for a header row. Let's run the next two steps of the pattern:

Step 5: Transpose the data back to its original form:

- Go to Transform → Transpose

Step 6: To finalize the header row, we can now review row 1 of the data set. For any column where row 1 contains only our delimiter, we will replace the delimiter with an accurate column name. In the case of the example:

- Right-click Column 1 → Replace Values → replace the **|** with **Class**
- Right-click Column 2 → Replace Values → replace the **|** with **Category**

The results of Steps 1 through 6 of this recipe are a perfect header row *which remains in the data table*:

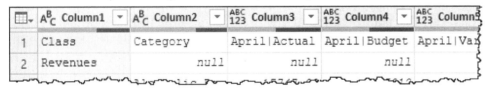

Won't row 1 make beautiful headers?

By virtue of using a delimiter that doesn't occur naturally in the data set, we have the ability to fill any headers which were originally undefined. And where we originally had two rows of detail to be combined into a single header we can see that Column3 now contains a single value for April|Actual, compared to the single April|Budget in Column4.

Things are shaping up well for us to run the recipe from step 7 through the final step:

Step 7: Promote row 1 to headers:

- Go to Home → Use First Row as Headers

Step 8: This step is reserved for general data cleanup prior to unpivoting the columns. Each data will have different requirements here depending on what it looks like. For this sample we need to fill the Class values into *null* values, as well as filter out the Totals and Subtotals that don't belong in a normalized data set:

- Right-click the Class column → Fill → Down
- Filter the Category column → uncheck *null*

As you can see, our data is fairly clean at this point, and finally ready to be unpivoted:

	A^B_C Class	A^B_C Category	⋎ 1.2 April|Actual	1.2 April|Budget	1.2 Ap
1	Revenues	Alcoholic Beverages	15747.28	25012	
2	Revenues	Food & Non-Alc Bever...	34523.71	44740	
3	Revenues	Incidental Revenue	237.79	3867	
4	Expenses	Cost of Sales	21977.81	24296	
5	Expenses	Labour & Benefits	35166.6	45327.25	
6	Expenses	Other Operational	10830.99	13210	

With header rows in place and a nice clean table, we're ready to unpivot

Step 9: It is finally time to unpivot the data:

- Select the Class and Category columns → right-click → Unpivot Other Columns

The results of the unpivot operation are shown here:

	A^B_C Class	A^B_C Category	A^B_C Attribute	1.2 Value
1	Revenues	Alcoholic Beverages	April|Actual	15747.28
2	Revenues	Alcoholic Beverages	April|Budget	25012
3	Revenues	Alcoholic Beverages	April|Variance ($)	(9264.72)
4	Revenues	Alcoholic Beverages	May|Actual	22133.53
5	Revenues	Alcoholic Beverages	May|Budget	41881
6	Revenues	Alcoholic Beverages	May|Variance ($)	(19747.47)
7	Revenues	Food & Non-Alc Bever...	April|Actual	34523.71

The Unpivoted data set still isn't properly normalized...

The important thing to realize here is that our headings and subheadings are still all contained within a single column. But that's not really an issue, as each is separated by a delimiter that doesn't occur anywhere else in our data set...

Step 10: Split the **Attribute** column by the delimiter used above:

- Right-click the Attribute column → Split Column → by Delimiter → | → at Each occurrence

The results are a pretty nice looking data set:

	A^B_C Class	A^B_C Category	A^B_C Attribute.1	A^B_C Attribute.2	1.2 Value
1	Revenues	Alcoholic Beverages	April	Actual	15747.28
2	Revenues	Alcoholic Beverages	April	Budget	25012
3	Revenues	Alcoholic Beverages	April	Variance ($)	(9264.72)
4	Revenues	Alcoholic Beverages	May	Actual	22133.53
5	Revenues	Alcoholic Beverages	May	Budget	41881
6	Revenues	Alcoholic Beverages	May	Variance ($)	(19747.47)
7	Revenues	Food & Non-Alc Bever...	April	Actual	34523.71

All done except for the cleanup!

Before we perform the final data cleanup, we want to call out something very important here. In the step above, we explicitly mention to split your data *at each occurrence of the delimiter* (one of the options on the Split By dialog). This is not an accident. Because you chose a character (or series of characters) that doesn't exist elsewhere in the data set, this allows you to split this column into as many levels as needed. In other words, this pattern will work for 2 levels of headings, or 20 levels of headings. (Although we hope you never have 20 levels of subcategorized data!)

Step 11: Perform any final data cleanup

The last step is all about performing the final data cleanup and loading it to your intended destination. For this example, we suggest:

- Renaming the Attribute.1 column → Month
- Renaming the Attribute.2 column → Measure
- Setting the data types

Optionally – if you have the skills to rebuild them using a PivotTable or DAX formula, you could also filter out the Variance $ items from the (newly named) Measure column.

Unpivoting Subcategorized Data Efficiently

Now that you know how the Unpivoting Subcategorized data pattern works, we need to talk about performance.

With small data sets, the pattern we outlined earlier works very well. If you are working with large datasets, however, you may encounter a couple of issues:

- Execution is very slow, and/or
- After transposing you only see a few rows (sometimes only 1 row) of data

While the first issue is more punishing to the end consumer, the second can be brutal for the developer. After all, how do you know if you should fill down if you can't see the values? (Rest assured that the recipe will still work when executed, it's just really hard to build.)

The reason these problems can occur are two-fold:

1. Power Query much prefers long and narrow tables (fewer columns) than short but wide tables, and
2. Transposing data is a computationally expensive operation that has to be done twice during this recipe.

Despite these considerations, not all is lost. The recipe still works, we just need to break things up a bit, and make sure that we are transposing as little data as possible when we need to do it. Assume for a second that you have 3 levels of headings, but 1 million rows. Rather than transpose 1 million rows into columns and back, we want to work with only the 3 rows that matter. That will be much faster, as Power Query has much less work to do.

In order to do this, we break the recipe down into four distinct queries, which turns out to be much faster than doing it all in one. If you anticipate that performance is going to be an issue, you can deal with this during the initial design. If not, you can always retrofit an existing query to follow this query structure:

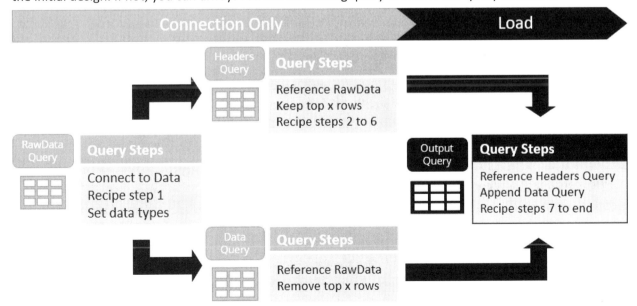

Overview of how to unpivot large datasets

If you recall, the original recipe steps were all numbered. The reason is that those step numbers tie directly into the image above and dictate which items are to be done where.

> ✎ If you do decide to create this query structure from scratch in Excel, we highly recommend that you choose to load your queries as connection only when you first commit them, then change the load destination of the Output query to a Table or the Data Model (as required.) If you skip that step, you run the risk of loading all four tables to separate worksheets, which causes your entire data set to load twice!

Retrofitting an Unpivoted Subcategorized Data Query

At this point, we are going to take the example we created previously and retrofit it so that it will perform better for large data sets.

> ✎ Should you need it, the completed query from the previous step is contained with the Ch13 Examples\Unpivoting Subcategories – Catchup file.

The first thing we will do is split out our Raw Data query. As this query is intended to follow the recipe up to and including Step 1, we will:

- Edit the Unpivoted query
- Right-click the Transposed Table step → Extract Previous
- Name the new query Raw Data

> ✎ The Extract Previous commands always extracts the commands previous to the step that you have selected. As we wanted to extract all items up to the end of Step 1, we select the first step in Step 2, which was Transposing the Table.

If you select the Raw Data query, you'll see that it now contains the data set with the header rows nested in the data.

Before we move on, let's create a duplicate of the Unpivoted query. This will allow us to keep the original query around (for review later), but will also allow us to build the more efficient version.

- Go to the Queries Pane (left side) → right-click Unpivoted → Duplicate
- Rename the "Unpivoted (2)" query as "Output"

Now, let's extract the portion that creates our header row. Make sure you are in the Output query and:

- Select and right-click the Promoted Headers step (this was Step 7) → Extract Previous
- Name the new query Headers
- Select the Headers query in the Queries Pane

So far, we have split the queries, but the Headers query is still transposing all of the data. We need to fix that.

- Select the Source step
- Go to Home → Keep Rows → Keep Top Rows → 2

The number is obviously dependent on your data set here. As we had two rows of headings, we used 2. If you step through the query at this point you'll see that it still performs steps 2 through 6 of the recipe, resulting in a single header row at the end:

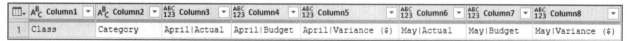

Column1	Column2	Column3	Column4	Column5	Column6	Column7	Column8
1 Class	Category	April|Actual	April|Budget	April|Variance ($)	May|Actual	May|Budget	May|Variance ($)

Our Headers query now contains a single header row

At this point – if you were to return to the Output query – you would see that it consists of properly named headers, but no data rows at all. This is to be expected, as we just removed all of the data. We need to get that back:

- Return to the Queries Pane → right-click the Raw Data query → Reference
- Rename this query to be "Data"

Make sure that the Data query is selected and...

- Go to Home → Remove Rows → Remove Top Rows → 2

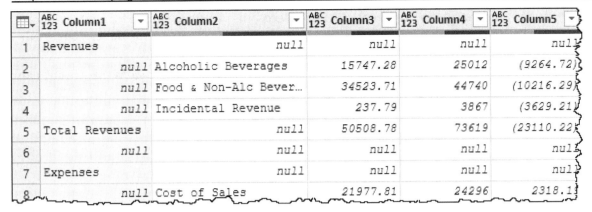

Column1	Column2	Column3	Column4	Column5
1	Revenues	null	null	null	null
2	null	Alcoholic Beverages	15747.28	25012	(9264.72)
3	null	Food & Non-Alc Bever…	34523.71	44740	(10216.29)
4	null	Incidental Revenue	237.79	3867	(3629.21)
5	Total Revenues	null	50508.78	73619	(23110.22)
6	null	null	null	null	null
7	Expenses	null	null	null	null
8	null	Cost of Sales	21977.81	24296	2318.1

Look ma, no headers!

Honestly, that's it for the Data query, but there are things to keep in mind here:

1. The number of rows to remove is always equal to the number of rows you kept for the Header query, and,

2. You want to ensure that this query loads as a connection only, or you will be waiting for it to load all of your data in addition to the Output query!

We now have all the pieces to put the solution back together. To do that:

- Select the Output query
- Select the Source step → Home → Append Queries → Data

🔪 Make sure you choose to Append Queries, not Append Queries as New here as this needs to be done within the Output query.

At the end of this process, we have split a single query into four distinct queries, but we have improved the performance of the overall solution. Despite this, the overall recipe works the same as for smaller data sets.

Keeping nulls During an Unpivot Operation

Another unpivot 'feature' that can cause you issues is the way that the unpivot operation deals with *null* values. Consider the following example where the analyst right-clicked the Product column and chose to "Unpivot Other Columns":

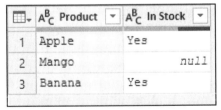

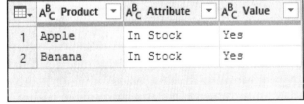

Has anyone seen my Mango?

In 99% of cases, we're more than happy for an unpivot operation to suppress the *null* records, but what if this is one of those cases where we actually do need to keep these records in our data set?

As it turns out, there is a recipe for that:

- Select columns with *null* values to unpivot
- Optional: Convert the column to a Text data type
- Right-click the column → Replace Values → Replace *null* with a ***placeholder value***
- Unpivot the column(s)
- Right-click the Value column → Replace Values → Replace ***placeholder value*** with *null*
- Rename the Attribute and Value columns
- Optional: Convert the Value column back to its original data type

Overall, the recipe is fairly easy with the exception of one piece... the value you choose for your placeholder value is restricted by the column's data type. This is not a problem for text based data, but can be for other data types, potentially leading to compromised data in certain situations.

Assume that we want to preserve our null values in the sample we provided above. Steps that we could use would be:

- Right-click the In Stock column → replace values → replace *null* with |
- Right-click the Product column → Unpivot Other Columns
- Right-click the Attribute column → replace values → replace | with *null*
- Rename the Attribute and Value columns as Status and Result

🔪 Each of the examples in this section are saved in the Ch13 Examples\Preserving Nulls – Complete file for your review.

As you can see, this simple recipe works very well to keep our Mango record in our data set after the unpivot operation:

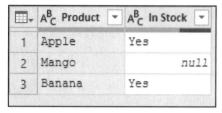

There's my Mango!

Like when unpivoting subcategorized data, the secret here is to pick a placeholder value that never occurs elsewhere in your data set. In this way we can run a replace operation without fear of accidentally compromising valid data.

Unfortunately, this can present a problem when confronted with non-text data as you are restricted to replacing your values with a data point that fits within the data type. In other words, if you have a column of whole numbers, the placeholder value must also be numeric. Why is this an issue? Assume that we have a different data set where sales have been defined with a numeric data type. People will commonly choose to replace a *null* with 0, as they are effectively the same. But look what happens when there actually is a 0 value in the data set:

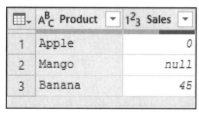

Aren't Apples supposed to be 0?

The challenge we have here is that 0 and *null*, while similar, are not the same thing. The 0 indicates a specific value has occurred, where *null* indicates the absence of a value. For this reason, replacing 0 with *null* at the end of the recipe actually compromises the data.

🔪 While it may seem strange, a sale of 0 units can occur via a positive sale followed by a negative sale (refund), yielding a net value of 0. Alternately, if we were tracking revenue, it is entirely possible to have a sale at $0 if we gifted it to a customer.

To be fair, you may very well want to skip the last replacement and leave both Apple and Mango with 0 values – after all neither actually had any quantity of sales. But what if it is important to actually record the 0 and *null* values as individual items like this?

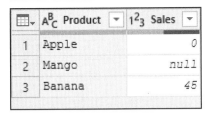

Keeping nulls during an unpivot of numeric columns

The output above is factually accurate based on the original data without compromising the original values. It was accomplished via the following steps:

- Change the type of the Sales column → Text
- Right-click the Sales column → replace values → replace *null* with |
- Right-click the Product column → Unpivot Other Columns
- Right-click the Attribute column → replace values → replace | with *null*
- Change the type of the Value column → Decimal Number
- Rename the Attribute and Value columns as Measure and Unit

⚓ This technique of converting to a Text based column will work for any non-text data type including numeric, date or other data types.

Advanced Grouping Techniques

In the example of grouping provided in Chapter 7, we showed how to use Power Query to group a basic data set. In this chapter we are going to look at a specific grouping aggregation operation called "All Rows". This aggregation is a bit mysterious at first, but once you see it in action, you'll realize it has incredible power.

Each of the examples in this section will begin with a fresh import of the following data from the Ch13 Examples\BeerSales.txt text file which contains the following raw data:

Class	Item	Sales
Lager	Member Lager	1,710
Lager	Bavarian Lager	958
Lager	Honey Brown Lager	951
Lager	Dark Lager	557
Ale	Winter Ale	557
Ale	Member Pale Ale	100
Ale	Pale Ale	96
Stout	Stout	96
Ale	Cream Ale	94

Raw data to be used for each of the advanced grouping techniques

Generating % of Total

To demonstrate the power of grouping, we will start by using Power Query to add a % of Total calculation to each of the rows in our data set. To do this, open a new workbook and:

- Create a new Query → From Text/CSV → Ch13 Examples\BeerSales.txt → Transform Data
- Go to Transform → Group By → Advanced

In order to work out the % of Total Sales we are going to need two things: the Total Sales for the data set as well as the individual row items.

To configure the grouping option correctly, we are going to need to do three things:

1. Mouse over the Class column → click the ... that appears → Delete
2. Configure the first column as Total Sales → Sum → Sales
3. Add a new column called "Data" which uses the All Rows operation

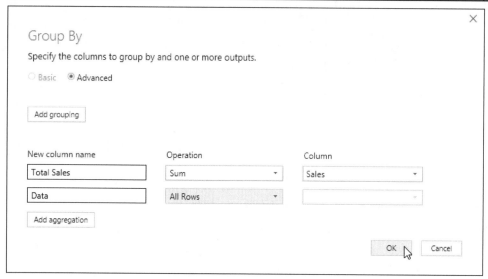

Generating Total Sales for the data set

This seems a bit strange at first, as we don't seem to be grouping by anything, and we've added this odd "All Rows" operation which doesn't even let us choose a column. By removing all of the grouping columns we should end up with a single value that reflects the sum of all values in the column(s) we choose to aggregate, rather than getting totals broken down by classes or sales items. With regards to the All Rows aggregation... its magic becomes evident upon clicking OK:

Total Sales (grouped by nothing) and a table which still contains our original data!

The All Rows aggregation is amazing; it preserves the original rows used to return the grouped value(s) in a Table. How cool is that? This means that not only can we calculate the Total Sales easily, but we can now expand the Table to get the original data rows back.

- Click the Expand arrow → uncheck the Column prefix option → OK

Getting our % of Total Sales is now as simple as dividing the Sales by the Total Sales:

- Select the Sales column → Add Column → Standard → Divide
- Change the Value dropdown to "Use values in a column" → Total Sales
- Rename the column as % of Total Sales

After following the above steps, you'll now have a column with the decimal values as shown below. All that is left is loading it to the destination and formatting them to show correctly:

	1.2 Total Sales	A_C^B Class	A_C^B Item	1.2 Sales	1.2 % of Total Sales
1	5119	Lager	Member Lager	1710	0.334049619
2	5119	Lager	Bavarian Lager	958	0.187145927
3	5119	Lager	Honey Brown Lager	951	0.185778472
4	5119	Lager	Dark Lager	557	0.108810315
5	5119	Ale	Winter Ale	557	0.108810315
6	5119	Ale	Member Pale Ale	100	0.019535065
7	5119	Ale	Pale Ale	96	0.018753663
8	5119	Stout	Stout	96	0.018753663
9	5119	Ale	Cream Ale	94	0.018362962

% of Total Sales generated via grouping

> ✎ It is worth noting that – in many cases – it is preferable to generate % of Total calculations using PivotTables or DAX measures, but Power Query gives you the ability to do it at a source data level if needed.

Ranking Data

There are many different ways to rank data, and grouping plays into most of them. We will illustrate this by ranking the previous data set using three different methods: ordinal ranking, standard competition ranking and dense ranking. To follow along, open a new workbook and:

- Create a new Query → From Text/CSV → Ch13 Examples\BeerSales.txt → Transform Data
- Select the Class column and delete it (as it is not needed for this example)

> ✎ Alternately – if you completed the following example you can edit your % of Sales query, select the Grouped Rows step and extract the previous steps into a new query called "Raw Data – Beer Sales". Once done, right-click the new query and choose Reference to create a new query to use for this example and remove the Class column.

We are going to start by creating a basic ranking where we rank the sales items in order from highest to lowest sales. Should we encounter two items with the same sales however, we want to sort the sales items in alphabetical order. This is called an Ordinal rank and it is accomplished via the following steps:

- Filter the Sales column → Sort Descending
- Filter the Item column → Sort Ascending (to order ties)
- Go to Add Column → Index Column → From 1
- Rename the Index column as Rank-Ordinal

As you can see, creating an Ordinal rank is fairly simple, and yields the results we expect:

	A_C^B Item	1²_3 Sales	1²_3 Rank-Ordinal
1	Member Lager	1710	1
2	Bavarian Lager	958	2
3	Honey Brown Lager	951	3
4	Dark Lager	557	4
5	Winter Ale	557	5
6	Member Pale Ale	100	6
7	Pale Ale	96	7
8	Stout	96	8
9	Cream Ale	94	9

Ordinal ranking where ties are broken via sorting

The important thing to realize about an Ordinal rank is that each item in the data set acquires a unique value. It makes no effort to break ties, with the ranks being assigned entirely on the sorted order of the data.

But what if we want to rank via what is called the Standard Competition Ranking method? In this method tied values are each ranked with the earliest tied rank, leaving gaps in the ranking numbers AFTER sets of equal-ranking items.

To accomplish a Standard Competition Rank, we must first create the Ordinal Rank illustrated above, but then we add some grouping steps:

- Select the "Fact" column (in this case Sales) → Transform → Group By → Advanced
- We now need to configure two aggregations:
- Rank-Std Comp which uses the Min operation on the Rank-Ordinal column
- Data which uses the All Rows operation
- Click OK

These steps help expose the next awesome power of the All Rows aggregation. Since the value created by the operation is a table, it means that it doesn't always contain a single row of data, but rather all rows that made up the grouped result. In addition, it also allows us to preview the results of the aggregation to ensure that it is correct.

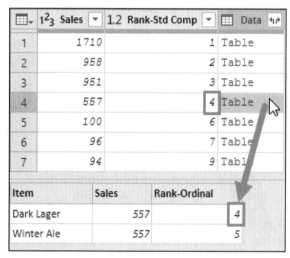

Verifying that our new rank is the Minimum value from grouped data

As we can see, two records tied with a value of 557, and we have indeed extracted the lowest numeric rank from those two records. The important part to realize here is that the new sales value (100), only had a single record in its grouped values, where the lowest rank was 6.

Let's extract these tables so that they inherit the primitive values displayed in the first two columns:

- Click the arrows at the top of the Data column
- Uncheck the preview option
- Expand only the Item and Rank-Ordinal columns (since we already have Sales displayed)

Your result set will now look as shown here:

⊞▾	1²₃ Sales ▾	1.2 Rank-Std Comp ▾	Aᴮ𝒸 Item ▾	1.2 Rank-Ordinal ▾
1	1710	1	Member Lager	1
2	958	2	Bavarian Lager	2
3	951	3	Honey Brown Lager	3
4	557	4	Dark Lager	4
5	557	4	Winter Ale	5
6	100	6	Member Pale Ale	6
7	96	7	Pale Ale	7
8	96	7	Stout	8
9	94	9	Cream Ale	9

Creating a Standard Competition Rank via Power Query

Notice how our first tied values are both ranked in 4th position, the next record is ranked in 6th, and the next two tied values are ranked in 7th position.

While there are other ranking methods that exist, there is one more that we would like to demonstrate: Dense ranking. The difference between Standard Competition and Dense ranking is that the Dense ranking doesn't skip the value after a tie.

Unlike Standard Competition ranking, Dense ranking doesn't require an Ordinal rank to be created, or data to be sorted at all. The recipe to perform a Dense rank is:

- Select the "Fact" column (in this case Sales) → Transform → Group By → Advanced
- Configure the aggregation to return a Data column which uses the All Rows operation
- Add an Index Column → From 1 and rename it as "Rank"
- Expand all columns except the "Fact" column from the Data column

Rather than recreate our example from scratch, we are going to just modify our existing example to add a Dense rank. This requires adding a new Index column *before* we expand the Data column:

- Select the Grouped Rows step
- Go to Add Column → Index Column → From 1
- Rename the column as "Rank-Dense"

   ✎ The main difference between the Standard Competition and Dense ranking methods is that – with the Standard Competition rank – the Index column is added before the grouping takes place, where the Dense rank adds it after the grouping is already done.

- Select the Expanded Data step

In the following image we have reordered the data to show the ranks in the order we created each. We have also highlighted the tied values, as well as the differences between the ranking values from one column to the next:

Item	Sales	Rank-Ordinal	Rank-Std Comp	Rank-Dense
1 Member Lager	1710	1	1	1
2 Bavarian Lager	958	2	2	2
3 Honey Brown Lager	951	3	3	3
4 Dark Lager	557	4	4	4
5 Winter Ale	557	5	4	4
6 Member Pale Ale	100	6	6	5
7 Pale Ale	96	7	7	6
8 Stout	96	8	7	6
9 Cream Ale	94	9	9	7

Comparing the 3 illustrated ranking methods

As you can see, the values vary slightly but they follow the goals that we outlined and in the case of the latter two ranking methods, were quite easy to accomplish via advanced grouping techniques.

Numbering Grouped Rows (aka Row Number with Partition)

For our final example in this chapter, we want to add an Ordinal rank to our Beer Sales data set, but with a twist. We want it to reset at each grouping level as shown in the image below:

	Class	Item	Sales	Group Rank
Group 1	Ale	Winter Ale	557	1
	Ale	Member Pale Ale	100	2
	Ale	Pale Ale	96	3
	Ale	Cream Ale	94	4
Group 2	Lager	Member Lager	1,710	1
	Lager	Bavarian Lager	958	2
	Lager	Honey Brown Lager	951	3
	Lager	Dark Lager	557	4
Group 3	Stout	Stout	96	1

Our goal is to add an Ordinal rank to each group of data

As you've probably already guessed, this will require grouping the data, but how would we add a ranking *within* one of the grouped tables?

To begin with, we are going to start against a fresh connection to the data source. Depending on whether you have been following along with the example you can either:

- Create a new Query → From Text/CSV → Ch13 Examples\BeerSales.txt → Transform Data
- Reference the Raw Data – Beer Sales query (if you created it in the previous example)

Once we have our connection to the data, we will start by preparing our data, then grouping it based on the "Class" column as this is the column which contains the values we wish to group by.

- Filter the Class column → Sort Ascending
- Filter the Sales column → Sort Descending
- Filter the Item column → Sort Ascending (to order ties)

- Select the Class column → Transform → Group by
- Configure the dialog to create a Data column using the All Rows operation → OK

At this point, you should have three rows of data with a column of table values containing the details of all rows used for each group:

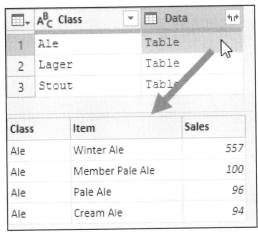

Reviewing the rows related to the Ale group

We're set up nicely so far, but now we want to number those rows within each table. The challenge is that there isn't a way to do this via the user interface – which means that we need to write a little formula to make this work. That formula is based on this pattern:

```
=Table.AddIndexColumn([Data], "<name for your column>", 1, 1)
```

🔦 You will learn all the mechanics of how this works as you move through the next few chapters, but for now rest assured that this is a pattern. So long as you called your "All Rows" column "Data", the only thing you need to change in this formula is the <name for your column>.

Let's put this into practice, with the intent of creating a new column called Group Rank:

- Go to Add Column → Custom Column
- Enter the formula below:

```
=Table.AddIndexColumn([Data], "Group Rank", 1, 1)
```

- Click OK (don't worry about changing the column name)

The result is a new column (called Custom) which contains a series of table values. Unlike the tables in the Data column (created by our grouping), these tables have a new Index column called "Group Rank" which acts as an ordinal rank for each row of each table:

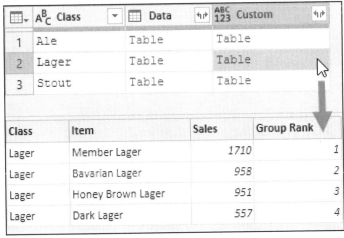

This table contains an Ordinal rank column which resets at 1 for each group!

✎ Let's just pause to recognize two very important things: Not only have we managed to accomplish the goal, but we have also seen that not everything can be accomplished through Power Query's user interface. Treat this as a bit of a sneak peek as to why learning about Power Query formulas and the M language can be very useful.

It's time to finish this example. As the Class used to perform the grouping was part of our original data set, the tables inside our Custom column contain not only the new Group Rank column, but also every piece of information we need to return to the end-user. That means that we only really need the Custom column (and the data within its tables.)

- Right-click the Custom column → Remove Other Columns
- Click the arrow to expand the Custom column → uncheck the prefix option → OK
- Select all the columns → Transform → Detect Data Types

	Class	Item	Sales	Group Rank
1	Ale	Winter Ale	557	1
2	Ale	Member Pale Ale	100	2
3	Ale	Pale Ale	96	3
4	Ale	Cream Ale	94	4
5	Lager	Member Lager	1710	1
6	Lager	Bavarian Lager	958	2
7	Lager	Honey Brown Lager	951	3
8	Lager	Dark Lager	557	4
9	Stout	Stout	96	1

Our rows are now properly sorted and numbered within each group

All that is left is to name your query and load it to your intended destination.

Chapter 14 - Conditional Logic in Power Query

As you build more solutions using Power Query, you're bound to come across scenarios where you need to perform some kind of logic in a column. In this chapter we will explore not only Power Query's Conditional Logic wizard – which allows you to easily build conditional logic rules – but also how to create the rules manually, allowing for the creation of even more complex rules.

Conditional Logic Basics

For this example we are going to look at the issues that present when importing the timesheet contained in Ch14 Examples\Timesheet.txt.

Data Set Background

This particular file has some challenges we are going to face when trying to normalize the data as shown below:

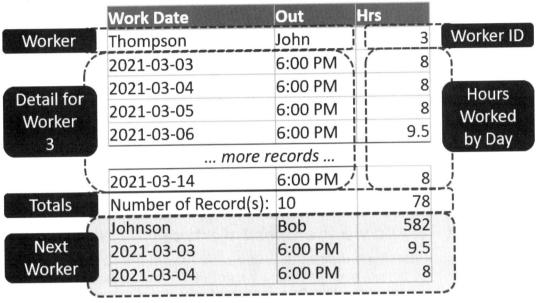

Decoding the structure of our Timesheet file

There is a lot going on here, but the key things to recognize are as follows:

- Each record starts with a header row where the worker's full name is spread across two columns, followed by a numeric Worker ID number. Unfortunately, we have no idea what the lower boundary of the Worker ID may be and – for all we know – Worker 1 may be part of the data set at some point.
- The detail rows for each worker could range between one and fourteen rows, depending on how many days the worker is scheduled during any given two-week period.
- The record ends with a Totals row that lists the number of records and total hours.

The challenge we have is that we need to normalize the data set into the following format:

Work Date	Out	Hrs	Worker
2021-03-03	6:00:00 PM	8.0	John, Thompson
2021-03-04	6:00:00 PM	8.0	John, Thompson
2021-03-05	6:00:00 PM	8.0	John, Thompson
2021-03-06	6:00:00 PM	9.5	John, Thompson

We are after this normalized data format

The challenge we have on our hands is that we need to get the Worker associated correctly with each of their individual rows. But the really tricky part is that there isn't really an easy data point to target to extract this information… we can't rely on a value from the Hrs column, as the numeric Worker ID can easily fall within a range of valid hours. We can't rely on the number of records, as that could vary from employee to employee within the same period. So how do we approach this task?

Connecting to the Data

The first step is to connect to the data to see how it looks in Power Query, as this may give us some ideas as to how to proceed. In a new workbook or Power BI file:

- Create a new query → From File → From Text → Ch14 Examples\Timesheet.txt
- Go to Home → Remove Rows → Remove Top Rows → 4
- Transform → Use Top Row as Headers

Also, to allow us to re-use this data for the next two examples, let's set this up as a staging query so that we can easily return to it:

- Rename the query as "Raw Data – Timesheet"
- Load the query as a Connection Only
- Right-click the query in the Queries pane → Reference
- Rename the new query as "Basics"

We should now have our raw data (and problem) exposed to us:

	A^B_C Work Date	A^B_C Out	1.2 Hrs
1	Thompson	John	3
2	2021-03-03	6:00 PM	8
3	2021-03-04	6:00 PM	8
4	2021-03-05	6:00 PM	8
5	2021-03-06	6:00 PM	9.5
6	2021-03-07	3:30 PM	6.5

John Thompson split across the "Work Date" and "Out" columns

Creating Conditional Logic via the User Interface

Successfully cleaning up misshaped data often takes some experimentation. So let's begin with what we know: we want a column that contains the worker name in a "last name, first name" format. We can accomplish that with a simple merge. We also know that the Work Date and Out columns should be date and time data typed. Let's take those steps now

- Select the Work Date and Out columns → Add Column → Merge Columns
- Leave the column name as Merged and use a custom separator of ", " (comma space)
- Change the data type of the Work Date column to Date
- Change the data type of the Out column to Time

The results at this point will look like this:

	Work Date	Out	1.2 Hrs	A^B_C Merged
1	Error	Error	3	Thompson, John
2	2021-03-03	6:00:00 PM	8	2021-03-03, 6:00 PM
3	2021-03-04	6:00:00 PM	8	2021-03-04, 6:00 PM
4	2021-03-05	6:00:00 PM	8	2021-03-05, 6:00 PM
5	2021-03-06	6:00:00 PM	9.5	2021-03-06, 6:00 PM
6	2021-03-07	3:30:00 PM	6.5	2021-03-07, 3:30 PM

Are we going in the right direction here?

At this point things may look very wrong, after all we have triggered data type errors and – while we do have our worker name in the correct format – the worker name is contained in a column with a bunch of other data. As it turns out, we did all of this deliberately.

🔨 Think back to Chapter 3 where we explored data types – specifically the section on errors being caused by invalid type conversions. That is exactly what happened here. By setting the Work Date column to a Date data type, we asked Power Query to convert "Thompson" to date data type. Plainly that isn't going to work, so it caused an error. The same is true of converting "John" to a Time data type.

The reason we did this is to get an entry point for our conditional logic. Due to the mixture of data within the Hrs column (Worker ID, actual hours and totals), we had no ability to write a reliable rule to figure out which line contained the worker ID. But one thing we can work on is based around the data type of the records. Basically, what we are doing here is deliberately causing an error to determine which values in the Work Date and Out columns are date or time based vs text based.

Now to be fair, no one wants to look at errors. Let's clean them up:

- Right-click the Work Date column → Replace Errors → null
- Right-click the Out column → Replace Errors → null

And at this point, we actually have something we can target for a conditional logic rule:

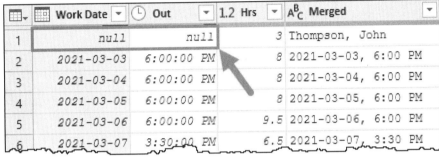

We have effectively moved our Worker to a new column and replaced them with null values

We are now able to take advantage of Power Query's Conditional Logic wizard:

- Go to Add Column → Conditional Logic
- Configure a new column called Worker using the following rule:

    If the **Work Date** column = *null* **then** the **Merged** column **else** *null*

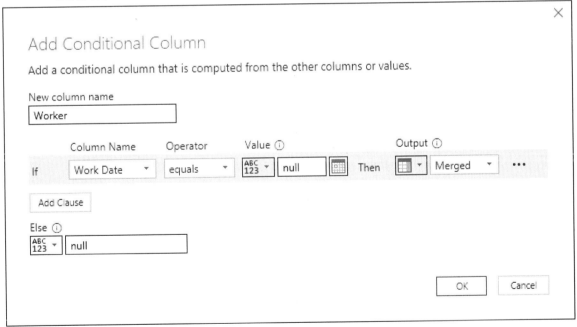

Configuring our Conditional Column

The tricky part of this configuration is that you'll need to change the drop-down for the Output section from the default selection (Enter a value) to Select a column before you can choose the Merged column.

🪶 While we can target a value of *null* in these rules, we cannot target an error. This is why we replaced the error values with *null* prior to creating our rule.

Upon clicking OK, we will now have a nice new column with our Worker names:

	Work Date	Out	1.2 Hrs	Merged	Worker
1	null	null	3	Thompson, John	Thompson, John
2	2021-03-03	6:00:00 PM	8	2021-03-03, 6:00 PM	null
3	2021-03-04	6:00:00 PM	8	2021-03-04, 6:00 PM	null
4	2021-03-05	6:00:00 PM	8	2021-03-05, 6:00 PM	null
5	2021-03-06	6:00:00 PM	9.5	2021-03-06, 6:00 PM	null
6	2021-03-07	3:30:00 PM	6.5	2021-03-07, 3:30 PM	null

Our Worker column now shows the worker name(s) followed by null values…

This is perfect. Our data cleanup is almost complete; we just need to replace each of the null values with the correct worker name:

- Right-click the Worker column → Fill → Down
- Filter the Work Date column → uncheck *null* values
- Remove the Merged column
- Change the Worker column to a Text data type

The result is a nice clean data set that will work upon refresh even when the dates and number of workers change:

	Work Date	Out	1.2 Hrs	Worker
1	2021-03-03	6:00:00 PM	8	Thompson, John
2	2021-03-04	6:00:00 PM	8	Thompson, John
3	2021-03-05	6:00:00 PM	8	Thompson, John
4	2021-03-06	6:00:00 PM	9.5	Thompson, John
5	2021-03-07	3:30:00 PM	6.5	Thompson, John
6	2021-03-10	6:00:00 PM	8	Thompson, John
18	2021-03-10	6:00:00 PM	6	Johnson, Bob
19	2021-03-11	6:00:00 PM	8	Johnson, Bob
20	2021-03-12	6:00:00 PM	8	Johnson, Bob

Complex data cleanup driven completely via the user interface

> ✎ As we proceed through this chapter we will look at additional options and methods to approach conditional logic. The key thing to remember is that there is often a user interface driven method to accomplish your goals if you dig hard enough to find it.

Creating Manual IF() Tests

While the Conditional Column dialog is fantastic, it does have one shortcoming: the output choice is limited to hard-coded text values, the results of a column or very simple formulas. If you want your output to use a formula, you are better off creating your conditional logic via a Custom Column. The challenge here however, is that the IF() formula doesn't use the same syntax as is used by Excel or DAX formulas.

Consider, for example, that we wanted to take our previous query and split the hours into regular versus overtime hours, where anything over 8 hours in a day is considered overtime. We could certainly do it via the following steps:

- Create a conditional column called **Reg Hours** column using the rule

      if [Hrs] > 8 then 8 else [Hrs]

- Subtract the new **Reg Hours** column from the **Hrs** to return the **OT Hours** column

This would take two steps but would work perfectly. But what if your requirements actually had no use for the Reg Hours column? In other words, what if you only cared about the OT Hours portion?

Ideally, you'd like to use the conditional column dialog to build a formula like this:

```
if [Hrs] > 8 then [Hrs] - 8 else 0
```

Since the various fields only seem to accept hard-coded values or column names, this doesn't appear to be possible via the conditional column dialog. And even if it were, would you want to write your conditional logic rules in such a tiny area? The good news is that we can write these rules, the bad news is that we actually have to write our complex logic manually via a custom column.

> ✎ In truth, you can perform complex logic in some of the conditional column fields. You just have to preface the formula with an operator and get the syntax exactly correct with no help. I.e. in the case of the example above, the Output would need to read `=[Hrs]-8` .

Let's work through the issue above, calculating the OT Hours first, and then using it to generate the Reg Hours portion. We'll duplicate the Basics query from the previous example and add this logic on at the end.

- Go to the Queries pane → right-click the Basics query → Duplicate
- Rename the query as "Manual Tests"
- Go to Add Column → Custom Column
- Set the new column name as OT Hours

Now the trick comes down to writing the correct formula...

If you have experience writing Excel or DAX formulas, your first temptation will be to write this:

```
=IF( [Hrs] > 8, [Hrs] - 8, 0)
```

Unfortunately, Power Query won't even let you commit this formula, telling you that "a Token Comma is expected". Even worse, Power Query's formula Intellisense doesn't recognize this, and also won't prompt you with the correct function for conditional logic at all.

The challenge here is that Power Query is case-sensitive and doesn't recognize IF as a valid function name. (If you were able to commit this, it would return an error asking if you spelled IF correctly!) Instead, we must provide the function as "if" (all lower case). In addition, unlike Excel and DAX formulas, Power Query doesn't enclose the parameters in parenthesis or separate them with commas. The correct syntax for our IF function is shown here:

```
=if [Hrs] > 8 then [Hrs] - 8 else 0
```

> ✎ An alternate method of writing the above formula would be to leverage the "not" keyword as shown here: `if not([Hrs] > 8) then 0 else [Hrs] - 8`

Here are a few things to keep in mind as you enter your custom column formulas:

- The key to working with Power Query's logic functions is to remember to spell them out in full, and make sure that you keep the function names in lower case
- You can use the Enter key to separate your formula into multiple lines
- Double clicking column names from the Available columns area injects the column into your formula and ensures its syntax is correct
- Pressing escape will dismiss the Intellisense, while typing a tab or enter will accept the Intellisense suggestion

Providing you separate your formula over three lines, it would look as follows:

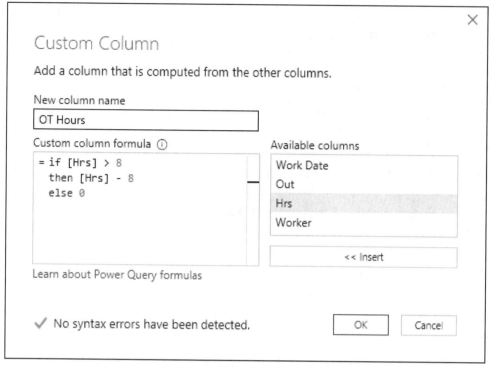

Creating the OT Hours column manually

We can now subtract this column from our Hrs column in order to generate the Reg Hours column:

- Select the Hrs column → hold down CTRL → select the OT Hours column
- Go to Add Column → Standard → Subtract
- Rename the Subtraction column → Reg Hours
- Remove the Hrs column
- Select all columns → Transform → Detect Data Types

Once complete, our data looks as shown here:

	Work Date	Out	Worker	OT Hours	Reg Hours
1	2021-03-03	6:00:00 PM	Thompson, John	0	8
2	2021-03-04	6:00:00 PM	Thompson, John	0	8
3	2021-03-05	6:00:00 PM	Thompson, John	0	8
4	2021-03-06	6:00:00 PM	Thompson, John	1.5	8
5	2021-03-07	3:30:00 PM	Thompson, John	0	6.5
6	2021-03-10	6:00:00 PM	Thompson, John	0	8

Hours are split between Regular and OT

At the end of the day, it is important to realize that this work could have been done completely via user interface commands. On the other hand, you will encounter scenarios where doing so will take many more steps. The skills to write your own conditional logic statements from scratch will provide you with the ability to perform much more complex logic in fewer steps.

Replicating Excel's IFERROR() Function

In our first example, we leveraged some tricks to trigger errors and replace them with *null* values to act as the basis of a conditional logic rule. In this example we will re-create the same output, but we will accomplish it in less steps. Let's see what we can do here:

- Go to the Queries pane → right-click the Raw Data - Timesheets query → Reference
- Rename the query as "IFError"

Our current state should look familiar:

	A^B_C Work Date	A^B_C Out	1.2 Hrs
1	Thompson	John	3
2	2021-03-03	6:00 PM	8
3	2021-03-04	6:00 PM	8
4	2021-03-05	6:00 PM	8
5	2021-03-06	6:00 PM	9.5
6	2021-03-07	3:30 PM	6.5

Remember this state?

Now, we know that converting the Out column to a Time data type would trigger an error in the first row, as John can't be converted to a time. Rather than duplicate a column to do so though, wouldn't it be nice if we could replicate Excel's IFERROR() function? That would allow us to try converting the column to a time, returning the time if it worked, and an alternate result if it didn't.

As you might expect already, Power Query won't recognize IFERROR as a valid function name. (And before you try it, iferror isn't valid either!) The syntax for this function in Power Query is:

```
try <attempted result> otherwise <alternate result>
```

🖎 The try syntax is reminiscent of other coding languages that leverage try/catch logic.

The way this works is that Power Query will "try" to do something. If it works, it will return that result, otherwise it will return the alternate result specified. Now the question is – what should we try to do?

In this case, we want to try converting a column to a specific data type, as that will tell us what to do next. Let's give this a shot:

- Go to Add Column → Custom Column
- Name the column Worker
- Enter the following formula: `try Time.From([Out]) otherwise null`

  🖎 Conversion from one data type to another can be accomplished by typing the data type, followed by `<data type>.From([Column])` as in `Time.From()`, `Date.From()`, `Number.From()`, etc… We chose to go with the Time format instead of dates to avoid the potential complexity of dealing with date locale issues.

The result should look like this:

	A^B_C Work Date	A^B_C Out	1.2 Hrs	ABC 123 Worker
1	Thompson	John	3	null
2	2021-03-03	6:00 PM	8	6:00:00 PM
3	2021-03-04	6:00 PM	8	6:00:00 PM
4	2021-03-05	6:00 PM	8	6:00:00 PM
5	2021-03-06	6:00 PM	9.5	6:00:00 PM
6	2021-03-07	3:30 PM	6.5	3:30:00 PM

Wait… that's not the Worker name…

It looks like the try statement worked, as we received a *null* value in place of the error, but this isn't exactly what we want, is it? We'd prefer to have the worker name in place of the *null*, and *null* values in place of all the dates. The secret? Let's wrap that try construct in a conditional logic framework to check if the result is null. If it is, then we will join the results of the Work Date and Out columns (using the & operator), and if not we will return a *null* value.

- Edit the Added Custom step you just created
- Adjust the formula as follows:

```
if ( try Time.From([Out]) otherwise null ) = null
then [Work Date] & ", " & [Out]
else null
```

> 🐌 In order to return the correct results, the original try statement must be wrapped in parenthesis. The spaces around the try statement are optional but help make the formula more readable.

After committing the formula, the results are exactly what we need:

	ABC Work Date	ABC Out	1.2 Hrs	ABC 123 Worker
1	Thompson	John	3	Thompson, John
2	2021-03-03	6:00 PM	8	null
3	2021-03-04	6:00 PM	8	null
4	2021-03-05	6:00 PM	8	null
5	2021-03-06	6:00 PM	9.5	null
6	2021-03-07	3:30 PM	6.5	null

That's way better!

We're now at a point where we can finish cleaning the data set via the user interface:

- Right-click the Worker column → Fill → Down
- Change the data type of the Work Date column to Date
- Select the Work Date column → Home → Remove Rows → Remove Errors
- Select all columns → Transform → Detect Date Types

The end result – as shown below – is identical to that achieved in the first example, however it was done in 5 steps versus 9.

	Work Date	Out	1.2 Hrs	ABC Worker
1	2021-03-03	6:00:00 PM	8	Thompson, John
2	2021-03-04	6:00:00 PM	8	Thompson, John
3	2021-03-05	6:00:00 PM	8	Thompson, John
4	2021-03-06	6:00:00 PM	9.5	Thompson, John
5	2021-03-07	3:30:00 PM	6.5	Thompson, John
6	2021-03-10	6:00:00 PM	8	Thompson, John
18	2021-03-10	6:00:00 PM	6	Johnson, Bob
19	2021-03-11	6:00:00 PM	8	Johnson, Bob
20	2021-03-12	6:00:00 PM	8	Johnson, Bob

Different method, same result

Working with Multiple Conditions

Our next goal also requires reaching to a custom column, as it is too complex to build using the conditional column dialog. In this case, we need to use logic that relies on multiple conditions:

Customer	Golf Dues	Option 1	Option 2	Curling Dues	Member Type	Pays Options
					Golf Dues and Curling Dues	Option 1 or Option 2
Berry, Cory	Season Pass		Power Cart	Member	All Access	Yes
Cameron, Averie	Member	Locker			Golf Course	Yes
Grimes, Sincere				Member	Curling Club	No
Oconnell, Raymond					None	No

We need to add the last two columns, depending on the results of multiple columns

Our challenge in this case is that the results we need depend upon meeting the results of one or more columns. For example: a member is only given an All Access pass if they pay (any type of) Golf dues AND (any type of) Curling dues. We also want to create a new column to indicate if they pay any optional dues at all.

Let's build this, starting from a new workbook or Power BI file:

- Create a new query → From Text/CSV → Ch14 Examples\DuesList.txt → Transform Data
- Rename the query as "Dues List"
- Promote the first row to headers
- Select all columns → Home → Replace Values → Replace blanks with *null* → OK

Once done, the raw data is prepared and ready to go:

	Customer	Golf Dues	Golf Option 1	Golf Option 2	Curling Dues
1	Berry, Cory	Season Pass		null Locker	Member
2	Cameron, Averie	Member	Locker	null	null
3	Gates, Emmanuel	Member	Power Cart	Locker	Member
4	Grimes, Sincere	null	null	null Member	
5	Jimenez, Jaime	null	null	null Member	
6	Mosley, Julianna	Season Pass	null	null	null

The data is ready, now how do we make our new columns

The first thing we need to do is work out the logic we want to create. Thinking through this one step at a time, we want to start with something like this:

```
if [Golf Dues] <> null and [Curling Dues] <> null
then "All Access"
else "Not sure yet..."
```

Shockingly, when you enter this in a new Custom Column (named Member Type), it works!

	Customer	Golf Dues	Golf Option 1	Golf Option 2	Curling Dues	Member Type
1	Berry, Cory	Season Pass		null Locker	Member	All Access
2	Cameron, Averie	Member	Locker	null	null	Not sure yet...
3	Gates, Emmanuel	Member	Power Cart	Locker	Member	All Access
4	Grimes, Sincere	null	null	null Member		Not sure yet...
5	Jimenez, Jaime	null	null	null Member		Not sure yet...
6	Mosley, Julianna	Season Pass	null	null	null	Not sure yet...

Well, that was easy...

Again, unlike the Excel and DAX formulas versions – which use upper case and precede the items to be tested, Power Query uses lower case and is entered between the logical tests as follows:

```
<test 1> and <test 2> (and <test 3>, etc...)
```

Like with Excel and DAX formulas, you can provide as many tests as you like, of which **all** must return a true result in order for the result to be treated as true.

> ✎ The only potential "gotcha" around the **and** operator is that you may need to wrap the logical tests before and after the operator in parenthesis. This becomes vitally important when you start nesting **and** tests with **or** tests!

Since that worked well, let's figure out what we need to do in order to replace the else clause with something more meaningful. What we are after here is the following:

```
if [Golf Dues] <> null then "Golf Course"
else if [Curling Dues] <> null then "Curling Club"
else "None"
```

🏌 Keep in mind that the Curling Dues logic is nothing more than an if statement nested within the else clause of the previous if statement. You may find it easier to place a line break after each of the if, then, else keywords to keep them straight, but there is no need to do so if you don't want to.

Taking the additional logic and editing the original Added Custom step, we can consolidate this into one complex if statement as follows:

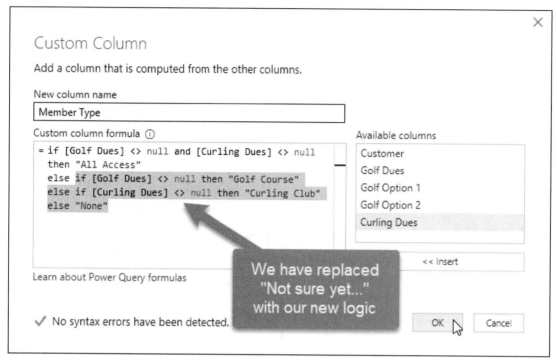

Updating our custom column formula

🏌 Not confident in your ability to write a perfect formula the first time? Don't sweat it! Create a new custom column to perfect the logic of each piece, then cut and copy them to consolidate them at the end. As long as you delete your steps, no one will have any idea!

	ᴬᴮC Customer	ᴬᴮC Golf Dues	ᴬᴮC Golf Option 1	ᴬᴮC Golf Option 2	ᴬᴮC Curling Dues	ᴬᴮC₁₂₃ Member Type
1	Berry, Cory	Season Pass		null Locker	Member	All Access
2	Cameron, Averie	Member	Locker	null	null	Golf Course
3	Gates, Emmanuel	Member	Power Cart	Locker	Member	All Access
4	Grimes, Sincere	null	null	null	Member	Curling Club
5	Jimenez, Jaime	null	null	null	Member	Curling Club
6	Mosley, Julianna	Season Pass	null	null	null	Golf Course
7	Oconnell, Raymond	null	null	null	null	None
8	Roberson, Sidney	Season Pass	Power Cart	null	Member	All Access

Our logic is looking good so far!

As you can see, this has worked nicely, so let's move on to the next challenge: determining whether a given customer pays any optional dues. In order to calculate this, we need to know if a customer has a value in either the Golf Option 1 or Golf Option 2 (or both) columns. We can accomplish this by using the "or" operator. It works the same way as the "and" operator used earlier but will return a true result if any of the provided conditions result in true.

- Go to Add Column → Custom Column
- Name the column "Pays Options" and use the following formula:

```
if [Golf Option 1]<> null or [Golf Option 2] <> null
then "Yes"
else "No"
```

The results give us exactly what we need:

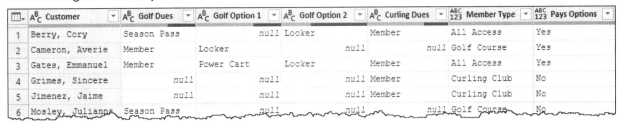

	A^BC Customer	A^BC Golf Dues	A^BC Golf Option 1	A^BC Golf Option 2	A^BC Curling Dues	ABC 123 Member Type	ABC 123 Pays Options
1	Berry, Cory	Season Pass		null	Locker	Member	All Access	Yes
2	Cameron, Averie	Member	Locker		null		null	Golf Course	Yes
3	Gates, Emmanuel	Member	Power Cart	Locker		Member	All Access	Yes
4	Grimes, Sincere	null		null		null	Member	Curling Club	No
5	Jimenez, Jaime	null		null		null	Member	Curling Club	No
6	Mosley, Julianna	Season Pass		null		null		null	Golf Course	No

A mixture of "and", "or" and "else if" logic yields our two columns

With our logic completed, the only thing left to do is set the data types and load the query.

Compare Against Next/Previous Row

One of the big challenges when working with Power Query is that there is no easy way to access the previous row. So how do you handle a scenario like this?

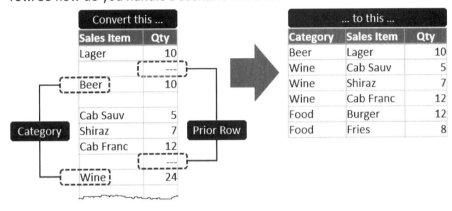

We need to extract data based on the previous row...

This solution uses a really cool trick that we can't wait to show you, so let's get to it:

- Create a new query → From Text/CSV → Ch14 Examples\Sales.txt → Transform Data
- Go to Home → Use First Row as Headers
- Select all columns → Home → Replace Values → replace blanks with *null*

The data will now look like this, presenting us with our challenge: how do we extract our category values based on a value in a different row?

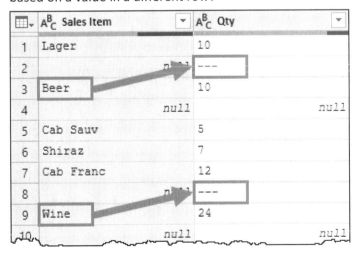

A common pattern exists in the row prior to our category value

> ✎ If you look carefully, the image shows only one commonality in this data set. Each category also shows null both before and after the data point in the Sales Item column as well as a null after the subtotal in the Qty column. Any one of these patterns would actually help us unwind this data set.

To access these values, we first need to add two index columns, so let's create those first:

- Go to Add Column → Index Column → From 1
- Go to Add Column → Index Column → From 0

And with those in place, we get to unleash the cool part of this pattern.

- Go to Home → Merge Queries (do not use the "as new" option!)
- Choose to merge the query to itself
- Select the Index.1 column in the top window, and the Index column in the bottom

Configuring the merge to compare against the prior row

Do you see where this is going?

- Click OK
- Expand the Qty column from the new Added Index1 column (without the prefix)
- Re-sort the Index column into ascending order

The results of the previous steps are shown here:

	A^B_C Sales Item	A^B_C Qty	1²₃ Index	1²₃ Index.1	A^B_C Qty.1
1	Lager	10	1	0	null
2	null	---	2	1	10
3	Beer	10	3	2	---
4	null	null	4	3	10
5	Cab Sauv	5	5	4	null
6	Shiraz	7	6	5	5
7	Cab Franc	12	7	6	7
8	null	---	8	7	12
9	Wine	24	9	8	---
10	null	null	10	9	24

We have successfully shifted the Qty column values to the next row

There are a few things worth commenting on with relation to what you have just seen:

1. The trick works whether you just want to shift one or more columns to a different row, or when you are trying to compare values against other rows as we are here.

2. To compare to the prior row, always select Index.1 in the top area of the merge dialog and Index in the bottom. If you want to compare to the next row instead, reverse that (select Index in the top window and Index.1 in the bottom.)

3. Comparing to the prior row always causes the data to re-sort when expanding one or more values from the merge result. This does not happen when comparing to the next row.

🐵 If you are using the prior row pattern to perform conditional logic, don't forget to re-sort the data after expanding the merge result!

We are now in a place where we can finish our data preparation:

- Create a new conditional column called "Category" with the following configuration

```
if [Qty.1] = "---" then [Sales Item] else null
```

- Right-click the new Category column → Fill → Up
- Filter the Qty.1 column and uncheck the "---" item
- Remove the Index, Index.1 and Qty.1 columns
- Filter the Sales Item column to remove nulls
- Select all columns → Transform → Detect Data Types

The result is a perfectly clean data set where the Category values have been extracted into their own column:

	$^{AB}_C$ Sales Item	$^{12}_3$ Qty	$^{AB}_C$ Category
1	Lager	10	Beer
2	Cab Sauv	5	Wine
3	Shiraz	7	Wine
4	Cab Franc	12	Wine
5	Burger	12	Food
6	Fries	8	Food

You'd never know that the Category values were nested in the Sales Item column!

🔍 The completed example file contains a version that uses the Next Row version of this technique. The only differences are that we switch the merge to join by Index and Index.1, and we target *null* values in our logic and filters instead of using "---".

Columns From Example

The final feature we are going to explore in this chapter is the Columns From Example. Like the previous technique, this isn't strictly related to conditional logic, but it is a logic-based expression builder. For that reason, we have included it in this chapter. It also happens to be capable of creating conditional logic rules as well, as you'll see.

To demonstrate the power of the Columns From Example feature, we are going to work with an assumption that we have a data set that is too complex for Power Query to import easily. Fortunately, a data set that imports incorrectly is actually becoming harder to find, so we are going to need to override Power Query's default interpretation of our file to force it back to a single column of text for this example. To do this:

- Create a new query → From Text/CSV → Ch14 Examples\FireEpisodes.txt
- Change the Delimiter to --Fixed Width-- and set the width to 0

While seldom needed, this handy trick allows you to override Power Query's defaults, returning a single column that you can manipulate as needed:

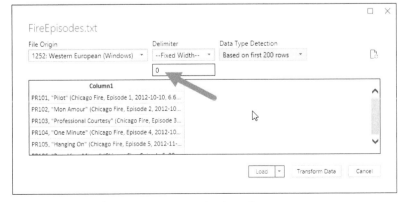

Forcing a text file to import as a single column

After clicking Transform Data, we will then find ourselves inside the Power Query editor, looking at a list of episodes and viewership statistics for the first few seasons of the Chicago Fire TV show. Our goal for this example is to extract data in the format of "<Episode Name>, <Episode Number>". The question is how?

There are a variety of ways to get this done, from splitting columns to writing custom formulas leveraging Power Query functions. Rather than spend a bunch of time trying to find an entry point however, we are going to leverage a new Power Query feature.

- Go to Add Column → Column From Examples

You will now be taken to this interface:

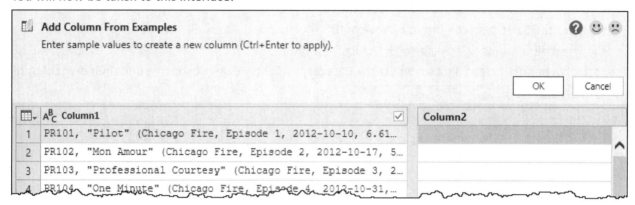

The Add Column From Examples interface

The idea here is that – in the empty Column2 – you just type the values you wish to extract from Column1. Let's give it a go and enter the first two values:

- Type **Pilot, Episode 1** in the first row
- Type **Mon Amour, Episode 2** in the second row

Upon completion of the second item, you'll see that Power Query immediately populates the entire column with values. While many of them look great, there is one that doesn't look quite right:

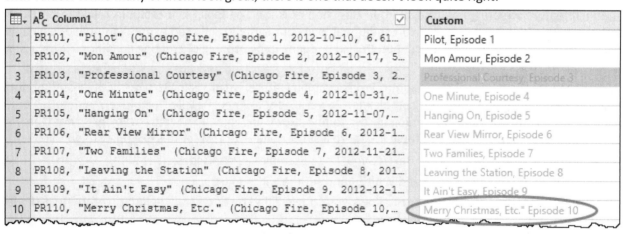

Why does Episode 10 have a " in it?

Let's fix that by just typing over it…

- Type **Merry Christmas, Etc., Episode 10** over row 10

Unfortunately, at this point something very bad happens… with the exception of the three records we typed manually, the entire column is populated with *null* values:

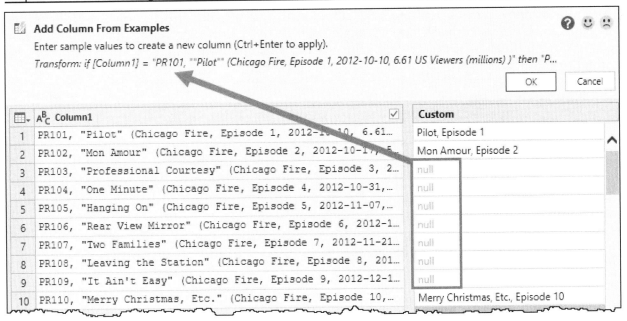

Uh oh... we broke Column From Examples...

What actually happens as you are typing the text to extract is that Power Query's engine builds the Power Query formula (shown in the top of the dialog) which is needed to extract your values. The issue we have here however, is that – based on the examples we have provided – the result has become too complex for Power Query to generate a reliable formula. In this case, Power Query falls back to creating a conditional column using if/then logic targeting the values we have specified manually. Plainly this won't scale as our data grows.

> ✎ The logic Power Query comes up with here is somewhat dependent on the order you enter your values. Depending on which items you type/replace, and the order you do it, you may actually get a working formula.

At this point, we are going to take another approach here.

- Delete all of the values we typed manually
- Enter **Pilot** in the first row
- Enter **Mon Amour** in the second row
- Double click the column header and change it to Episode Name

These results are much more promising as all of the values appear to be correct – even "Merry Christmas, Etc." You can also see that the formula no longer relies on conditional logic at all, but rather extracts the text using the Text.BetweenDelimiters() function to extract our episode names from within the quotes that surround each of them:

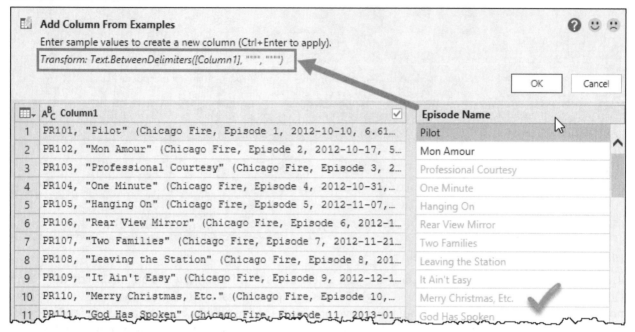

Power Query has leveraged a function to perfectly extract our episode names

Let's commit this and see if we can also extract the Episode Number.

- Click OK (to save this column)
- Go to Add Column → Column From Examples
- Type **Episode 1** on the first row of the new column
- Type **Episode 2** on the second row

The results are close, but the Merry Christmas episode is still causing us an issue, so we will need to type over it manually as well.

- Replace **Etc." (Chicago Fire** (on row 10) with **Episode 10**
- Rename the column **Episode Nbr**

Now, the results look perfect, and Power Query shows that it is using the Text.BetweenDelimiters() function to read all the values between "Fire, " and the next comma. How cool is that?

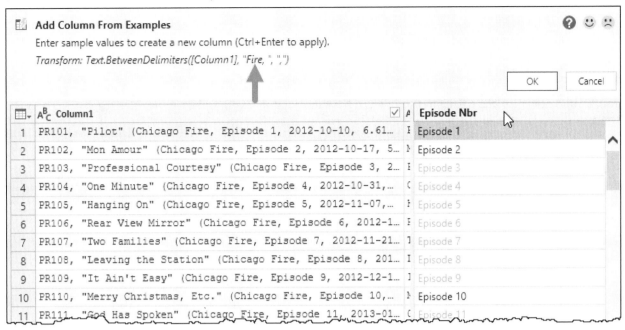

Would you have thought of using "Fire, " as a delimiter?

> 🔧 We love this feature, particularly because you don't need to know which functions exist to use them. In fact, you don't need to know anything about Power Query functions at all!

Let's commit this, and see if the work we have done has influenced our ability to achieve our original goal...

- Click OK to save this column
- Go to Add Column → Column From Examples
- Type **Pilot, Episode 1** in the first row

Unlike the first time we tried this, it immediately returns results – correct results – down every row of the column. Why? Because it is also reading from the columns we created previously:

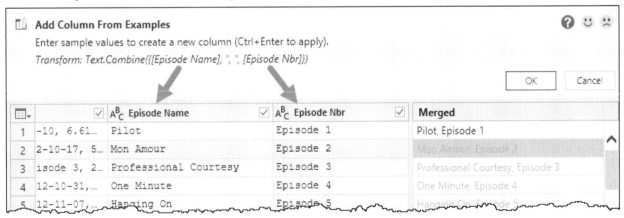

The Text.Combine() function is exactly what Power Query uses when you Merge columns

The most important parts to realize about what just happened here are:

- You could have selected the Episode Name and Episode Nbr columns → Add Column → Merge Columns, and merged them with a custom delimiter of ", " (comma space)
- Had you done so, Power Query would have recorded the exact same formula as you see in the top of the Add Column From Examples dialog
- Should you wish to exclude results of columns from the Column From Examples dialog, you can just uncheck the boxes next to their headers.

🍌 Seriously, how cool is this? If you can't find or remember the command for something, try doing it via Column From Examples. You might just find that it makes your life easier!

Let's do our final cleanup:

- Rename the Merged column to Episode and click OK to save it
- Right-click the new Episode column → Remove Other Columns
- Load your query to a worksheet or the data model, as desired

Your data is now nice and clean, and no one will have any idea that you took intermediate steps to accomplish the goal!

Chapter 15 - Power Query Values

Before we take a closer look at programming with M – the Power Query formula language – we first need to take a detailed look at how values and the overall data and functions are presented to us in Power Query. Having a sound understanding of these values will be useful when working with more advanced programming concepts.

Be aware that the focus on this chapter is not how to use these new-found powers in anything extremely practical. This chapter focuses on understanding how everything ties together in this language.

If you're following along on your own computer, you'll notice that all of the structured values in this chapter (tables, lists, records, values, binaries, and errors) show up in a colored font (green for Excel, yellow for Power BI) when included in a column. In addition, each can be previewed by clicking the whitespace beside that word in the results pane.

> ☎ In an attempt to balance accuracy with accessibility, we need to disclose that some of the resources that we've created for this book are based on our interpretations of the official Power Query specification document. While we have tried to stay as true to the documentation as possible, a few terms we use may not be "technically perfect". This was intentional in order to simplify and/or explain some of the jargon of the M language.

Types of Values in Power Query

We've been working with Power Query for quite some time now and inside the Data Preview section we've seen a preview of our data, displayed as a collection of "values". You'll also have noticed that some of the values in that view show data in a colored font such as *Tables, Lists, Records, Binaries* and even *Errors*. Why are they different than the rest of the values?

> ⚒ Note that, instead of referring to "objects" as we would in a language like VBA, Power Query is focused on interpreting "values".

In Power Query we have two types of values:

- **Primitive** — which classify primitive values (binary, date, datetime, datetimezone, duration, logical, null, number, text, time, type)
- **Structured** — which appears in a colored font font such as table, list, record and even function. They are constructed from primitive values.

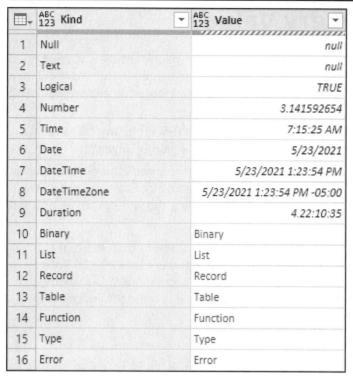

	ABC 123 Kind	▼	ABC 123 Value	▼
1	Null			null
2	Text			null
3	Logical			TRUE
4	Number			3.141592654
5	Time			7:15:25 AM
6	Date			5/23/2021
7	DateTime			5/23/2021 1:23:54 PM
8	DateTimeZone			5/23/2021 1:23:54 PM -05:00
9	Duration			4.22:10:35
10	Binary		Binary	
11	List		List	
12	Record		Record	
13	Table		Table	
14	Function		Function	
15	Type		Type	
16	Error		Error	

Miscellaneous values shown in Power Query

While it's easy for us to understand the primitive values, the structured values are something quite unique to Power Query. The reason why structured values exist is to perform operations based on rows, columns, or other aspects only possible through structured values.

> ✎ If you're familiar with Python and the pandas dataframes, then you'll feel right at home while trying to understand the following sections, but we've written this chapter assuming that you have no prior knowledge of any of those technologies.

Let's dive into these structured values one by one and see how everything ties together.

Tables

A Power Query "Table" is a structured value which contains rows, columns and metadata such as column names and their data types. A table value can show up in numerous places in Power Query, and we always appreciate it when they do, as they are very easy to work with.

- Open Ch15 Examples\Power Query Values.xlsx
- Create a new query → From Other Sources → Blank Query
- Type the following formula in the formula bar

      =Excel.CurrentWorkbook()

And we can see that there is one table in the workbook:

The sole table in the workbook being previewed

The benefits of the table value are numerous in Power Query. We know that:

- We can preview the data in the table

- The data contained in a table will have rows and columns, (even though we can't guarantee that a header row will already be in place)
- We can drill into specific tables listed in the column or expand them all
- Once we've expanded our table, we will have a full set of transformation ribbon tabs available to us in order to further transform and manipulate the data

Tables do not, of course, only mean Excel workbook Tables. Far from it, in fact. We can find tables in many data sources, including those extracted using formulas like Csv.Document(), Excel.CurrentWorkbook(), database tables and more, as you've seen in earlier chapters.

Let's finalize this query before we move on:

- Rename the query to Table
- Go to Home → Close & Load To... → Only Create Connection

Lists

Power Query "List" values are incredibly robust and useful, and in many cases are required in order to use some of Power Query's most powerful formulas.

The main way that list values differ from table values is that, when viewed, lists only ever have a single column of data. If you picture a list as being equivalent to your grocery list, you would simply list the names of the items you wish to purchase. (A list is basically a single column of a table, but with no header.) As soon as you start adding price comparisons between different stores you have moved to a table, not a list.

Syntax

When working with Power Query, a list can be identified by the presence of curly braces, with each list item separated by commas. In addition, textual items must be surrounded by quotes, just as they would need to be in an Excel formula:

```
={1,2,3,4,5,6,7,8,9,10}
={"A","B","C","D"}
```

Lists are not restricted to containing only numeric values, however. They can mix any data type at all, including other lists:

```
={1,465,"M","Data Monkey",{999,234}}
```

The key items to remember here are that the individual list items are separated by commas, and each individual list is surrounded by curly braces.

Creating Lists from Scratch

Let's create some lists from scratch to see how they work.

- Create a new query → From Other Sources → Blank Query
- In the formula bar, type the following formula
  ```
  ={1,2,3,4,5,6,7,8,9,10}
  ```
- Press Enter

You'll now have a nice list from 1 through 10:

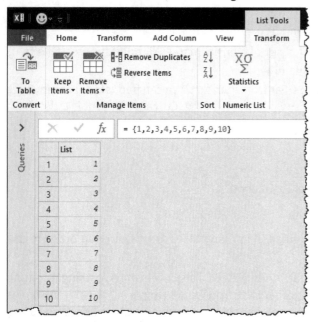

Creating a list from scratch

In addition to the fact that you've created a list of (primitive) values, you'll also notice that you're now working with the List Tools → Transform contextual tab active. Virtually all of the commands on the other tabs will be inactive at this point, making this feel like a very limited experience. Despite this, you'll see that you still have access to keep/remove rows, sort, de-duplicate and even perform some basic statistical operations on your data.

Now, as great as it is to be able to create a list from scratch like this, creating a list of numbers from 1 to 365 would be a bit of a pain. For this reason, we also have the ability to use a coding shortcut to create a consecutive list from one number through another. Change the formula in the formula bar to read as follows:

```
={1..365}
```

And you'll see that you get a nice consecutive list from 1 to 365.

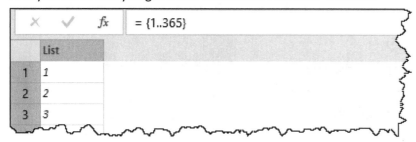

Using the .. characters to create a consecutive list

> ✎ You can create consecutive alphabetical lists in this manner as well, providing that you wrap the characters in quotes and only use a single character. I.e. `={"A".."Z"}` will work, but `={"AA".."ZZ"}` will not

We can also use commas inside our lists, providing they are inside the quotes. Replace the formula in the formula bar with the following:

```
= {"Puls,Ken","Escobar,Miguel"}
```

Upon committing it, you'll find that you get two list items, showing the names of the book authors:

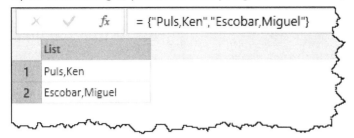

We can still use commas in our list output

Converting Lists into Tables

At this point, we really want to split this data into two columns, but that is not possible with a list as lists are restricted to a single column of data. We really need the richer transformational toolset that tables offer us.

Not to worry, as it is super easy to transform a list into a table. Just click the big "To Table" button in the top left of the List Tools contextual tab.

Doing so will present you with an interesting dialog:

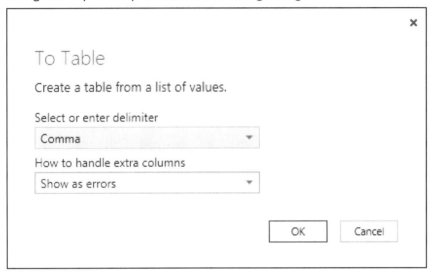

What's this about delimiters?

We can set the delimiter setting to Comma, click OK, and our data will load nicely into a two column table:

Data loaded from a comma separated list

> ✎ This dialog will show up whether there are delimiters in your data or not. If you don't have delimiters, just click OK and it will go away.

Let's finalize this query

- Change the query name to List_Authors
- Go to Home → Close & Load To… → Only Create Connection

Creating Lists from Table Columns

There are occasions where you'll want to extract the data from a single column of your query into a list. To demonstrate how this works, let's connect to the Sales table.

- Go to the Sales worksheet and select any cell in the Sales table
- Create a new query → From Table

You'll notice that you now have the full table showing:

The raw table of data

Now, what would we do if we wanted to get a unique list of the Inventory Items? If we were comfortable leaving it in the form of a table, we could simply remove all the other columns, then go to the Transform tab and remove duplicates. The challenge here is that it would still be in table form, and we wouldn't be able to feed it into a function if we need to. Instead, we'd like to get those unique items, but as a list, allowing us that flexibility.

- Remove the Changed Type step from the Applied Steps pane
- Right-click the Inventory Item column → Drill Down

You'll now be looking at a list of all the Inventory items:

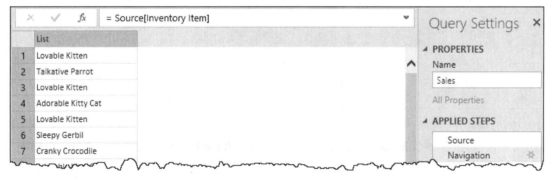

Our column, extracted to a list

Before we move on, look at the formula bar. In there, you'll see a line of code that reads:

```
=Source[Inventory Item]
```

This line of code refers to the Inventory Item column, as it was calculated during the Source step of this query. This gives you the M code shortcut to extract all column values into a list without using the user interface commands; something you'll find **very** useful later.

> ⚓ Another way to accomplish this with just a line of code is to use the Table.Column() function which requires a table as its first parameter and the name of the column to extract from the table as the second parameter. The output of this function is a list from the values from the column entered in the second argument. For this example, the formula will read **Table.Column(Source, "Inventory Item")** and provide the exact same result as that formula is the equivalent of using **Source[Inventory Item]**.

With our column contents extracted to a list, we are able to perform further list operations on it, such as de-duplicating the data.

- Go to List Tools → Transform → Remove Duplicates

And we've now got a list of unique items that we could feed into a different function.

Let's finalize this query:

- Rename the query to List_FromColumn
- Go to Home → Close & Load To… → Only Create Connection

Creating Lists of Lists

We mentioned earlier that it was possible to create lists of lists. This might seem like an odd concept, so let's explore this scenario.

We have four employee ID's (from 1 through 4) involved in this sales table. These values represent Fred, John, Jane and Mary, in that order. Wouldn't it be nice to be able to convert those values to their names, without having to create a separate table? Let's explore whether we can use a list to do this.

- Create a new query → From Other Sources → Blank Query
- Create a new list in the formula bar as follows:

```
= {{1,"Fred"},{2,"John"},{3,"Jane"},{4,"Mary"}}
```

Notice here that we have four separate lists, each surrounded by curly braces and separated by commas. These four lists are in turn surrounded by a single set of master curly braces, defining a master list made up of four sub lists. When committed to the formula bar, they return a list containing four lists:

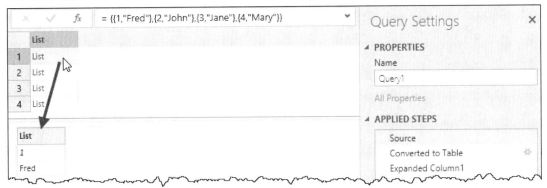

A list of lists

As you can see, previewing the first list shows us that it is a list which holds the values 1 and Fred. This is interesting, but can we use this?

Converting this list to a table returns a single column that still contains lists, but it has an expansion arrow in the top right. Let's click that and look at the results:

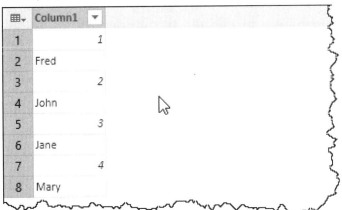

Our lists have expanded vertically, not horizontally!

Plainly, aggregating our lists combines them by stacking the rows, not treating each as an individual row. While we could transform this using the Index/Modulo/Pivot approach from Chapter 13, it is a bunch of extra work that we should be able to avoid.

🔍 In order to make this work, we would have needed to define our list as we did for the author example above; not as a list of lists, but rather as a list of items with the commas inside the quotes.

Let's close off this example:

- Rename the query to List_of_Lists
- Go to Home → Close & Load To... → Only Create Connection

There are two key things to recognize here when working with lists:

- Lists **can** be created which contain other lists, and
- Expanding lists of lists does not change their orientation

An alternative to reach the same output, while keeping things in the List realm, is to use a function called **List.Combine()**. It is as simple as clicking the fx icon from the formula bar to add a custom step and then just wrapping the code shown in the formula bar with List.Combine() as shown below:

```
= List.Combine ( Source )
```

Using List.Combine() to combine a list of lists

The way that List.Combine() works is that it combines a list of lists into a single list. It's basically like the equivalent of the Append query operation but for Lists.

However, what we're after is more in the lines of having each list become a row. For that use case, there's a function called **Table.FromRows()** which requires a list of lists to create a table. Similar to what we did before, all we need to do is simply wrap our List of Lists into the aforementioned formula as shown below and voila:

fx	= Table.FromRows(Source)

	ABC 123 Column1	ABC 123 Column2
1		1 Fred
2		2 John
3		3 Jane
4		4 Mary

Table created from a list of lists using the Table.FromRows() function

Records

While Power Query's "List" values can be described as a single vertical column of data, "Record" values are their horizontal, multi-column counterparts. A record can be visualized as a table with just one row, containing all the pertinent information related to that customer or transaction.

In Power Query, records can appear in table columns or lists as you retrieve data. They can also be created on the fly if needed.

Syntax

Records are slightly more complex than lists in that they need to not only have a value of some kind, we must also define the column names:

```
=[Name="Ken Puls", Country="Canada", Languages Spoken=2]
```

The key syntax points you want to observe here are:

- Every complete record is surrounded by square brackets
- Every record field (column) needs a name defined, followed by the = character
- The data for the field is then provided, surrounded by quotes for textual data
- Each field name and data pair is then separated by commas

✎ Field (column) names do not need any punctuation surrounding them, whether they include spaces or not.

But what happens when you need to create multiple records at once? The answer is that you reach to a list:

```
={ [Name="Ken Puls", Country="Canada", Languages Spoken=2],
   [Name="Miguel Escobar", Country="Panama", Languages Spoken=2] }
```

Creating a Record from Scratch

Let's circle back on our prior attempt at building the records for an employee ID table.

- Create a new query → From Other Sources → Blank Query
- Now, we'll start by creating a single record. In the formula bar, enter the following formula:
  ```
  =[EmployeeID=1,EmployeeName="Fred"]
  ```

When we hit Enter, we see that Power Query returns our record:

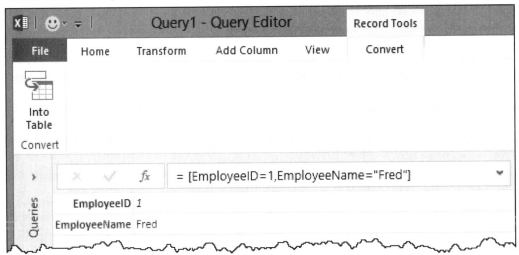

Our first record

As we can see, the record's field names are listed down the left, with the corresponding data down the right. Interestingly enough, the data is arranged vertically, not horizontally, as we'd expect. This isn't an issue, just something to get used to.

You'll also notice that you have a new Record Tools → Convert contextual tab and, if you explore the rest of the ribbon tabs, you'll find out that they are all greyed out.

Converting a Record into a Table

Since there's obviously not a lot that we can do with records, we'll just go ahead and turn this into a table, to see what happens.

- Go to Record Tools → Convert → Into Table

The result isn't exactly what you'd expect:

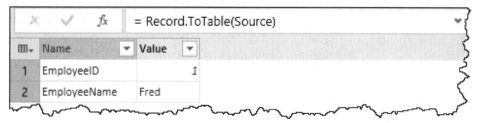

A single record converted to a table

If you expected that this would show up with the field names across the top and the values in the first row, you're not alone. Regardless, it's easy to fix since it's now a table:

- Go to Transform → Transpose
- Transform → First Row as Headers

The result is a bit more synonymous to what we would have originally expected:

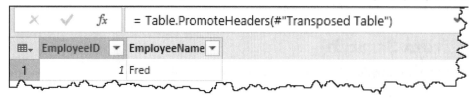

Our record now looks like a proper table

Now this is fine, but what is going to happen if we have a bunch of records that we need to convert to a table? Let's find out.

- Rename the query to Record_Single
- Go to Home → Close & Load To… → Only Create Connection

Creating Multiple Records from Scratch

This time, we want to build our table out so that it encompasses all the employees. We'll need to build a list of records to do that.

- Create a new query → From Other Sources → Blank Query

```
= { [EmployeeID=1,EmployeeName="Fred"],
[EmployeeID=2,EmployeeName="John"],
[EmployeeID=3,EmployeeName="Jane"],
[EmployeeID=4,EmployeeName="Mary"]  }
```

Notice that we are still using the same format for a single record, but we've separated each record with commas and surrounded them in the curly braces needed to indicate that they are part of a list.

Upon committing the formula above, you'll see that it returns a list of Records:

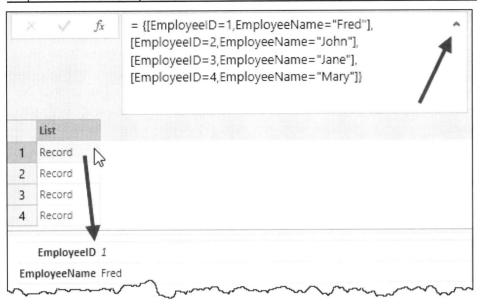

A list of records, with the preview showing we got it right

> 👠 The arrow in the top right of the formula bar will allow you to expand it to show multiple lines at once.

Converting Multiple Records into a Table

Now, let's convert this list of records to a table and see what kind of a disaster we have on our hands...

- Go to List Tools → Transform → To Table → OK

And the result is a column of records which can be expanded. Interestingly, clicking that Expand icon indicates that there are columns to be expanded...

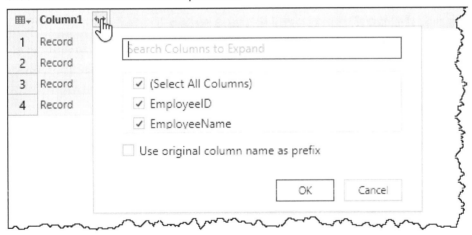

This is looking better...

And clicking OK returns a nice set of columns and rows, exactly as we were looking for with the single record!

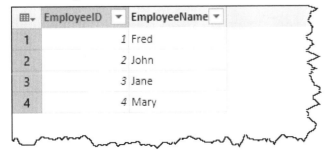

We just built a table from scratch!

It goes against conventional wisdom, but creating multiple records actually feels like it unwinds into a table more logically than a single record. The true difference is that we convert a *list* of *records* into a *table* in the second instance, not a single record into a table. With the records in a table column, it then reads the record information correctly in order to expand it into the requisite column and rows.

We're now at a stage where this table can be saved, and even merged into other queries if we so choose.

However, there's also another way to transform a list of records into a table with just a single line of code.

- Create a new blank query and enter the same list of records previously entered
- Click the fx icon in the formula bar to create a new custom step
- Change the formula to the one below

```
Table.FromRecords(Source)
```

And afterwards you'll notice that table has been created without any issues just from a list of records. The Table.FromRecords() function is widely used in the documentation to showcase sample tables written completely in the M Language, so it's really helpful to get acquainted with this formula early on and what it does.

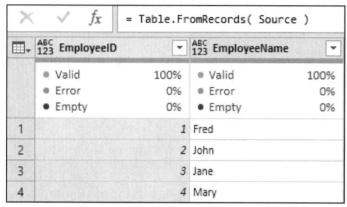

Using Table.FromRecords() to extract values from a list of records

Accessing Table Records by Position (Row Index)

When we were working with lists, we showed how you can convert a column into a list if you ever needed to do this for any reason. You can also convert a row into a record. To do this, we will start with a new query.

- Go to the Sales worksheet and select any cell in the Sales table
- Create a new query → From Table

As with earlier examples, you now have the full table showing. To extract the first record, we'll need to create a blank query step. To do this:

- Click the fx button next to the formula bar

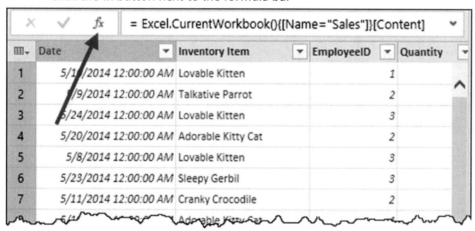

Creating a blank query step

You'll now get a new step with the following formula in the formula bar:

```
=Source
```

Modify this formula to add {0} to it:

        =Source{0}

The result is our first record:

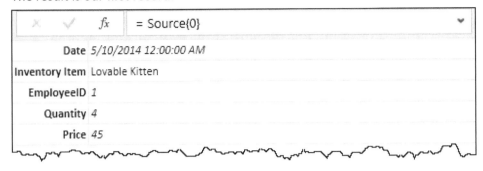

{0} = Record 1?

What just happened here?

When treated in this way, the Source step returns a record. The secret is to pick up the correct number that retrieves the indexed row of the Source step we wish to drill into. Because Power Query is Base 0, record 0 returns the first value in the table. (If we'd made this =Source{1} we would have retrieved the record for the Talkative Parrot.)

> ⚓ This is not only possible against tables, but also against lists. In other words, you could refer to List{0} and it would give you the first value from that list. It is not applicable to records as a record is essentially a table with just one row. However, you can always access a field from a record, as described later in this chapter.

Even more interesting, we can drill in even further by appending the field name in square brackets. Try modifying the query to the following:

        =Source{0}[Price]

As you can see, we just drilled right in and extracted the Price for the first record in the table:

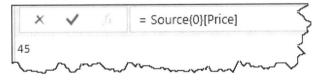

Drilling into record 0's price

To understand the relevance of this, consider a situation where you need to drill into a specific record in order to control filters. In the next chapter you'll see where this technique allows you to do exactly that.

- Rename the query to Record_From_Table
- Go to Home → Close & Load To… → Only Create Connection

Accessing Table Records by Criteria

There is also another way to navigate directly to a specific record in a table. Rather than drilling in by index position, it is to drill into the table where one or more fields match certain criteria. In fact, this is what Power Query typically records when we click on a structured value and generate a "Navigation" step.

Going back to our original query where we connected to the Sales table, make sure that we define the data types as follows:

- **Date** as date type
- **Inventory Item** as text
- **EmployeeID**, **Quantity**, and **Price** as Whole Number

	Date	A^B_C Inventory Item	1^2_3 EmployeeID	1^2_3 Quantity	1^2_3 Price
1	5/10/2014	Lovable Kitten	1	4	45
2	5/9/2014	Talkative Parrot	2	2	32
3	5/24/2014	Lovable Kitten	3	4	45
4	5/20/2014	Adorable Kitty Cat	2	2	35
5	5/8/2014	Lovable Kitten	3	1	45

Data types defined for the Sales table

Create a new custom step by clicking the fx icon from the formula bar and then write the following formula:

```
= #"Changed Type"{[Inventory Item= "Lovable Kitten", EmployeeID = 1,
Quantity = 4]}
```

What this formula is doing is effectively defining a logic to navigate to a specific row of a table that matches the criteria defined. In other words, we have a record inside of a list, preceded by a table value, that helps us navigate or drill down to a specific value that matches the criteria.

In this case it basically translates into a navigation to a specific row from the table for the #"Changed Type" step where:

- **Inventory Item** is "Lovable Kitten"
- **EmployeeID** is 1
- **Quantity** is 4

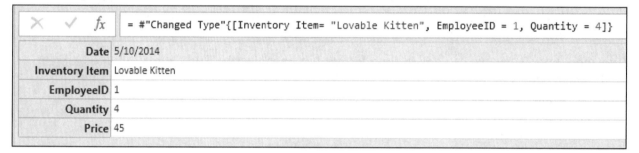

Navigating to a specific record from a table using the Table{[Field = Criteria]} method

The most important aspect of this pattern is that the record logic works like a filter to the table. However, in order for this to work you must provide a "Key" (logic or criteria) that will give you a single record. In this case, there is only one record that meets all of the provided criteria.

If multiple records in the table meet the key that you've defined then you'll get an error similar to the one below:

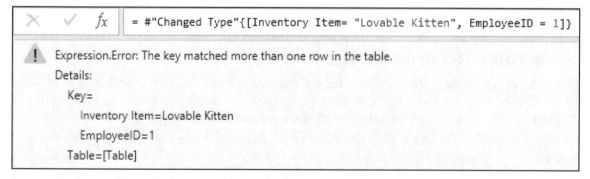

Expression.Error where the key defined matched more than one row in the table

This error indicates that there must be more than one record in our complete dataset where Employee 1 has sold a Lovable Kitten.

> ✎ One easy way to overcome this issue is to make sure that your table has a Key column with unique values. If you don't have one, create a new Index column, and simply use the value from that column as your key for the record navigation.

After we've navigated to the specific row of our table, we can then navigate to a specific field from that record using the following formula:

```
= Custom1[Price]
```

With that, we will be reaching the same output from the previous method but using a completely different approach.

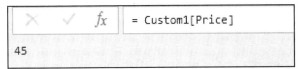

Accessing the Price field from the record that we navigated to

There is no right or wrong way to do it as it all depends on your use case. However, one thing that you'll notice throughout your experience using Power Query is that Power Query usually uses the last method shown. For example, if you go back to the Source step of our query you'll see that specific pattern being used with the formula:

```
= Excel.CurrentWorkbook(){[Name="Sales"]}[Content]
```

To put it in simple terms:

- **Excel.CurrentWorkbook()** - produces a table with the available objects from within the active workbook
- **{[Name = "Sales"]}** - is the key or filter logic for the record that we're trying to access which is the record that has the value "Sales" in its Name column.
- **[Content]** – once we've navigated to the row where the value "Sales" exists in the Name column, we will drill down, navigate or access the contents inside the [Content] column which in this case happens to be a table value and that's why we see a full-blown table.

	ABC 123 Date	ABC 123 Inventory Item	ABC 123 EmployeeID	ABC 123 Quantity	ABC 123 Price
1	5/10/2014 12:00:00 AM	Lovable Kitten	1	4	45
2	5/9/2014 12:00:00 AM	Talkative Parrot	2	2	32
3	5/24/2014 12:00:00 AM	Lovable Kitten	3	4	45
4	5/20/2014 12:00:00 AM	Adorable Kitty Cat	2	2	35

Formula bar: `= Excel.CurrentWorkbook(){[Name="Sales"]}[Content]`

Record access and field access automatically created by Power Query

> 🔍 Understanding the concepts of **record access** and **field access** is key to understanding M (the Power Query formula language).

Creating Records from each Table Row

To convert each row in a table into records, we have a couple of options. Let's see how to do that with a nifty little trick.

- Go to the Sales worksheet and select any cell in the Sales table
- Create a new query → From Table

Now, we want to convert each row in the table to a record. The challenge is that we need the index number of each row to do that. So let's reach to the Index column:

- Go to Add Column → Add Index Column → From 0

Now we are going to rename this **step** (not the column) in the Applied Steps window:

- Right-click the "Added Index" step → Rename → "AddedIndex" (no space)

The query will now look as follows:

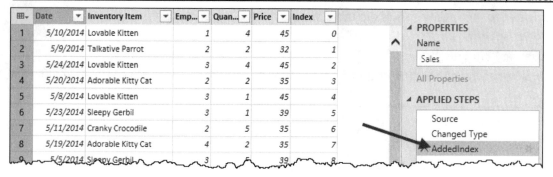

The Index column has been added, and the step renamed to remove the space

With that done, let's reach to a Custom Column to convert our rows to records. The trick in this was creating an Index column, as we now have the value we need to extract our records. The reason we need this trick? We're not going to operate on the current row, but rather on the AddedIndex step's output. This way, rather than getting a specific value (such as the 1st row), we can dynamically feed it into the query to get each row.

- Go to Add Column → Add Custom Column
- Name the column "Records"
- Use the following formula:

    =AddedIndex{[Index]}

And the result is that a new column is created which contains the rows as records:

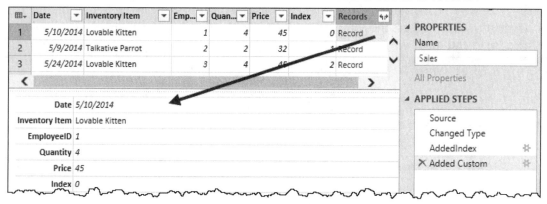

A column of records

> ✎ Strictly speaking, we didn't need to rename the Added Index column to remove the space, it just makes things a lot easier in the user interface.

At this point, we could remove all other columns, and we'd simply have a column of records.

- Right-click the Records column → Remove Other Columns
- Rename the query as Records_From_Table
- Go to Home → Close & Load To... → Connection Only

Another even more simple way to reach this same state is to skip adding the Index column, creating a Custom column only using this formula:

    =_

And the result is exactly the same as in the previous column that we created:

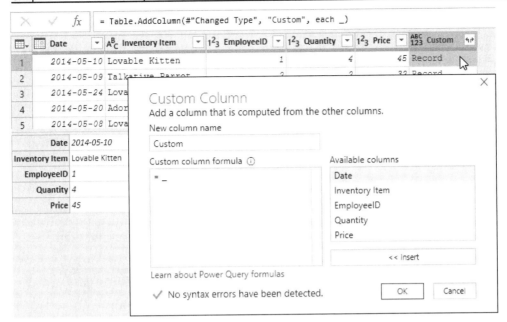

Creating a record from each table row using the underscore method

🔧 The underscore is a specific keyword in the M language and when used in combination with the word *each* in a custom column, it effectively refers to the current element in a collection which, in this case is the current row of the table.

🔧 We will cover this concept and the concept of functions more in-depth later in this book, but this is one of those nifty little tricks that you can start using without having to know everything about the M language.

Values

If you are working with relational data sources like OData or databases, you will occasionally see columns containing Values:

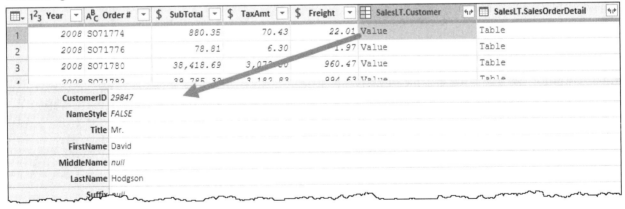

The elusive Value

This particular value only shows up in certain cases. In order for it to appear you must be working with a relational data source that has a Primary Key and Foreign Key relationship set up between tables. What's really strange is that a Value is just the way a database returns a Record.

Once you know what you have, then working with them is the same as the other data types that they are related to.

🔧 The cardinality, such as one to many or many to one in a relationship, will determine what is returned to a related column when working with a relational data source. If you are in a Fact table, and the link is going to the Dimension table, you'll receive a Value (record). If you are in a Dimension table and the link is going to a Fact table, you'll receive a table.

Binaries

Power Query displays files as "Binary" values. The contents of these files can be accessed via Power Query's various connectors (functions) which interpret and displays the file's data.

For example, you could interpret the binary file as an Excel workbook, CSV / TXT file, JSON file, XML file, PDF file, webpage and more as more connectors are being added and will be added even after this book gets released.

Errors

There are two types of error messages that you can encounter in Power Query: Step Level errors, and row level errors.

Row Level Errors

These are the type of errors that typically occur when trying to convert data to the wrong data type or when trying to operate on data before it has been converted to the correct type. You've seen several examples of these types of errors throughout this book.

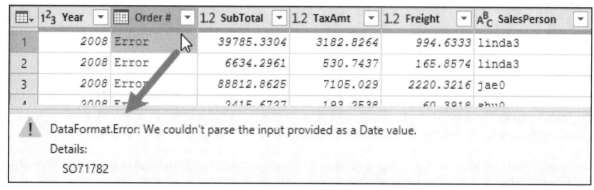

A row level error triggered by trying to convert Order # to a Date data type

These errors generally aren't show stoppers, and can even be very useful when cleaning data, as they can be treated in two ways:

1. Used as filters to keep/remove rows
2. Replaced with other data using the Transform → Replace Errors command

Despite the fact that there is no debugging engine, these are usually identifiable, and often (although not always) are related to incorrect data types.

Step Level Errors

Step level errors are a bit more serious to deal with. These messages block your Power Query from showing anything in the output window except the error.

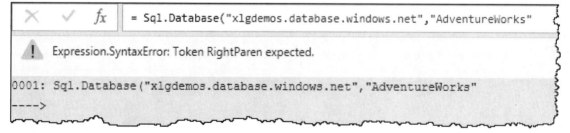

An Expression Syntax Error, triggered by a missing) at the end of the line

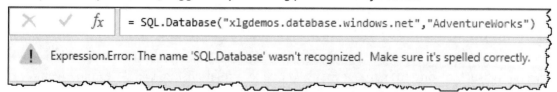

A general Expression Error, triggered by referring to SQL rather than Sql

Unfortunately, Power Query's debugging tools are particularly weak at this point, as is evidenced by the following issue:

```
!  Expression.SyntaxError: Token Comma expected.

0001: Table.Group(#"Inserted Year", {"Year", "SalesOrderID" ,
0002:        {{"Sales", each List.Sum([TotalDue]), type number}})
---->                                                              ^
```

A syntax error caused by a missing } character, but asking for a comma

The first issue you'll see here is that the error message is presented on a single row (it had to be cut and wrapped for this image). At the very end of the string is a helpful ^ character indicating where Power Query thinks you need to place your comma. The issue, however, is that a curly brace was not provided to close the YTD Sales list as indicated by the vertical red arrow.

These issues today are challenges. While we do have an implementation of Intellisense and coloring today, it is far from perfect. As Power Query is receiving frequent updates, we do hope to see that change in future. Until such time, however, debugging must be done the painful way of reviewing the line, watching for key opening and closing syntax marks, commas and the like.

Functions

The last type of value that you will encounter in Power Query is a Function. A function value is a value that maps a set of arguments to a single value. You will more frequently find these values in one of three places:

1. Inside a database, indicating a function at the database level

2. By returning a list of functions from Power Query

3. By manually referring to a function

You'll learn more about using and invoking functions later in the book, but there is a trick that we can use to demonstrate how functions manifest, and also help you discover the Power Query function list.

- Create a new query → From Other Sources → Blank Query
- In the formula bar enter the following formula:

    `=#shared`

- Go to Record Tools → Convert → Into Table

This will generate a table of all Power Query queries in the current workbook, but more importantly it also gives us the ability to access the documentation for all functions included in the product:

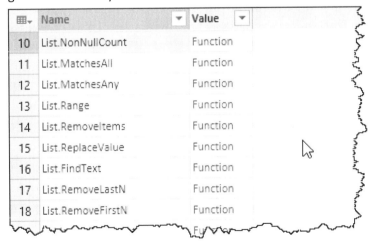

Name	Value
10	List.NonNullCount	Function
11	List.MatchesAll	Function
12	List.MatchesAny	Function
13	List.Range	Function
14	List.RemoveItems	Function
15	List.ReplaceValue	Function
16	List.FindText	Function
17	List.RemoveLastN	Function
18	List.RemoveFirstN	Function

A table of Functions

✎ The #shared keyword allows us to access the same documentation as we can find for Power Query M Functions as at `https://docs.microsoft.com/en-us/powerquery-m`

How do we use this? Let's filter the first column for "Max" (with an upper case "M").

- Filter the Name column → Text Filters → Contains → Max

Our search turns up four offers:

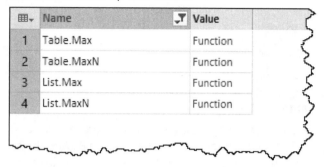

	Name	Value
1	Table.Max	Function
2	Table.MaxN	Function
3	List.Max	Function
4	List.MaxN	Function

All functions containing Max

If you click on the Function beside Table.Max, you'll see two things happen; you'll see documentation pop up behind and an Invocation box pop up in front:

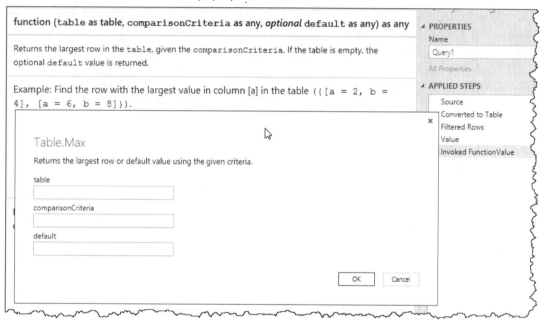

An Invocation box appears in front of our documentation

The purpose of this box is to allow you to test the function out, but hitting Cancel will make it go away. Behind it you'll find the full documentation for the function, so you can determine if it does what you need.

As a handy tip, you're not restricted to using this from blank queries. Any time you want to check the documentation, you can do the following:

- Click the fx on the formula bar to add a new step
- Replace the code in the new step with =#shared
- Convert the records to a table
- Drill into the function you want to explore

You can then step back into the earlier Applied Steps to implement it, deleting all the #shared steps when you are finished.

> ✎ There are over 600 functions in any given product integration of Power Query. We encourage you not to try and memorize these functions whatsoever – we certainly haven't (and won't) – as your knowledge of any programming language is not really determined by how good you are at memorizing things, but rather how good you are at interpreting these functions and applying them into your solutions.

While we don't advocate memorizing all the Power Query functions, we do suggest skimming through the list to see what functions exist, as well as understand how they seem to be categorized based on their prefix or their goal with a format of **Category.Action**. Here are some examples of function categories:

- **Data source:** these are commonly the functions that connect to a data source such as `Excel.Workbook()`
- **Table**: Functions that work over tables or try to work in relationship to tables. These commonly start with the prefix Table like `Table.PromoteHeaders()`
- **List**: Functions that work over a list or try to work in relationship to lists. These commonly start with the prefix List as seen in `List.Sum()`
- **Record**: Functions that work over a field or try to work in relationship to fields. These commonly start with the prefix Record like `Record.FieldNames()`
- **Text:** Functions that work on text-based values. These commonly start with the prefix Text like `Text.Contains()`

🪓 There are other function categories that were not mentioned in the list above, but we've provided these examples just to showcase that these categories do exist and that there is a way to discover new functions that could help you with your specific transformation needs.

Keywords in Power Query

In the M language there are some specific words that are reserved – these words are called keywords and can only be used in specific contexts.

Some examples of keywords are:

```
and as each else error false if in is let meta not null or otherwise
section shared then true try type #binary #date #datetime
#datetimezone #duration #infinity #nan #sections #shared #table #time
```

While some of these keywords are specifically used for the nitty gritty code of Power Query, we've already seen some of these keywords in previous chapters such as:

- if, else, then, true, false, and, or, not, try, otherwise – In the chapter for Formulas and Conditional Logic.

While some other keywords will be covered later in the book, it is quite important that we cover some of them now – specifically the ones that have the pound sign before them. Excluding #shared and #sections, each of these keywords help you create a specific value that conforms to a data type. Let's see how they work.

☎ Remember that correct punctuation and casing are imperative when writing any type of code in the M language. This means that these keywords need to be typed exactly as showcased in this book or your Power Query environment will not recognize them.

#binary

While you will most commonly see binaries when using a connector that displays the file system view (such as the Folder, SharePoint, and Azure Data Lake connectors), you can create a binary value from "thin air" purely with code.

The #binary keyword expects any value and it will try to transform the value provided into a binary value. The most practical approach that we've seen is when you pass a base 64 encoded text value. For this example, we have chosen to add a new blank query and add the code in the first step of the query:

```
#binary("TWlndWVsIEVzY29iYXI=")
```

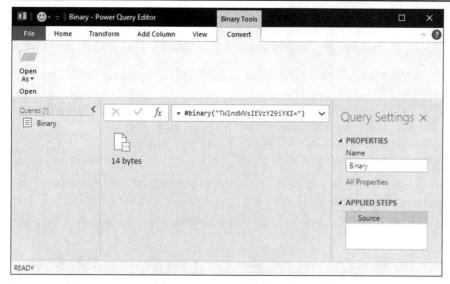

A binary value created with the usage of the keyword #binary

If you click on the *Open As* option in the top left and select the option to interpret the binary as a Text file then Power Query will do just that:

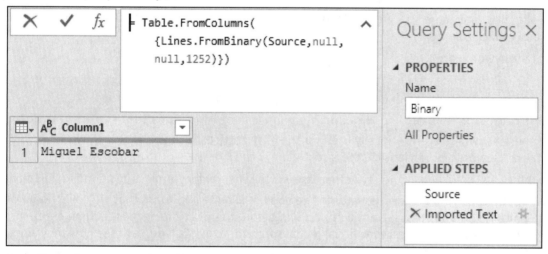

Decoding a base 64 encrypted Binary into its text equivalent

> ✎ There are also some functions that can help you interpret other values as Binary values. Be sure to check out the Binary.From(), Binary.FromText(), and Binary.FromList() functions, which are a more explicit way of doing what we're trying to accomplish with the #binary keyword.

#date, #datetime, and #datetimezone

We're grouping all of these keywords into a single section because they all build on top of each other. Each of these can be valuable whenever you are trying to create a value from other values in your query, such as from other columns in your query.

The pattern is the following:

```
#keyword(year, month, day, hour, minutes, seconds, time zone hour, time
zone minutes)
```

However, depending on the value that you're trying to create, you may only need to provide a few of these arguments. For example:

- When you want to create a #date you only need to use the year, month, and day parameters.
  E.g.: May 23rd, 2021 would be written as `#date(2021,5,23)`

- When you want to create a #datetime you'll need to provide all of the parameters listed in the #date keyword as well as the hour, minutes, and seconds parameters.
  E.g.: May 23rd, 2021 at 1:23:54 PM would be written as `#datetime(2021,5,23,13,23,54)`

- Finally, if you want to create a #datetimezone then you'll need to provide all of the parameters from the pattern provided.
  E.g.: May 23rd, 2021 at 1:23:54 PM for the Time Zone UTC-05:00 would be written as
  `#datetimezone(2021,5,23,13,23,54,-5,0)`

If you manually enter the code provided in the examples above into a custom step in the formula bar, you'll notice that Power Query automatically transforms that keyword into the actual representation of the value. However, your code has not been deleted – this is just a by-design visual feature by the Power Query team. You can jump into the Advanced Editor view to check that your code is still intact.

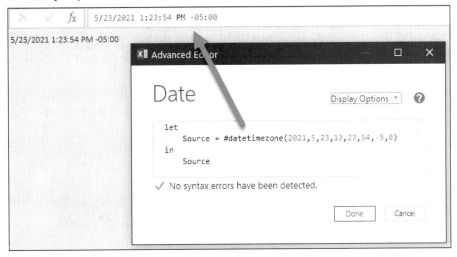

Keyword #datetimezone (as per the Advanced Editor) displayed as a primitive value

The main practical approach for these keywords, as mentioned before, is when you're trying to construct either one of these values from known values in your query. For example, you might already have the Year, Month, and Day values in separate columns in one of your queries and you want to create a new custom column that combines all of those values into a data value. You could use the keyword `#date( [Year Number], [Month Number], [Day Number])` in order to create that value. One thing that is crucial about these keywords is that they only accept integer numbers – text or decimal values are not allowed and will yield an error during the evaluation of the formula.

#time

It is quite important to remind ourselves that data types are not the same as data format. Power Query primarily cares about the data types, but its user interface does display some specific formats as previously seen in this book.

The time data type is effectively the times that you see on your clock – its values can range from 00:00:00 until 23:59:59.

As an example, let's say that we want to write 2:36:54 PM in the M language. In order to do so, we'll use the #time keyword, which requires passing the time parts in a 24-hour format (14:36:54):

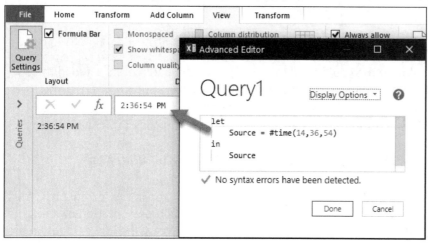

Using the #time keyword to return a time of 2:36:54 PM

🖈 Similar to the parameters used in the #date, #datetime, and #datetimezone keywords, the #time keyword only accepts integer values. Anything other than integer values will yield an error.

#duration

While #time refers to the time of a particular day (from the time 00:00:00 until 23:59:59), duration refers to a specific data type that refers to the length of time. In other words, it's the data type that answers the question: "What's the duration between datetime A and datetime B?".

For example, imagine that you want to say that you need a duration of 4 days, 22 hours, 10 minutes, and 35 seconds. To write that in M you'll need to write #duration(4,22,10,35).

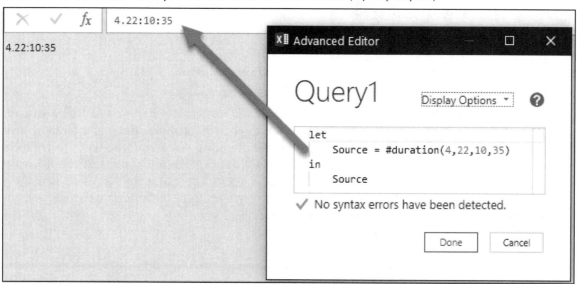

Using #duration to create a duration value for 4 days, 22 hours, 10 minutes, and 35 seconds

The most common practical application is when you combine a duration with something like a date, datetime, and / or datetimezone. For example, let's say that we have the date value of May 23rd, 2021 and we want to add 12 days to that date. To do that we can use the following formula:

$$= \text{\#date(2021,5,23)} + \text{\#duration(12,0,0,0)}$$

×	✓	*fx*	= #date(2021,5,23) + #duration(12,0,0,0)
6/4/2021			

Adding 12 days to the date value of May 23rd, 2021 which yields Miguel's birthday (June 4th)

Of course, you can use this technique with a datetime value to add not only days but also hours, minutes and seconds as you see fit.

> 🔧 As with both the #date and #time keywords, the #duration keyword only accepts integer values as parameters.

type

Data types in Power Query are very important. Not only do they help you take advantage of what the user interface has to offer, but they can also affect how the M engine functions when executing a query step or even a specific function.

You've seen us define data types throughout this book quite a few times but, what are types? The following is an excerpt taken directly from the official Power Query formula language documentation to help us understand what they are:

A type value is a value that classifies other values. A value that is classified by a type is said to conform to that type. The M type system consists of the following kinds of types:	
[various] types	which classify primitive values (binary, date, datetime, datetimezone, duration, list, logical, null, number, record, text, time, type) and also include a number of abstract types (function, table, any, and none)
Record types	which classify record values based on field names and value types
List types	which classify lists using a single item base type
Function types	which classify function values based on the types of their parameters and return values
Table types	which classify table values based on column names, column types, and keys
Nullable types	which classifies the value null in addition to all the values classified by a base type
Type types	which classify values that are types

Type values as per https://docs.microsoft.com/en-us/powerquery-m/m-spec-types

One important note regarding terminology is that, unlike values, which are classified as primitive or structured, all naturally occurring types – including Record, List, Function, Table, Nullable and Type types – are considered to be primitive types. While "complex" data types can exist, they must be defined by the user.

> 🔧 Naturally occurring tables do not contain the data types of their columns by default and are therefore classified as a primitive type of table. If the table definition is adjusted to contain properly typed columns – as you will see in Chapter 16's "Create a Dynamic List of Headers with Typed Columns" example – then it would be classified as a complex type. As it is, the table value contains a mixture of defined data types across the columns.

While you are used to seeing a variety of data types by now, there is one that is worth a specific mention: any. This data type most commonly occurs when data cannot be conformed to a specific type. It often manifests on table columns which have not yet had their data types explicitly defined, or where a column contains a mixture of different data types.

So how do you know which data type has been applied to each column of your data set?

The most visible way is to scan and interpret the icons in the top left corner of each column. But for really wide tables this may not be desirable. Another simple and cool way to check the data types of a table is by using the **Table.Schema()** function. To better demonstrate this, let's use the table from the image below:

Sample table with three columns and two rows

This table has three columns / fields:

- **id** with integer data type
- **Patient Name** with text as data type
- **First Vaccine Shot Date** with date as data type

When we create a custom step via the fx button and wrap that previous step name (Source) inside of the Table.Schema(), it gives us a report of all the metadata for that particular table:

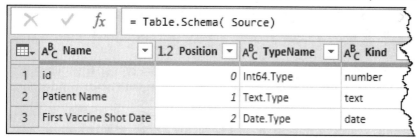

Using the Table.Schema() function to see the metadata of a table

Check both the TypeName and Kind columns, as these provide you with different ways to set your data types. In the case of the image above either of the following are perfectly valid ways to set the data type of the id column:

```
= Table.TransformColumnTypes(Source,{{"id", Int64.Type}})
= Table.TransformColumnTypes(Source,{{"id", type number}})
```

🔖 As you'll learn later in this chapter, type number will actually return a decimal data type rather than a whole number data type.

There is also another way to check the data type of any value and that is by using the Value.Type() function, which will return the data type as per the "Kind" column shown above. For example, the following formula would return "text" as a result of targeting the table shown above:

```
= Value.Type(Source[Name]{0})
```

While this is a lot of info, it's usually better to see this within the context of the Power Query editor to see how things work. If you write a custom step with the formula type number, it will give you just that data type and nothing else.

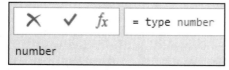

The data type for number written through the usage of the keyword type

The main use case of the type keyword is when it is being used with a table when you want to define the data types and the columns for your table.

🔖 When you get into the realm of trying to create a Power BI Custom Connector, the schema of a particular column or value is imperative. Outside of that scenario, however, it is unlikely that you'll need to refer to the type keyword often.

#table

While it is entirely possible to create tables using a list of records and the Table.FromRecords() function, as showcased earlier in this chapter, we have another option as well; using the #table keyword. We've left this one for last, as it is the only keyword that helps create a structured value via a keyword. It is not better, or worse, than the previously illustrated option, simply another tool to keep in your toolbelt.

The #table keyword requires two parameters:

1. **The table columns:** we can provide a list of column headers, or pass a table type with the metadata in it for the column names and their respective data types.

2. **The data for the rows of the table:** as a list of lists where each nested list is effectively one row of the table.

As an example, you could create a new blank query and replace the first step with the following formula:

```
= #table( {"id", "Patient Name", "First Vaccine Shot Date" },
    { {1, "Ken", #date(2021,5,20)},
    {2, "Miguel", #date(2021,4,4)} }
)
```

You'll notice one thing right away and that is, while the table looks pretty great, it doesn't have the correct data types defined for each of the columns. We can tell by the icon that is right before the name of the fields which is the icon for the *any* data type.

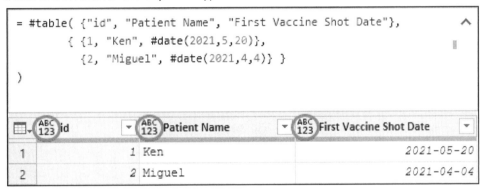

A table created using the #table keyword using a list of field names

☎ It is critically important that the data in your fields is provided in the same order as your column header list since Power Query fills the fields based on column positions, not names.

While you can add a Changed Type step to set the data types, what if your goal was to do it all in one single step? That's where the other method using a table type comes in.

So, what is a table type? A type is just the name that we have for data types. We've been working with data types for primitive values, but this will be the first time where we try to define the data type of a structured value.

Let's change the previous code that we used to this:

```
= #table( type table [ id = Int64.Type, Patient Name = Text.Type, First
Vaccine Shot Date = Date.Type],
    { {1, "Ken", #date(2021,5,20)},
    {2, "Miguel", #date(2021,4,4)} }
)
```

Notice how the only thing that changed was the first parameter? This is quite different to the list we provided previously, as the list cannot define any data types. Instead, we defined data types for the columns by using *type table* with a record to act as it's data-typed headers:

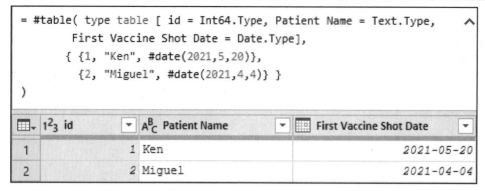

A table created using the #table keyword using a table type

> 🔧 Just as before, the order of the fields added via the subsequent list of lists does matter, as the fields are populated by position, not by column name.

When providing a record for the *type table* data type, you can use either the explicit TypeName or the Kind for it. For example, try replacing your current formula with the one below:

```
= #table( type table [ id = number, Patient Name = text, First Vaccine
    Shot Date = date],
        { {1, "Ken", #date(2021,5,20) },
          {2, "Miguel", #date(2021,4,4) } }
    )
```

The result will be a bit different in the sense that the id column will no longer be an integer (whole number), but rather now of the decimal data type. We can see this by simply looking on the icon in the column header of the id field.

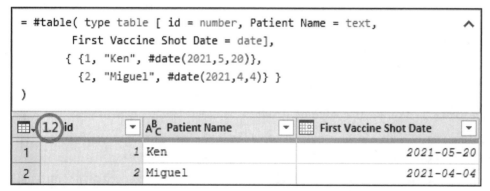

New formula for creating a table using the #table and type keywords with data type kinds

> 🔧 The *number* kind is an umbrella for all data types related to numeric values. Given that a number may or may not have decimals associated with it, Power Query has to play it safe to ensure it won't lose any precision. For this reason a type of *number* gets converted to the decimal data type.

It is often easier to use the data type Kinds than the more explicit TypeNames, so you'll see us using the data type kinds more often than not, unless we have a specific use case where the more explicit Type is required. In other words, when setting data types via code, we will typically use *type number* to assign a data type to a numeric column instead of using *Int64.Type* unless we specifically need to force a column to an Integer data type, limiting or removing the decimal precision.

Chapter 16 - Understanding the M Language

Now that we've explored the different values that we can use in Power Query, it is time to take a deeper look at the M language that is used to perform Power Query's magic. While it isn't truly necessary to master M, it will certainly add some incredible power to your arsenal and allow you to work with situations that others can't.

M Query Structure

To get started, we'll pull a table into Power Query, and then examine the code that is working behind the scenes.

- Open a blank file
- Create a new query → From SQL Server Database → Use the server and database information from Chapter 12

  ✎ If you previously completed Chapter 12 then you'll automatically reach the Navigator window. Otherwise, be sure to check Chapter 12 in this book to get the username and password to connect to the sample database.

- Now inside the Navigator window, select the **SalesLT.Customer** table and hit the Transform button at the bottom right corner of the window.
- Filter the table using the field **CompanyName** and the value "Friendly Bike Shop"
- Select the columns CustomerID, FirstName, LastName and remove other columns
- Rename the query to be named "Sample Query"

The outcome of all of these transformations will be a table with only 4 rows and 3 columns as shown below.

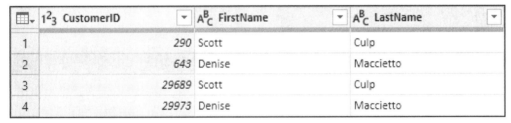

	1²₃ CustomerID	AᴮC FirstName	AᴮC LastName
1	290	Scott	Culp
2	643	Denise	Maccietto
3	29689	Scott	Culp
4	29973	Denise	Maccietto

Output of the sample query

If you look at the Applied Steps pane, you'll see that it currently contains 4 steps:

- **Source** – The connection to the database
- **Navigation** – Drills down (navigates) in to the SalesLT.Customer table
- **Filtered Rows** – Filters the table to rows where CompanyName equals "Friendly Bike Shop"
- **Remove Other Columns** – Keeps only the CustomerID, FirstName, and LastName columns

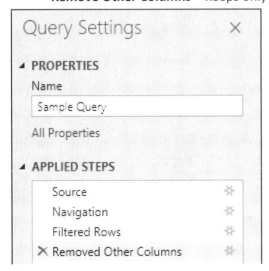

The applied steps pane of our sample query

Query Structure

So far, everything you've seen has been driven through the user interface. You've seen Power Query act as a macro recorder and have been able to interact with it via the Applied Steps window, as well as some limited interaction via the formula bar. What you haven't seen yet is the programming language that resides underneath the covers of this incredible tool. It's time to change that.

- Go to Home tab → Advanced Editor

This will launch the Advanced Editor window, the interface we use to write or customize our M code. It offers Intellisense as well as syntax highlighting and has a few additional display options that you can toggle via the drop-down menu in the top right corner of the window. In order to make our code samples a bit easier to read, we have enabled the following options for the code samples in this chapter:

- Display line numbers
- Render whitespace
- Enable word wrap

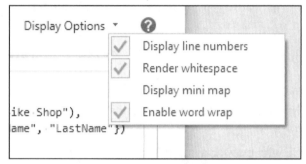

Display options available inside the Advanced Editor

With this done, the code for our entire query created to date looks as shown below:

```
1  let
2      Source = Sql.Database("xlgdemos.database.windows.net", "AdventureWorks"),
3      SalesLT_Customer = Source{[Schema="SalesLT",Item="Customer"]}[Data],
4      #"Filtered Rows" = Table.SelectRows(SalesLT_Customer, each [CompanyName] = "Friendly Bike Shop"),
5      #"Removed Other Columns" = Table.SelectColumns(#"Filtered Rows",{"CustomerID", "FirstName", "LastName"})
6  in
7      #"Removed Other Columns"
```

The Advanced Editor

Let's focus on the code inside this window, which is made up of four core components:

- **Start of the Query** – this is defined by the **let** keyword at the top of the query (line 1 in this case).
- **End of the Query** – this is defined by the **in** keyword (line 6) which is usually found one line short of the end of the code.
- **Query definition** – is everything that we see in between the **let** and the **in** keywords and dictates what the query will do. In this case, the definition spans from lines 2 through 5 of the query.

- **Query output** – After the **in** keyword we need to define what the output of the query will be. For this case this is defined in line 7 and returns the value from the last step in the query which is `#"Removed Other Columns"`.

🪃 It is important to realize that the Query Output usually refers to the last step of the query definition but is not required to do so.

As a simplified example, check this other query to see how those 4 components come into play:

```
let
    Source = 1
in
    Source
```

Notice how there is a **let** that defines that the query definition is about to start. Then in a new line we have a new step with the name **Source** followed by an equal sign and then the value 1. In the next line we have the **in** keyword which finalizes the query definition and finally we have the line which defines that the results of the **Source** step will be the output of the query.

Obviously, our original query has many more steps than just one in its Query Definition. As that is the magic part of the query, we are going to take a closer look at what happens within that component.

The Query Definition Section & Identifiers

The next thing to understand is how the individual lines (steps) link to each other.

In Power Query, much like algebra and functional programming, we use words to refer to values. For example, the name of a step in a query or the name of the query itself. These names are called identifiers in Power Query and can be written in two ways:

1. **Regular Identifiers:** Have no spaces or any sort of special characters in their names. For example, a step called `StepName` would be written in M as follows: `StepName`

2. **Quoted Identifiers:** Could have spaces, special characters, or reserved keywords in its name. For example, a step called `Step Name` would be written in M as follows: `#"Step Name"`

🪃 Remember that we have provided a list of reserved keywords in Chapter 15.

This is effectively the mechanism that Power Query uses to protect itself from having ambiguities at the code level and prevent conflicts against reserved keywords. In short, any sort of name at the code level that contains a space, a reserved character or keyword, or any special character would be encapsuled in quotes preceded by a pound sign and will be categorized as a quoted identifier.

As you'll see this concept in play throughout the language, let's compare the names in the Applied Steps pane to how they show up in the M code:

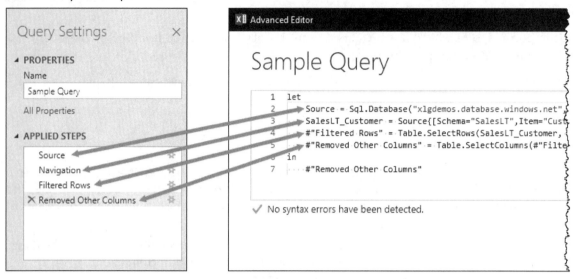

Comparing the M code to the labels used in the Applied Steps section

As you can see, the Applied Steps section contains friendly names that describe what is actually happening behind the scenes in the M code. You can see that the first step is exactly the same in both the M code and the Applied Steps shown as **Source**, but then the second step shown as **Navigation** is simply not present in the M code. (That is because this step was automatically created by Power Query and behind the scenes is written in M code by the name of **SalesLT_Customer**.) This Navigation step is usually the exception to the rule but check out the rest of the steps where the names are almost the same as what you see in the Applied Steps pane. The notable difference is that in the M code they are within quoted identifiers such as #"Filtered Rows" and #"Removed Other Columns" due to the spaces in their names.

The next thing to recognize is that the Query definition has similarities to a record. As explained in Chapter 15, when creating a record we first define the field name, then place an equal sign, an expression for the value inside that field and then a comma if you're about to add more fields to your record. But if it is the last "Field" of your record you omit the comma. The same is true of query steps: if it is the last step of your query definition, you simply omit the comma. That is why the components inside the **Query definition** will look familiar, but the formulas might not.

> 🐵 While you can modify your step names inside the Advanced Editor, it is far easier to modify them through the user interface as Power Query will make sure to update the identifier everywhere where it is being used in your query. If you make your modifications manually, remember that your new term must be identical in all instances (no case changes). Also, don't forget to update the query output if you rename the last step!

About Generalized Identifiers

There are exceptions to these naming conventions where no quoted identifiers are needed, allowing us to use regular identifiers even when the name of the values have special characters or spaces. These special scenarios are called **Generalized Identifiers** and there are only two places in the M language where you will see them:

- **Field names inside a record:** When you create a new record you don't need to use the quoted identifiers. For example, you can write a record with the field name "Base Line" as follows:

```
[ Data = [Base Line = 100, Rate = 1.8] ]
```

- **Field access operators:** When you are trying to access fields from any other value, you don't need to use quoted identifiers. For example, using the previous example, we can create a new field that accesses the Data field and multiplies the *Base Line* by the *Rate* to get the new *Progression* field value:

```
[
    Data = [Base Line = 100, Rate = 1.8],
    Progression = Data[Base Line] * Data[Rate]
]
```

🖐 Essentially this means that there are two places inside the M language where you can use column names which contains spaces, without wrapping them in the #" " structure of a quoted identifier.

Generalized Identifiers are also the reason why – when creating a Custom Column – you don't see the names of the fields using quoted identifiers.

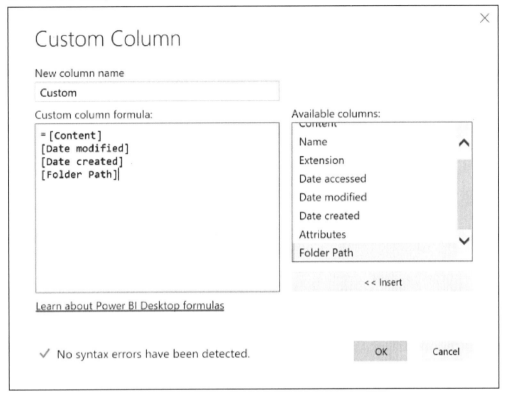

Quoted identifiers are not required when referring to columns in the Custom Column dialog

Code Comments

There are multiple ways to add comments to your query, but by far the easiest way is to do it through the user interface. To make this happen, all you need to do is right-click a step from your query, select the Properties… option at the bottom and then add a Description inside the **Step Properties** dialogue as shown in the image below.

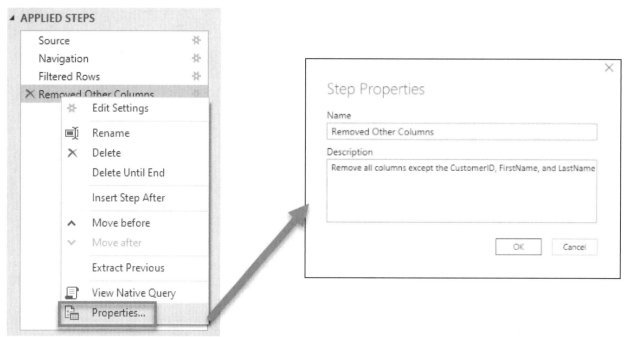

Adding a comment to a step through the user interface

Once you do this, Power Query will display a little information icon right in the step to denote that it has a description. Behind the scenes, it will add that description as a comment at the code level as shown in the image below:

Comment shown in the user interface and the Advanced Editor

It is also possible to create multi-line comments in your M code, but these take a different form. Where single-line comments must be prefaced by two slashes at the beginning of the line, multi-line comments are initiated by typing **/*** prior to the code we don't want executed, and ***/** at the end of the section as shown below:

Multi-line comment added to our sample query from lines 5 through 7

Tying Everything Together

While the Query that we currently have is fully functional, let's add a new step to it to see how things function and how Power Query automatically updates the code in the Advanced Editor.

- Filter the FirstName column to the value "Scott"

This will yield a table with only two rows but, more importantly, let's check the Advanced Editor and see how Power Query changed our code.

New "Filtered Rows1" step added to our query to filter the FirstName field with the value "Scott"

If we compare this code against the previous image, we can see that we haven't just added a new line to our code:

- A comma has been added to the end of line 8,
- Line 9 now shows the #"Filtered Rows1" step we injected, and
- You'll also notice that final line of the query after the **in** keyword (which is now line 11) is referencing the #"Filtered Rows" step instead of #"Removed Other Columns".

It is also worth noticing that these are the only changes to the query, and all of the previous steps remain intact.

Understanding Query Evaluation

One thing that we haven't yet discussed in detail is the magic that happens at each step of a query. To truly understand each step, we need to read the documentation for each function used in that step of the query (as showcased in Chapter 15). This will allow us to understand the required parameters, as well as the expected output of the functions. One thing that we can easily see is how these steps are chained between each other as if there was a dependency between them – especially when reviewing queries that were created via the user interface. As an example, let's check our final code, specifically the last two steps (from the bottom up):

- `#"Filtered Rows1"` – this step uses the `Table.SelectRows()` function which requires a table as its first parameter. The value passed to this first parameter is the value from the previous step: `#"Removed Other Columns"`

- `#"Removed Other Columns"` – this step uses the `Table.SelectColumns()` function which also requires a table as its first parameter. The value passed to this first parameter is the value from its previous step: `#"Filtered Rows"`

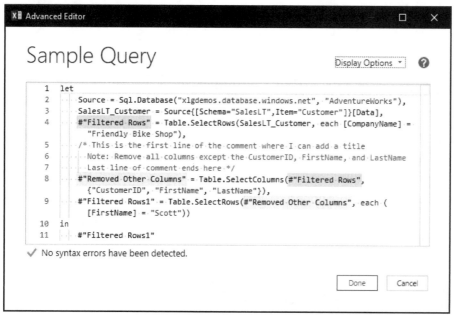

Highlighting the dependencies between steps and how values from other steps are passed to functions in other steps

To truly understand how a query is evaluated, it is usually a better idea to look at the query from the bottom up, as this is effectively how Power Query evaluates things. It looks at the output of the query, figures out all the precedents of that value (and its precedents) before finally evaluating the query.

What is Lazy Evaluation?

In Power Query the evaluation of your queries can be different, depending upon where it will be evaluated:

- **Data Preview view:** This is the most common view that you'll see in Power Query where your data is previewed for you.

- **Query output:** This scenario is where you load the data to its intended destination, executing a full query load or refresh.

The main difference between these two is that in the Data Preview, Power Query will try to stream a portion (usually the top 1000 rows) of the data to you without fully evaluating your query against the entire data set. This, in essence, is one of the major benefits of how Power Query works as a functional language using **lazy evaluation**. The way lazy evaluation works is – if something is not needed – it will not be evaluated at the time. In other words, only what's truly needed to create your data preview will be executed.

This also works in combination with another major key component of Power Query called **Query Folding** which is the process that Power Query uses to translate your M code into a native query against your data source. We briefly mentioned this in Chapter 12 as well as with the options to showcase the **View Native Query** and the **Step Folding indicator** features.

Lazy Evaluation and Query Folding help us work better with Power Query, saving you from downloading all the data from the database or selected table as you are building your query. Instead, Power Query usually tries to evaluate the first (or top) 1000 rows from your data source and create a cache (basically a local copy which is also encrypted) of that evaluation. This is what is presented in the preview, allowing you to build your transformations on a smaller subset of the data. (Consider a database with a billion-row table, and you can easily see the benefits of this approach!)

Of course, when we try to evaluate the Query Output, we do need Power Query to evaluate the whole dataset – not only the rows that would be needed for the data preview. And that is exactly the point of lazy evaluation. When the full dataset is needed, that is what Power Query delivers.

> 🪝 For a SQL Server database, you could use a tool like SQL Server Profiler to monitor the requests being made by Power Query to the database to see how the data preview gets evaluated. The main difference between the requests of a Data Preview versus the Query output against a SQL Server database is that the Data Preview usually has a SELECT TOP 1000 for the data preview and the full evaluation doesn't have this TOP 1000 clause.

Query Plan

Going even deeper into the concept of **Query Folding**, not all transformations can be translated into a native query for your data source and the options vary from connector to connector and even from data source to data source depending on how each source is configured.

> 🪝 This is where a new feature called Query Plan comes into play which – at the time of writing – is in preview within the Power Query Online experience.

The Query plan is nothing more than just that: a plan or a hypothesis of how the query will be evaluated. The goal is always to push as much work as possible to the data source and that is Query Folding's job.

> 🪝 For the purposes of this section, we will illustrate this as if you are working within the Power Query Online experience, or assuming that the feature has arrived in the Power Query product you are using.

Assume we return to our initial Sample Query from this chapter – which connected to the database and filtered the data set to include only Friendly Bike Shop sales – you can right-click the last step of your query and select the option that reads "View query plan", returning the following diagram:

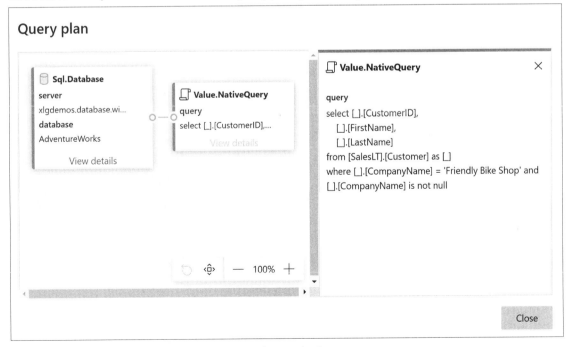

Query plan and SQL statement for our initial Sample Query

This Query plan is telling us that the whole query can be offloaded to the data source, meaning that we will only receive the table with 3 columns and 4 rows instead of having to download all the data from the table and perform the transformations locally. Furthermore, it is also telling us what query will be sent to the data source and which data source it will be sent to.

Let's add a new step to the query that we know will break its ability to fold: Keeping the bottom rows. We will set this to keep only the bottom 2 rows:

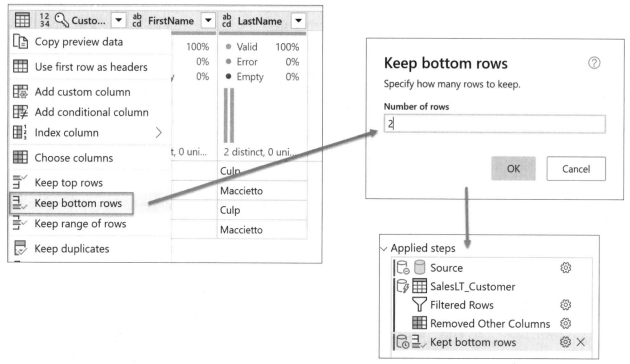

Adding a new step to keep the bottom 2 rows from the table

> 🐵 Since a SQL database has no operator to select the bottom rows of a table, this command will always break query folding.

As shown in the previous image, after taking this step, the new **Kept bottom rows** step shown in the Applied Steps pane has an indicator that it can't be folded. Right-clicking this step and launching the Query plan view yields the following updated view:

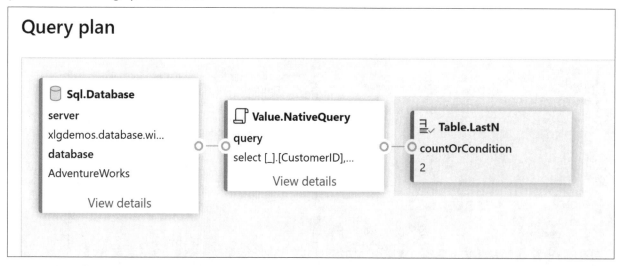

Query plan after adding the Kept bottom rows step

While this query plan looks quite similar to the previous one, note that a new event or task has been added called Table.LastN. This is the name of a function, more specifically the function used in the **Kept bottom rows** step. We can now see that a query will still be sent to the data source (the same one from the previous query plan), but after Power Query downloads that data, a Table.LastN transformation will be evaluated locally using the Power Query engine.

> ✎ The Query plan is an incredibly helpful tool when you're trying to understand and fine tune your queries. It is still in its early stages, but we have high hopes for it and cannot wait to see how it evolves!

Iterators (Row by Row Evaluation)

There is one more very important skill to get into your toolkit when working with M, and that is understanding how to read and modify code that operates on each row in a column.

In the M language we have multiple ways to iterate over a set of values. In simple terms, an iteration is a process that occurs in somewhat of a cycle or repetitive process. As an example, imagine when we add a new column to a table. That new column needs to be evaluated on a row-by-row basis following a single formula or function. (This is quite similar to how a column gets evaluated in an Excel defined table.) In this section we will investigate how Power Query does just that, the rules that it follows, and how we can leverage that knowledge.

A Note on Power Query's Recursive Functions

This book will focus on standard functions in the M language, but please be aware that there are advanced functions that can help you create more advanced Power Query solutions similar to a for-loop or do-while-loop in the M language. The primary recursive functions that you might find in Power Query are:

- `List.Generate()` which is commonly used in the context of Power BI Custom Connectors for Pagination purposes.
- `List.Accumulate()` which works similarly to a for-loop where you have a set of values that you need to iterate through to aggregate. Think about how you can have a list of values and this iteration could perform a calculation, for example, like how a factorial gets calculated.

While we know this will disappoint some of our readers, we have elected to omit detailed examples of these two functions in this book. The reality is that – while they do have uses – we can count the number of times on one hand that we have actually needed to use them. In almost all practical cases, we have always been able to discover other ways to keep our code friendly, optimal, and foldable.

> ✎ There is also another reserved keyword in the M language which is the @ sign. This can be used to create a recursive function, but in our experience we believe using `List.Accumulate()` or `List.Generate()` yields better performance.

Keywords *each* and _

Let's continue with our sample query and create a new column that will concatenate the FirstName and LastName. To do this:

- Delete any steps after the Removed Other Columns step
- Go to Add Column → Custom Column
- Name the column FullName and use the following formula:

```
[FirstName] & " " & [LastName]
```

With this formula we're effectively concatenating these two fields into a new one that we are creating. The big question though, is how does Power Query know that it needs to create a new column and use this formula to populate it?

The answer always lies in the formula bar or the Advanced Editor. For our example, we can simply look at the formula in the formula bar for this step and notice that Power Query used a function called `Table.AddColumn()` as shown in the image below.

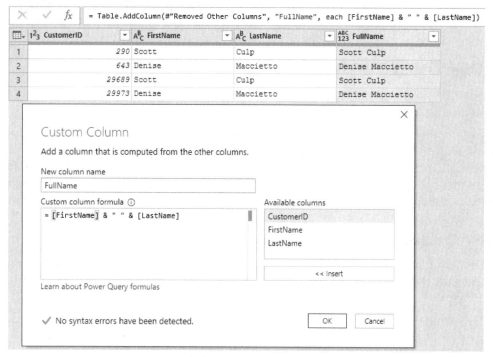

Creating a new custom column for the new field FullName

As you can see, the entire formula generated via the Custom Column dialog gets added as:

```
=Table.AddColumn(#"Removed Other Columns", "FullName",
each [FirstName] & " " & [LastName])
```

If we look at the Intellisense for this function – which you can trigger by deleting and then re-typing the (in the formula bar – we can see the parameters needed for the Table.AddColumn() function. Let's have a look at them, and what has been passed for each:

Official Parameter	Requires	Input
table as table	Table where the new column will be added	The table from the step #"Removed Other Columns"
newColumnName as text	The name of the new column	The text value "FullName"
columnGenerater as function	A function to create the new column	each [FirstName] & " " & [LastName]

Mapping the parameters of Table.AddColumn() function

> 🖋 Think about a function as a step or query that could accept arguments being passed to it, returning a dynamic result. Table.AddColumn() is a native function, but we can also define our own functions; something we will look at in greater detail in Chapter 17. But for now it's only important that we know what a function is as well as their main use case.

The component that might be new to us is the keyword **each**. This gets pre-appended to the formula that we defined for our custom column. But what is this keyword and what does it do?

If you remove this keyword from the formula in the formula bar, then an error will arise. Let's try doing that just to see what the step level error message says.

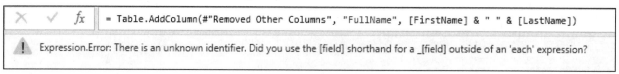

Error message after removing the each keyword from the formula bar

The error says something about a [field] being referenced outside of an 'each' expression. While correct, this error message is pretty cryptic and not super helpful to someone new to the M language. The issue is that the third parameter for the function requires a *function* to be passed and – by removing the *each* keyword – we simply provided a bunch of field names as *text*.

Let's try something else. Go back to the formula in the formula bar again and make another edit. Where we originally had the *each* keyword that we deleted, insert **(_)=>** into the formula as follows:

	fx	= Table.AddColumn(#"Removed Other Columns", "FullName", (_)=> [FirstName] & " " & [LastName])

	1²₃ CustomerID ▾	ABᶜ FirstName ▾	ABᶜ LastName ▾	ᴬᴮᶜ₁₂₃ FullName ▾
1	290	Scott	Culp	Scott Culp
2	643	Denise	Maccietto	Denise Maccietto
3	29689	Scott	Culp	Scott Culp
4	29973	Denise	Maccietto	Denise Maccietto

You'll notice right away that the step is now working as intended, but without the each and with something new. What does this mean? It means that **each** and **(_)=>** are equivalents from a syntax perspective for Power Query.

> 🗶 The ***each*** keyword is what we called "syntax-sugar" in programming. It is essentially a constant that is easier to type than its equivalent syntax.

Okay great... but what does (_)=> do? It is actually declaring a custom function.

A function can be defined by first a set of parentheses, then an equal sign followed by a greater than sign. For example, here's a function that takes two numbers and then multiplies those two numbers to achieve its output:

```
(x, y) => x*y
```

The key thing to recognize about the (_)=> function is that it is passing the underscore keyword as its parameter (a keyword that we first saw when creating records in Chapter 15). Let's just do that again quickly:

- Add a new column called Custom which uses the following formula: = _

The results will look as shown here:

	fx	= Table.AddColumn(#"Added Custom", "Custom", each _)

	1²₃ CustomerID ▾	ABᶜ FirstName ▾	ABᶜ LastName ▾	ᴬᴮᶜ₁₂₃ FullName ▾	ᴬᴮᶜ₁₂₃ Custom ⁴ᵗ
1	290	Scott	Culp	Scott Culp	Record
2	643	Denise	Maccietto	Denise Maccietto	Record
3	29689	Scott	Culp	Scott Culp	Record
4	29973	Denise	Maccietto	Denise Maccietto	Record

CustomerID	290
FirstName	Scott
LastName	Culp
FullName	Scott Culp

Creating a new custom column using only the underscore keyword

> 🗶 When you create a new column using nothing but the underscore keyword then the value from the current row will be showcased as a record, because we're in a table.

Going back to our sugar syntax and equivalencies, the 3 following formulas are completely equivalent:

```
(_)=> _[FirstName] & " " & _[LastName]
(_)=> [FirstName] & " " & [LastName]
each [FirstName] & " " & [LastName]
```

This first is the most explicit way to define a function where we are using the shorthand _ to refer to a specific field within the record. In short, we pass the underscore which holds a record to the function and then we access a field from that record as it was showcased in Chapter 15 where we simply use the square brackets and the name of the field from the record.

This second option is valid and it works, it just isn't as explicit as the previous one because we're assuming that we're only accessing those fields from the record that we passed to the function using the underscore keyword.

The final option is the way that Power Query automatically creates a new custom column and it is the easiest way to work with functions in Power Query. Having said that it is not always the best method when used outside of the context of the Table.AddColumn() function.

> 🐵 We recommend using either the first or last options as they are the most explicit.

It is important to realize that everything that we've covered in this section not only applies to the Table. AddColumn() function, but also to other functions. For example, imagine that we have a list of numbers like {1,2,3,4,5} and we want to modify that list by multiplying each of the numbers in the list by the number 2. To do that we can create the following formula:

```
= List.Transform( {1..5}, each _ * 2)
```

> 🐵 You may have noticed that we don't have to include any square braces in the formula above. This is because we have a list of primitive values that we are iterating through. If our list contained structured values such as records or tables, we would have to include some kind of navigation by saying each [value].

The List.Transform() function requires first a list and then a transform function, returning a list at the end which – in the case of the function above – would yield {2,4,6,8,10}. Notice how even in a list function we can use the each and underscore keywords to iterate through all values in the list.

One way that we think about the underscore is that it retrieves the current element. In some cases that might be a record – like when used with Table.AddColumn() – and in other cases – like with this list – it could just be the value within the list.

> 🙈 You cannot nest an each within another each as Power Query will only return the top level or outermost each in the formula. If you are trying to deal with multiple levels of iteration, you will have much more success with a custom function.

One thing to note is that the following two formulas are also an equivalent of the previous List.Transform() formula:

```
= List.Transform( {1..5}, (r)=> r * 2)
= List.Transform( {1..5}, (_)=> _ * 2)
```

> 🐵 The underscore just happens to be the character that the Power Query team chose to standardize upon. If you wrote this function manually you could use any letter or series of letters instead of the underscore (although we don't recommend doing so.)

	List
1	2
2	4
3	6
4	8
5	10

fx = List.Transform({1..5}, (_)=> _ * 2)

Using the underscore as an argument to a function inside a List.Transform() function

The bottom line is that you shouldn't feel intimidated by the each or underscore keywords in the formula bar. They are there to make your life easier and even make things easier to read by simplifying the code. Understanding these concepts is the first step into understanding how functions work in Power Query and a prerequisite before jumping into the creation of custom functions.

Other techniques

While this book doesn't try to cover every single function or every piece of code that has ever existed, this book does try to give you the foundation for the M language and also a couple of techniques and best practices that we've learned throughout the years.

The next few sections in this chapter will try to drive home everything that we've seen in the current and previous chapters, as well as add some new patterns that we hope you'll find useful when implementing your next Power Query solution.

Get the First Value From a Table Column

Imagine a scenario where you have a table with a column called Content that holds binary values and where you want to create a dynamic solution that will always access the Content field from the first row of the table.

Let's take a look at a sample scenario, found in the "First Value" query of the Ch16 Example file:

```
let
    Source = #table( type table [Content= binary, Value = text], {
        {#binary("Rmlyc3Q="), "First"},
        {#binary("U2Vjb25k"), "Second"},
        {#binary("VGhpcmQ="), "Third"}
    }),
    Data = Source{[Value="First"]}[Content],
    #"Imported Text" = Table.FromColumns(
      {Lines.FromBinary(Data,null,null,1252)})
in
    #"Imported Text"
```

The Source step of the query (pictured below) creates a replica of what you would see if you connected to folder or similar data source before navigating into the contents of the first file:

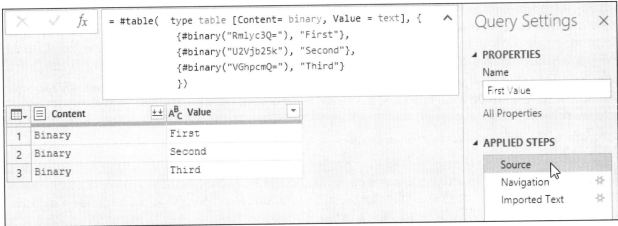

A sample query that mimics the contents of a "From Folder" query

The challenge with the current definition of this query, however, is that the formula of the Navigation step (which drills into the data) reads as follows:

```
= Source{[Value="First"]}[Content]
```

This formula states that Power Query needs to get the record where Value is equal to "First" and then drills down to the Content field of that record. This is not dynamic as it explicitly relies on the word "First" being present in the values for the navigation to work. So, what happens if it doesn't? To answer this question:

- Go to the Source Step → filter the Value column → uncheck "First"

Upon selecting the navigation (Data) step, you will be greeted with the following error:

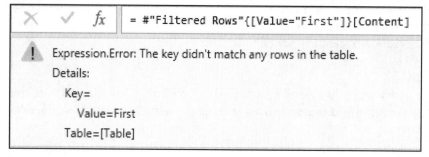

Step level error where the key didn't match any rows in the table

We can improve this by modifying the navigation (Data) step so it doesn't rely on any specific data point, instead ensuring that it always returns the first row from the table. As we saw in Chapter 15, all we need to do is remove the `[Value="First"]` from the formula and replace it with the number 0 to denote that we want the first row (or record) from the table as follows.

```
= Source{0}[Content]
```

At this point, you'll notice that everything still works, and that the query will always return the contents of the first binary, no matter which you filter out via the Filtered Rows step.

We cannot stress enough how incredibly helpful numeric row navigation can be when you are creating more dynamic solutions with Power Query.

> 🔧 As it happens, this behavior is exactly what Power Query configures for you in the Sample File query when combining files, ensuring that the Transform Sample is always based on the first file in the (filtered) folder.

> 🐵 When you click a Binary value, Power Query automatically interprets that you want to navigate to that specific value, so it creates a bunch of steps for you. Some of those steps may have identifier references, rather than navigation that targets the first item in the list as we have shown here. For that reason, it is always a good idea to check what Power Query did and tweak the code to fit your needs.

Replace with *null* if Navigation Fails

While we've just seen how to dynamically refer to a specific row, there is one thing that we can't make dynamic and that is the reference to the Content column. Power Query always requires referring to columns by name; there is no way to connect to a column via an indexed position. You could argue that it is a good thing since we need to have a clear understanding of what field we need to access or where exactly we find the data that matters to us. On the other hand, what happens if the name of the field changes?

Ignoring the dynamic row for a minute, consider what will happen to our original query if someone renames the Content column to Data. Of course, it will cause another step level error telling us that the [Content] field doesn't exist.

Using one of the structures we learned in Chapter 14, we could handle this using as follows:

```
try Source{[Value="First"]}[Data] otherwise null
```

While this is perfectly valid, there is another option that might be helpful depending on your specific case. It works well when you want to use it for navigation through values in Power Query. Simply add a question mark keyword (?) at the end of original code, like this:

```
Source{[Value="First"]}[Data]?
```

As you can see it functions equivalently to the previous try statement as shown here:

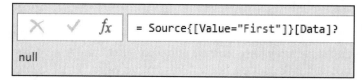

Using the question mark keyword when accessing a field

This is really valuable when you want to test things out or want to make your solution more robust as this is "syntax sugar" for a full `try x otherwise null` logical structure. And if the column gets renamed back to Content either of the two previous options will work as expected since the Content field again exists in the Source table.

Where this structure becomes even more valuable is when you try to access or navigate through a table, list or other structured values. For example, replace the formula in the Navigation step with this:

```
= Source{[Value="1"]}?[Content]?
```

This formula is trying to find a record in the Value column of the Source table where the text value equals "1" and then access the Content field related to that record. We've added another question mark keyword right after the table navigation since that's the first evaluation that happens to get a record, but since that record doesn't exist in the table it yields an error, so we catch that error with this keyword and output a null. If no errors occur during the evaluation, it will simply output the result of the evaluation.

Putting this technique together with that from the previous section, the code below will return the first row from the Content column, and will return null if the Content column is not found:

```
= Source{0}?[Content]?
```

⚓ You can complement your query by checking if the result from this step was a null and then act accordingly based on that information. That would by far make it more robust and make sure that you are ready for cases where the query might generate errors during the navigation phase for whatever reason.

Create a Dynamic List of Headers with Typed Columns

The following scenario is based upon the following code, found in the "List of Headers" query in the chapter's example file:

```
= #table( type table [Data=record, Title = text], {
        {[First="Bill", Last="Jelen"], "First"},
        {[First = "Miguel", Last= "Escobar", Country ="Panama"],
            "Second"},
        {[First = "Ken", Last= "Puls", Country ="Canada",
            #"Tall?" = true], "Third"}
    } )
```

Since it contains records, we can expand the Data column using the button at the top right:

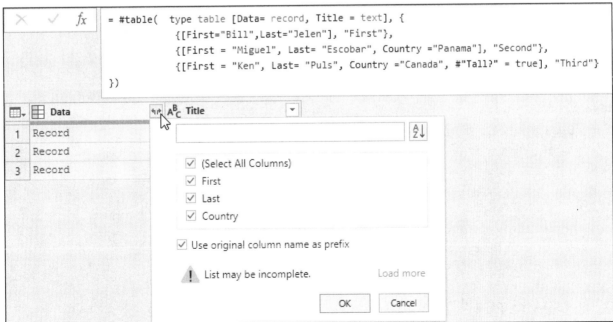

Triggering a Table.ExpandTableColumns() operation on the Data column

You'll notice that the menu, triggered when we attempt to expand the records in the Data column, shows a warning which reads "List may be incomplete" with clickable text next to it reading "Load more". Upon clicking the *Load more* option we are presented with the following:

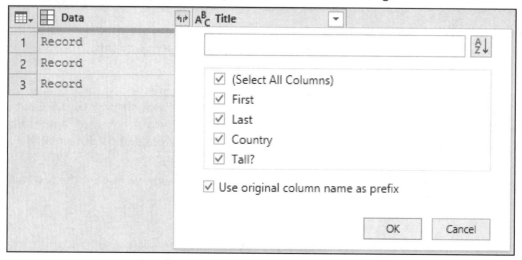

A new field appears after clicking the load more option

If you've ever seen this, you may wonder why Power Query didn't show ALL of the fields that were available in the first place. To answer that question, we first need to review how Power Query gathers the information for this menu.

In short, Power Query can figure out this information in two ways:

1. **It already has this info** – where the data type for the column already has the metadata about what fields are supposed to be in each of those records.

1. **It needs to calculate this info** – where there is no explicit data type defined for the record, Power Query needs to do some introspection on the values that it finds in the Data Preview view.

> ✎ The first scenario is actually quite common. For example, whenever you use the Merge operation, creating a new column with table values, the expand dialog will automatically load the full list of the fields without issue.

But how can we make it work for our case? The answer to this question is that we need to explicitly define our data types; an action that we will accomplish in two steps:

Step 1: Create a new query that holds our custom record types:

- Create a new blank query and call it "MyRecordType"
- Enter the following formula in the formula bar for the first step:

```
= type [First= text, Last=text, Country=text, #"Tall?"=logical]
```

Step2: Update the query to use the new MyRecordType.

- Duplicate the List of Headers query and call it "Dynamic Headers – Typed"
- Replace the word "record" in the Source step with "MyRecordType" as shown below:

```
= #table( type table [Data= MyRecordType, Title = text], {
        {[First="Bill", Last="Jelen"], "First"},
        {[First = "Miguel", Last= "Escobar", Country ="Panama"],
            "Second"},
        {[First = "Ken", Last= "Puls", Country ="Canada",
            #"Tall?" = true], "Third"}
    } )
```

- Select the Expanded Data step (or expand all fields from the Data column if it doesn't already exist.)

🖎 This whole process is effectively a more precise method to define the data types of your table, and results in data that is classified as a complex data type. This approach is not commonly seen in live solutions, except when creating custom connectors where fully defined data types are required.

The great benefits of this approach are:

1. All columns are immediately shown when performing the expand operation, and

2. The columns keep their data types when expanded.

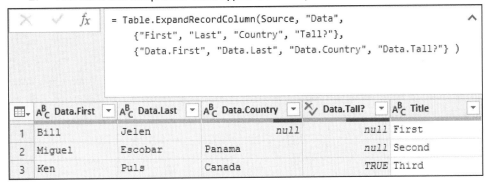

All record values expanded from the table with correct data types in place

In the real world, we often don't know what fields might be in your records or tables in advance, so how can we make it more dynamic? This is where Power Query can help you calculate that on the fly doing its own introspection.

The only caveat is that Power Query, as mentioned before, tries to work in a smart fashion using lazy evaluation to its advantage. That's why the first time that we clicked the expand button, it only did the introspection of the fields in the record values of the first few records, but not on the last. This is pretty important because the last record in the table had a field that the rest of the records didn't have. We had to force Power Query to do a full introspection on the available data by clicking the Load More option.

🖎 Can we create our own introspection of records and table fields? We sure can, and we can use this to provide a dynamic list of items when using the Table.ExpandTableColumn(), Table.ExpandRecordColumn() and Table.ExpandListColumn() functions.

Create a Dynamic List of Headers with Untyped Columns

As an alternative to creating a dynamic list of headers with fully data-type columns, let's create a new query that does the same thing, but with an untyped record set:

- Create a new query by duplicating the List of Headers query
- Name the query "Dynamic Headers – Untyped"
- Delete the Expanded Data step (if you added it to the List of Headers earlier)
- Right-click the Data column and select the Drill Down option

This will transform your table column into a list as shown below.

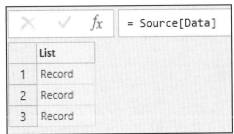

We now have a list of records

Hit the fx button in the formula bar to create a custom step and write the following formula:

```
= List.Transform( Data, each Record.FieldNames(_))
```

This will transform that list of records into a list of lists where each list contains the Field Names for each of the records.

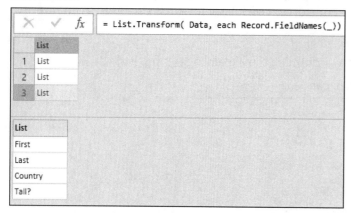

A list of lists which contain the column names from each record

Create a new custom step to keep things clean and then write the following formula:

```
= List.Combine( Custom1 )
```

> 🔧 List.Combine() appends all elements from each list into a single list with all the elements. This means that we'll have a list with all the field names from all of our records.

Finally, go to the List Tools → Transform tab and choose Remove Duplicates:

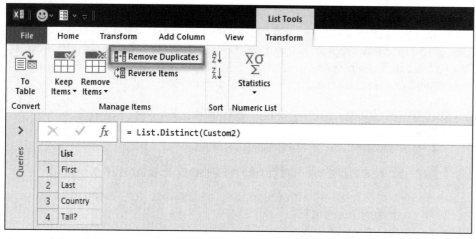

A consolidated list of our unique column headers

> 🔧 Make sure that the name of this step is **Removed Duplicates** as we will be using it later!

We now have a query that is effectively calculating a dynamic list of (unique) headers and can pass it into the Table.ExpandRecordColumn() function:

- Press the *fx* button to create another custom step
- Change the formula in the formula bar to =Source (returning its original results)
- Expand all fields from the Data column

The results and formula are shown below:

```
fx    = Table.ExpandRecordColumn(Custom3, "Data",
              {"First", "Last", "Country"},
              {"Data.First", "Data.Last", "Data.Country"})
```

	ABC 123 Data.First	ABC 123 Data.Last	ABC 123 Data.Country	A B C Title
1	Bill	Jelen	null	First
2	Miguel	Escobar	Panama	Second
3	Ken	Puls	Canada	Third

Our records have been expanded with static column names

⚓ Both the Table.ExpandRecordColumn() and Table.ExpandTableColumn() functions require a table as the first argument, followed by the name of the column which holds the fields to be expanded, and finally a list of the fields you wish to expand from the column of fields. As an optional fourth argument you can pass the new names for the fields that you are expanding. (The reason our code shows each field name prefaced with "Data." is due to the fact that we left the option to add a prefix checked when expanding the records.)

The next and final step is simply to remove those last two arguments of the Table.ExpandRecordColumn() function and replace them with the formula below:

```
= Table.ExpandRecordColumn(Custom3, "Data", #"Removed Duplicates")
```

And just like that, we now have a solution that will scan or have some sort of introspection for the record values in the Data column. As the list of columns is dynamic, it will never miss a new column added to one of the records, with all columns showing up automatically during a refresh.

```
fx    = Table.ExpandRecordColumn(Custom3, "Data",
              #"Removed Duplicates")
```

	ABC 123 First	ABC 123 Last	ABC 123 Country	ABC 123 Tall?	A B C Title
1	Bill	Jelen	null	null	First
2	Miguel	Escobar	Panama	null	Second
3	Ken	Puls	Canada	TRUE	Third

Final output with all fields expanded

🐵 While this is an incredibly helpful technique, bear in mind that if your list contains field names that already exist in your table, then that would create a conflict and would raise an error. Be sure to use this technique when you know that there won't be a conflict of field names between the fields expanded and the fields already in the table.

⚓ Please note that while we demonstrated this technique using a column with record values, this same pattern works for a column with table values. All that you'll need to change is the usage of `Record.FieldNames()` for `Table.ColumnNames()` and instead of using `Table.ExpandRecordColumn()` you'll be using `Table.ExpandTableColumn()`. Everything else would remain exactly the same.

Chapter 17 - Parameters and Custom Functions

Back in Chapter 9 we saw a pretty cool example of combining multiple files together. In order to do so, Power Query created a custom function allowing you to work with a separate data sample, and then apply that to a table of files. The greatest thing about this, however, is that we aren't limited to the functions that Power Query already provides or can build for us. We can build our own.

In this chapter we will explore the method that Power Query used in order to generate its function, so that you can see how the pieces are derived and fit together. We will then work through other examples to show how we can adapt these pieces for different scenarios.

Re-Creating the Combine Files Experience

In this section, let's begin by recreating the mechanics of Power Query's Combine Files experience. While we won't perform the data transformation of the individual files, we will still follow the FilesList recipe we introduced in Chapter 9 for combining files. To get started, open a blank workbook and build the FilesList query as follows:

- Create a new query → From File → From Folder
- Select the Ch17 Examples\Source Data folder → Transform Data
- Right-click the Extension column → Transform → lowercase
- Filter the Extension column → Text Filters → Equals → Advanced → set the filter as follows:
- Extension → equals → .xlsx
- And Name → Does not begin with → ~
- Rename the query as FilesList and load it as a Connection Only query

Next, let's create the Orders query, just as we did in the original recipe:

- Right-click the FilesList query → Reference
- Rename the new query as Orders

At this point we should have a simple listing of all files in the folder and are ready to combine all of the files in the folder:

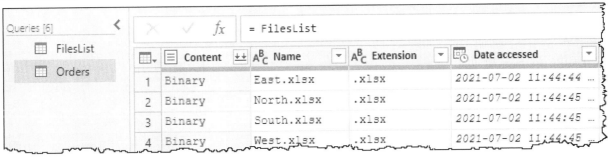

At this point we could just click the Combine Files button, but where is the fun in that?

> 🔍 Remember that we split the query prior to combining files – something you can recognize since the Formula Bar shows =FilesList instead of a more complex M code formula.

Rather than take the easy way out, let's manually re-create the magic that happens when you click the Combine Files button. This will involve the manual creation of the Sample File, Sample File Parameter, Transform Sample and Transform Function.

Creating the Sample File

To create the sample file, we start from the Orders table and:

- Right-click the first Binary in the Content column → Add as New Query
- Rename the new query as "Sample File"

What you'll notice is that this query now has two steps:

1. Source, which references the Orders table, and
2. Navigation, which drills into the file we referenced.

The challenge here is that the file path to the file has been hard-coded, which isn't very dynamic:

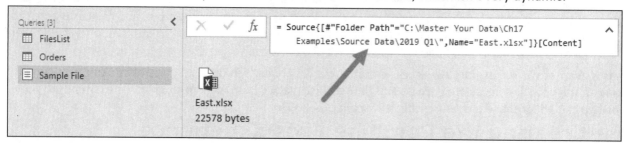

The sample file contains a hard-coded file path

We want this file to dynamically refer to the first file in the Orders table, something that we can accomplish using a trick that we learned in Chapter 16:

*   Replace the file path with 0 so that the formula reads =Source{0}[Content]
*   Delete the new step that Power Query automatically creates to drill in to the file

We now have our Sample File query set up as required:

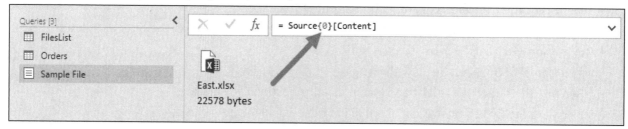

Our Sample File now dynamically pulls from the first row of the Source step (Orders)

Creating the Sample File Parameter

This step isn't difficult, but it does involve a manual creation of the parameter. To do this:

- Go to Home → Manage Parameters → New Parameter
- Name the parameter "Sample File Parameter"
- Set the Type to Binary
- Set the Default and Current values to Sample File

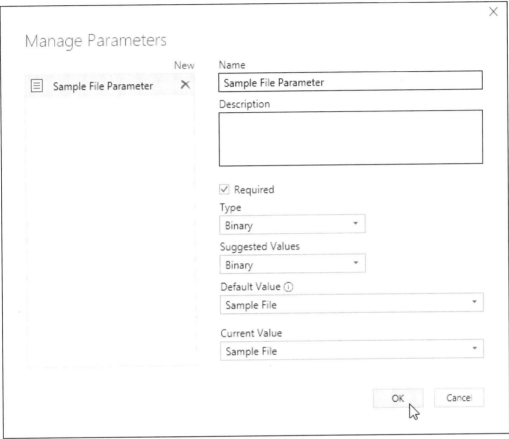

Configuring the Sample File Parameter

> 🔧 The name of this parameter is not truly important, we are simply following the naming convention laid out in Chapter 9. You could leave it as Parameter1 if you chose and everything would work without issue.

Upon clicking OK, you'll be greeted with a very simple display that shows the current value of the parameter is our Sample File:

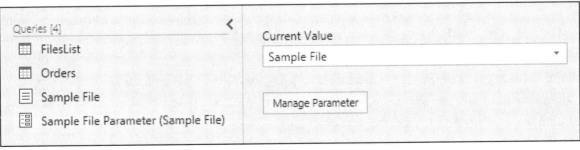

Our previews will reference the Sample File

Creating the Transform Sample

The next thing we need to do is create the Transform Sample – the workhorse that you use to build the data transformation pattern. As mentioned previously, we won't actually perform any manipulations, as that isn't the point of this chapter, but we will build the framework that allows you to do so.

To create your Transform Sample query:

- Right-click the Sample File Parameter → Reference
- Rename the query as Transform Sample

At this point, you should notice a couple of things. First, the Transform still points to the Sample File Parameter in the formula bar. Second, it shows an image representing our binary file. To drill into the file itself, we can right-click it and choose how to interpret the file:

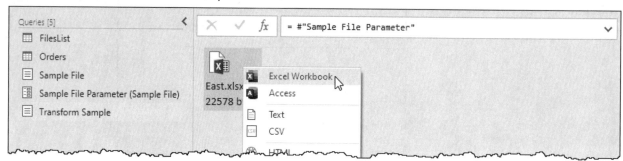

Building our Transform Sample

Let's drill into our file now:

- Right-click the East.xlsx file → Excel Workbook

Upon doing so, you'll notice that Power Query doesn't add a new step, but rather modifies the Source step to use the Excel.Workbook() function to enumerate the list of values you can play with.

- Click the Table value related to the Parts table (on the 3rd row)

At this point we should now see the contents of the Parts table from our sample file (East.xlsx):

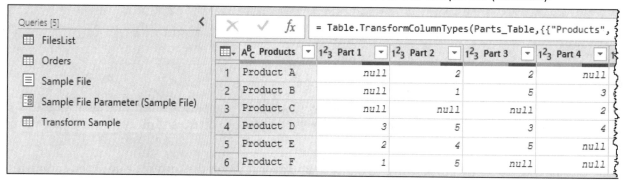

Our Transform Sample file has been created

Obviously, we could now do more work here, but at this point we are not going to do that. Instead, we want to create the Transform Function that can be applied to all files in the folder.

Creating the Transform Function

Given that this query uses a parameter to drive its binary file, this next step is actually easy:

- Right-click the Transform Sample query → Create Function
- Name the new function Transform Function → OK
- Optionally, you may also want to drag the Sample File into the new folder

Believe it or not, we have now re-created all of the pieces that Power Query generates when you click the Combine Files button (we just haven't actually used them yet):

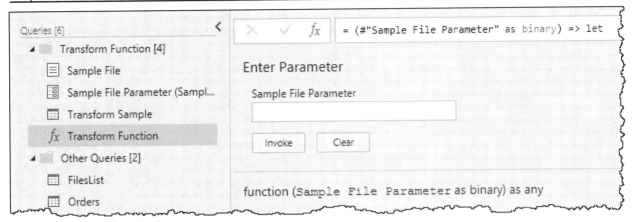

All of our components have been successfully created

Invoking the Transform Function

Now it is time to prove that everything has been hooked up correctly:

- Select the Orders query → go to Home → Choose Columns → select only Content and Name
- Go to Add Column → Invoke Custom Function → choose the Transform Function → OK
- Preview the second table (the transform related to North.xlsx)

At this point you should recognize that our Transform Function appears to be working for not only the East.xlsx file, but also the North.xlsx file:

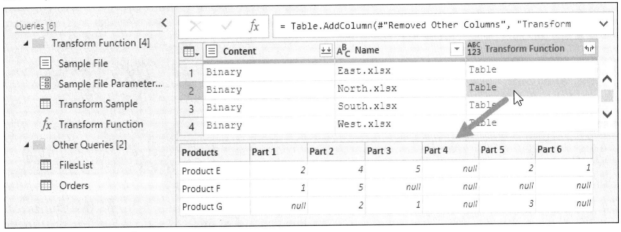

Our Transform Function appears to be extracting details for each file

Updating the Transform Function

So far, so good, but did this actually all link up the same way as Power Query's magic Combine Files button? In other words, if we update the Transform Sample, will it update the Transform Function? Let's find out:

- Select the Transform Sample
- Right-click the Products column → Unpivot Other columns
- Rename Attribute as Part and Value as Units
- Return to the Orders table
- Preview the results for the North file again

As you can see, the changes we made are coming through without issue:

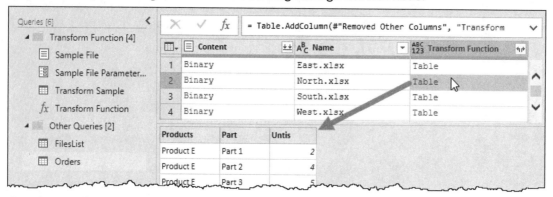

Our changes have come through perfectly!

Knowing this, we can expand the data for loading:

- Expand the Transform Function column
- Remove the Content column
- Set the data types for each column

The final step of this process is to load the data so that we can use it but beware of a potential pitfall here.

We have created five new queries in this session, without choosing a load destination. In Power BI this is easy to resolve, just make sure that all of the queries have the Load Enabled property unchecked before you commit them. But in Excel? When you choose to load your queries, you only get to pick one destination and – should you accidentally choose to load to a worksheet or the data model – you may get an error telling you that the Sample File cannot be loaded (since it is a binary value).

> ✎ In Excel we highly recommend that you go to Close & Load To → Only Create Connection at this point and – once the queries are all saved – change the load destination of the Orders table to load to the required destination.

Key Observations

The first thing you should recognize about what we have just accomplished is that the Combine Files button is essentially a macro that builds all of the required components for you. You click a button, and magic just happens, which is great!

One danger from this process however is that it may lead you to a false observation as to how these functions need to be set up to work. We are going to look at building our own functions shortly, but there are some things we want to call out before we get there:

1. The Transform Sample is fully editable and provides write-back capability to the Transform function. This means that you can add or remove additional parameters to the Transform Sample, and they will get incorporated into the Transform Function.

2. While the Transform Sample can be used to drive the Transform Function, the Transform Function doesn't actually have a dependency on the Transform Sample. You could actually delete the Transform Sample if you chose to do so, and it wouldn't have any effect on the query's ability to refresh. Of course, if you did this, you would lose the ability to easily update your function via the user interface and Applied Steps window.

1. Not every function requires a dynamic sample as we have with the Sample File. In fact, it becomes very easy to violate privacy and Formula.Firewall rules if you try to provide one.

2. Do not get hung up in trying to make your Parameters dynamic. The Sample and Current values you see are only used in the preview window for debugging your Transform Sample. At runtime they will be populated with whatever you pass into them.

3. Don't feel that you have to use a Parameter to drive your custom function either. Custom Functions can rely on queries or parameters to drive their logic, or neither of these elements!

🔦 Custom Functions can be very powerful, just don't get stuck thinking that they have to work following the exact same methods used in the Combine Files experience!

Building a Custom Function Using Parameters

In this example we will look at a rather common scenario: someone has built a transformation against a single text file, thinking it was a one-time job. They've now realized that they need to apply the same transformation to each file in a folder. Rather than rebuild the entire solution from scratch, they want to retrofit the file, turning their original query into a function, and then use that function to import and transform each file.

Ideally, we'd like to have a Transform Sample query, as well as the Transform Function. But most important – the Timesheet query is already loaded to a worksheet, with business logic based upon that table. We cannot afford to blow that up, so that query must remain as the one that loads our finalized data.

We will start from the Ch17 Examples\Retrofitting-Begin.xlsx file, which contains two queries:

- **Timesheet** reshapes the 2021-03-14.txt file contained in the Timesheets subfolder
- **FilesList** contains a simple query that lists all files in the TimeSheets subfolder, returning a simple list of consolidated file paths and names as shown below:

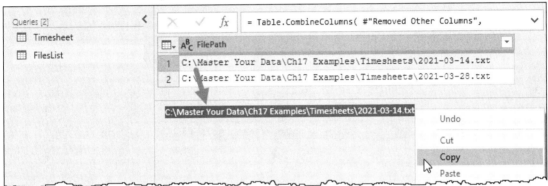

Copying the first value from the FilesList query…

🙈 Remember that the file paths in both the Timesheet and FilesList queries are hard-coded at this point. Make sure you update them to where they live on your PC or you will get errors when you try to follow the examples!

In this solution we will need to take four steps:

1. Create a FilePath parameter
2. Create a new Timesheet transform (based on the original query) to leverage the parameter
3. Create a new Timesheet function
4. Retrofit the original Timesheet query to invoke the new Timesheet function

Creating the FilePath Parameter

Let's get started by creating a simple parameter that will hold the complete file path as text:

- Select the FilesList query → copy the path to the first file (as shown in the previous image)
- Go to Home → Manage Parameters → New Parameter
- Name the parameter FilePath
- Set the Type to text → paste the file path into the Current Value area → OK

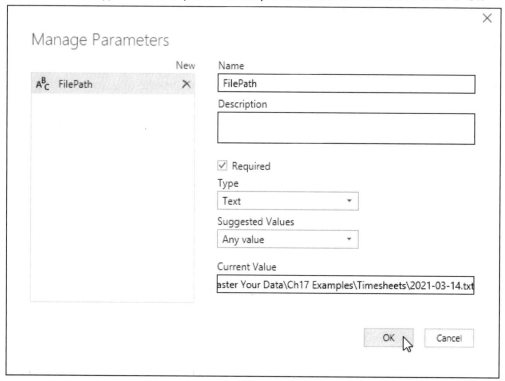

Configuring a text-based parameter

> ⚒ Remember that the current value is only used to drive the results in the preview, and you can always update it to use a different file later via the Manage Parameters dialog.

Creating the Timesheet Transform

With our Parameter created, we now need to create a new Timesheet Transform based on the original Timesheet query and update it to use the new FilePath parameter. This is actually much easier than it sounds:

- Right-click the original Timesheet query → Duplicate
- Rename the Timesheet(2) query as Timesheet Transform
- Select the Source step of the Timesheet Transform → Edit Settings
- Change the drop-down under File path to Parameter

> ⚒ This is where a Parameter really shines. Many input areas in the Power Query user interface provide an option to change from a primitive value to a column and/or a Parameter. Unfortunately, queries rarely ever show up in this list of options, even if they evaluate to a primitive value.

If you only have one parameter in your solution, it will be selected automatically, but if not, you'll have to select it:

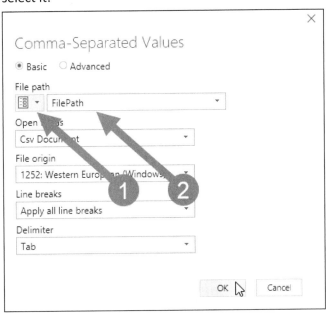

Configuring the Source step of the Timesheet Transform query

Believe it or not, that's all you have to do in order to create a new Transform Sample query. So long as you provided a valid path (including the file name and extension) to the Current Value of the FilePath parameter, the preview should show data after clicking OK:

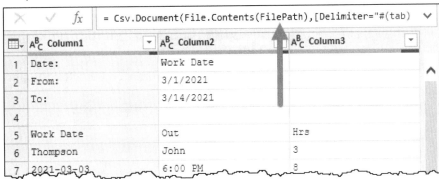

Our file path has been replaced by the FilePath parameter, and the preview still shows data

> 🐵 Is the preview showing an error? Go to Home → Manage Parameters → Filepath and ensure that the "Current Value" contains the complete file path to one of the two timesheet files.

Creating the Timesheet Function

With the Timesheet Transform relying on the parameter, creating the Transform Function is deadly simple:

- Right-click the Timesheet Transform → Create Function → name it Timesheet Function → OK

Seriously. That's it!

> 🖋 The secret to enabling the Create Function button is to have at least one Parameter used within the query. As long as you do, you'll be able to create a new function from it and keep the original as a "Transform Sample".

Updating the Timesheet Query

The final part of retrofitting our solution is the trickiest. If we get it wrong, it will blow up the business logic that relies on the structure of the original Timesheet table, so we need to be careful. Fortunately, our new Timesheet Transform query contains the required column names for our original table, so we can always check back against that to confirm our updated query is correct.

In order to update the Timesheet query, we need to do the following:

- Delete all the current steps
- Repoint the query to read from the FilesList query
- Invoke the new Timesheet Function and remove all columns except the Function results
- Expand the results of the Timesheet Function
- Set the data types

In theory, if we do all of that, we should have the same columns that we had previously and – when loaded – we shouldn't compromise any of the existing business logic created against the original Timesheet table.

Probably the easiest way to start this process is actually to edit and clear out the contents of the existing Timesheet query. To do that:

- Select the Timesheet query → View → Advanced Editor
- Replace all of the code in the query with the code shown below

```
let
    Source = FilesList
in
    Source
```

☎ Don't forget – if you called your query "Files List" – it would need to be referred to as #"Files List". In addition, you must make sure that the query name is spelled and cased correctly or Power Query won't recognize it.

Upon clicking Done, you will now have a fresh query ready, just as if you had referenced the FilesList query directly in a new query:

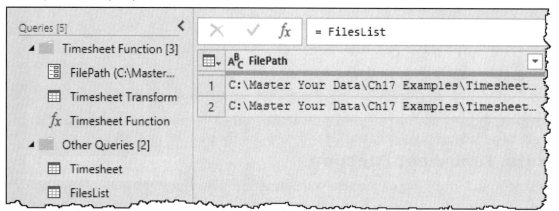

Our Timesheet query now refers to the FilesList query

Let's finish this off:

- Go to Add Column → Invoke Custom Function → Timesheet Function
- Select FilePath → OK

And… oh no…

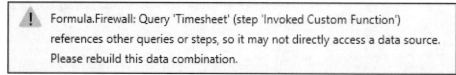

The dreaded Formula.Firewall refuses to let us invoke our custom function

This is a super frustrating error message and one that we were honestly hoping to avoid.

> 🖋 While the formula firewall tries to protect you from combining data with incompatible privacy levels, that is not the only thing it protects against. You might be tempted to solve this issue by disabling the privacy settings, but it won't have any effect here.

We are going to look at the formula firewall in more detail in chapter 19, but for now, can we do something to skip this issue? Disabling privacy won't fix it, so what can we do?

The error message seems to be complaining about referencing another query, so could we eliminate that issue and do this in the query we referenced? In other words, if we try to invoke the function within the FilesList query, will it work? Let's try it...

- Delete the Invoked Custom Function step from the Timesheet query
- Select the FilesList query
- Go to Add Column → Invoke Custom Function → Timesheet Function → Select FilePath → OK

And how about that? It works nicely!

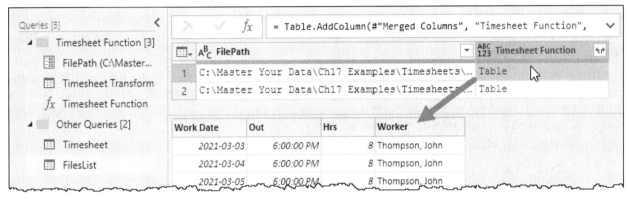

Our custom function can be invoked within the FilesList query

At the end of the day, this isn't a huge issue for us. With the function invoked in the FilesList table, we have avoided the formula firewall issue, and now have a list of the files and their contents nested within Table values in the FilesList query. There is nothing saying that we have to expand those tables within this query. In fact, this could actually be helpful to us if we need to spin off another query with a different view of that information.

Let's go back to the Timesheet query and finish extracting our columns:

- Select the Timesheet query
- Right-click the Timesheet Function column → Remove Other Columns
- Expand all columns from the Timesheet Function column (with the prefix option unchecked)
- Set the data types on all of the columns

The final thing to watch out for here is the load destinations when we load the query. We have again created multiple queries in this one Power Query session. The thing is that the original Timesheet query was already set to load to a worksheet, so we are only going to be able to choose the load destination for the new queries – none of which are needed in the worksheet.

- Go to Home → Close & Load To → Connection Only

At this point the data table will update to show the records from both timesheet files in the Timesheets subfolder, and the formulas targeting the table will update flawlessly:

The business logic (formulas) built against the Timesheet table update without issue

Building a Custom Function Manually

So far, things seem fairly easy. Create one or more parameters, use one (or more) in a query, and then create a function from that query. Unfortunately, it won't take long for you to run into a scenario where this isn't possible.

If you open Ch17 Examples\Pivoting Tables-Begin.xlsx, you will find that there are two tables living in the first worksheet. Our goal is to unpivot each table, as shown here:

Our goal is to be able to unpivot the data prior to appending it

Of course, we could connect to each individual table, unpivot it, then append them all together. But what if the transformations were even more complex? We'd much rather build a single function that can be applied to each of the tables consistently.

Based on the previous examples, this shouldn't appear too difficult, except that we have one big issue… currently you can only create Parameters that hold primitive values. As we would need to pass a table (a structured value) to our function, we cannot leverage a parameter to do this. What this means is that we are going to need to build a custom function from scratch.

In order to build a custom function, we basically follow a three-step process:

1.   Build a single use scenario first,
2.   Convert the single use scenario into a function, and
3.   Call the function from another query.

This sounds easy enough in practice. Let's take a look how we put it all together.

Build a Single Use Scenario

In order to get started, open the Ch17 Examples\Pivoting Tables-Begin.xlsx file and:

- Create a new query → From Other Sources → Blank Query
- Type =Excel.CurrentWorkbook() in the formula bar
- Rename the query as Sales
- Filter the Name column → Does Not Equal → Sales

   🐵 Don't forget the lesson we learned in Chapter 8 when using Excel.CurrentWorkbook() to consolidate tables: Always filter out the table you will be creating!

With our future-proofing done, we can now build a single-use scenario to unpivot one of the two tables. To do this:

- Right-click on either of the Table values in the Content columns → Add as New Query
- Rename the new query fxUnpivot
- Right-click the Date column → Unpivot Other Columns
- Rename Attribute to Product and Value to Units
- Set the data types to Date, Text and Whole Number

Providing that you started with Table2, your output should now look like this:

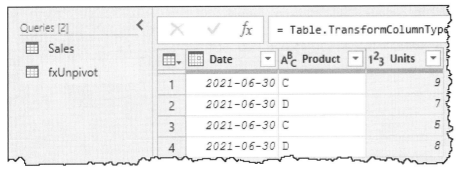

Okay… that's one table unpivoted… now how do we make this a function?

Converting the Query into a Function

The next step in the process is to convert the query into a function. This involves three steps:

1. Come up with a name for the variable that will hold the data you wish to replace
2. Edit the query and place the following text at the beginning: **(variable_name)=>**
3. Scan your query for the data you wish to replace and overwrite it with the variable name

> ⚒ Note that placing spaces around your variable name is optional, but we like to do this as it makes the code easier to read.

It's a good idea to come up with a variable name that is somewhat descriptive of the data it will hold, as this helps self-document your M code. As our goal is to convert our single use scenario into a function where we can pass it a table, we will use the variable name **tbl.**

Now that we've determined our variable name, let's edit the query to turn it into a function.

- Right-click the fxUnpivot Query → Advanced Editor
- Place your cursor right in front of the **let** statement
- Type in **(tbl)=>** and press Enter

Your code should now start like this:

```
1  (tbl) =>
2  let
3      Source = Excel.CurrentWorkbook(),
4      #"Filtered Rows" = Table.SelectRows(Source, each [Name] <> "Sales"),
5      Table1 = #"Filtered Rows"{[Name="Table2"]}[Content],
6      #"Unpivoted Other Columns" = Table.UnpivotOtherColumns(Table1, {"Date"}
7      #"Renamed Columns" = Table.RenameColumns(#"Unpivoted Other Columns",{{"A
8      #"Changed Type" = Table.TransformColumnTypes(#"Renamed Columns",{{"Date"
```

Our variable is now in place

> ⚒ At this point, you've already converted your query into a function. As we haven't subbed the variable name into the code, however, the function won't actually change anything.

For the next step, it really pays to understand the M code behind the query. What we need to do is figure out where to put our variable. Our intent is to pass a table value into the query, so we need to know which step should consume that table.

If we look carefully at the code, the first two steps connect to the Excel workbook, and set a filter to remove the Sales table, leaving behind the two tables from our worksheet. The next row – which starts with Table1 – navigates in to Table2's content. So we *could* assign the Table1 step to set it equal to the tbl variable, like this:

```
Table1 = tbl ,
```

While this would work, it isn't truly necessary, as all this step does is record the value of the table so that it can feed it to the next line of code:

```
Table.UnpivotOtherColumns(Table1, {"Date"}, "Attribute", "Value"),
```

We know that UnpivotOtherColumns requires a table as the first parameter, which is what our tbl variable will hold. So rather than pass tbl to Table1, and then pass Table1 into the following line, why don't we just feed the tbl variable directly into the Table.UnpivotOtherColumns() function?

```
1   (tbl) =>
2   let
3       Source = Excel.CurrentWorkbook(),
4       #"Filtered Rows" = Table.SelectRows(Source, each [Name] <> "Sales"),
5       Table1 = #"Filtered Rows"{[Name="Table2"]}[Content],
6       #"Unpivoted Other Columns" = Table.UnpivotOtherColumns(Table1, {"Date"}, "Attribute"
7       #"Renamed Columns" = Table.RenameColumns(#"Unpivoted Other Columns",{{"Attribute", "
8       #"Changed Type" = Table.TransformColumnTypes(#"Renamed Columns",{{"Date", type date}
9   in
10      #"Changed Type"
```

Let's put our tbl variable here...

In fact, if we do that, we don't even need the first three rows of the query definition anymore, so why don't we just remove them?

```
1   (tbl) =>
2   let
3       #"Unpivoted Other Columns" = Table.UnpivotOtherColumns(tbl, {"Date"}, "Attribute
4       #"Renamed Columns" = Table.RenameColumns(#"Unpivoted Other Columns",{{"Attribute
5       #"Changed Type" = Table.TransformColumnTypes(#"Renamed Columns",{{"Date", type d
6   in
7       #"Changed Type"
```

Our function is shorter, but does it work?

At this point you can click OK, and you'll notice that your query changes into the view you would expect to see for a function:

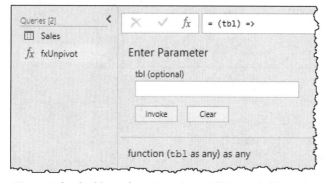

Nice... it looks like a function, but will it work like a function?

Calling the Function

If your parameter required a primitive value, such as a piece of text or a value, you could enter that into the dialog and then press Invoke. This would allow you to easily test your function to make sure it is working correctly. Unfortunately, with a structured value this is a bit more difficult to do.

> ✒ Sadly, you can't even trick this dialog by preceding it with the = character, like you can when creating a custom column. Feeding it =Excel.CurrentWorkbook(){0}[Content] just treats the formula as text.

The easiest way to test this function is just try and invoke it, passing it some tables to work with.

- Select the Sales query → Add Column → Invoke Custom Function
- Choose the fxUnpivot column → make sure the tbl is set to Content → OK
- Preview the results for Table1

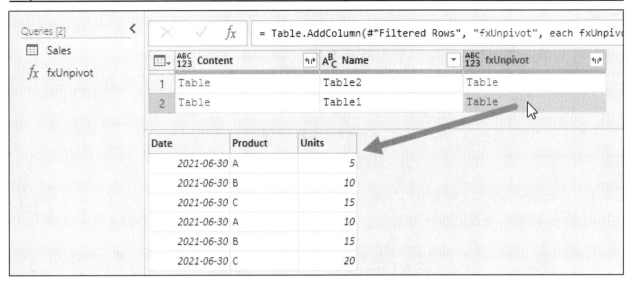

It looks like our custom fxUnpivot function is working!

As you can see, while Parameters can be quite helpful, they aren't actually necessary if you want to build a custom function. Let's finish this query:

- Right-click the fxUnpivot column → Remove other Columns
- Expand the fxUnpivot column (with the prefix option unchecked)
- Set the data types for each of the columns

At the end of the process, our data looks perfect and – if someone adds another table of products – it will be included in the unpivot operation.

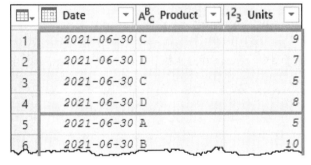

The results of our unpivot operation

Debugging Custom Functions

One of the things that you may have noticed is that without creating a Parameter, we don't get to keep a copy of our Transform Sample. This is one of the painful pieces of working with custom functions: we lose the ability to step through them easily. That makes debugging custom functions a bit of a challenge.

While not ideal, there is a way to convert your function back into a query so that you can test it. The unfortunate part of this process is that it is a temporary state, as converting the function into a debuggable state converts it out of function mode, breaking any subsequent queries during the debugging process. Despite this, it is the only way to accomplish the goal, so we'll explore it here.

In order to restore the Applied Steps window so that you can debug your function, we actually need to turn it back into a query. To do this we need to do two things:

1. Comment out the line that turns the query into a function
2. Duplicate the variable used in the initial line and assign it a value

Failure to do either of the above will cause us to end up with a query or function that returns the wrong results at best, or errors at worst.

To comment out a line in M code, we insert the characters // at the beginning of the line. This tells the Power Query engine that the remaining characters on the line should not be executed.

To duplicate our variable, we need to set up a new step *after the initial let line* which creates and assigns a value to the variable. That line must be built using the following syntax:

```
Variable_name = assign_value_here ,
```

The variable name must be the variable that is currently enclosed in the opening parenthesis for the function, and the line must end with a comma. Let's go and take a look.

- Right-click the fxUnpivot query → Advanced Editor
- Modify your query so that the first three lines read as follows:

```
//( tbl )=>
let
tbl = Excel.CurrentWorkbook(){0}[Content] ,
```

> 🐵 Don't forget the final comma at the end of the line, or your code won't work!

> 🐵 Be warned that if you ever do invoke a custom function, it will wrap the entire function in a new let/in structure. In this case you'll need to comment both the first two and last two lines of the function in order to set it back to a query.

When you're done, the code should look similar to this:

```
1  //(tbl) =>
2  let
3      tbl = Excel.CurrentWorkbook(){0}[Content],
4      #"Unpivoted Other Columns" = Table.UnpivotOtherColumns(tbl, {"Date"}, "Attribute
5      #"Renamed Columns" = Table.RenameColumns(#"Unpivoted Other Columns",{{"Attribute
6      #"Changed Type" = Table.TransformColumnTypes(#"Renamed Columns",{{"Date", type d
7  in
8      #"Changed Type"
```

The modified code to convert this back into a query

And when you click OK, you'll see that you can step through and verify what is happening in your query:

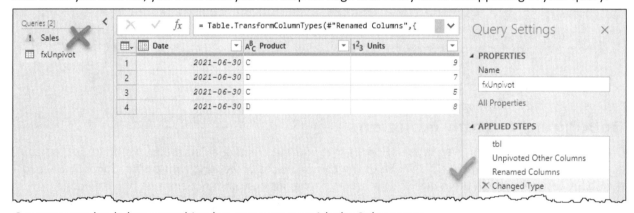

Our steps are back, but something has gone wrong with the Sales query

The nice thing here is that you can walk through each step, including the value you assigned to tbl for debugging. But there is some bad news...

> 🐵 While your function is in debug mode any queries that refer to it will not function!

Restoring "Function"ality

To turn the query back into a function you again need to edit the M code to do two things:

1. Remove the // characters from the initial row
2. Place the // characters in front of the row that is currently declaring the temporary variable

Once done, your function will resume its normal operation method, and all queries using this function will be able to use it again.

As a final thought on creating custom functions, it is not required, but it is a smart practice, to declare the data types of each variable. To do this, we would simply add "as <type>" to the variable declaration line. If we were to do this prior to setting the function back into its usable state, our code would then look as shown here:

```
1   ( tbl as table )=>
2   let
3   //    tbl = Excel.CurrentWorkbook(){0}[Content] ,
4       #"Unpivoted Other Columns" = Table.UnpivotOtherColumns(tbl, {"Date"},
5       #"Renamed Columns" = Table.RenameColumns(#"Unpivoted Other Columns",{{
6       #"Changed Type" = Table.TransformColumnTypes(#"Renamed Columns",{{"Dat
7   in
8       #"Changed Type"
```

Data-typing our variable when restoring functionality

🐵 Forgetting to comment out the temporary variable line will result in that line overwriting any variable passed into the function. You don't want to forget to comment that line!

Dynamic Parameter Tables

When we think about Parameters, we see a lot of potential for what they can do, beyond just a dynamically changing file path or table. For example, wouldn't it be nice if you could just change your parameter to easily filter your data to a specific business unit or department?

While Parameters are great, there are a couple of things that are a bit frustrating about working with them: The first is that they encourage static values. We really want to be able to drive a Power Query Parameter via an Excel formula, passing the current value from the spreadsheet at run time. The second is that, in order to update a Parameter's value, you have to use the Manage Parameters button which is only found inside the Power Query editor. That means extra clicks and wait time every time you want to make a change. In addition to being slow, it's not user friendly at all.

This section is going to show how we can set up a table and a function called fnGetParameter to solve these issues. While it is particularly useful in Excel, the technique can also be used in Power BI if you maintain a table of parameter and value pairs. There are two main drawbacks for Power BI however:

1. You will still need to enter the Power Query editor to update those "parameter" values, and

2. There is no facility for a user to dynamically change these parameters after a Power BI model is published, as the end-user cannot access or modify the M code in a published model.

The upside is that it keeps all of your "parameters" in one nice easy-to-review table for the model developer.

🔑 As you will see, we will not be creating true Parameters, but rather extracting primitive values from table and passing those to other queries.

The Dynamic File Path Issue

When working with web-hosted data, sharing files is relatively easy. You can simply share the file via any method. When the user opens the file at the other end, they may be prompted to enable data connections, set privacy levels or authenticate, but those questions are to be expected. Since the data is web-hosted access can be given without updating any of the data source connectors in the file.

But what happens when you've built an Excel-based solution like the Timesheet example we retrofitted earlier in this chapter? The data is stored in folders on the local computer, or network drive. Now you zip up the solution and share the entire folder with someone else – just as we have done with the example files for this book.

When the user receives the file, they unzip them into a folder, open the solution and trigger a refresh. What will happen? The answer depends on whether the end-user unzipped the files to the exact same path as the author or not. If they did, then the refresh will work. If not, they will get an error message and need to update the file paths to all of the "local" resources.

🖎 This problem definitely affects Power BI users who build their solutions against local data sources, but it affects Excel users far more often as they have a much higher propensity to use locally hosted data files.

Let's put our Timesheet example into a real-world business context: You've built the master consolidation file, saved it in H:\Payroll, and for months have been storing the timesheets in the subfolder which resides in H:\Payroll\Timesheets. After working hard all year, you finally get a few weeks off and have to pass the solution to someone else to maintain while you're gone. There's a problem though... their system has the path to your solution mapped as J:\HR\Payroll. Rather than recode the solution for your replacement, and then have to recode it again when you return, you'd really like to make the path relative to where the workbook is located. That way, if the user opens it up from J:\HR\Payroll or H:\Payroll or something else, it shouldn't make a difference.

The real challenge? There is currently no function in the M language that allows you to work out the path to the workbook you're using. Interestingly, an Excel formula can do this work.

🖎 Power BI doesn't have a function that can enumerate the source file's location, like Excel does. If this were a Power BI solution, we would ensure that we were storing the files in a SharePoint folder and connecting to that, as it is a web-hosted data set where the path won't change.

Implementing Dynamic Parameter Tables

Let's return to our previous Timesheet example and see if we can make the file path truly dynamic so that a refresh can be performed by anyone opening the file.

🖎 You can catch up by opening the `Ch17 Examples\Retrofitting-Complete.xlsx` file.

There are three steps to implementing parameter tables into your solution:

1. Creating a parameter table in Excel
2. Creating the function to extract the values from the table
3. Retrofitting your existing queries to call the function

Creating the Parameter Table

The first thing we need to do is to create a table to hold our parameters. In order to use the function we are going to provide, this table takes a specific form, and needs to have certain components set up correctly.

Create the table shown below in cell F9:G10 of the Timesheet worksheet:

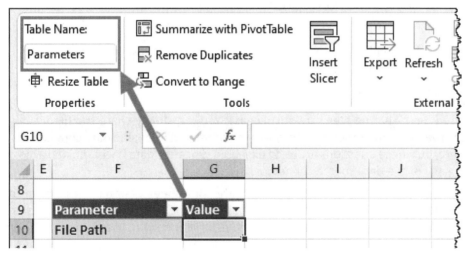

The bare bones Parameters table

Notice that this table has several key characteristics:

*   The first column's header is: Parameter
*   The second column's header is: Value
*   The table has a name of: Parameters

🐵 This is an official "CTRL+T" table, and it is critical to get each property correct in order to use the function provided in the download files. If even one of these items is spelled differently, you will need to debug the table and/or the function.

This table is now set up to hold every piece of data that you want to use as a dynamic variable in your solution. Simply provide the name of the parameter on the left, and the value for the parameter in the Values column.

👠 The items in the Values column can be hard-coded text or values, be driven by data validation lists, or can use formulas. How you get the correct value in the cell is completely up to you as the solution designer.

Next, we need to determine the file path to the current workbook. Enter the formula below into cell G10:

```
=IFERROR(LEFT(CELL("filename",A1),FIND("[",CELL("filename",A1),1)-1),
"Workbook needs to be saved!")
```

👠 If you haven't saved your file this function won't return the path as it can't determine where the workbook lives. The final parameter of the IFERROR() function helps you in this case, as it tells you how to solve the issue instead of showing an error.

Upon doing so, you should see the file path to the workbook listed. The only challenge is that we actually want this file path to point to the TimeSheets folder, as that is where the timesheets are stored. Update the formula to add the folder path as shown below:

```
=IFERROR(LEFT(CELL("filename",A1),FIND("[",CELL("filename",A1),1)-1),
"Workbook needs to be saved!")&"TimeSheets\"
```

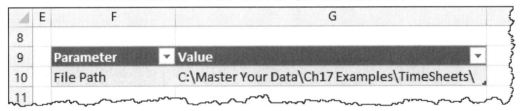

Dynamically returning the file path using an Excel formula

🐵 One irritating feature in Microsoft 365 is that files stored in a folder synced to OneDrive or SharePoint will return the https:// path to the file instead of the local file path. The issue with this is that you need a different connector to access the file contents. If you need to block this 'smart' switch and force the solution to use the local file path, you can do so by temporarily pausing OneDrive's syncing, and then re-opening the file from the local path.

Implementing the fnGetParameter Function

With the parameter table now in a state that can hold any variable we need we just need to give Power Query a method to read those values. This portion can be done by using the following custom function:

```
( getValue as text ) =>
let
  ParamTable = Excel.CurrentWorkbook(){[Name="Parameters"]}[Content],
  Result = ParamTable{[Parameter=getValue]}?[Value]?
in
  Result
```

👠 This function is contained in the fnGetParameter.txt file in the Ch17 Examples folder. In addition to the code, it also contains instructions to use the function, as well as the formula to return the file path from a cell. The file was provided in an attempt to give you a template you can store and use multiple times.

This code connects to the Parameters table in the workbook, then selects the row of the table where the dynamic parameter's value matches the record in the Parameter column of the Excel table. With that match in place, it then returns what it finds in the Value column. It is because each of these names is hard-coded in the function that both the table and column names for the Excel table match what was specified above.

Rather than retype this entire block of code, open the Ch17 Examples\fnGetParameter.txt file and copy all lines inside the file. With those in the paste buffer, it will be deadly simple to implement this function into your solution.

- Create a new query → From Other Sources → From Blank Query
- Go to Home → Advanced Editor → highlight all rows of code in the window
- Press CTRL + V to paste in the content of the text file
- Click Done
- Change the function's name to fnGetParameter

And you're done.

Calling the Function

With the parameter table built, and the function in place, the last step is to retrofit our existing query to actually use it. Doing so will allow us to source the file path from the cell and use that in our query. As the file path updates when the workbook is recalculated, it will always be accurate, meaning that the solution will always look for the timesheet files in the subdirectory of where the solution resides.

To retrofit the Timesheets query we don't even have to leave the Power Query editor:

- Select the FilesList query → right-click it → Advanced Editor
- Insert the following line of code immediately after the let line

```
fullfilepath = fnGetParameter("File Path"),
```

The query should now look as follows:

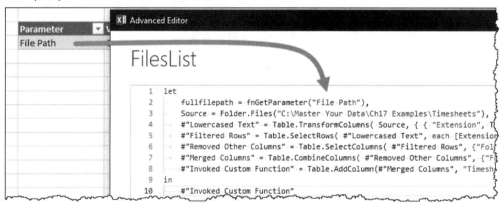

Calling the fnGetParameter function

Notice here that we have created a new variable called *fullfilepath* to hold the value from the *File Path* row of our Excel table.

> 🐵 While you *could* skip this step and just nest the fnGetParameter call in place of the file path on the next row, we advise that you don't. Creating a separate step for each fnGetParameter at the beginning of the function, helps avoid the Formula Firewall issue we triggered in the previous example, where we were prevented from accessing a data source in a later query step.

In addition, by adding this call on a separate line, we make the query much easier to debug, as we'll see now.

- Click Done
- Select the fullfilepath step in the Applied Steps window

The full file path to the folder is displayed nicely in the editor, giving us the comfort that we've got that part correct:

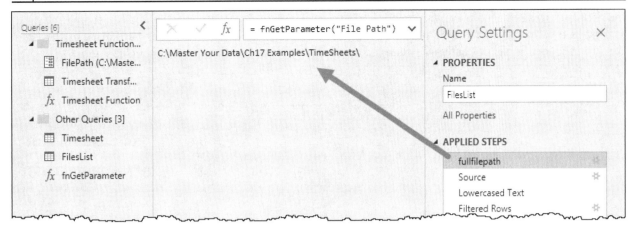

The fullfilepath variable is correctly pulling the file path

Now that we've got comfort that the function is returning the correct path via our Excel formula, we can slipstream the variable in place of the hard-coded file path in the Source step.

- Go to Home → Advanced Editor → locate the file path in the Source line
- Select the entire file path (including the quotes) and replace it with *fullfilepath*

The first three lines of the query should now read as follows:

```
let
    fullfilepath = fnGetParameter("File Path"),
    Source = Folder.Files(fullfilepath),
```

> ✎ You must edit the M code manually to make this work via the Advanced Editor or the formula bar. It can't be accomplished by clicking the gear icon next to the Source step, as fullfilepath is not a valid parameter or folder of the Windows operating system.

When you've made the modifications, you can click Done, and you'll see that every step of the query still functions correctly.

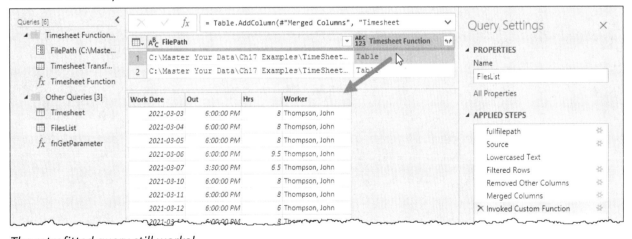

The retrofitted query still works!

Implications of Parameter Tables

Particularly when working with Power Query in Excel, referencing a parameter table gives us a huge amount of flexibility when building solutions. If you are building solutions internally in your company and need to share them with team members or other divisions, you can now set them up to read from dynamic folder structures relative to your solution path. If – on the other hand – you are a consultant who develops solutions for clients, this technique is hugely impactful, as it is doubtful that you'll ever have exactly the same file structure on your system as your client does. The last thing you want to do in either of these situations is send the end-user a file with instructions on how to edit the M code.

You can actually see this in play by opening the Dynamic FilePath-Complete.xlsx file and refreshing the data. As long as the TimeSheets folder (and files) are stored in the same location on your hard drive as the Excel file, (and the location is not actively syncing to OneDrive or SharePoint), the refresh will just work!

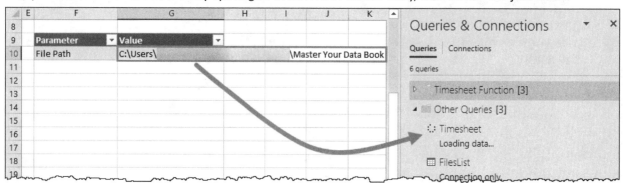

A completely different (local) file path doesn't affect our ability to refresh!

But the power of parameter tables doesn't end there. Consider each of the following tasks that you may wish to perform:

- Build a calendar table based on the dates in cells in an Excel worksheet
- Drive a filter for a table based on the value in an Excel cell
- Determine which of four Excel tables to load into a solution

By setting up and using a custom function to read from an Excel table, we can accomplish any of these goals. This affords us not only the ability to dynamically drive our content, but also gives us the ability to generate data in an environment more familiar to us, and in some cases do things that Power Query wouldn't otherwise allow us to do.

Chapter 18 - Date and Time Techniques

When performing any type of analysis or reporting that slices data by date, you generally need a calendar table in your solution. Many Excel Pros will build a hard-coded calendar table in a worksheet to solve this need, linking it to their data via formulas or pulling it into the data model. The challenge however, is that these tables often require manual updates at the end of the fiscal year. Wouldn't it be nice to remove this manual update requirement once and for all?

In this chapter, we will look at different methods for building complete calendar tables, as well as generating tables with individual records based on defined schedules.

Now let's be honest, building a calendar on the fly with Power Query sounds like work, and is bound to take resources to refresh. You might be asking if it wouldn't be better to just pull the calendar table directly from the corporate database? The answer is absolutely yes, it would... if you have one provided to you. If you have access to the calendar from corporate, use it. But what if you don't? What if you're served up a diet of Excel or text files, and don't have access to a calendar that is blessed by corporate IT. THAT is when the steps in this chapter open things up for you.

When building calendar tables, there are three important pieces to consider: the date the calendar table will start, the date it will end, and the "granularity" needed. In other words, does the calendar need daily records, weekly, monthly or something different. In this chapter, we will provide options for generating each of these components, which we hope you will be able to leverage to satisfy your date-based requirements.

Generating Calendar Boundaries

Every calendar requires boundaries: a date that the calendar will start, and the date that the calendar will end. As it turns out, we have a few ways of generating these to drive our date-based solutions. We could use:

- Parameters
- Dynamic Parameter Tables (as shown in Chapter 17)
- Data dynamically generated from the data set

The challenge with using Parameters is that the values are hard-coded and will require a manual update inside the Power Query editor. Dynamic Parameter Tables are great – for Excel – but by far our preferred way to build a calendar is by dynamically sourcing our dates directly from the data. In that way, a refresh will always ensure that the calendar covers the required boundaries.

> 🔧 The Calendar section of this chapter is highly recipe driven and covers multiple different calendar formats. In an effort to keep the chapter concise, we aren't providing step by step walk throughs of creating these tables based on sample data. We have however, provided a complete example file with all of the different calendars included. You'll find that in Ch18 Examples\Calendar Tables.xlsx

Dynamically Generating a Calendar StartDate (or EndDate)

Generating the boundaries for a calendar is actually relatively easy with Power Query if you follow the recipe that we are about to introduce you to. Before we do that however, we want to call out a couple of practices that we follow:

1. We highly recommend making your calendars span the entire fiscal year for your data,
2. Source your StartDate from the table that will always hold the earliest possible date in your data. (A Sales table is usually a good choice for this.)
3. Source your EndDate from the table that will always hold the latest possible date in your data. (A budget table is a good choice for this – providing that your budgets are always uploaded to your database BEFORE sales take place!)

Given the above (and assuming that the name of the column which holds your dates is called "Date") the recipe to create calendar boundaries is as follows:

Step	StartDate Recipe	EndDate Recipe
1	Reference the table with earliest date	Reference table with latest date
2	Remove all except the [Date] column	Remove all except the [Date] column
3	Filter [Date] → Date Filters → Is Earliest	Filter [Date] → Date Filters → Is Latest
4	Remove duplicates	Remove duplicates
5	Transform date to Year → **Start of Year**	Transform date to Year → **End of Year**
6	Optional: Shift the date for non-standard year-ends. See the "Adjust the Start/End Date for Non-Standard Fiscal Years" section below.	
7	Change the data type to Date	Change the data type to Date
8	Right-click the date cell → Drill down	Right-click the date cell → Drill down
9	Name the query **StartDate**	Name the query **EndDate**
10	Load as Connection Only	Load as Connection Only

Calendar StartDate and EndDate recipes

🐵 Be aware that this recipe will break Query Folding. Again, if your corporate IT provides you with a calendar table in your SQL database, you should be using that. This recipe is for people who cannot do this and just need to get their job done!

The majority of these steps are fairly straightforward, but there are three that we want to specifically call out:

Step 6: For a 12-month calendar that ends on December 31 you can just skip this step. We will expand on this step for alternate fiscal year-ends in the next sections.

Step 7: The reason we redefine the date in step 7 is to ensure that step 8 correctly drills into the data using the {0} format. (On occasion this does not happen when you skip step 7.)

Step 8: When performing your drill down, it is very important that you right-click the date, not the column header to perform the drill down as shown here:

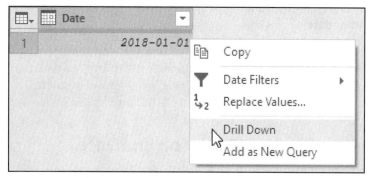

Drilling down on the StartDate

If you perform step 8 correctly, you should end up with the date shown as a primitive value, as shown below:

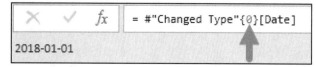

The StartDate should be based on {0} and show as a primitive Date data type

🖋 The date will be displayed based on your default date format, so may not match ours!

🐵 If you right-click the column header instead, you will receive a list, which won't work for the rest of the recipes in this section.

Adjusting Start/End Dates for Non-Standard Fiscal Years

By far the most common format of calendar used in the world is a 12-month calendar, but of course not everyone ends their fiscal year on December 31. The good news is that it is very easy to shift the StartDate and EndDate of your calendar to match the fiscal year-end you use.

To make this as easy as possible, we recommend creating a **YEMonth** query as follows:

- Create a new blank query
- Rename the query to YEMonth
- In the formula bar enter the numeric value of the final month of your year-end
- Load the query as Connection Only

Assuming that your company has a September 30 year-end, your query would look as follows:

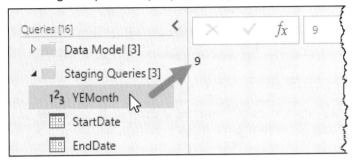

Setting up for a Sep 30 year-end

With the YEMonth query created, you can then follow (or modify) the StartDate and EndDate recipe illustrated above where step 6 expands to include the following steps:

Step	StartDate Recipe	EndDate Recipe
6A	Go to add Column → Custom Column	Go to add Column → Custom Column

6B	Name the column Custom and use the formula:
	`=Date.AddMonths(`
	`    [Date], YEMonth - 12)`
		Name the column Custom and use the formula:
		`=Date.AddMonths(`
		`    [Date], YEMonth )`

6C	Right-click [Custom] → Remove Other Columns	Right-click [Custom] → Remove Other Columns
6D	Rename the [Custom] column to Date	Rename the [Custom] column to Date

Step 6 of the StartDate and EndDate recipe for non-standard 12-month calendars

> ✎ If you already created the StartDate and EndDate queries and need to insert these steps, make sure you start at the Calculated Start (End) of Year step.

The image below compares the results of the original StartDate pattern against a FiscalStartDate generated with step 6 followed in full. The important thing to recognize about this data set is that the earliest Sale transaction is Jan 1, 2018, so the pattern shifts the dates to cover the entire fiscal year – whether that runs from Jan 1 – Dec 31, or Oct 1 – Sep 30:

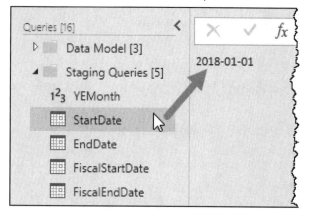 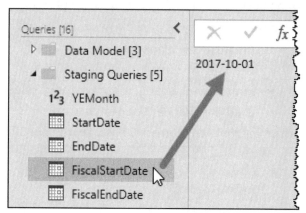

Comparing the results of the original StartDate vs a FiscalStartDate for a Sep 30 year-end

> 🖐 In order to showcase both regular and fiscal year-ends in the same file, the completed example file contains FiscalStartDate and FiscalEndDate queries that rely on the modifications shown in this section.

Adjusting Start/End Dates for 364-Day Calendars

While there is no end to corporate calendar formats, the next most popular to use after a 12-month calendar are 364 day calendar structures including 4-4-5, 4-5-4, 5-4-4 and 13 x 4 weeks. While each is defined based on the number of weeks used to derive the quarters or years, the one thing they all have in common is that they span 364 days per year, with a different year-end date annually.

Once again, we will need to make an adjustment to the original StartDate and EndDate recipe in order to make this work. And again, in order to make this as easy as possible, we recommend creating a new query to do so. This time we will name the query **Start364** and will use it to record the first day of *any* valid fiscal year from your corporate history. To do so:

- Create a new blank query
- Rename the query to Start364
- In the formula bar enter the date for the first day of any fiscal year
- Load the query as Connection Only

Assuming that the corporate years began on 2017-01-01, 2017-12-31 and 2018-12-30, (each of which is a Sunday), we could use any of those values for our Start364 query:

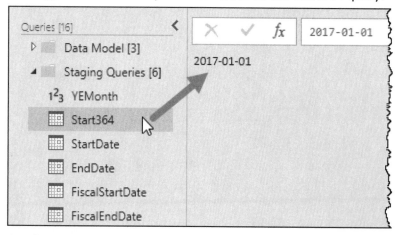

Sunday, January 1, 2017 is a valid starting date for this company's fiscal year

👞 If your query doesn't show the date icon in the Queries pane, try entering it in the following format: =#date(2017,1,1)

With the Start364 query in place, we can now take the original recipe and generate our StartDate and EndDate queries using the following for version step 6:

Step	StartDate Recipe	EndDate Recipe
6A	Go to add Column → Custom Column	Go to add Column → Custom Column
6B	Name the column Custom and use the formula: `=Date.AddDays( Start364, 364 * Number.Round( Duration.Days( [Date] - Start364 ) /364 , 0 ) )`	Name the column Custom and use the formula: `=Date.AddDays( Start364, 364 * Number.RoundUp( Duration.Days( [Date] - Start364 ) / 364 , 0 ) -1 )`
6C	Right-click [Custom] → Remove Other Columns	Right-click [Custom] → Remove Other Columns
6D	Rename the [Custom] column to Date	Rename the [Custom] column to Date

Step 6 of the StartDate and EndDate recipe for calendars based on 364-day year-ends

In the case of our sample data, the earliest data point is Jan 1, 2018. This means that based on the date pattern defined above, our 364-day calendar pattern must start on Dec 31, 2017, as that is the first date of the fiscal year that includes the earliest record. And as you can see, that is exactly what happens:

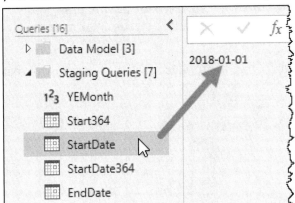 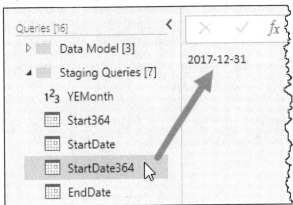

Our StartDate364 is correct even though Start364 was the first date of the prior fiscal year

👞 Again, in order to allow comparison of all calendars in the same file, the completed example provides these queries as StartDate364 and EndDate364.

Calendars with Consecutive Dates

Now that we know how to generate the beginning and ending date for a variety of different calendar patterns, let's build a calendar table. This calendar will span from the StartDate through the EndDate, with daily granularity. (One record per day with no gaps.)

Building the Calendar Table

Once you have the StartDate and EndDate defined, you'll find that creating a calendar follows a very simple recipe:

- Create a new blank query
- In the formula bar enter the following formula:

```
= { Number.From( StartDate ) .. Number.From( EndDate ) }
```

- Go to List Tools → Transform → To Table → OK
- Rename Column1 to Date
- Change the data type of the Date column to Date
- Rename the query as "Calendar" (or whatever you prefer)

> 🖐 Unfortunately, we cannot create a list of dates using the { .. } structure, but we can create a list from one number to another. For this reason we convert the dates into their serial number equivalents using Number.From(). While we could have converted our individual queries into numeric values, this approach preserves the display of the staging queries as dates, making them easier to review later.

The end result is a completely dynamic table of dates with daily granularity which span the entire (fiscal) year for which you have data:

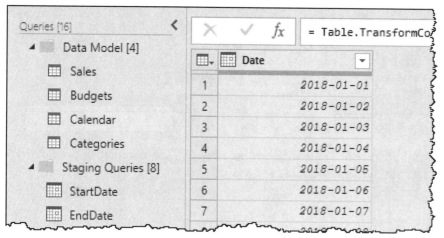

A 100% dynamic thing of beauty

At this point, we want to make sure you recognize something very important. While the image above was generated using the StartDate and EndDate for a standard year-end that runs from Jan 1 through Dec 31 of each year, we also calculated various other start and end dates in the previous section. Had we used those instead, the calendar would span that range.

> ☎ If you provide an EndDate that is earlier than your StartDate, your table will generate an empty list, and then return a step level error when trying to rename the non-existent Column1. For this reason you need to be careful when basing your StartDate and EndDate on different queries, making sure that you pick columns that will never lead to this situation.

The other thing that we want to make sure you recognize here is that this scenario is a practical application of filling consecutive dates between two dates. It is not limited to Calendar tables at all, as you'll see later in this chapter.

Enriching the Calendar with Period Columns

If you are planning to do any real analysis with your calendar table, then you will need some additional columns to denote the periods: things like Month, Month Name, Year and the like. Fortunately, Power Query makes this pretty easy, as it contains a collection of built-in date transforms within easy reach. To leverage them, follow this 3-step process:

1. Select the Date column → Add Column → Date

2. Choose the period you need

3. Return to Step 1 as many times as needed

The image below shows the results of adding Year, Month and Month Name columns to our query:

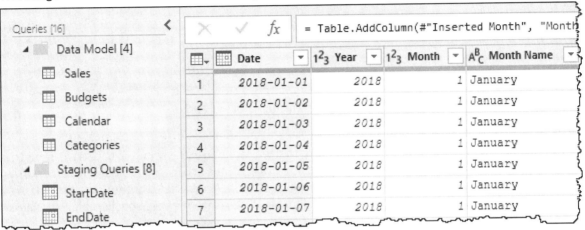

Adding a few useful columns to our Calendar table

☎ Don't forget to return to Step 1 if you create a column that returns a date like an End of Month column. It's super easy to create your next transform and realize that you just extracted data from the newly created column instead of your original Date column!

Fiscal Period Columns – 12 Month Calendars

While the built-in Date transforms are really handy, they can break down when applied to calendars which use a year-end other than Dec 31. Fortunately, calculating fiscal periods (such as the Fiscal Month) can be done via a formula in a custom column.

The table below contains some key formulas that you may find useful if you need to extract reporting periods for a 12-month year-end that ends on a date other than Dec 31 of each year:

Column Name	Required Columns	Formula
Fiscal Year	[Date]	`Date.Year(Date.AddMonths([Date],12-YEMonth))`
Fiscal Month	[Date]	`Date.Month(Date.AddMonths([Date],-YEMonth))`
Fiscal Quarter	[Fiscal Month]	`Number.RoundUp([Fiscal Month]/3)`

Fiscal Month of Quarter	[Fiscal Month]	`if Number.Mod([Fiscal Month],3) = 0`
		`then 3`
		`else Number.Mod([Fiscal Month],3)`

End of Fiscal Year	[Date], [Fiscal Month]	`Date.EndOfMonth(Date.AddMonths([Date],` `12-[Fiscal Month]))`
End of Fiscal Quarter	[Date], [Fiscal Month of Quarter]	`Date.EndOfMonth(Date.AddMonths([Date],` `3-[Fiscal Month of Quarter] ) )`

Some helpful Fiscal Period formulas for 12-month year-ends

The results shown here were generated by using the Fiscal Year and Fiscal Month formula above, with Month Name using the standard Name of Month transform targeting the Date column:

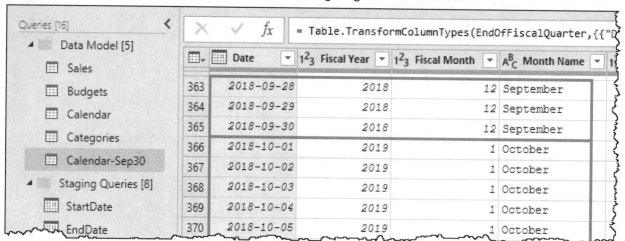

Fiscal Year and Fiscal Month columns which reset after the Sep 30 year-end

Period ID Columns for 364-day Calendars

The biggest challenge when building 364-day calendars is that we cannot use the standard date transforms that work for 12-month calendars. Instead, we need a special set of columns in order to drive the fiscal reporting years for the specific variant of the 364-day calendar we are using. No matter whether that calendar is a 4-4-5 variant or based on 13 months that are 4 weeks long, it all starts from a very specific column: DayID.

The DayID column essentially represents a row number for the calendar which increases daily, and never resets throughout the entire table. It is then used to drive every other reporting period you need. Fortunately, it is super easy to create. After generating the column that spans the calendar date range (as shown previously), we can create the DayID column as follows:

- Go to Add Column → Index Column → From 1
- Rename the new column to "DayID"

With that critical column in place, you can then add the remaining PeriodID columns you need. Each requires using a custom column – the trick is knowing the formula to use. The table below contains the column formulas for each of the 4-4-5 calendar variants, just pay attention to which variant you need, as the MonthID formula is different for each calendar variant:

Column Name	Required Columns	Formula
WeekID	[DayID]	`Number.RoundUp([DayID]/7)`

MonthID
 	
(for 4-4-5 Calendars)
	[DayID]	`Number.RoundDown([DayID]/91)*3+`
		`( if Number.Mod([DayID],91)=0 then 0`
		`else if Number.Mod([DayID],91)<= 28 then 1`
		`else if Number.Mod([DayID],91)<= 56 then 2`
		`else 3 )`

MonthID
 	
(for 4-5-4 Calendars)
	[DayID]	`Number.RoundDown([DayID]/91)*3+`
		`( if Number.Mod([DayID],91)=0 then 0`
		`else if Number.Mod([DayID],91)<= 28 then 1`
		`else if Number.Mod([DayID],91)<= 63 then 2`
		`else 3 )`

MonthID
 	
(for 5-4-4 Calendars)
	[DayID]	`Number.RoundDown([DayID]/91)*3+`
		`( if Number.Mod([DayID],91)=0 then 0`
		`else if Number.Mod([DayID],91)<= 35 then 1`
		`else if Number.Mod([DayID],91)<= 63 then 2`
		`else 3 )`

MonthID (for 13x4 Calendars)		`Number.RoundUp ([DayID]/28)`
QuarterID	[DayID]	`Number.RoundUp([DayID]/91)`
YearID	[DayID]	`Number.RoundUp([DayID]/364)`

Key PeriodID columns for driving 364-day calendars

🥿 If you are familiar with Rob Collie's GFITW (Greatest Formula In The World) DAX pattern, you'll realize that these columns are key to generating cross period time intelligence measures for 4-4-5 calendars in the DAX formula language.

	Date	1²₃ DayID	1²₃ WeekID	1²₃ MonthID	1²₃ QuarterID	1²₃ YearID
363	2018-12-28	363	52	12	4	1
364	2018-12-29	364	52	12	4	1
365	2018-12-30	365	53	13	5	2
366	2018-12-31	366	53	13	5	2
367	2019-01-01	367	53	13	5	2
368	2019-01-02	368	53	13	5	2

PeriodID columns shown at end of year 1 for a 4-4-5 Calendar

The key thing to recognize about these columns is that they are not used for reporting, they are used for driving additional logic.

🐵 The patterns provided previously do not take into account variations of the standard 364-day calendar patterns. If your organization practices a "catch-up" year where an extra week is added every x years, you will need to adjust the logic used in order to reflect that.

Fiscal Period Columns – 4-4-5 Calendars (and their variants)

Unlike 12-month calendars, which can use Power Query's standard date transforms, custom calendars require writing a custom formula for each reporting period that you wish to generate. Fortunately, with the PeriodID columns in place, we are now in a position to do just this.

As we know how difficult generating this logic can be, we have provided a collection of formulas that will allow you to generate the columns you'll need to report by fiscal periods for 4-4-5 calendars (as well as their 4-5-4 and 5-4-4 variants). Just make sure, as you work through these formulas, that you pay very careful attention to the Required Columns section, as many of these require the additional queries or columns to be created first.

🥿 Don't want or need one of the required columns in your final table? No worries. Just remove it at the end. Power Query won't mind!

Column Name	Required Columns	Formula
Fiscal Year	StartDate445, [YearID]	`Date.Year(Date.From(StartDate))+[YearID]`

Formula for the Fiscal Year column

One consideration to keep in mind is that, depending on the first date used and the fiscal year you wish to represent for it, you may need to add or subtract 1 from the end result.

Column Name	Required Columns	Formula
Quarter of Year	[QuarterID]	`Number.Mod([QuarterID]-1,4)+1`
Month of Year	[MonthID]	`Number.Mod([MonthID]-1,12)+1`
Week of Year	[WeekID]	`Number.Mod([WeekID]-1,52)+1`
Day of Year	[DayID]	`Number.Mod([DayID]-1,364)+1`

Formulas for the x of Year columns

🐒 Don't forget that Power Query is case-sensitive, meaning that 'Day Of Year' is not the same as 'Day _of_ Year'. If you receive an error that your field doesn't exist when you know you have created it, check the casing and spelling as it is likely this causing the issue.

Column Name	Required Columns	Formula
Month of Quarter	[Month of Year]	`Number.Mod([Month of Year]-1,3)+1`
Week of Quarter	[Week of Year]	`Number.Mod([Week of Year]-1,13)+1`
Day of Quarter	[Day of Year]	`Number.Mod([Day of Year]-1,91)+1`

Day of Month
 	
(for 4-4-5 Calendars)
	[Day of Quarter], [Month of Quarter]	`if [Month of Quarter] = 1`
		`then [Day of Quarter]`
		`else if [Month of Quarter] = 2`
		`then [Day of Quarter] - 28`
		`else [Day of Quarter] - 35`

Day of Month
 	
(for 4-5-4 Calendars)
	[Day of Quarter], [Month of Quarter]	`if [Month of Quarter] = 1`
		`then [Day of Quarter]`
		`else if [Month of Quarter] = 2`
		`then [Day of Quarter] - 28`
		`else [Day of Quarter] - 63`

Day of Month
 	
(for 5-4-4 Calendars)
	[Day of Quarter], [Month of Quarter]	`if [Month of Quarter] = 1`
		`then [Day of Quarter]`
		`else if [Month of Quarter] = 2`
		`then [Day of Quarter] - 35`
		`else [Day of Quarter] - 63`

Week of Month	[Day of Month]	`Number.RoundUp([Day of Month]/7)`
Day of Week	[Day of Year]	`Number.Mod([Day of Year]-1,7)+1`

Formulas for the x of Quarter, x of Month and x of Week columns

Column Name	Required Columns	Formula
Days in Year	N/A	`364`
Days in Quarter	N/A	`91`

Days in Month
(for 4-4-5 Calendars)
	[Week of Quarter]	`if [Week of Quarter] > 8`
		`  then 35`
		`  else 28`

Days in Month
(for 4-5-4 Calendars)
	[Week of Quarter]	`if [Week of Quarter]>4 and`
		`    [Week of Quarter]<10`
		`  then 35`
		`  else 28`

Days in Month
(for 5-4-4 Calendars)
	[Week of Quarter]	`if [Week of Quarter] < 5`
		`  then 35`
		`  else 28`

Days in Week	N/A	`7`

Formulas for Days in x columns

Column Name	Required Columns	Formula
Start of Week	[Date], [Day of Week]	`Date.AddDays([Date],-([Day of Week]-1))`
End of Week	[Start of Week]	`Date.AddDays([Start of Week],6)`
Start of Month	[Date], [Day of Month]	`Date.AddDays([Date],-([Day of Month]-1))`
End of Month	[Start of Month], [Days in Month]	`Date.AddDays([Start of Month],[Days in Month]-1)`
Start of Quarter	[Date], [Day of Quarter]	`Date.AddDays([Date],-([Day of Quarter]-1))`
End of Quarter	[Start of Quarter]	`Date.AddDays([Start of Quarter],91-1)`
Start of Year	[Date], [Day of Year]	`Date.AddDays([Date],-([Day of Year]-1))`
End of Year	[Start of Year]	`Date.AddDays([Start of Year],364-1)`

Formula for Start of x/End of x columns

What Is In the Example File?

Inside the completed example file, you will find each of the following complete versions of each of the following calendar tables built using the techniques illustrated in this chapter:

- Calendar: A standard 12-month calendar that ends on Dec 31 of each year
- Calendar-Sep30: A 12-month calendar with a fiscal year-end of Sep 30 of each year,
- Calendar-445: A 364-day calendar using the 4-4-5 week pattern,
- Calendar-454: A 364-day calendar using the 4-5-4 week pattern,
- Calendar-544: A 364-day calendar using the 5-4-4 week pattern,

Each of the tables is loaded to the data model and linked to the Sales and Budgets tables as shown here:

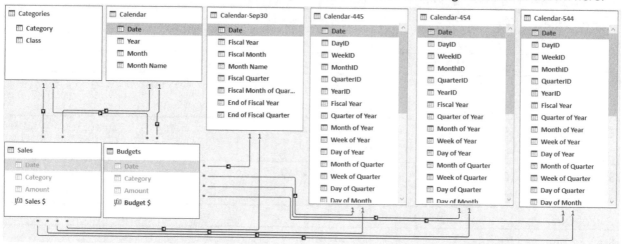

5 different calendar tables linked to the Sales and Budgets table via the Date columns

There are also Sales $ and Budget $ measures created in the file, as well as some samples on the Comparisons page, which compare the results, allow you to spot the similarities and differences between how the calendars report the data.

For the custom calendars, each of the steps has also been named within the Power Query applied steps window, allowing you to easily identify which formulas were used in each step.

Filling Specific Date/Time Ranges

While the Calendar patterns above are very useful, it targets filling complete fiscal years between two dates. In this section we will look at alternate methods to generate date and time based tables.

Fill x Number of Days

The solutions we looked at previously showed how we can fill dates between two specific dates. But what if you only have the start date and you want to figure out a specific set of dates from that start date? Consider the sample below which is based on the data saved in the Visitors table of the Ch18 Examples\Fill Dates-Begin. xlsx file. In this scenario, we need to generate a daily listing to track which visitors are on-site on any given day:

Convert this ...		
Visitor	**Arrival**	**Days on Site**
Miguel	2021-06-30	2
Ken	2021-06-27	5
Matt	2021-07-02	4

... to this ...	
Pass Date	**Visitor**
2021-06-28	Ken
2021-06-29	Ken
2021-06-30	Miguel
2021-06-30	Ken
2021-07-01	Miguel
2021-07-01	Ken
2021-07-02	Ken
2021-07-02	Matt

We need to generate a list of Visitors by date...

The output we are after isn't very complicated... We know which date the visitor is arriving, how many times they will be visiting and that each visit will be a full day.

As it turns out, we have a function we can use to get what we need here: List.Dates(). If you check the List. Dates() documentation, not only does it tell us exactly what we need to provide to this function, it also shows what we can expect to get back. And that output description looks very promising:

```
List.Dates(start as date, count as number, step as duration)

date

Generates a list of date values given an initial value, count, and incremental
duration value.
```

The List.Dates() documentation which appears in the formula Intellisense

The only tricky part around this is the final parameter, which requires a duration. The easiest way to get a daily duration value is to declare one using the following code:

```
#duration(1,0,0,0)
```

✎ The four parameters of a duration value are Days, Hours, Minutes, Seconds.

Let's give this a shot:

- Create a new query that reads from the Visitors table
- Go to Add Column → Custom Column
- Name the column "Pass Date" and use the following formula:
  ```
  =List.Dates( [Arrival], [Days on Site], #duration(1,0,0,0) )
  ```
- Select the Pass Date and Visitor columns → Remove Other Columns
- Expand the Pass Date column into new rows
- Set the data types

The output, as you can see, works perfectly:

	Pass Date	Visitor
1	2021-06-30	Miguel
2	2021-07-01	Miguel
3	2021-06-28	Ken
4	2021-06-29	Ken
5	2021-06-30	Ken
6	2021-07-01	Ken
7	2021-07-02	Ken
8	2021-07-02	Matt
9	2021-07-03	Matt
10	2021-07-04	Matt
11	2021-07-05	Matt

We have two entries for Miguel, five for Ken, and four for Matt

✎ The reason we don't recommend using List.Dates() to generate full Calendar tables is that the final parameter takes a duration. Unfortunately, there is no duration for "months". Given that months have differing numbers of days from month to month (and in the case of February, year to year), it is just easier to use the previously demonstrated pattern.

Fill x Hours per Day

This previous example works very well, but one important thing to recognize about using List.Dates() is that the "counting" of the durations starts from the hour 0 of the start date. You can see this, as the first record for each of our visitors is the same as the Arrival date contained in the table.

This can actually have an impact if you use durations of less than one day. For example, notice the different result you would have received if we had set the duration at 1-hour intervals by providing #duration(0,1,0,0) instead:

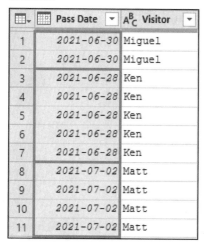

	Pass Date	Visitor
1	2021-06-30	Miguel
2	2021-06-30	Miguel
3	2021-06-28	Ken
4	2021-06-28	Ken
5	2021-06-28	Ken
6	2021-06-28	Ken
7	2021-06-28	Ken
8	2021-07-02	Matt
9	2021-07-02	Matt
10	2021-07-02	Matt
11	2021-07-02	Matt

We have the correct number of intervals, but all on the start date – and where are the times?

What is happening behind the scenes here is that Power Query is creating a list of dates that repeat every hour for x hours, starting at midnight of the start date. Unfortunately, this is a bit difficult to see, as List.Dates() only returns the Date portion, cutting off the precision that makes this clear.

So, what if we wanted to take our dates, as we did in the previous example, but also wanted to add 8 hourly entries starting at 9:00 AM every day? We obviously can't use List.Dates(), so we need to reach to List.Times(), starting the list from:

```
#time(9,0,0)
```

> 🦶 The three parameters of a duration value are Hours, Minutes, Seconds. Keep in mind that this function relies on 24-hour time, so 1:00 PM is achieved with #time(13,0,0).

To put this in place, we can:

- Duplicate the previous query and name it "Pass Times"
- Go to Add Column → Custom Column
- Name the column Hour and use the following formula

```
=List.Times( #time(9,0,0), 8, #duration(0,1,0,0) )
```

At this point, we can preview the newly created lists to verify that we have indeed created the correct times for each date. And since the lists have been created at the daily level, expanding the Hour column into new rows will give us the correct times for each day in the Pass Date column.

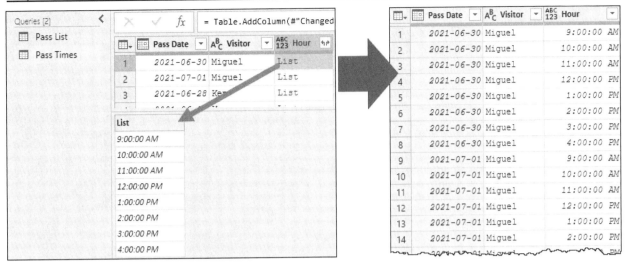

We have just added 8 hourly records for each date in the data set

> ⚓ There is also a List.DateTimes() function that will allow you to provide a complete #datetime value as the starting point.

One of the challenges of working with dates is the variability as the number of days is inconsistent between months and even years. Times generally don't have this issue, as every day contains 24 hours of which each contains 60 minutes which are 60 seconds long. For this reason, using List.Times() is the preferred way to build tables that involve time segments.

Fill x Dates at y Intervals

The next challenge we are going to explore is where we need to convert our data as shown here:

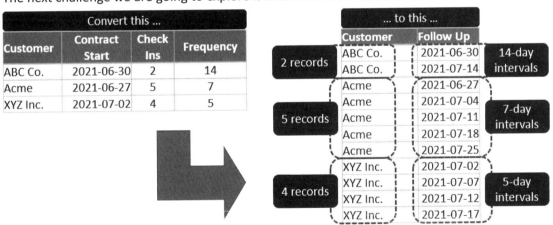

How do we generate a table of dates that repeats x times at y intervals?

What may be surprising is that we already have the answer to this. We use the same List.Dates() formula that we used previously. We just have to modify the final parameter to feed it the intervals instead of repeating every one day. The only real trick is that the final parameter of List.Dates() requires a Duration data type, so we will need to create a duration which equals the number of the days indicated in the Frequency column. This can be done by leveraging the Duration.From() formula.

Assuming that you have created a query that connects to the "Contracts" table of the Ch18 Examples\Fill Every x Dates-Begin.xlsx file, we can accomplish our goal via the following steps:

- Add a new Custom Column called Follow Up which uses the following formula:

```
=List.Dates( [Contract Start], [Check Ins],
        Duration.From([Frequency]) )
```

- Expand the new Follow Up columns to new rows
- Select the Customer and Follow Up columns → Remove Other Columns
- Set the data types

And the results are exactly what we need:

	A^B_C Customer	Follow Up
1	ABC Co.	2021-06-30
2	ABC Co.	2021-07-14
3	Acme	2021-06-27
4	Acme	2021-07-04
5	Acme	2021-07-11
6	Acme	2021-07-18
7	Acme	2021-07-25
8	XYZ Inc.	2021-07-02
9	XYZ Inc.	2021-07-07

We have created x records that repeat every y days

🖉 This technique is not limited to just working with List.Dates(). It can be applied to List.DateTimes() or List.Times() as well, should you need to do this with time values!

Allocations Based on Date Tables

Another question that we encounter quite frequently is how to apply the techniques listed above to allocation schedules, particularly when trying to allocate revenues or expenses over multiple month-ends.

To be fair, there are countless nuances to this issue depending on the exact needs of the business, but in this section we will look at two common ways to approach this task. We have provided a single table called Sales in the Ch18 Examples\Allocations-Begin.xlsx file which contains all columns to drive the examples in this section and we will remove the unneeded columns in order to showcase each specific technique we are illustrating.

To make life easy, we will need a staging query that we can connect to for each example:

- Create a new query that reads from the Sales table
- Change the data types of the Start Date and End Date columns to Date
- Name the query "Raw Data"
- Load it as a Connection only

Allocate by Days

The first scenario leverages the list concepts we looked at when generating calendar tables earlier in the chapter, and can be used to allocate transactions over a given number of days as illustrated here:

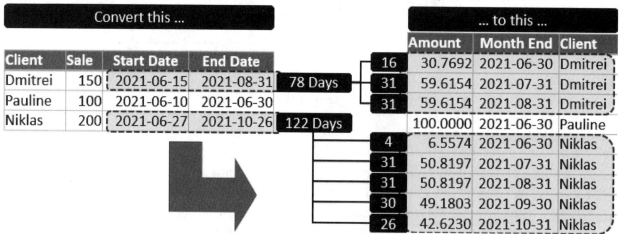

Allocating over month-ends based on total days by month

🖉 While the allocation of the other clients may immediately make sense, the records for Niklas could look a bit strange. We are allocating $200 over four months, so why don't we see $50 per month? The key thing to recognize here is that we are allocating over the days in the period, which vary from month to month.

The big challenges that we are facing within this scenario are: how do we create the correct list of month-ends, and how do we work out how much to allocate to each of those periods based on the days in the period?

We are going to start by working out the amount of the transaction that should be allocated to each day. To calculate this, we need to know the total number of days that have elapsed from the Start Date through End Date periods. And while Power Query won't let us just subtract one date from another, we already know how to convert dates into their serial number equivalents:

- Reference the Raw Data query
- Remove the Months column (as it is not needed for this example)
- Add a Custom column called "Amount" that uses the following formula:

```
= [Sale] /
    ( Number.From( [End Date] ) - Number.From( [Start Date] ) + 1 )
```

🐵 Don't forget to add one to the result when subtracting one day from another!

	A^B_C Client	1²₃ Sale	Start Date	End Date	ABC 123 Amount
1	Dmitrei	150	2021-06-15	2021-08-31	1.923076923
2	Pauline	100	2021-06-10	2021-06-30	4.761904762
3	Niklas	200	2021-06-27	2021-10-26	1.639344262

We have calculated the amount to be allocated per day

With our daily allocation calculated, we can now proceed to the next step: expanding the table to contain a record for each allocation day by client:

- Add a Custom column called Date that uses the following formula:

```
= { Number.From( [Start Date] ) .. Number.From( [End Date] ) }
```

- Expand the new Date column to new rows
- Change the data type of the Date column to Date

Leveraging the list technique we used when creating calendar tables, we now have a full table of daily transactions:

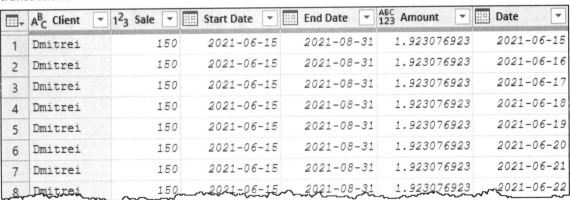

	A^B_C Client	1²₃ Sale	Start Date	End Date	ABC Amount	Date
1	Dmitrei	150	2021-06-15	2021-08-31	1.923076923	2021-06-15
2	Dmitrei	150	2021-06-15	2021-08-31	1.923076923	2021-06-16
3	Dmitrei	150	2021-06-15	2021-08-31	1.923076923	2021-06-17
4	Dmitrei	150	2021-06-15	2021-08-31	1.923076923	2021-06-18
5	Dmitrei	150	2021-06-15	2021-08-31	1.923076923	2021-06-19
6	Dmitrei	150	2021-06-15	2021-08-31	1.923076923	2021-06-20
7	Dmitrei	150	2021-06-15	2021-08-31	1.923076923	2021-06-21
8	Dmitrei	150	2021-06-15	2021-08-31	1.923076923	2021-06-22

Allocations by day

At this point you have two different directions you could take. If you want your data at this level of granularity, then you simply need to remove the Sale, Start Date and End Date columns and set your data types. You are then good to load your data. For this example, however, we want this data summarized by Month End, so we are going to do a little bit more:

- Select the Date column → Transform → Date → Month → End of Month
- Select Client, Sale, Start Date, Date → Transform → Group By
- Add an aggregation called Amount to Sum the Amount column
- Click OK

- Remove the Sale and Start Date columns

Once complete, the data should look as shown here:

	Client	Date	Amount
1	Dmitrei	2021-06-30	30.76923077
2	Dmitrei	2021-07-31	59.61538462
3	Dmitrei	2021-08-31	59.61538462
4	Pauline	2021-06-30	100
5	Niklas	2021-06-30	6.557377049
6	Niklas	2021-07-31	50.81967213
7	Niklas	2021-08-31	50.81967213
8	Niklas	2021-09-30	49.18032787
9	Niklas	2021-10-31	42.62295082

Success! Our sales are now allocated to the correct months based on the days in the period

> ✎ The reason we grouped by so many fields is to reduce the chance of aggregating two client contracts together in error. If your data contains a unique identifier for each item you are allocating – such as a contract number – you would only need to group by that column (unless you wanted to keep the other columns in your final table).

One thing to recognize about this technique is that we did not round the daily allocation in any way, as this increases the chance of rounding errors. Should you need to round your data, we highly recommend performing this operation at the very end to reduce the likelihood that the sum of the allocations won't add up to the original amount.

Allocate by Whole Months

The next allocation method is a little bit different in that it requires allocating the Sale amount evenly based on the total number of months from the start through end dates. Note that it doesn't matter how many days into the month the sale happened, or how early the end date is within the month – if it overlaps with the month in any way we will consider it as a valid allocation month. An illustrated example of how this would be applied is shown here:

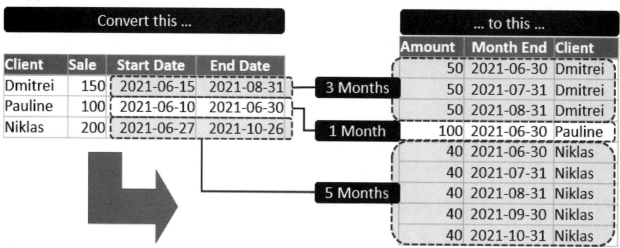

Allocating evenly over the number of months in the period

The frustrating thing about this scenario is that this would be super easy if Power Query just had a function that could create a list of Month End dates. The good news however, is that we can easily create one using a custom function. So let's do that first, building up a sample transform based on two parameters.

- Open the Power Query editor
- Go to Home → Manage Parameters → New Parameter
- Create two new parameters as follows:

- FromDate as a Date type with a current value of 2021-06-01
- ToDate as a Date type with a current value of 2021-08-31

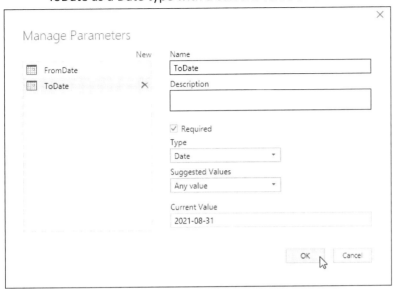

Creating the required parameters for our function

Now that we have our parameters, we can build the getMonthEnds query as follows:

- Create a new Blank Query and call it getMonthEnds
- Enter the following in the formula bar:

    ```
    = { Number.From( FromDate ) .. Number.From( ToDate ) }
    ```
- Go to List Tools → Transform → To Table → OK
- Set Column1 to a Date data type
- Select Column1 → Transform → Month → End of Month
- Right-click Column1 → Remove Duplicates
- Rename Column1 to Month End

The result is a short table of month-end dates between the FromDate and ToDate parameters:

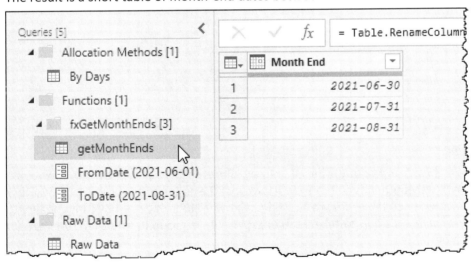

We've generated a table of Month End values between two dates

As we know from Chapter 17, the steps we have followed so far allow us to keep the getMonthEnds query as a Sample Transform query, while easily converting it into a function, which we will do now:

- Right-click GetMonthEnds → Create Function → fxGetMonthEnds → OK

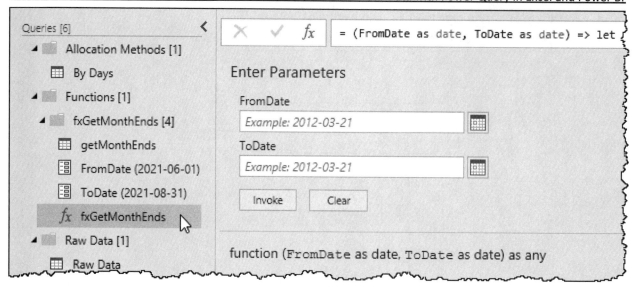

Our fxGetMonthEnds function accepts two parameters, and is ready for use

> 🖈 At this point it would be a very good time to save your progress, loading all of the newly created queries as connection only queries as we don't need to load any of them to a worksheet or the data model.

With our new function in place, we can now set to generating our allocation by month:

- Reference the Raw Data query
- Remove the Months column (as it is not needed for this example)
- Go to Add Column → Invoke Custom Function → fxGetMonthEnds
- Set FromDate to the Start Date column and ToDate to the End Date column

After committing the invocation, we can now preview the results of our function applied to our data set:

	A^B_C Client	1²₃ Sale	Start Date	End Date	ABC 123 fxGetMonthEnds
1	Dmitrei	150	2021-06-15	2021-08-31	Table
2	Pauline	100	2021-06-10	2021-__-30	Table
3	Niklas	200	2021-06-__	2021-10-26	Table

Month End
2021-06-30
2021-07-31
2021-08-31

Our custom function is working perfectly

At this point what we really want to do is work out the value to be allocated to each month. But how would you do this? If you expand the fxGetMonthEnds column you'll have lost the ability to easily count the number of Month End values nested within each table. Yes, you could use Power Query's Group By functionality to count the rows, but doesn't it seem a bit odd to take a table, expand it, re-group it, and then re-expand it again? Surely there must be a better way...

Of course, there is – leveraging the Table.Rowcount() function in a custom column:

- Add a custom column called Amount that uses the following formula
    ```
    = [Sale] / Table.RowCount( [fxGetMonthEnds] )
    ```
- Select the Client, fxGetMonthEnds and Amount columns → Remove Other Columns
- Expand the fxGetMonthEnds column to new rows (without a prefix)
- Set the data types of each column

And the results are perfect. The Table.Rowcount() function counts the number of rows returned by the fxGetMonthEnds function for each client and divides that into the Sale amount. After expanding the results, the net effect is that the sales for each client are allocated evenly across all months in the range:

	AᴮC Client	Month End	1²3 Amount
1	Dmitrei	2021-06-30	50
2	Dmitrei	2021-07-31	50
3	Dmitrei	2021-08-31	50
4	Pauline	2021-06-30	100
5	Niklas	2021-06-30	40
6	Niklas	2021-07-31	40
7	Niklas	2021-08-31	40
8	Niklas	2021-09-30	40
9	Niklas	2021-10-31	40

Our values are now allocated as desired

🔍 This is another one of those scenarios where a quick stroll through the documentation can be super useful to us. We knew we were working with a Table value, so scanned the Table section of the M documentation looking for something that sounded promising.

Remember that custom functions are a life saver when trying to do things that aren't natively supported by Power Query, or where you need to generate reusable logic for complex patterns. If you are trying to build more complicated logic in order to get your allocation methods working correctly for your scenario, don't forget that you have this tool in your toolbox!

Allocate Over x Months From Start Date

The final challenge we are going to explore adds an additional nuance to the previous scenario. The finance department requires allocating a full month of revenue in the starting month if the transactions start date is before or equal to the 15th of the month but allocating the first month to the month following the start date if incurred after the 15th. For this scenario, we are also going to assume that we have been provided a Start Date and the number of months to allocate, but no specific End Date column as shown here:

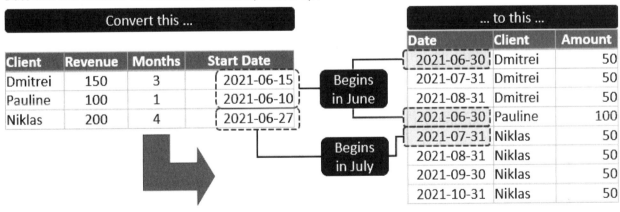

How do we allocate our revenues over x month-end dates?

In order to solve this scenario, we will need to combine the list technique we used for creating calendar tables, a couple of date formulas, and some conditional logic.

Let's get started by calculating the amount of our sales that should be allocated to each month:

- Reference the Raw Data query
- Remove the EndDate column (as this scenario doesn't leverage this column)
- Select the Sale and Months columns → Add Column → Standard → Divide
- Rename the new Division column to Amount

The results should look like this at this point:

	A^B_C Client	1²₃ Sale	Start Date	1²₃ Months	1.2 Amount
1	Dmitrei	150	2021-06-15	3	50
2	Pauline	100	2021-06-10	1	100
3	Niklas	200	2021-06-27	4	50

We have calculated the monthly allocation amount

With the amount we need to allocate calculated, we now need to expand our table to generate a new row for each required month. We know how many records we need – that is indicated in the Months column – but we have a couple of challenges here. We can't use List.Dates() to create this, as there is no "month" duration, and we can't use a simple {1 .. [Months] } setup either, as the list requires a different offset based on the day of the month contained in the Start Date column. So here's what we need to do:

- Go to Add Column → Custom Column called "Custom" which uses the following formula:
  ```
  =if Date.Day([Start Date]) <= 15
  then { 0 .. [Months] - 1 }
  else { 1 .. [Months] }
  ```
- Expand the Custom column to new rows

At this point we can see the results of the conditional column we created:

	A^B_C Client	1²₃ Sale	Start Date	1²₃ Months	1.2 Amount	ABC 123 Custom
1	Dmitrei	150	2021-06-15	3	50	0
2	Dmitrei	150	2021-06-15	3	50	1
3	Dmitrei	150	2021-06-15	3	50	2
4	Pauline	100	2021-06-10	1	100	0
5	Niklas	200	2021-06-27	4	50	1
6	Niklas	200	2021-06-27	4	50	2
7	Niklas	200	2021-06-27	4	50	3
8	Niklas	200	2021-06-27	4	50	4

The results of our new Custom column displayed for easy review

There are two important things to notice about this data set at this point:

1. Each client now contains the number of rows that were dictated by the number of months for which we need an allocation,
2. The Custom column values start at 0 for the first two clients but start at 1 for the 3rd client.

Let's leverage this new column to take our start date and create a new date that represents the Month End for each record:

- Create a new Custom column called Date that uses the following formula:
  ```
  = Date.EndOfMonth( Date.AddMonths( [Start Date], [Custom] ) )
  ```
- Select the Date, Client and Amount columns → Remove Other Columns
- Set the data type of each column

As you can see, the trick here was all about generating the list of months needed (with the correct offset for each month) and feeding that into the Date.AddMonths() function.

▦▾	▦ Date ▾	A^B_C Client ▾	1$^2_3$ Amount ▾
1	2021-06-30	Dmitrei	50
2	2021-07-31	Dmitrei	50
3	2021-08-31	Dmitrei	50
4	2021-06-30	Pauline	100
5	2021-07-31	Niklas	50
6	2021-08-31	Niklas	50
7	2021-09-30	Niklas	50
8	2021-10-31	Niklas	50

Our records allocated over and into the correct months

> ⚒ Not interested in forcing the dates to month-ends? No problem, just drop the Date.EndOfMonth() from the formula used to generate the final dates. It will then return the same day of the month x months from the Start Date provided.

Final Thoughts on Allocations

As mentioned earlier, there are countless ways that you may need to allocate your data – these are just the most common methods we have seen in practice. Our hope is that the scenarios that we have outlined above give you the tools to be able to creatively approach your own scenarios and build the perfect allocation method that your business requires.

Chapter 19 - Query Optimization

Power Query is an amazing product that can let you transform data more quickly than you ever could before. Despite this, it is no secret that it is easy to build slow queries or suffer latency as we are building queries. This chapter is dedicated to helping you get the most out of your Power Query environment so that you can develop queries more quickly, as well as get them running faster.

Optimizing Power Query Settings

The first thing you may want to check is the default settings that you have configured within your Power Query environment. These are accessed via the Query Options dialog, which can be found in the following locations:

- Excel: Get Data → Query Options
- Power BI: File → Options & Settings → Options

We will look at a few tabs within this dialog and share how we set up our environments.

Global Data Load Options

The first two groups in this dialog are related to Type Detection and Background Data. As these are both useful, we recommend leaving these as the default (middle) setting which leaves them active by default, but changeable at a file level. This gives you the best mix of functionality and control for specific scenarios where you need to override the defaults.

The next two settings are only available in Excel, and we change each of them:

- **Default Load Settings**. We recommend a Custom default load setting, with both the Load to Worksheet and Load to Data Model checkboxes **unchecked**. The reason for this is simple: when creating multiple queries in one Power Query instance, you only get to choose one load destination. No matter how many queries we have created in one session, we've never seen it take more than a couple of seconds to "load" them all as Connection Only. Compare that with the default which will load each query to a new table on a new worksheet. Not only do you have to wait for the data to load, but you then have to remove each query you didn't want loaded (waiting for it to 'un-load') and finally remove the worksheets as well. It is much faster to create all queries as Connection Only and then toggle the ones you DO need to load to a destination afterwards.
- **Fast Data Load**. We make sure this box is **checked**. (I mean, who wants their data to load slowly, right?) The reality is that this may lock Excel's window while the data is refreshing, but we generally don't care, as we want our data fully loaded before we move on to our next task anyway.

Global Power Query Editor Options

We'll make this one super easy on you – every checkbox on this page should be checked.

Global Security Options

If you follow our advice from Chapter 12, and never provide a custom SQL statement when connecting to a database, the "Native Database Queries" approval setting won't matter to you, as you won't be sending native queries.

If – on the other hand – you ignore our advice and provide your own SQL statement to the database connector, you may be tempted to turn this setting off to avoid the nagging messages that come up. It is unfortunate that this option is only provided at a global level, as there is no way anyone should be turning this off globally. You want to know about this in most solutions!

The reason why this setting is important to leave checked is due to the fact that Power Query does not restrict you to sending SELECT statements via a database connector. This setting is the **only** warning that you are going to get when someone changes the SQL query from a SELECT statement to a DROP TABLE statement on April Fool's Day.

> ✎ To be fair, it is the responsibility of your IT department to make sure that the correct people have Read/Write vs Read Only access to the database. Despite that, who is going to wear the blame if the command is executed under your user credentials?

Take our advice, leave this checkbox enabled, and let Power Query build your SQL for you.

Global Privacy Settings

As we showed in Chapter 12, Privacy Settings can have a real impact on both query refresh speed as well as your ability to combine data. Many users come straight to this setting and set it to Always ignore Privacy Level settings at a global level. **Don't do this.**

We understand that Privacy can be frustrating but disabling privacy at this level means that you'll get no prompting or protection, even when you do need it. Toggling privacy settings is fine but do it on a solution-by-solution basis when you know what data sources are in play. This setting should be left as the default option: **Combine data according to each file's Privacy Level Settings**.

Current Workbook (File) Settings – Background Data

While there are a host of options on the Data Load tab of the Current Workbook (File) tab, they are mostly self-explanatory. One that we specifically want to call out, however, is "Allow data previews to download in the background", also known as "Background Refresh".

This option is always selected by default, and controls whether Excel or Power BI attempts to automatically load the data required to correctly display the icons and previews shown in the Queries & Connections pane and Power Query editor.

While these previews are useful, in large files they can be particularly punishing due to the resources required for the application to generate them. Should you find that your file grinds to a halt when you load a workbook containing a large number of complex queries, it may be a good idea to turn these previews off.

> 🏌 Keep in mind that disabling the background load of preview doesn't actually make your queries refresh faster – it simply stops Power Query from loading them in the background. While this reduces the resource drain on the application during normal use, this can make the query editing experience feel much slower, as the previews won't already be there for you and will need to be calculated when you access them.

Before you do disable background refresh, be aware that this can cause some ugly visual side effects. The image below was taken from a very complex solution where the background refresh was disabled. While it makes the workbook more responsive, many of the queries show a question mark (?) in their icon (since the preview wasn't generated), and the query preview is filled with an intimidating information message.

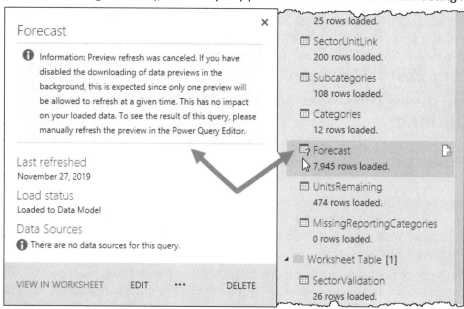

Background query has been turned off globally in this workbook

As the message indicates, there is no actual issue with the data. A refresh operation will continue to execute correctly, but inside the Power Query editor you will need to force a refresh of the previews by clicking the Refresh Preview button found on Power Query's Home tab.

🐾 As a general rule, we leave this setting enabled unless we start experiencing performance issues or long freezes when we are not editing queries.

Current Workbook (File) Settings - Other

Many of the previous options from the global settings are found within these tabs, and this is the appropriate place to toggle them, as it can be done only where needed for each specific project. Items that you may wish to change in this section include:

Regional Settings → Locale: This can be quite helpful if you need to override the default Locale settings in a solution so that you can share the solution with others.

Privacy: Privacy was discussed in detail in Chapter 12. The thing we want to recognize about this setting is that this area is the appropriate place to disable privacy when warranted, as it will not accidentally affect how privacy impacts other files.

Leveraging Buffer Functions

When Power Query tries to evaluate a value, it tries to use a combination of lazy evaluation and query folding; the mechanisms that we discussed in Chapter 16. Effectively, this is the way that Power Query translates your M code into the query plan which evaluates your query, deciding which things will be pushed to the data source and which transformations will run through the local Power Query engine.

By default, when you create a query, any steps which can be folded will be offloaded to your data source with un-foldable steps then being processed locally. But what happens if you either want to force things to be evaluated solely via the local Power Query engine or you want to optimize a query that relies on a value that will be read / accessed multiple times?

This is where Buffer functions come in to play. These functions share the same two objectives:

1. Force the evaluation of a value
2. Buffer the evaluation of a value

In Power Query, "buffering" overrides the lazy evaluation engine, forcing the evaluation of the value(s) of that step, and only that step (the precedent steps themselves are not buffered and will continue to be evaluated as normal if referenced by other query steps). The result of the buffered step is then stored in memory, isolating it from external changes during evaluation. This could potentially be a good thing or a bad thing depending on your query and the amount of data that would need to be stored in memory.

🐾 At the time of writing this book, there were three buffer functions available in Power Query: Table.Buffer, List.Buffer and Binary.Buffer, each of which is used to buffer the results of the prefacing value.

Let's explore the main use cases for Buffer functions and look at some examples which demonstrate when you might want to use one and why.

Force Evaluation of a Value

The first use case we will explore is using a Buffer function in order to force the evaluation of a value.

For our example, we will attempt to use Power Query to generate a random number on each row of our data set. To do so, lets start with a blank query and put the following code in the Advanced Editor:

```
let
    Source = Table.FromList( {"A" .. "E"}, null, {"Column1"} ),
    #"Added Custom" = Table.AddColumn(Source, "Random Value",
      each Number.RandomBetween(1,10))
in
    #"Added Custom"
```

The result is shown here:

	ABC 123 Column1	ABC 123 Random Value
1	A	5.883
2	B	5.883
3	C	5.883
4	D	5.883
5	E	5.883

Well, that's random all right – you didn't see that coming, did you?

> ⚓ If you are using an older version of Excel, you may find that the preview shows random numbers on all rows with the initial code. Despite this, it will load to your worksheet or data model as a single column of values as shown above. We recommend following the steps in this section in order to "future proof" your solutions so that they work when upgrading to newer versions of Excel or Power BI.

This is a frustrating issue with Random numbers inside Power Query. When the lazy evaluation engine kicks in, it only generates one random number and uses it for each "random" value. To fix this, we will need to modify the Custom Column, generating an individual list of (a single) random number for each row:

- Modify the Custom Column so that the formula reads as follows:

```
= { Number.RandomBetween(1,10) }
```

At first glance, things look good. Each of our previews now generates a distinct value:

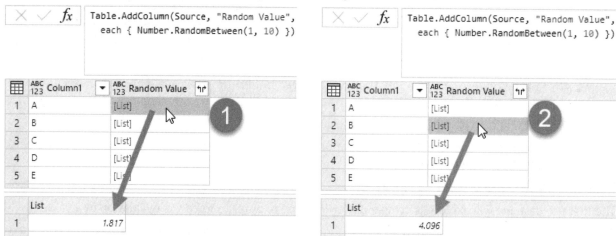

That's better – now we have random numbers per row... or do we?

Upon expanding the Random Value column, we are right back where we started, with a single repeating value on all rows.

This is one of those scenarios where we need to force the evaluation of the list items so that it "locks in" the values we see in the preview. To do that, we will:

- Return to the Added Custom step
- Wrap the formula in the formula bar in a Table.Buffer() function so that it reads:

```
= Table.Buffer( Table.AddColumn(Source, "Random Value",
each { Number.RandomBetween(1, 10) } ) )
```

Upon returning to the final step of the query, you'll now notice that things are exactly as we intended, with a random number per row:

	ABC 123 Column1 ▼	ABC 123 Random Value ▼
1	A	3.157
2	B	7.335
3	C	6.769
4	D	7.827
5	E	6.623

That's what we expected to happen in the first place!

> 🔦 While we demonstrated this scenario based on random numbers, it is also VERY common to see the sorting order of a table change when you add a new step – especially when grouping data – even if there is no random number component to the query. Should you encounter this scenario, try buffering the table prior to whatever step you added, and it will most likely prevent the re-sorting from happening.

Buffer the Evaluation of a Value

For the next scenario, imagine a situation where your queries simply cannot be folded back to the data source. For example, using the From Folder connector to read from CSV, TXT or Excel files, none of which have any query folding capabilities. What this means in terms of performance is that the query which enumerates the Source Files will be referenced multiple times across the solution, and therefore read multiple times.

When executing query chains, Power Query does try to cache shared nodes (queries or steps that are referenced by multiple other queries or steps). When successful, this allows a query (or step) to be evaluated once and then used in any queries that rely on the result of it. However, in some cases these shared nodes are simply not enough. In those cases, we may be able to optimize our queries by buffering either the entire query or the values within the query.

> 🔦 As a useful tip, try to always imagine that there are counters on your queries in the number of read and transform operations that they need to do. (The lower the number of read operations the better.) As you start adding more transformation steps and read operations then you'll start to notice performance slowing down.

Assume we have a collection of approximately 240 Excel files in a folder on our hard drive, from which we need to extract two tables each. We may set up our queries based on the structure shown here:

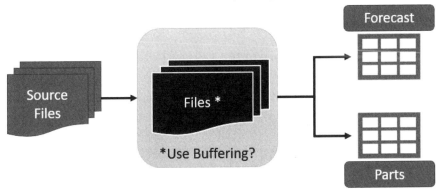

Flow chart of the queries in the provided sample file

At first glance, it may look like there are four queries here, but there are actually five components in total, as follows:

- **Source Files** – this query points to the original folder which contains all the binary files which will be processed. Each binary represents an Excel file in the folder and each Excel file has multiple sheets with different data that we need to get.

- **Use Buffering** – a Parameter that allows us to flip quickly between using the Buffered or Un-Buffered files list in the next three queries.
- **Files *** –this query essentially references the Source Files query and distills it into a simple list of only the binary files from the source folder. (* To allow for easy comparisons, the example file contains two versions of this query: **Buffered Files** and **Un-Buffered Files**.)
- **Forecast** – dynamically references the correct list of binary files (based on the value of the **Use Buffering** parameter) extracting only the Forecast data from each file.
- **Parts** – dynamically references the correct list of binary files (based on the value of the **Use Buffering** parameter) extracting only the Parts data from each file.

The key thing to recognize about these queries is that the ONLY difference between the two **Files** queries is in the final step. Where the Buffered Files query contains the Binary.Buffer() call in the Content step (as shown below), this is omitted in the Un-Buffered Files query:

```
= List.Transform( #"Removed Other Columns"[Content], each Excel.
Workbook ( Binary.Buffer( _ ) ) )
```

> ✎ Despite the fact that we are using buffer functions here, the lazy evaluation engine is still in play and works backwards from the Forecast and Parts queries, checking the value of the Use Buffering parameter. If that value is true, the Buffered list will be evaluated, but the Un-Buffered list will not. If the Use Buffering parameter is false, then the Un-Buffered list will be loaded instead.

Let's have a look at what happens when we run 10 refreshes over this solution with buffering active, versus another 10 tests without buffering:

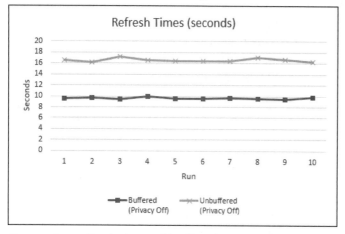

Comparing refresh times of buffered vs unbuffered files from folder

In the case of our tests, the buffered queries refreshed in an average of 9.6 seconds (with a standard deviation of 0.16 seconds), while the un-buffered queries took an average of 16.6 seconds (with a standard deviation of 0.33 seconds). The takeaway here is that the buffered version refreshed 30% faster, with half of the variability in refresh times.

> ✎ These tests were conducted using 64-bit Excel, version 2107 from the beta channel of Microsoft 365. The hardware in use was a dual core i7-7600U CPU @2.8GHZ, with 16GB of RAM. But keep in mind that your performance tests will vary from day to day and from machine to machine, as Power Query doesn't get exclusive access to your RAM or processor. The more programs you have competing for those resources, the slower your queries will refresh.

While the performance benefits might be inspiring, the challenging part is that discovering if you would benefit from buffering is a simple trial and error process. At the time of writing, there were no debugging tools – in Power Query or from a 3rd party – which could tell us how to speed things up. We have little choice but to test things manually to reach our own conclusions.

In normal scenarios, we would never set up a series of queries to allow dynamic switching between buffered and un-buffered files. We would test the timing of the current state of the query, modify the queries to add or remove any Buffer functions, and then test the refresh time again.

Looking for tools to benchmark query refresh times? You have three options:

1.   Manual timing. Certainly, the least accurate and most painful way of timing queries.

2.   Query Diagnostics in Power BI Desktop. Records refresh times at step level detail but leaves you to interpret the data. (Found in Power BI under Tools → Start Diagnostics.)

3.   Excelguru's Monkey Tools add-in. This tool can benchmark and chart the results of refreshing specific queries or the global Refresh All operation in Excel, as well as chart the results for interpretation. (Find more at https://xlguru.ca/monkeytools)

🐵 Beware that buffering a value is only recommended when you know that you can't take advantage of query folding or lazy evaluation. Using buffer functions unnecessarily can actually have a negative impact on performance.

🔪 It is never a good idea to buffer an already buffered value using a combination of buffer functions. Always pick the correct buffer function for your scenario by understanding how the navigation or flow of values go from one query to the other.

Reducing Development Lag

One thing that can be frustrating when developing Power Query solutions is the lag that you experience after adding new steps. Even worse, the bigger the data set is, the more you feel it. This is another issue that comes down to lazy evaluation, but this time strictly related to generating Power Query previews.

In order to illustrate the scenario, let's make the following assumptions related to a (fictitious) data set:

*   The source data table holds 70 million rows of data
*   The Power Query preview populates with the top 1000 rows

Now, let's walk through a typical query development:

*   The user connects to the data set
*   Power Query pulls the first 1000 rows and loads them to the preview window
*   The user filters out all records for dept 105, removing half the rows in the data set

At this point, what happens? We know that Power Query won't leave you with only the 500 rows that meet the current filtering criteria. Instead, it will attempt to fold the new step into a single query and will go and grab an updated preview of the top 1000 rows.

Next, the user drops 20 columns and… Power Query does the same action again. Fold the query, retrieve a new preview from the data source based on the new criteria, and re-populate the preview window.

In fact, almost every action taken to add or reconfigure a step in the Applied Steps window drives an update which forces a refresh. And since the dataset in question here is 70 million rows, getting that preview back involves a long wait. This can be intensely frustrating.

🔪 Before you ask "why not just add a Table.Buffer() command in there?"… it won't help. If you are inside the query editor, the Buffer commands get ignored (at best), or re-executed, which just adds time to the process as the data is loaded to memory. In other words, while it may help at run time, it won't help as you are building your queries, as the preview needs to reload the data to reflect the changes you are making.

One of the things that we'd love to see in Power Query is the ability to effectively buffer steps within the preview window only; a mechanism to "pin" a step, forcing a buffering in the preview window. From that point, we envision that any subsequent steps would read from that pinned step until you hit the Refresh Preview button, forcing a complete re-calculation of all steps in the query window. This would allow us much more granular control over how previews refresh when working with large data sets. Unfortunately, at this point, that is just a dream, so we need a way to cope with the way Power Query currently works.

A Strategy to Reduce Development Lag

One method of dealing with development lag is to set up a temporary stage for your data that doesn't constantly call back to the full data source. This involves a 6-step process as follows:

1. Connect to the Data Source
2. Reference the Data Source query, creating a Data Staging query and load it to an Excel Table
3. Load the Excel Table to Power Query, creating a Connection Only query (Temp Data)
4. Reference the Temp Data query and develop your Output query
5. Re-point the Output query against the Data Source query
6. Delete the Data Staging and Temp Data queries, as well as the Excel Table

A diagram of the Development vs Release query chain is shown below:

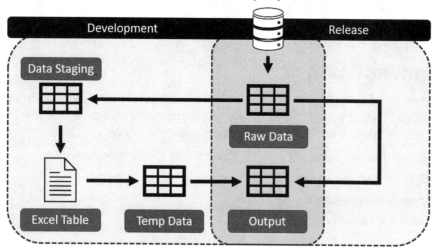

Visual comparison of Development vs Release query architecture

If you study the image above, you'll recognize that the "Release" path is generally the way that we build our queries in the first place. And honestly, in most cases the release path can be used during query development unless you anticipate (or experience) significant lag during the query construction process. This is where the Development path can add some value.

The way it works is that we temporarily load a set of sample data to an Excel table, and then refer to that table as we build our query. Assume for a second that our database has 70 million rows of data that we keep calling back to, but we land 2000 rows of that to the Excel worksheet. When we then build a query against the Excel table, our preview is now only pulling from that 2000 row sample, not reaching back to the full database. While it doesn't stop the preview from refreshing, it certainly limits the amount of data that needs to be read upon each update.

> 🗲 Since Excel tables do not support query folding, we will not be able to leverage that technology as we are building our Output query. Upon repointing the Output query to call from the Raw Data query at the end of the process however, query folding capabilities (if available in the data source) will function as normal.

Experiencing Development Lag

While the above process may make sense conceptually, the reality is that you are rarely going to anticipate that you'll need to set things up in this way. What this means to you is that it is most likely that you'll be part way through the development of a query and getting very frustrated with waiting as you modify or add new steps to your query. At some point, you'll decide you've had enough, and decide that you really need the query set up in this fashion. So how do you retrofit a query to take advantage of this structure?

Assume our goal is to create a summary of total sales by product name by year. In the Ch19 Examples\ Development Lag-Begin.xlsx file, you'll find a Connection Only query called "Output" which does the following (so far):

- Connects to the AdventureWorks database (using the credentials from Chapter 12)

- Navigates into the Sales Order Detail table
- Removes all but four columns

And leaves us in the following state:

ModifiedDate	OrderQty	ProductID	UnitPrice	SalesLT.Product
1	2008-06-01 12:00:00 ...	1	836	356.90	Value
2	2008-06-01 12:00:00 ...	1	822	356.90	Value
3	2008-06-01 12:00:00 ...	1	907	63.90	Value
4	2008-06-01 12:00:00 ...	4	905	218.45	Value
5	2008-06-01 12:00:00 ...	2	983	461.69	Value
6	2008-06-01 12:00:00 ...	6	988	113.00	Value
7	2008-06-01 12:00:00 ...	2	748	818.70	Value
8	2008-06-01 12:00:00 ...	1	990	323.99	Value

The current state of our query

Before we go further into the example, we need to disclose that there is actually one more step in the sample file... Due to the cost of hosting a massive database which would replicate performance issues, we were unable to provide a real data sample to work with. In order to artificially slow things down to a painful point, we've added an additional step (immediately prior to setting the data types) called Custom1 which uses the following code:

```
= Table.Repeat(#"Removed Other Columns",1000)
```

This code will pull the 542 rows of the table, and repeat them 1,000 times, yielding a dataset that is 542,000 rows long. Naturally, this slows down processing quite a bit.

> 🔧 Table.Repeat basically appends your data set x times. It can be a very useful function for artificially increasing your dataset size should you need to do any performance testing.

> 🐵 Should you receive an Expression.Error message during this process indicating that the Evaluation ran out of memory, reduce the Custom1 step to use a value less than 1,000.

We'll now execute two more steps towards our output goal, and will experience some significant lag as we do so:

- Expand "Name" (only) from the SalesLT.Product column
- Set the data types for all columns

While the data looks great, the issue we have here is that each action took in excess of 5 seconds to execute, which feels like an eternity.

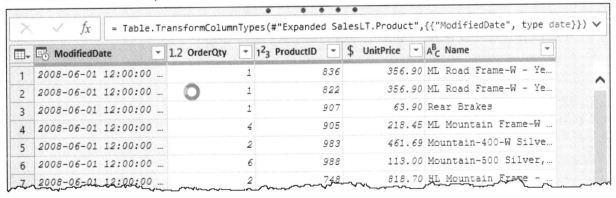

Waiting as we convert the ModifiedDate column to a Date data type

As we still have several steps left to do in order to transform this data, this is an ideal time to retrofit our query in order to make our further development/debugging faster.

RetroFitting an Existing Solution to Reduce Development Lag

The primary thing we want to do during this process is ensure that our existing Output query still loads to its intended destination, as there may be business logic based upon it. For this reason, we don't want to build a new query based upon it, but rather, we want to split the previous steps into a new query:

- Right-click the Changed Type step → Extract Previous → name the query "Raw Data"
- Reference the Raw Data query to create a new query called Staging Data
- Select the Staging Data query → Home → Keep Rows → Top Rows → 1000
- Load all queries as Connection Only queries
- Change the load destination of the Staging Data query to load to a new worksheet

This entire process is likely to take a while due to the fact that Power Query will attempt to generate previews for the Raw Data and Staging Data queries. You may also find that the preview needs to refresh completely for the Staging Data query before you can filter to the top x rows within it.

> 🐵 Be careful when loading these queries. You're already going to have to wait for the Output query to load in full. If you forget to change the load destination, Raw Data will essentially triple the load time as it will load the same number of rows to the data model as the Output Query, and the Staging Data still needs to be processed in full. On top of that, you'll then need to adjust queries to load as connection only and to the worksheet, causing even more lag time.

Once complete, we should have a 1,000 row Excel table containing the information we are after, replicating what we would normally see in the Power Query preview:

▲	A	B	C	D	E	
1	ModifiedDate ▼	OrderQty ▼	ProductID ▼	UnitPrice ▼	Name ▼	
2	2008-06-01 0:00	1	836	356.898	ML Road Frame-W - Yellow, 48	
3	2008-06-01 0:00	1	822	356.898	ML Road Frame-W - Yellow, 38	
4	2008-06-01 0:00	1	907	63.9	Rear Brakes	
5	2008-06-01 0:00	4	905	218.454	ML Mountain Frame-W - Silver, 42	
6	2008-06-01 0:00	2	983	461.694	Mountain-400-W Silver, 46	
7	2008-06-01 0:00	6	988	112.998	Mountain-500 Silver, 52	
8	2008-06-01 0:00	2	748	818.7	HL Mountain Frame - Silver, 38	

We now have a 1,000 row "preview" of our data to work with

> ✎ Keep in mind that you must expand any primitive values you need from all columns which contain Value or Table values, as Excel cannot manifest the structured values in the worksheet grid.

The next step is to create a query which reads from this table, and repoint our Output query to use it while we are developing the rest of the solution:

- Select any cell in the table → create a new query → from Table
- Rename the query "Temp Data"
- Select the Output query and modify the Source step's formula to read `=#"Temp Data"`
- Select the final (Changed Type) step of the Output Query

What you should notice is that we are right back in the same place we were before splitting our queries apart, but that the previews are refreshing much more quickly.

At this point we can finish developing our query with much less lag time:

- Select OrderQty and UnitPrice → Add Column → Standard → Multiply
- Select the ModifiedDate column → Transform → Date → Year → Year
- Rename the ModifiedDate column to be "Year"
- Select the Year and Name columns → Transform → Group By
- Configure the New column to be called Revenue and Sum the Multiplication column

With this work done, the output looks as shown here:

▦▾	1²₃ Year ▾	Aᴮ_C Name ▾	1.2 Revenue ▾
1	2008	AWC Logo Cap	557.0204
2	2008	Bike Wash - Dissolver	511.185
3	2008	Chain	194.304
4	2008	Classic Vest, M	2590.8
5	2008	Classic Vest, S	6242.05
6	2008	Front Brakes	1533.6
7	2008	Front Derailleur	1427.244

Our data is now grouped to summarize revenue by year and product

If you followed through this example, you'll have noticed that the actions during this past phase were quite responsive, as compared to the incredible lag we experienced previously. There are only a couple of things left to do, starting with repointing the Output against the original data:

- Select the Source step of the Output query
- Point the formula back to the original Raw Data query: =#"Raw Data"
- Go to Home → Close & Load

> 🔦 You do not need to wait for the query to refresh the preview before triggering the Close & Load action! It is also worth noting that – upon triggering the Close & Load action – Power Query will force the Output query (only) to refresh, as we never modified the Staging Data query.

As the Output query is now pointed against the full database, it will take some time to finish re-loading to the data model. Once it has finished, we can then delete the worksheet used to house the Staging Data output, as well as the Staging Data and Temp Data queries.

> 🔦 In the completed sample file, we have repointed the Output query against the Raw Data query. We have left the Staging Data and Temp Data queries, as well as the Staging Data worksheet table in the file for your review.

Adjusting the Preview Data

The reason that this technique allows us to work faster is that it essentially freezes the state of the source data at a specific step. So, what happens if you need to expand or change the source data during the development process?

The answer to this question is that you modify the Data Staging query to load different (or more) data to the Excel table. In order to:

- Use different data: Inject a new step to Remove Top Rows *before* the Keep Top rows step. This will essentially allow you to move to the next block of rows in your data set.
- Use more data: Modify the Keep Top Rows step to increase the data sample to include more rows.

Just remember, the Data Staging query still targets the entire database, so the modifications you make to this query will suffer the lag as you build and load the data. But once done, your Output query's previews will be based on the updated data sample.

Dealing with the Formula Firewall

Typically found when combining data from different sources, and by far the most dreaded error message in all of Power Query is the Formula.Firewall error message. It's not well understood, looks intimidating, and always ends with the message "Please rebuild this data combination."

One of the biggest issues with this error message is that it actually manifests in different instances, for completely different reasons.

Formula.Firewall Error 1: Privacy Level Incompatibilities

The first Formula.Firewall issue is caused when – within the same query – you're trying to access multiple data sources that have incompatible privacy levels:

Formula.Firewall: Query 'Events' (step 'Added Custom') is accessing
data sources that have privacy levels which cannot be used together.
Please rebuild this data combination.

Formula firewall issue related to incompatible data sources

We explored this issue in detail in Chapter 12 in the section on Data Privacy Levels. If you encounter this error, we recommend reviewing that section to resolve the issue.

Formula.Firewall Error 2: Data Source Access

Compare the previous message to the following version of the Formula.Firewall error:

 Formula.Firewall: Query 'Timesheet' (step 'Merged Queries') references
other queries or steps, so it may not directly access a data source.
Please rebuild this data combination.

Formula firewall issue related to data source access

At first glance, you can understand why anyone would think that all Formula.Firewall errors are the same. It starts with the same message and ends with the same five-word direction. And let's be honest – does anyone actually read the stuff between those two bookends? Not likely. You'd probably just grab the last few words, throw it into your favorite search engine and see what comes up.

The challenge here is that the text in the middle of this error describes the root issue you are facing and affects what you need to do in order to solve the issue. And while disabling privacy will sometimes solve the issue, that is not always the case. In cases where you either cannot disable the privacy settings or disabling privacy doesn't fix the issue you only have one option; rebuild the data combination. But how?

Triggering the Rebuild Data Combination Error

This error is frequently triggered when trying to use values from one data source to dynamically retrieve/ combine and/or filter data from another data source. It is quite commonly experienced when working with Excel Parameter tables, as well as web-based data sources or databases.

The root cause of this issue is that before Power Query evaluates the results of a query, it scans the entire query in order to discover what data sources are in use and check their privacy compatibility. This process is called the static analysis where Power Query finds the data source functions and the arguments passed to those data source functions.

The issue around "Dynamic data sources" – where a key component of the data source function is not a static value, but rather a dynamic one – is that an argument of a data source function is not static in the sense that it needs to be evaluated first in order for Power Query to know where exactly it needs to connect to and its impact on data privacy. As this violates the core methodology and structure of the lazy evaluation engine, we get a Formula.Firewall error instead.

> ✎ In short, trying to pass a dynamic value into any of the M functions classified as an "Accessing Data Functions" is very likely to throw this error. For a complete list of these functions, see: https://docs.microsoft.com/en-us/powerquery-m/accessing-data-functions.

To demonstrate the issue, as well as some potential ways to work around Data Source Access errors, we are going to explore the queries that have been created in Ch19 Examples\Firewall-Begin.xlsx. This file contains four key components to be aware of:

- The fnGetParameter function (as per Chapter 17)
- A table of parameters (shown below)
- A Timesheet query which retrieves and reshapes the data from a specific text file. The full file path for this file is dynamically generated based on the combination of the File Path, Timesheet and Date parameters from the parameter table, and fed into the Timesheet query in the FilePath step.

- An EmployeeDepts query, which sources its data from an Excel workbook called Departments.xlsx. The file path to this workbook is also dynamically generated via the FilePath step in the EmployeeDetps query and – like the Timesheet query – leverages the fnGetParameter function to do so.

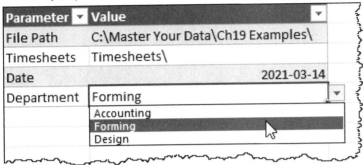

This parameters table makes use of Data Validation on the Date and Department fields

Currently, both the Timesheet and EmployeeDepts queries are loaded as connection only, and the Timesheet function already dynamically sources the correct timesheet based on the date drop-down in the Parameters table. The goal now is to merge the Departments table into the Timesheet – so that we can see which department an employee belongs to – and add the ability to dynamically filter the query from the worksheet as well.

- Edit the TimeSheet query → Home → Merge Queries
- Choose to merge Worker against Employee Depts → Employee

Right away, you'll get an indication that something isn't quite right:

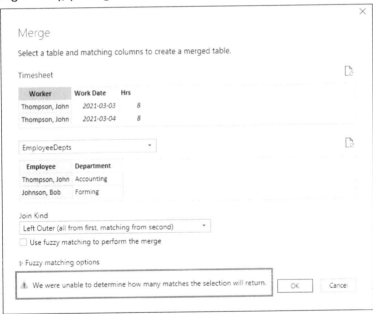

What do you mean you can't work out the match quantities?

We can plainly see that **Thompson, John** exists in both tables, and yet Power Query seems to be having trouble. Never mind though, let's just soldier on and click OK:

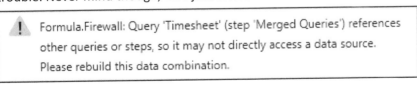

Plainly, Power Query is not happy

To be a bit more explicit, the Merged Queries step references another query, which directly accesses a data source – something it does in the second line of the M code:

EmployeeDepts

```
let
    FilePath = fnGetParameter("File Path"),
    Source = Excel.Workbook(File.Contents(FilePath & "Departments.xlsx"), null, true),
    EmployeeDepts_Table = Source{[Item="EmployeeDepts",Kind="Table"]}[Data],
    #"Changed Type" = Table.TransformColumnTypes(EmployeeDepts_Table,{{"Employee", type text}}
in
    #"Changed Type"
```

The EmployeeDepts query references a data source directly via File.Contents()

Regardless of the reason, this obviously isn't working so we need to delete the step. And now the question becomes – how can we get this to work to achieve our goals?

Rebuild Data Combinations via Query Chaining

If you follow the multi-query architecture that we laid out in Chapter 2, it's likely that you wouldn't have hit this issue. Why? Because instead of trying to merge the data right inside the Timesheet query, we would have done this instead:

* Right-click the Timesheet query → Reference → rename the new query "Output"
* Perform the merge in the Output query
* Expand the Department field from the EmployeDepts column

As you can see, the results are perfect, with no Formula.Firewall issues at all:

	A^B_C Worker	Work Date	1.2 Hrs	A^B_C Department
1	Thompson, John	2021-03-03	8	Accounting
2	Thompson, John	2021-03-04	8	Accounting
3	Thompson, John	2021-03-05	8	Accounting
4	Thompson, John	2021-03-06	9.5	Accounting
5	Thompson, John	2021-03-07	6.5	Accounting
6	Thompson, John	2021-03-10	8	Accounting
7	Thompson, John	2021-03-11	8	Accounting

This is what we were hoping for the first time...

This is one of the reasons we separate queries into separate components.

Now, let's take this a bit further... we want to add a filter to be able to dynamically choose which department gets shown. Let's try this:

* Filter the Department column to only "Accounting"
* Replace `"Accounting"` in the formula bar with `fnGetParameter("Department")`

And great, we have another error:

 Formula.Firewall: Query 'Output' (step 'Filtered Rows1') references other queries or steps, so it may not directly access a data source. Please rebuild this data combination.

Yet another error when "accessing a data source"

So, what is this about? This query doesn't access a data source, although it references two that do. But they aren't actually the issue here, this step is. The reason? The fnGetParameter function – by its very nature – accesses a data source (the Parameters table in the Excel worksheet) to return a value.

The solution to this issue? Isolating the parameter retrieval into its own step. We can do this by invoking our fnGetParameter function to generate a new query:

- Select the fnGetParameter function
- Enter Department for the getValue parameter → Invoke
- Rename the new query to call it "Department"

The result is a fairly simple query that extracts the Department from the Excel table and returns its result as a primitive value:

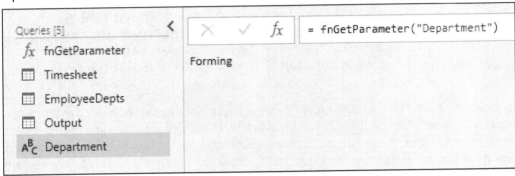

The Department query created by invoking the fnGetParameter function

Now, let's see how this helps with our previous issue:

- Select the Output query → select the Filtered Rows step → modify the formula
- Replace `fnGetParameter("Department")` with `Department`

Not only do the results show up (avoiding the Formula.Firewall error), but they are also correctly filtered to the Forming department, as indicated in the Excel worksheet table:

Our results are now dynamically filtered by file name (date) and department

There is one final consideration that we want to add to this solution, and it comes down to the way that the filter was created for the Department filter. In Excel, a user could select a single department, but we also want to give them the option to clear the filter and return all departments. Should they clear the filter by deleting the cell value, the Department query will return a value of *null*. We need to make the entire Filtered Rows step dynamic, so that it only executes when the value of the Department query is **not** null. If the Department query is equal to null, we don't want to do anything – something that can be accomplished by returning the results of the previous step (Expanded EmployeeDepts). To that end, we will update the formula of the Filtered Rows step from this:

```
= Table.SelectRows(#"Expanded EmployeeDepts",
    each ([Department] = Department))
```

To this:

```
= if Department <> null
then Table.SelectRows(#"Expanded EmployeeDepts",
    each ([Department] = Department))
else #"Expanded EmployeeDepts"
```

At this point, you'll find that you can load the Output table to the Excel worksheet. You can then:

- Choose which file you want to retrieve by selecting the Date from the dropdown that appears when you select cell C7, and/or
- Select which (if any) department you'd like to see by choosing from the dropdown in cell C8 (or clearing it all together)

Your choices should refresh without issue providing that your file path indicates that it is not stored in an https:// location.

> ✎ The date variable doesn't drive a filter, it forms the name of the file to be retrieved. For this reason, you will get an error if you try to delete the date variable from the Parameters table prior to initiating a refresh. It is also worth noting that this is only due to the way that we built the example file – it could certainly be rebuilt in order to call data from a folder and use the date field as a dynamic filter.

The benefits of this approach are that – with the exception of some minor tweaks we made for filtering – everything can be built via the user interface. In addition, following this structure will allow you to circumvent Formula.Firewall errors in *most* cases. But while we wish we could say that the Query Chaining approach is 100% reliable, this unfortunately isn't true; there are some instances where alternate approaches are necessary.

Rebuild Data Combinations via Query Flattening

Another option is "flattening" all of your data calls into the same query. While it is possible to make this happen via the user interface by leveraging the fx button to create new steps, the realities are that you are far more likely to do this if you are comfortable editing your M code in the Advanced Editor window.

A complete code sample is contained in the Ch19 Examples\Firewall-Complete.xlsx file under the name "All_In_One". As its name suggests, it could act as a standalone query to perform the complete logic that was implemented in the previous section. In fact, you could delete every other query in the workbook, and the All_In_one query would load results identical to the Output query built in the previous section.

The general method behind this approach is to set up steps to connect to each of the data sources you want to use within the same query. The trick is to do this at the very beginning, before you do anything with them.

An annotated version of the All_In_One approach is shown here:

All_In_One

```
1   let
2       //Define fxGetParameter function
3       fxGetParameter = ( getValue as text ) =>
4           let
                ParamTable = Excel.CurrentWorkbook(){[Name="Parameters"]}[Content],
                Result = ParamTable{[Parameter=getValue]}?[Value]?
7           in
8               Result,
9
10      //Variables from Worksheet
        FilePath = fxGetParameter("File Path"),
12      TimeSheetPath = FilePath &
13          fxGetParameter("Timesheets") &
14          Text.From(Date.From(fxGetParameter("Date"))) & ".txt",
15      Dept = fxGetParameter("Department"),
16
17      //Departments file
        DeptFile = Excel.Workbook(File.Contents(FilePath & "Departments.xlsx"), null, true),
19      EmployeeDepts_Table = DeptFile{[Item="EmployeeDepts",Kind="Table"]}[Data],
20      EmployeeData = Table.TransformColumnTypes(EmployeeDepts_Table,{{"Employee", type te
21
22      //Timesheet file
        TimesheetFile = Csv.Document(File.Contents(TimeSheetPath)[Delimiter=" ", Columns=
24      #"Changed Type1" = Table.TransformColumnTypes(TimesheetFile,{{"Column1", type text}

35      //Merge and filter
        #"Merged Queries" = Table.NestedJoin(TimesheetData, {"Worker"}, EmployeeData, {"Empl
37      #"Expanded EmployeeDepts" = Table.ExpandTableColumn(#"Merged Queries", "EmployeeDept
38      Final = if Dept <> null then Table.SelectRows(#"Expanded EmployeeDepts", each ([Dep
39  in
40      Final
```

A "flattened" solution that does everything in a single query

The specific things we would like to call attention to are:

1. We nested the "fnGetParameter" function (renamed to fxGetParameter to avoid conflicts with the original function) right inside the query. This wasn't truly necessary – as we could have kept references to fnGetParameter – but we elected to make this a truly all-in-one solution. Should you decide to do this, we recommend including all of your functions at the very beginning of the query.

2. Next comes the declaration of each data source call that we needed to drive the File Path, Timesheet Path and Dept which drive the query results.

3. This section replicates the original EmployeeDepts query, updated only to clearly define the step names.

4. This section uses the exact same steps as the original Timesheet query, but with the steps renamed to avoid any conflicts.

5. The final section – which was previously accomplished in the Output query – is shown nested within the same query.

The benefits of this approach over the previous approach is that it makes it much easier to copy from one solution to another, as it is wholly contained.

Rebuild Data Combinations when Passing Values to SQL

On occasion, you will run into scenarios where it is not possible to flatten or separate the queries. One specific use case here is feeding a filter from an Excel table into a custom SQL query. Consider a case where a user wants to return a sample of transactions where the line-item total falls within a specific range. They have created a custom SQL query, and are attempting to pass it values sourced via the fnGetParameter function:

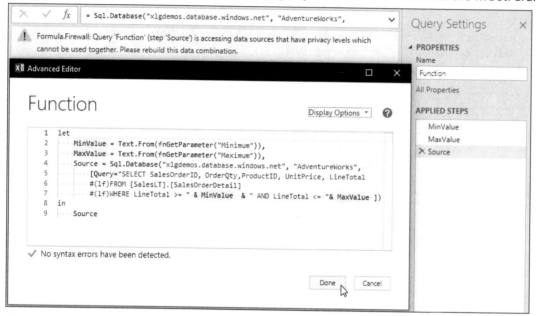

Violating the formula firewall while passing variables to a SQL statement

Because they dynamically access data sources, the MinValue and MaxValue steps cannot be passed into an "Accessing Data Function" like the SQL.Database() function. And while the query shown here is a flattened query – where all data sources are contained within the same query – it is important to realize that it would react the same if you set the MinValue and MaxValue as separate queries. The Formula.Firewall will complain when you try to pass dynamically generated components into a function that accesses a data source.

> 🏂 We still recommend that you use Power Query to connect to the data source and perform your filtering via the user interface, allowing it to fold your query steps for you to avoid this issue. Having said that, your solution is your solution, and there are scenarios where you must pass a pre-formed query to your SQL database.

The good news is that there is a function called Value.NativeQuery() which was specifically designed for this task. It acts as a safe handler which allows you to declare and pass values dynamically into a SQL query. In order to make use of it however, we need to do a little prep work.

Inside the ch19 Examples\Dynamic SQL.xlsx file, you'll find the following parameter table:

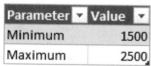

Parameter	Value
Minimum	1500
Maximum	2500

A basic parameter table that drives the min and max values for our query

The first thing we need to do is set up two queries to retrieve the minimum and maximum values we wish to pass to our function. The query names, and their formulas, are shown here:

- **valMin** `=Text.From(fnGetParameter("Minimum"))`
- **valMax** `=Text.From(fnGetParameter("Maximum"))`

> 🏂 The example file contains a query called "NativeQuery-Flat" which attempts to do this all within the same query. Sadly, this still violates the Formula.Firewall.

With these two queries retrieving the values from the Excel worksheet, we can now create a new query that leverages the Value.NativeQuery() function. The M code of this query is shown here:

```
let
    Source = Sql.Database(
        "xlgdemos.database.windows.net", "AdventureWorks"),
    Return = Value.NativeQuery(
        Source,
        "SELECT SalesOrderID, OrderQty,ProductID, UnitPrice, LineTotal
        FROM [SalesLT].[SalesOrderDetail]
        WHERE LineTotal >= @Minimum AND LineTotal <= @Maximum",
        [Minimum=valMin, Maximum=valMax] )
    in
    Return
```

If you know your SQL, you'll recognize what is happening here. The final parameter of the Value.NativeQuery() function acts as an implied DECLARE statement, defining each of the variables we wish to use in the SQL statement, and assigning them a value. The values assigned here (via our valMin and valMax queries) are then passed into the SQL statement via the @Minimum and @Maximum variables. This generates the complete SQL SELECT statement we have provided, and issues it against the database defined in the Source step.

> ✎ When you attempt to load a query that leverages the Value.NativeQuery() function, you will be prompted to approve each unique instance of SQL that will be sent to the database. While you can disable this prompting, make sure you review the Global Security Options section of this chapter before you do so.

100% compatible with the Formula.Firewall, the results are displayed below:

	1^2_3 SalesOrderID	1.2 OrderQty	1^2_3 ProductID	1.2 UnitPrice	1.2 LineTotal
1	71780	2	748	818.7	1637.4
2	71782	4	959	445.41	1781.64
3	71783	7	998	323.994	2267.958
4	71783	5	999	323.994	1619.97
5	71783	2	718	858.9	1717.8
6	71784	4	889	602.346	2409.384
7	71784	5	963	445.41	2227.05
8	71784	3	953	728.91	2186.73

Our query leverages a dynamically crafted SQL statement to return its results

> ✎ The example file contains examples of both valid configurations for dynamically driving SQL queries, as well as those which violate the Formula.Firewall.

The implication of the Value.NativeQuery() function is actually much bigger than just using SELECT statements. It can be used to trigger stored procedures as well!

Final Thoughts on the Formula.Firewall

While privacy errors are fairly easy to handle, data source access errors are tricky to deal with. It involves building your queries in a way that data sources are isolated from each other. In many cases this can be achieved by restricting the queries to separate data sources, or by loading them into steps earlier in the process. It is also worth recognizing that leveraging custom functions and parameters can also be useful to separate data sources from each other, particularly if you need to return a value for each row of a table.

Chapter 20 - Automating Refresh

As you build more and more solutions that leverage Power Query, and realize how much time it saves you, you're bound to become hungry for more automation in your life. Yes, we can click the Refresh All button, but even that will begin to feel so... manual. Wouldn't it be better if you could just schedule an update, or maybe control the order things update?

Options for Automating Refresh in Excel

We actually have a few different methods of automating the refresh of Power Query solutions:

- Refreshing when the workbook is opened
- Refreshing every x minutes
- Refreshing a connection on demand via VBA
- Refreshing all connections on demand via VBA
- Scheduling refreshes via a 3rd party add-in

Each works differently and has its own benefits and drawbacks, as you'll see in this chapter.

Scheduling Excel Refreshes Without Code

The first two methods that we'll explore are both set through the user interface without requiring any VBA code whatsoever. They can be configured on a connection-by-connection basis and can even automate the refresh to Power Pivot if desired. Each of these connections is controlled by navigating to the Workbook Connections dialog:

- Go to the Queries & Connections pane → right-click your query → Properties

This will take you into the following dialog, where we have a variety of options we can control.

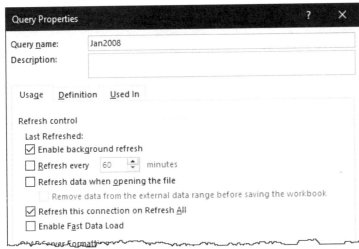

Setting Connection Options

Background Refresh

The concept of Background Refresh was introduced in Chapter 19, and can be enabled/disabled in three scopes:

- **Query level**: toggled via the properties of the individual query as per the previous image
- **Workbook level**: via the Query Options dialog → Current Workbook → Data Load
- **Application level**: via the Query Options dialog → Global → Data Load

  🖱 To access the Query Options dialog, go to Get Data → Query Options

It is unlikely that you'll be toggling this setting here, as users typically want to turn off background refresh for the entire solution, not one specific connection. Having said that, should you need it suppressed for a single connection, this is where you make that happen.

Refreshing Every x Minutes

The next available setting in the dialog is the ability to refresh the data set every x minutes. Upon checking the box you can set how often you'd like the data to be refreshed. This setting is fantastic if you're pulling data from a web source that is constantly changing, or you are targeting against a database that is being updated on a regular basis. You can work with the assurance that your data is always kept up to date while you're in the file.

Keep in mind that the workbook does need to be open in order for this refresh to occur. And if you're going to be scheduling frequent refreshes while you are actively working in the workbook, you'll want to make sure the background refresh setting is enabled.

> 🔧 Valid values for this setting run from 1 to 32,767, allowing you to refresh once every minute up to once every 22.75 days.

Refreshing When the Workbook is Opened

In this selection there are actually two components:

- Refresh the data when opening the file
- Removing the data before saving

The first one is rather self-explanatory and checking the box will change the behavior of the workbook to do exactly what it says: refresh the data each time you open the file. This helps ensure that your data is always up to date when you start working with your file.

If you have a significant amount of data sources, or the data takes a significant amount of time to refresh, then it may be a good idea to leave the Enable Background Refresh setting enabled so that you can use the workbook while the refresh is occurring.

The second choice in this section relates to the question if you'd like the data saved in the workbook, or only the query definition. This setting is actually a security setting, as it ensures that your users have access to the data source when they open the workbook. If they don't, they'll be greeted by a blank table, as the connection cannot be refreshed. If they do have access, the query will run and bring the data in.

Fast Data Load

This setting allows you to determine if you'd like to keep working in Excel while the data refreshes. If you uncheck this box, you could potentially decrease the amount of time it takes to refresh your solution, but you'll also lock out your user interface, preventing you from doing other things until it is complete.

Should you wish to prevent users from working with the data until it is fully refreshed, this can be a great setting to toggle. If you need to do other things while you wait, however, it is best left alone.

> 🔧 This setting can be controlled globally via the Query Options dialog.

Automating Query Refresh with VBA in Excel

The options above will allow you to refresh Power Queries with no macro security warnings at all. In addition, workbooks using the options above are easier to port to Power BI, as they don't cause any blocking issues.

If you're working purely in a desktop Excel instance, however, there are times where you may want to give a user an easy to use and obvious way to update your Power Query solutions. This can be accomplished via recording VBA macros.

Refreshing a Single Connection

Let's take a look at how to build a macro to refresh a single Power Query connection. Open Ch20 Examples\
Automating Refresh.xlsx and navigate to the Transactions worksheet.

On this worksheet you'll find a Transactions table, as well as a PivotTable. Assume now that we'd like to create a macro to update the Transactions and then the PivotTable.

To do this, we will record a simple macro using the following steps.

- Navigate to the Developer tab

    🦶 If you don't see the Developer tab, right-click any tab on the ribbon and choose Customize Ribbon. Check the box on the right hand side next to Developer, then click OK

- In the upper left, click Record Macro

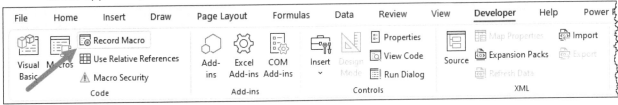

Start recording a macro

    🐵 Once you've clicked this button, Excel will start recording every worksheet click, every keystroke and every mistake you make. Follow the steps below with precision to make sure you get a clean macro!

- Name the Macro "Refresh" and store it in "This Workbook" → OK
- Go to the Data tab → Refresh → Refresh All
- Go to the Developer tab → Stop Recording

    🦶 The Refresh All button refreshes all connections in the workbook, as well as all PivotTables that are connected to tables generated by Power Query. If you choose to refresh the Power Query alone, you will also need to update any PivotTables which source their data from Worksheet tables separately.

The macro is now recorded and ready to use. Let's test it out:

- Go to the Developer tab → Macros

This will launch a dialog that allows us to see what macros are in our file and run any one of them. As there is only one – our Refresh macro – let's select it and click Run.

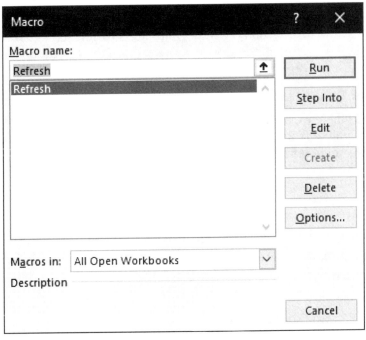

Running our macro

When you run the macro, you can see that the Transactions table will refresh, followed by the PivotTable. (Of course, this would be more obvious if the data changed, but the data source is static.)

As great as this is, sending your users back to the Developer tab to run the macro on a regular basis is a little scary. Rather than do that, why not give them a button to refresh the macro?

- Go to the Developer tab → Insert → choose the top left icon

- Find an empty space on the worksheet
- Hold down the left mouse button → drag down and right → let go of the mouse

At this point the Assign Macro dialog will pop up with our macro in it.

- Select the Refresh macro
- Click OK
- Right-click the button → Edit Text
- Rename it to Refresh
- Click any cell in the worksheet

You've now got a nice, shiny, new button, all ready to use:

▲	A	B	C	D	E	F	G
1	Date ▼	Account ▼	Dept ▼	Amount ▼			
2	2008-01-02	61510	150	-26.03		Sum of Amount	Column Labels ▼
3	2008-01-02	61520	150	-55.07		Row Labels ▼	110
4	2008-01-02	61530	150	-10.6		⊟ 2008	-86148.0
5	2008-01-02	61540	150	-0.29		Jan	-7568.
6	2008-01-02	61550	150	-48.02		Feb	-32777.2
7	2008-01-02	61560	150	-1.35		Mar	-45802.5
8	2008-01-02	61570	150	-77.04		Grand Total	-86148.0
9	2008-01-02	62010	150	-305.95			
10	2008-01-02	62020	150	-95.15			
11	2008-01-02	62099	150	8.79		Refresh	
12	2008-01-02	62510	120	56.74			

Launch button ready to activate!

Go ahead and click the button, and revel in the fact that any user can now refresh your query.

> 🖉 If you ever need to edit the button, right-click it. When the little white bubbles surround it, it is in design mode and can be modified. Select a cell in the worksheet to remove the selection handles and put it back into active mode.

Refreshing in a Specific Order

The next concern that we may wish to tackle is where we need to take explicit control of the order that your queries will refresh. By default, your queries will refresh in alphabetical order, unless they have already refreshed by another (parent) query. While we could rename our queries to preface them with a number, this is obviously not desirable.

Let's set up an explicit query refresh order:

- Go to the Developer tab → Record Macro
- Name the Macro "Refresh_Explicit" and store it in "This Workbook" → OK
- Go to the Queries & Connections pane → right-click Transactions → Refresh
- Right-click a cell in the PivotTable (we used G6) → Refresh
- Go to the Developer tab → Stop Recording
- Go to the Developer tab → Macros → Refresh Explicit → Edit

At this point you'll be taken into the Visual Basic Editor, where you will see code like that below:

```
Sub Refresh_Explicit()

' Refresh_Explicit Macro

'

'

    ActiveWorkbook.Connections("Query - Transactions").Refresh
    Range("G6").Select
    ActiveSheet.PivotTables("PivotTable1").PivotCache.Refresh
End Sub
```

🔏 The word Query is localized depending on the language of the Excel installation where the query was created. Each of the existing queries in this workbook will be prefaced by the word "Query" as the queries were created using an English version of Excel. New queries created in German Excel versions however would be prefaced with "Abfrage" instead.

Breaking this macro down:

- The first four lines after the Sub Refresh_Explicit() line are simply comments, so we really don't need to keep them.
- The line that starts ActiveWorkbook is the one that refreshes the connection
- The next line selects a range on the active worksheet
- The final line refreshes the PivotTable on the active worksheet

We can make some modifications to this macro to not only control the order all of the connections refresh, but also make the code a bit more bulletproof, as right now it would fail if someone tried to run it from a different worksheet (since it wouldn't have the PivotTable on it.)

The revised code will look like this:

```
Sub Refresh()
    ActiveWorkbook.Connections("Query - Jan2008").Refresh
    ActiveWorkbook.Connections("Query - Feb2008").Refresh
    ActiveWorkbook.Connections("Query - Mar2008").Refresh
    ActiveWorkbook.Connections("Query - Transactions").Refresh
    Worksheets("Transactions").PivotTables("PivotTable1") _
        .PivotCache.Refresh

End Sub
```

Notice that we removed the unneeded code comments first. After that we simply injected new lines in order to refresh the specific connections in the order we wanted them refreshed.

In addition, by specifying the name of the Worksheets("Transactions") in place of ActiveSheet, we removed the need to select the PivotTable, as well as ensure that we are always refreshing the PivotTable on the Transactions worksheet.

You'll find that when you click the Refresh button now, each query refresh will be kicked off in turn, and the PivotTable refreshed afterwards.

🔏 This example was done for academic illustration only, as it causes the data to update twice: once for each of the monthly queries and then a second time since each monthly query is a child of the Transactions query. We would normally only use this technique if we were refreshing a query that needed to load to a worksheet before being loaded into another query.

☻ One thing to be aware of is that you **cannot** save your workbook in an .xlsx format once you have a macro inside it. Instead, you'll need to save the workbook in an .xlsm format to preserve the macros. This will prompt users with a macro security warning message when they open the workbook before they can use your button to refresh the data.

Refreshing All Power Queries

In order to refresh just the Power Queries in the workbook, we need to use a slightly different block of code. This macro will look through all connections in the workbook, identifying if they are created by Power Query (ignoring all others).

```
Public Sub RefreshPowerQueriesOnly()
    Dim lTest As Long, cn As WorkbookConnection
    On Error Resume Next
    For Each cn In ThisWorkbook.Connections
        lTest = InStr(1, cn.OLEDBConnection.Connection, _
            "Provider=Microsoft.Mashup.OleDb.1")
        If Err.Number <> 0 Then
            Err.Clear
            Exit For
        End If

        If lTest > 0 Then cn.Refresh
    Next cn
End Sub
```

This macro can be stored in the same workbook as the one created in the previous section, or it can replace the previous code as well (although you'd need to relink your button to the new macro instead).

🐵 Remember that the code above will not necessarily refresh the queries in the order that they need to be refreshed, as Excel refreshes the queries in alphabetical order. In order to override the order, use the previously illustrated technique.

Issues with Synchronous Refresh

The macros above assume that your end goal is simply refreshing your data. If you are building more complex scenarios and you require Power Query to completely finish loading the query output to the worksheet or data model before moving on to the next step, then the code above may not be sufficient for you.

As this is an issue that only affects a small set of developers – typically those who are creating new queries on the fly via VBA – we won't cover it in detail here. Having said that, if this is something that resonates with you, be aware that Power Query seems to finish its processing in an asynchronous manner, and then continues on with the next line of VBA code before the load destination object (worksheet or data model table) has finished actually loading the data. If this causes you issues, consider using the Refresh method on the destination table to "pull" the refresh, rather than automating the refresh of the Power Query to "push" the data to the table.

Scheduling Refresh in Power BI

While Power BI doesn't have a macro language to automatically update data, it does have the ability to schedule a refresh within the Power BI service. In an ideal world, every one of your data sources is web based, meaning that you can publish your Power BI file, and then just schedule the refresh entirely via the Power BI web portal. On the other hand, if you have local files acting as source, all is not lost, as you have the ability to install a data gateway to act as a tunnel between the Power BI service and your desktop.

To schedule the refresh of your Power BI solution in the Power BI service, you need to:

- Publish the solution to Power BI
- Log in to the Power BI service → select the appropriate Workspace for your data set
- Go to Datasets + Dataflows → find the dataset → click the Schedule Refresh button

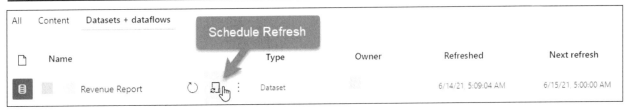

Accessing the refresh scheduler in the Power BI service

This will take you to a screen where you can configure the refresh options for your data set. In order to do that, you will need to either:

- Configure your Data source credentials (for your web-hosted sources), or
- Install a Gateway (for locally hosted sources)

After configuring one (or both) of the options above, you should be able to schedule the refresh of your solution as shown here:

Enabling scheduled refresh in the Power BI service

    ✎ The Gateway connection menu contains links to the documentation and installer for the Gateway software. We recommend reading the current documentation prior to installation as installing and configuring data gateways is outside the scope of this book.

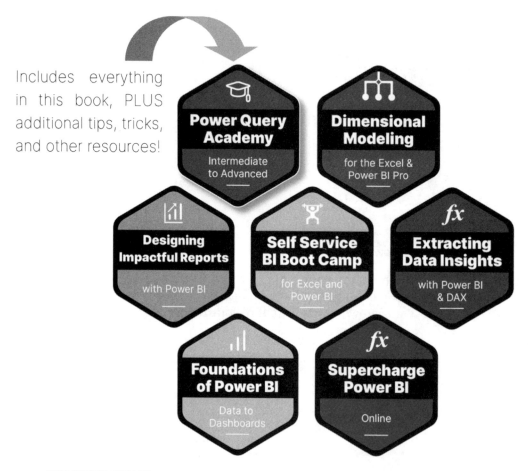

Index

Monkey Tools

Build better models faster!

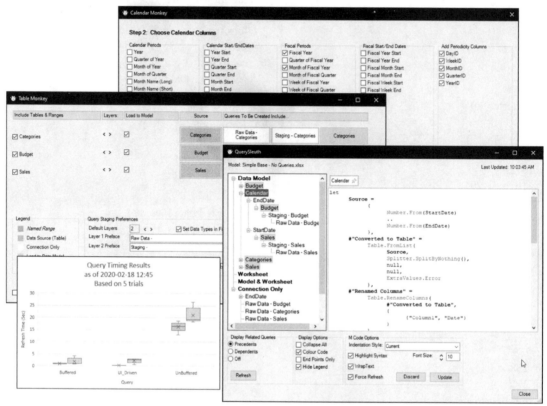

Our Excel add-in provides you, the business intelligence author, a good set of tools to:

- Quickly create multi-query architectures
- Build complete calendars in seconds
- Trace query dependencies
- Audit and edit queries from Excel
- Chart query refresh speeds in Excel

- Create a complete fnGetParameter setup in 2 clicks
- Create and manage DAX measures
- Document your work
- Import models from Power BI to Excel
- Do so much more!

Check it out at **https://xlguru.ca/monkeytools**

Powered by:

www.excelguru.ca